The Painful Transition

The Painful Transition

Bourgeois Democracy in India

ACHIN VANAIK

VERSO

London · New York

First published by Verso 1990
© Achin Vanaik 1990
All rights reserved

Verso
UK: 6 Meard Street, London WIV 3HR
USA: 29 West 35th Street, New York, NY 10001–2291

Verso is the imprint of New Left Books

British Library Cataloguing in Publication Data
Vanaik, Achin
   The painful transition : bourgeois democracy in India.
   1. India.   Politics, history
   I. Title
   320.954

   ISBN 0-86091-288-4
   ISBN 0-86091-504-2 pbk

US Library of Congress Cataloging-in-Publication Data
Vanaik, Achin.
      The painful transition : bourgeois democracy in India / Achin Vanaik.
         p. cm.
      Includes index.
      ISBN 0-86091-288-4 (hardback) — ISBN 0-86091-504-2 (paperback)
      1. India—Politics and government—1977-2. Political leadership—
India.   I. Title.
JQ281.V34   1990
954.05'2—dc20

Typeset by Selectmove Ltd, London
Printed in Great Britain by Bookcraft (Bath) Ltd

For Pamela

Contents

Acknowledgements

This book constitutes a very substantial reworking and extension of ideas first tentatively addressed in two articles in *New Left Review*. My thanks first to Robin Blackburn and Tariq Ali, who were sufficiently enthused by these early explorations to urge me to embark on a larger project. It would have been impossible for me to carry it out without the financial and institutional support of the Centre for Social Studies (CSS) in Surat, Gujarat. My appointment as Visiting Senior Fellow gave me the necessary space and time as well as the opportunity to benefit intellectually from exchanges with fellow colleagues at the Centre. I am especially indebted to the Director of CSS, Dr S.P. Punalekar, and to Senior Fellow, Dr Ghanshyam Shah.

Perry Anderson's comments on the *NLR* articles helped to clarify my thinking at an important stage in the construction of the general architecture of this study. Krishna Raj, Praful Bidwai, Romilla Thapar and Fred Halliday sifted through earlier drafts of Chapters 1, 3, 4 and 6 respectively. Mike Marqusee went through the full manuscript offering numerous valuable comments. Many of their criticisms and suggestions were incorporated. They have all helped to improve the final product. Responsibility for the remaining deficiencies is mine alone. Being in the early stages of computer literacy I had to rely heavily on the technical expertise of K.M. Bhavsar, V. Dayanandan, S. Chandrasekhar and K.S. Raman at CSS. My grateful thanks to them.

My biggest debt, and one that it is impossible to repay in proper measure, is to Pamela – for her unfailing support, for enduring the bouts of excessive self-preoccupation that occasionally afflicted me in the course of writing, and for her willingness to discharge me of my household responsibilities whenever I had to spend time away from home, which was often.

Preface

The bulk of this book was completed some months prior to the general elections held at the end of November 1989.

I would contend that the results of these elections strongly confirm the basic postulates as laid down in Chapter 2 on the 'Crisis of Bourgeois Leadership'. (See especially the sub-section on 'A System in Transition', in which I deal with the plebiscitary character of Indian politics, the possible emergence of a victorious electoral alternative to the Congress, and the question of Congress survival and longevity in the face of such a reversal.) A post-election analysis making these and other points is presented in a postscript at the end of the book. The reader may, if he or she wishes, read this immediately after completing Chapter 2.

Unavoidably, the momentous implications of Eastern Europe's upheavals and the collapse of bloc rivalry on the Indian left and on the future evolution of India's foreign policy could not be addressed.

Introduction

The central theme of this book is simple enough; it is of an India in transition, both externally and internally. The external transition is the subject matter of the last chapter, 'India in the World'. The fundamental proposition held is that the Indian state is in the process of becoming an ever more dominant power in South Asia and will derive from this growing regional hegemony greater global prestige and status. This conclusion already enjoys widespread acceptance among both Marxists and non-Marxists.

My analysis and critique of Indian foreign policy and behaviour – stated from a clear position on the left – differs from both bourgeois and previous left (Stalinist and Maoist) studies in its assessment of the relative weight and importance of the components and relationships that make up the story told in this book, and also in some of the evaluations I have finally arrived at. At least to my knowledge, for example, no one else has ever argued (perhaps wisely) that some of the very factors that make it possible for the Indian state to achieve regional eminence also make it difficult for it to achieve real global authority. Global prestige as a result of regional preponderance it can certainly have; but a commensurate extra-regional capability and activity is an altogether more difficult proposition. The fact that nonalignment has endured is tribute to its specific compatibility with India's search for power. But the point at which the Indian state seeks to break out of the confines of what is now the beckoning horizon of regional 'fulfilment' will be the time when the inadequacies of the ideology of nonalignment will be most sharply revealed. Till then it will continue to serve its Indian masters well.

The methodological approach adopted for the study of India's external relations is perhaps the most conventional and in that sense un-Marxist part of the book. The concepts and formulae used and the objects of investigation (relations with Pakistan, China, the superpowers, and regional neighbours) are all familiar enough. Though these perspectives are common among analysts of left, liberal and right persuasions, their use here needs some explanation. In the realm of foreign policy the relative autonomy of the state from domestic class dispositions and tensions is, in 'ordinary' times, seen most clearly. Even in a bourgeois democracy, the structures of decision-making in foreign affairs are always more autocratic, more insulated from the everyday pressures of domestically engaged social forces than structures governing internal policy-making.

The fundamental Marxian notion that foreign policy is an extension of domestic preoccupations – that is to say, the (class) structure of the state has a determining effect on that state's behaviour vis-à-vis other states in the international arena – operates at a certain remove. Once this is understood, it remains a valuable corrective to the conventional wisdom of the dominant paradigm – Political Realism – used to explicate contemporary international relations. This model disregards almost totally the socio-economic character of the international system as a whole (capitalism) and its parts, the capitalist or post-capitalist states, and is incapable of dealing with the complex hierarchy of imperialist and dependent states. Instead, it presents us with an intra-system structure of competing states where the only meaningful concept of hierarchy is the unequal distribution of power.

The weaknesses of Political Realism have been repeatedly exposed. Far too much responsibility is given to statecraft and diplomacy as a determining variable of international politics. No wonder then that the more 'historical' examples of these studies are excessively imbued with the spirit of diachronic diplomacy. There is a bias towards such normatively loaded terms as 'stability' and 'order', which become all too easily a means of rationalizing 'great-power politics' and the hegemonic aspirations and activities of these 'great powers'. The dialectic between profound internal transformation within states – that is, revolutions – and changes in the international political environment and structure is minimized or ignored. Its philosophical premises about the Hobbesian nature of man and society are, of course, extremely dubious.

Marxism has a very powerful case when it argues that the overall shape of the modern global system has been decisively established by the successes and failures of revolutions, both bourgeois and proletarian, and in the power of ideas released by them. This is a 'disequilibrium' theory of the march of history and of the evolution of global political arrangements, in contrast to the 'general equilibrium' vision of Political Realism (with Morgenthau's 'moral consensus' playing the crucial role of moderator).[1] But Marxism's strengths are also its weaknesses. So impressive in its analytical depiction of the large sweeps of history and in the elucidation of the objective determinants of major conflicts and wars, it does not as yet have any 'distinctive' concepts which furnish a way of grasping the more subjectively influenced 'nuts and bolts' of inter-state behaviour in 'normal' times. For some countries such normal times can span decades, punctuated perhaps by unsuccessful revolutionary or pre-revolutionary upheavals. This lacuna exists in respect of both bourgeois states and post-revolutionary regimes which, by pursuing 'socialism in one country', have substantially narrowed (though not eliminated) the gap between the operational premises of their external behaviour and those of their ideological opponents.

Thus concepts like 'national interest' and 'national power' continue to dominate much of the discussion on the foreign policy of *particular* countries. This is all the more so for a state like India which is not post-revolutionary, not decisively dependent, and not imperialist. Nonetheless, the issue of revolutionary change is always there, lurking in the shadows. The struggle between revolution and its containment, between capitalism and socialism, is very much the central axis of global and regional politics, not just of the politics internal to any given state. If South Asia is a region of little intrinsic strategic importance to the USA or Western imperialism in comparison to other regions (hence the relative equanimity with which imperialism can cede to India its regional goal), it is so because of the absence of a post-revolutionary state.

The *strategic* importance of Central America, its standing challenge to imperialism, its location as a point of tension in Soviet–American relations, is not a function of its natural economic wealth or of the existence of the Panama Canal as ocean link. Rather, it has everything to do with the existence of Cuba, Nicaragua, the struggle in El Salvador and the continent-wide impact of the Castroist and Sandinist experiences. Similarly, the stakes of the global and regional game, the configuration of dominant and subordinate balances of power – so important to practitioners of Political Realism – would be dramatically altered by a successful revolutionary upsurge in any of the countries of South Asia. Socialism's victory as a global system might owe just as much to success in New Delhi as to conquest in Bonn, Tokyo or Washington.

The exploration of India's second, internal transition constitutes the central arch of the book. India is in movement from one variant of bourgeois democracy to another. This has been expressed in an unceasing political instability which nonetheless remains contained within a framework of quite remarkable durability. Both terms in this paradox require explication. Chapter 2 seeks to establish the ground rules for understanding this phenomenon, and argues that the principal social force exercising influence on both sides of this dialectic is the agrarian bourgeoisie supported by its rural allies. This class is, at one and the same time, the major factor behind the micro-level erosion of the norms of bourgeois democratic functioning and its macro-level anchorage. The principal internal mechanism for the preservation of a non-democratic form of bourgeois rule is the police. The most striking trait of the internal apparatus of repression in India is that its structural infirmities make decentralized brutality in the service of class oppressors almost inevitable but the stabilization of centralized authoritarianism extremely difficult.

'Authoritarian democracy' is one way of describing the drift but parity of emphasis must be maintained. Three crucial characteristics of the transition process are investigated in Chapters 2, 3 and 4.

At the national level, Indian bourgeois democracy shows no signs of developing a stable two-party system of governmental alternation or even of coalition rule based on stable party components. What has emerged has been aptly termed 'plebiscitary politics', though the political tones which this term takes on in the course of this exposition may not all be to the liking of those who have previously made use of the concept.

India's federalism and communalism have also been investigated in some depth. These have, of course, been the subjects of much debate, but invariably in a discrete and one-sided manner. In consequence, there has been much exaggeration of their destabilizing impact and potential. Unless these analyses are situated in a larger study of the politico-economic framework, the controls necessary to prevent such imbalances are likely to be absent. India is still far from being balkanized or lapsing into prolonged authoritarian rule, let alone fascism or semi-fascism. In this book, with whatever measure of success or failure, I have made a conscious attempt to provide such an overarching framework in order to achieve a more nuanced and accurate evaluation of the threats of communalism and Hindu nationalism and of the implications of what the Indian left has called the 'nationalities question'.

Communalism is connected to religion in a much deeper way than most Indian Marxists have been prepared to concede. The scandalous attitude of Iran's Islamic fundamentalist regime to Salman Rushdie's *The Satanic Verses* is a tragic reminder of the power of religious appeal. Such intolerance cannot simply be reduced to a case of political manipulation (though it is also most certainly that). An earlier draft of the chapter on the nationalities question was released separately for seminar discussions and for publication in the *Economic and Political Weekly*.[2] It is perhaps the most controversial section of the book as far as the Indian left is concerned. In all acts of authorship one risks being criticized for what one has not said or meant, as well as for what one has stated or implied.

It is not my contention that the 'multi-national state' or 'multi-national nation-state' are misleading or inapt characterizations in general which should never be applied to countries or territorial expanses. It *is* my contention, however, that, as generally understood, this is a false and misleading characterization of the Indian situation.

The point of departure for the journey which led to this conclusion was Benedict Anderson's *Imagined Communities*, a work of stunning brilliance, originality and compressed power.[3] Following Anderson, Kohn and a few others, I argue that, if nationalism is understood above all as a collective state of mind, it must then be seen to possess an inherent fluidity utterly incompatible with rigid Stalinist conceptualizations which even when substantially modified have left such a negative mark on the thinking of Marxists on this question. The excessive emphasis given to the centrality of the language–nationality link is an example of this rigidity, especially when applied to the 'newer' nations of the third world and to the post-colonial era of nation-states. The confusions that this can create when dealing with a multi-lingual formation such as India can be glimpsed. Anthony Smith has correctly pointed out that while language played a big role in the rise of 'old' nations it has not been so important in the rise of modern national movements and therefore of those nations and nation-states which emerged from them.[4] Both Hugh Seton-Watson and Horace Davis have shown commendable caution in hesitating to endorse the conventional wisdom that India's main linguistic communities constitute nationalities.[5]

There is also no consensus on what constitutes a 'national movement'. Some analysts, Marxists and non-Marxists, use this appellation to describe subnational movements for autonomy, especially if the degree of autonomy demanded is substantial. This makes clarification of the issue more, not less difficult. For this reason, rather than out of fidelity to canonical texts, it is better to follow Lenin's use of it to describe those mass movements with a clear tendency towards political independence even if that demand was never clearly articulated. This may still raise problems of judgement about what is a clear tendency, but these are surely of a much reduced order.

Most of the movements for autonomy in India since independence do not constitute national movements in the Leninist sense. Undoubtedly certain mass movements (for example, Nagaland) have arisen with a definite thrust towards secession which justifies their designation as a national movement and their participants as a nationality. Elsewhere in the subcontinent, the national question is crucial – there are nationalities within the multi-national nation-state of Pakistan and there is the emergence of the Tamil nationality of Sri Lanka. But, since such entities as nationality or nation are 'states of mind', they are all subject to potential transformation, to birth and to disappearance. The state can become a nation-state. And the nation-state, with more difficulty, can regress to simple statehood.

The point about India, then, is that, recognizing the inherent fluidity of states of consciousness, one cannot theoretically rule out the possibilities of India becoming more (or less) multi-national than it actually is or even of language-based national movements (having a clear tendency to political independence) arising within it. But what actually is India today? What has it been since independence? What is likely to happen in the future within a time-scale suitable for the purposes of intelligent speculation?

In India the linguistic community as an imagined community did not so much precede the rise of nationalist consciousness and nationalist struggle as develop along with and through it. Leaders in the National Movement were often also leaders of the regional movements of linguistic consciousness and commonality, which is why the desire for a linguistic division of states was so urgently expressed after independence. Once achieved, however, linguistic consciousness in these states lost its 'movement' character. In fact, the most powerful candidates for nationhood in India have been religious, not linguistic communities. This is evidenced not only by the partition of colonial India along religious lines but also by the fact that Hinduism, not Hindi, became crucial to the formation of nationalist consciousness, leading to the emergence of the Indian nation and nation-state and of a pan-Indian nationality. Religion-based nationalism can be said to be bad because it is non-secular and anti-democratic. But it cannot be said to be false – the very existence of such a nationalism or of a religion-based national movement cannot be denied. Incidentally, once it is accepted, as it should be, that there is an Indian nation (and therefore nation-state), then the assumed centrality of the language–nationality link is vitiated. For what was or is the single language of Indian nationalism and of the Indian nation?

The point can be further illuminated through the history of post-independence India. The four states which have had the most tenuous relationship with the Indian Union, which have caused the most trouble for the central government because of separatist movements or popular anti-Indian or non-Indian sentiment, have been Kashmir, Punjab, Mizoram and Nagaland. In the case of the first two, not language (Kashmiri or Punjabi) but religion lies at the heart of their separatist or even autonomist tendencies. In the cases of Mizoram and Nagaland, Christianity may not have played a role of comparable importance, but it is a more important factor than language in promoting a Mizo or Naga cultural unity and identification. With respect to the Nagas it has had to be. After all, 800,000 Nagas are divided into over 40 tribes speaking at least half as many languages (not dialects). At the elite level English has some value as an inter-tribal medium of communication; at lower levels this role is played by a bazaar Assamese. If there are certain common patterns of tribal behaviour, the tribes also have so many distinctive forms of cultural expression that their broad anti-Indian unity and struggle over many years is a remarkable tribute to the mobilizational capacities of the first major leader of the Nagas, Phizo, in exile in Britain for over two decades. But for all their linguistic heterogeneity, the Nagas are an oppressed nationality and theirs has been a national movement fully deserving of left support.

Can it not be said that a dual nationality or national consciousness dominates in India? That most Indians have a *linguistic* national consciousness as well as a *pan-Indian* national consciousness? Is it merely a quibble over terminology to dispute the identification of multi-linguism as also multi-nationalism? But by ascribing nationality status to a linguistic community as well as to a larger community, the problematic character of the relationship between the two identities in the Indian context is not adequately addressed. To call the linguistic community a nationality is to imply an inevitable tension between the two 'national' identifications; it is to imply that the linguistic identification is somehow deeper and more basic. Not only is this analytically and historically misleading in the Indian case (although it can be apt elsewhere), it is also politically misleading. It tends to give a principled character to the general conflict between the centre and the states, to make it an aspect of the nationalities question. It also tends to the view that, should a future rupture of sufficient dimension take place in the Indian political system, then the 'natural' fault lines of the fissuring process will coincide with the linguistic boundaries dividing the population, as is happening today in the Soviet Union, itself a multi-national state. This is to misunderstand fundamentally the historical process of cultural, linguistic and political integration in India, whose strengths, infirmities and tensions are of a qualitatively different kind from those of the Soviet Union. A comparative survey of the two lies outside the scope of this study. But what is said about India here should suffice to show that there is indeed such a qualitative difference and that radical ruptures in India will evoke qualitatively different socio-political responses.

Chapters 1 and 5 gird the central arch of this study of Indian internal transition. Chapter 5, on 'Agencies of Change', traces the development of the left, of the oppressed classes of town and country and of the new social movements. Questions of revolutionary strategy are addressed, such as the 'permanent revolution' thesis, and a judgement on the prospects for radical advance is put forward. Chapter 1 on 'State and

Economy' seeks to establish the class character of the Indian state, to delineate the strengths and weaknesses of the economy, and to investigate the nature of the relationships within the dominant coalition.

Many will dispute my exclusion of the representatives of foreign capital from this dominant coalition. It may be argued that the autonomy of the Indian state and bourgeoisie is exaggerated. India, it is true, is a dependent capitalist country. But the real question is: how dependent? The Indian left has already done too much damage to its cause by underestimating the economic and political resilience of the Indian bourgeoisie and the strengths of its offensive and defensive fortifications. In emphasizing this resilience and strength there is always a danger of bending the stick too far in the other direction. But the Indian state has played a decisive role in constructing the most self-reliant and insulated capitalist economy in the third world. This was not done in accordance with imperialism's wishes but in spite of them. This in itself is a powerful argument for excluding imperialism from the dominant coalition.

But – and this is an important but – what was true in the past need not remain true in the future. From the late seventies (sharply accelerated since the mid eighties) the Indian state and bourgeoisie have turned towards closer reintegration into the world economy. This reintegration is being conducted in a manner which is intended to strengthen the Indian bourgeoisie's position both domestically and internationally. However, desire alone cannot be father to the fact. Though the Indian bourgeoisie operates from a stronger relative base than in the past, the conscious strategy of opening out to the world market in order to strengthen the country's technological base carries onerous risks to Indian economic dependence.

Two areas will need to be watched closely. Can India avoid a debt trap or, having fallen into one, will it be able to escape from it, as it has in the past and as South Korea has done more recently? How successful will it be in using import liberalization and foreign collaboration to transform its capital goods sector, especially in consumer and industrial electronics, so that a sufficiently wide range of advanced skills and goods, hardware and software, can be indigenously produced and reproduced?

That there will be some erosion of economic autarky is not in dispute. The Indian state and bourgeoisie have already chosen to move in this direction. The question is how serious and how permanent will be the erosion of a self-reliance which, when all is said and done, must always be seen as relative? This is a matter of judgement on which there will inevitably be some disagreement. It is never a simple question of fact but a matter of weighing different factors and potentials in order to arrive at summary conclusions. Any generalization about the character of Indian dependency is contingent on an assessment of the *degree* and *manner* of articulation of India's economy in the world economy, bearing in mind that this articulation is a dynamic process subject to constant shifts and alterations.

It is, therefore, entirely possible (some would say probable) that imperialism's representatives may have to be accommodated in the dominant coalition at some future date as subordinate partners, especially if foreign equity investment is to be encouraged in a manner qualitatively beyond anything in the past. Private foreign investments are expected to rise from $208m in 1986–87 to $646m in 1994–95 or approximately 9 per cent of its current account deficit.[6] What would be the economic and political implications of such a development? Much would depend on the homogeneity of origin of foreign capital. The more heterogeneous the sources, the more room for manoeuvre for the Indian bourgeoisie and its principal unifier, the state. In fact, the real heterogeneity of existing foreign capital over the four decades since independence has weakened its ability to control sectors and sub-sectors of the Indian economy, further justifying the exclusion so far of its representatives from the ruling coalition. There is another important consideration. We are well into the age of imperialist and Stalinist decline. America's imperial decline has not so far been compensated by the rise of German and Japanese imperialism, whose growing economic strengths are not paralleled by any commensurate rise in political and military strength. What *has* increased is imperialist competitiveness in the economic field, which, even as it expands the range of linkages between imperialist and dependent countries, also helps reduce the *political* force or consequence of those linkages for the dependent country. The earlier and closer correlative between economic and political dependence can no longer be so readily assumed.

This book has been conceived as an act of intervention and exploration. It is an intervention in the debates of the Indian left which tries to sweep away some of the debris and cobwebs accumulated there. It has sought to establish a case against defining India as a semi-colonial country, for defining it a nation-state and a bourgeois democracy, and against any notion that it is subordinated to that mythical creature, Soviet Social Imperialism. All these misconceptions should be discarded. But if intervention had been my sole or primary purpose, then the polemical charge would have been greater and more care would have been taken to present in full measure the contested side of the argument. Such an effort may or may not have been more useful. Certainly it would have resulted in a different kind of book.

But as an exploratory study of the concrete nature of the Indian social formation this book must also extend an invitation. Marxist thought must try to paint the large picture as well as devote appropriate attention to the smaller parts of the canvas in an ongoing and combined process of constant refinement. Any claim to originality that this work can make lies in its attempt at this particular synthesis. Such an approach carries its own strengths and weaknesses. The panoramic view, even if it succeeds in appearing reasonably symmetrical or coherent from afar, will on closer inspection reveal clumsy brush strokes, patchiness and downright ugly blotches. Such blotches are bound to occur. If, however, this study has some compensatory merits and if it can stimulate others on the Indian left to play the surveyor with better and more accurate effect, then it will have served its purpose.

Notes

1. H. Morgenthau's *Politics Among Nations*, 3rd edn, Sadhna Press, Pune 1966 remains the classic text of Political Realism. Given competing states, 'balance-of-power' politics is unavoidable and eternal. Morgenthau recognizes that the pursuit of balances of power leads to the pursuit of maximum power by individual states which is constantly unsettling and destabilizing of the system as a whole. If Morgenthau was often accused of an excessive emphasis on the necessity to use power, he also cautioned against the abuse of power. His fundamental stabilizing mechanism was a 'moral consensus' which would moderate and check the excessive drive for power by one or more political units/states.

His belief in Political Realism as the best assurance of equilibrium stands refuted by his own terms of reference. A moral consensus cannot be abstracted from specific socio-economic structures having their distinctive set of moral and ideological values. Thus the post-capitalist societies (in howsoever distorted and partial a way) and revolutionary struggles represent an enduring challenge to capitalism's moral consensus. Only a universal moral consensus resting on a universal socio-economic system can establish the desired equilibrium.

2. A. Vanaik, 'Is There a Nationality Question in India?', in *Economic and Political Weekly*, 29 Oct 1988.

3. B. Anderson, *Imagined Communities*, Verso, London 1983.

4. A.D. Smith, *Theories of Nationalism*, 2nd ed, Duckworth, London 1983.

5. H. Seton-Watson, *Nations and States*, Methuen, London 1977; H. Davis, *Towards a Marxist Theory of Nationalism*, Monthly Review Press, New York 1978.

6. A.K. Bhattacharya, 'India May Return to Regime of Controls', in *The Economic Times*, 14 September 1989.

1

State and Economy

There is no major capitalist country in the third world which has a more powerful state than India's or an indigenous bourgeoisie with more autonomy from foreign capital. Brazil may have gross output slightly higher than that of India; South Korea may be the fastest expanding economy of the eighties. But India's premier ranking is fully justified. No evaluation of the overall strength of a specific capitalist state can afford to ignore such questions as the autonomy of that state and of the indigenous bourgeoisie (whose interests it represents) from the imperialist states and bourgeoisies. Nor can it ignore such crucial non-economic factors as the territorial size, resources and population over which that state authority is exercised, and its military strength and potential, particularly in relation to neighbouring rival states which might hope to challenge its regional eminence (see Table 1).

The exceptional autonomy of the Indian state is reflected in a striking and unique fact: there is no other *capitalist* country in the developing world which has had such a sustained and close economic relationship with the USSR or such an enduring political friendship with it. This has been possible precisely because the tensions of serious dependency have been absent and the equality of mutual benefit so marked. It is ironic that what both American conservatives and Maoists would cite as evidence of the weakness or absence of Indian autonomy in foreign policy is in fact the most positive proof of what they would deny. Leaving aside for the moment the misleading character of the term 'nonalignment', there is little doubt that in the developing world India is easily the most 'nonaligned' of the 'nonaligned'. This political status is not and cannot be unconnected to its economic status. It is clearly associated with the particular nature of India's place in the world economy, with the specific strengths of the Indian state and its autonomy even from the dominant classes whose interests it represents.[1]

11

Indian Autonomy

There have been major transformations of the world economy, basic shifts in the international division of labour and very substantial industrialization in many parts of the third world. These developments have pushed Marxists, even those adhering to classical Leninist perspectives, into new evaluations of the nature of 'dependency' of some backward or developing states, even while preserving an insistence on the 'irreducible' dependency on and domination by imperialism. One such effort, by the well-known Belgian economist, Ernest Mandel, can serve as a useful starting point for an examination of the Indian case.[2] After arguing forcefully that the term 'semi-colonial' can no longer be applied to certain countries – for example, South Korea, Brazil, Mexico, Argentina, India, Algeria, Egypt, OPEC, Hong Kong – Mandel proposes instead the term 'semi-industrialized dependent countries'. The principal factor in this transition to a new status is the rise of autonomous financial capital in these countries which has facilitated the dramatic decline in imperialist property and the emergence of heavy industry. This has usually been organized through some mix of state capital and private capital (dominated by the monopolists) or through a combination of domestic and foreign capital.

But these countries remain dependent on imperialism and, therefore, their ruling oligarchies include a bigger or smaller segment of the representatives of foreign, multi-national, imperialist capital, even if foreign capital can no longer hegemonize the ruling oligarchy as it can in semi-colonial countries. Nevertheless, in the semi-industrialized dependent countries, the indirect hold and influence of foreign capital/ imperialism remains powerful and inescapable. This dependence takes five basic forms, one or more of which are supposed to be found in decisive measure in all semi-industrialized dependent countries: (1) the hold of foreign capital remains powerful in numerous branches, so the call for expropriation is still valid; (2) there is domination through indebtedness; (3) there is technological dependence and transfer of outdated technologies; (4) dependence on the world market remains fundamental and there is substantial transfer of value through unequal exchange; (5) there is substantial military and diplomatic dependence on imperialism.

The weight of these indirect forms of control in India has so far been so limited that it is extremely difficult to justify any allocation of space to 'representatives of foreign capital' in the 'ruling oligarchy', 'power bloc' or 'dominant coalition'.[3] It does not follow, of course, that this is a permanent condition. It is an historically provisional conclusion based on an assessment of the pattern of development to date. Foreign investment as a proportion of total investment fell between 1948 and 1974. In the seventh plan period (1986–90) total foreign inflows will not amount to more than 6 per cent of total investment, public and private. Foreign aid which averaged 3.2 per cent of NNP between 1956 and 1968–69 fell to 1 per cent NNP between 1969–70 and 1977–78. Since 1953 foreign trade accounts for between 10 and 13 per cent of GNP. In 1986 exports were 6 per cent of GDP. Total long-term debt service as a percentage of GNP was 1.1 per cent in 1970 rising to 1.6 per cent in 1986. As a percentage of exports of goods and services it was 27.3 per cent in 1970 and down to 24.6 per cent in 1986. But for most of the intervening years it was much lower. The equivalent figures for Brazil are 0.9 per cent rising to 4.1 per cent and 12.5 per cent rising to 41.8 per cent; for Mexico, 3.7 per cent rising to 10.2 per cent and 44.3 per cent rising to 51.5 per cent; South Korea, 3.1 per cent rising to 10.8 per cent and 20.4 per cent rising to 24.4 per cent (see Table 2).[4] Between 1969 and 1980 India was probably the only developing country from which direct equity investment abroad ($122 million) exceeded investment by foreigners ($70 million). Brazil in 1978 alone had a net inflow of $2.2 billion.[5]

Foreign capital in India has tended to come into the most profitable but not the key sectors, for example, capital goods. The areas where foreign capital had a significant presence were oil, drugs and pharmaceuticals, rubber goods, cigarettes, soaps and detergents, typewriters, batteries and bulbs, glycerine and explosives. But in 1976 the Indian state nationalized the assets of foreign oil companies. In rubber and household consumer goods like soaps and detergents, Indian competitors have greatly reduced the market share of foreign firms while even in drugs and pharmaceuticals (a foreign stronghold) domestic firms have taken over 30 per cent of the market, which is better than a number of advanced countries, such as Belgium and Australia, have done. Between 1951 and 1979 Indian dependence on capital goods made abroad declined rapidly. India accounts for 90 per cent of its own domestic fixed investment. The dynamic of Indian industrialization is essentially internal with an indigenous consumer goods sector closely articulated with an indigenous capital goods sector.

Foreign banks account for around 9 per cent of total deposits. Between 1969 and 1981, while the number of Indian bank branches rose from 8,262 to 35,707, the number of foreign bank branches rose from 130 to 132.[6] The one area where the dependency argument has force is that of high technology. But the typical Indian response has been foreign collaboration which does not so much involve equity control as licensing and to a lesser degree outright purchase of equipment or design. Domestic R & D levels of investment are poor by international standards largely because the private sector has little involvement in it. Also multi-national corporations do not transfer the latest technologies – witness the Indian failure to get the latest, state-of-the-art Cray-XMP 'supercomputer' model from the USA.

But in spite of this, the Indian economy has shown impressively consistent growth. The period of long-term capitalist decline in the world economy beginning roughly in the early seventies has left its mark on virtually all the semi-industrializing countries, though at different times and with differing intensities of impact. But in this same period, Indian economic growth had a small but significant acceleration which has become particularly marked in the eighties. It has broken away from the low-level equilibrium that was scathingly called the 'Hindu rate of growth' – 3.5 per cent per annum or thereabouts. South Korea has had an even more impressive acceleration but this has clearly been tied to its export expansion and rising share of the world market. In India accelerated growth has taken place even while the Indian share of world exports has progressively declined. It fell from 1.05 per cent in 1960–61 to 0.65 per cent in 1970–71 to 0.44 per cent in 1986–87. The insulated character of the Indian economy hardly needs clearer verification.[7]

The Indian economy is now beginning to open up, to reorganize its integration in the world economy, but from a relatively stronger position than in the past and in a careful and cautious manner.[8] To overcome or at least significantly narrow the technology gap, India needs to import certain capital goods it cannot yet produce on its own. To finance these imports it needs to export more. But there is no danger of the Indian economy being anything other than overwhelmingly oriented to the domestic market. When allowances are made for opportunity costs, an average annual increase in real terms of as much as 10 per cent in exports would add barely 0.3 per cent to GDP growth.

The Indian government's willingness to liberalize broadly echoes the desires and ambitions of domestic capital. The industrial bourgeoisie, even its monopoly sectors, want liberalization and greater domestic competition. The big business houses recognize that if they themselves are to expand they have to have the freedom to enter on reasonable terms sectors where other monopoly houses have dominated production and marketing. Thus foreign collaboration is to be encouraged with a view to getting foreign know-how and technology to help produce superior and more competitive final products in areas such as consumer durables, but not to encourage entry of finished final goods from abroad.

This is liberalization aimed at strengthening the hold of indigenous capital in the domestic market with the help of foreign capital.[9]

In any sober analysis of dominant class relationships in India as they have emerged and matured one cannot find a meaningful place for imperialism or foreign capital. It is not surprising, therefore, that outside the ritual incantations of the Indian Communist parties' theorists against the 'hold of foreign capital' and the necessity of a 'first stage' struggle against an imperialist–feudalist alliance, there is widespread agreement that the two dominant classes of the Indian social formation are the agrarian bourgeoisie – or rich capitalist farmer class – and the industrial bourgeoisie led by big capital. Beyond this, the exceptional autonomy and strength of the Indian state has posed serious problems and considerable disagreement on what social groups constitute in full the 'ruling oligarchy' and therefore, on how best to characterize the Indian state.

Problems of Characterization

Broadly speaking, there can be two approaches within Marxism to the problem of the non-neutral class state. That which dissolves state power into class power, and that which refuses to do so. The first approach literally defines away the problem of establishing the class character of the state. But the great merit of this approach is that by focusing attention on the question of how the capitalist state acts to reproduce capitalist relations it has stimulated the development of concepts which have become indispensable tools for investigating and understanding the class nature of the state. The seminal writings of Nicos Poulantzas, for example, sparked a veritable take-off of Marxist theorization on the state.

For post-colonial societies – even in the case of India, where the indigenous bourgeoisie was relatively well developed – the state has to be seen, as Skocpol has argued, in 'organizational' and 'realist' terms, as actual organizations with certain interests distinct from those of the dominant classes controlling real peoples and territories.[10] Hamza Alavi is surely right in his insistence that both the colonial and post-colonial state were overdeveloped and have consequently had to play a major role in the accumulation process and in developing and expanding capitalist production relations, in consolidating (and sometimes even creating from scratch) capitalist ruling classes.[11] The substantial and necessary autonomy of the overdeveloped post-colonial state (which must mediate between distinct ruling classes and not just between different fractions of a single ruling class) poses in a particularly sharp way the issue of the third-world 'intelligentsia', the 'state bureaucracy', or in another formulation of similar vagueness, the 'middle classes'. This is partly because the state is manned by members of this middle class and partly because it pursues many policies which do not meet with the approval or support of the industrial or agrarian bourgeoisies but apparently become more easily explicable if they are seen as promoting the interests of those who man the state and who seem to benefit from the extension of the state's role in the economy.

In the Indian case, the urban middle class played a major role in the National Movement. It provided a disproportionate number of the leaders of the Congress Party at all levels. It was the source from which the cadres of the civilian and military bureaucracy were drawn both before and after independence. Time and again, the question of middle-class incorporation in the ruling coalition has surfaced and resurfaced. One early expression of this was the speculation on how applicable to India was Kalecki's concept of the 'intermediate regime'. In this regime, the ruling classes were the lower middle class and the rich peasantry. They organized an appropriate arrangement with the upper middle class. The state was the dynamic entrepreneur and state capitalism served the interests of the lower middle class.[12] Surprisingly, this concept enjoyed currency in the early and mid seventies when the strongly capitalist character of the Indian economy, the growing weight of the industrial bourgeoisie, and the unimportance of foreign capital should have become self-evident. Unsurprisingly, the thesis suffered a rapid demise and is now largely ignored or dismissed.

But the middle class cannot be treated so cavalierly. Both its huge size in absolute terms and its growing prosperity over time have demanded that it be given close attention. No other capitalist country in the developing world has either a total population or a middle class that is in any way comparable in magnitude.[13] There is not enough recognition of the fact that this demographic uniqueness (the sheer size of the domestic market for even a narrow-based elite-oriented industrialization process) has played a significant role in enabling the Indian economy to pursue an internally oriented path of growth with considerable insulation from the world economy, thus reinforcing the state's autonomy. The state and the middle class would thus seem to have been part of a single dialectic of mutual benefit.

Nevertheless, this does not justify attempts to include the middle class in the ruling coalition. Of all the various terms that have been used to describe the social apex – ruling oligarchy, power bloc, ruling-class alliances, dominant coalition/ruling coalition – the last would appear to be most appropriate because of the considerable tension among its various components, above all the tension between the industrial *idiological - cultural elite* [handwritten annotation]

and agrarian bourgeoisie. 'Coalition', rather than 'bloc', 'oligarchy' or 'alliance', better captures the looseness of this arrangement and the pivotal, mediating role that its third component, the apex of the state bureaucracy, has played and continues to play. It is also appropriate to attach to this third component of the dominant coalition the upper echelons of the non-state professional strata, who play a significant ideological–cultural role in civil society, such as senior lawyers and journalists, establishment professors and educationalists, media stars, and so on.

Why not then include the 'middle classes' as a whole in the dominant coalition or an even broader social category incorporating a larger or smaller segment of the 'working class'? And how justified is it to argue that the Indian state represents the interests of this ruling (but not governing) coalition of two exploiting classes and a third social group which does not in itself constitute a distinct class in the precise Marxist sense of the term?

There is an unresolved problem in the Marxist theory of the state. There is still no way of establishing beyond reasonable doubt or valid criticism the class character of the modern state. An empirical investigation of the social origins and background of senior state personnel, their values and motives, their ideological preferences, can at best give powerful weight to the argument that state managers will be favourably inclined to the dominant classes. Detailed study of the ways in which dominant and dominated classes organize themselves to influence the state apparatuses will confirm the immensely superior access that, for example, business and rich farmers have to the Indian state compared to labour and the poor peasantry; or the ways in which they create obligations through campaign contributions, corruption and favours to senior bureaucrats and politicians.[14] Even an analysis of the content of state policies showing how the specific interests of the dominant classes are regularly served and their class power strengthened cannot be taken as decisive proof of the state's class character. This would be functionalist explanation at its crudest. All these approaches can do is show that the practice of the state displays a consistent and cumulative class bias which renders liberal notions of the neutral state so implausible as to be untenable. But that is a separate issue.

Perhaps the most promising methodological approach – one which can show that class power does 'determine' state power – is to *specify* the filtering, selection and transmission mechanisms through which the exercise of such power governs personnel recruitment and training, the examination and choice of policy options, state revenue sources, decision-making sources, and so on.[15] This needs to be done for different

class character of state [handwritten annotation]

historical periods so that a dynamic element is introduced into the analysis and it becomes possible to visualize how shifts in the relationship of class forces even within the ruling coalition affect state structures and activities and through them the economy. As far as the Indian social formation is concerned, this is still an unexplored research agenda, at both the theoretical and empirical levels. All that can be offered here as a clearly inadequate substitute for this critical task are some observations and generalizations whose plausibility must be measured against similar, broadly Marxist attempts by others to elucidate the nature of the ruling coalition and its relationship to the state.

The Dominant Coalition

The most important effort in this direction was undertaken by Pranab Bardhan in his Radhakrishnan Memorial lectures at Oxford University in 1984, subsequently published as *The Political Economy of Development in India*.[16] This short work (barely 100 pages) set new standards in elegance and terseness of exposition, while retaining an impressive sweep and synthetic appeal. More recently, Ashok Rudra, in an article of much narrower focus, has also sought to present a case for considering the 'intelligentsia' a ruling class.[17]

Bardhan starts off by arguing that the state should be seen as an autonomous actor which, in certain historical cases – for example Meiji Japan and India – has been far more important in shaping and moulding class power than vice versa. Without explicitly saying so, he seems to be far happier with Skocpol's concept of 'potential autonomy' than Miliband's or Poulantzas's concepts of 'relative autonomy'.[18] In the first decades after 1947, the personnel of the state elite in India enjoyed an independent authority and prestige that made them both the main actors in and principal directors of the unfolding socio-economic drama of Indian development, though class constraints existed.[19] Over time, however, with the strengthening of the main proprietary classes (the industrial and agrarian bourgeoisies), the autonomous behaviour of the state became confined more and more to its 'regulatory' rather than its 'developmental' functions.[20]

Bardhan offers convincing factual evidence to support identification of the industrial bourgeoisie (as a whole) as the dominant proprietary class and the principal beneficiary of state policies. This class, under the leadership of the top business houses,

> supported the government policy of encouraging import substituting indus-
> trialization, quantitative trade restrictions providing automatically protected

domestic markets, and of running a large public sector providing capital goods, intermediate products and infrastructural facilities for private industry, often at artificially low prices. Since the mid-fifties the government has created several public lending institutions loans from which form the predominant source of private industrial finance. . . . an elaborate scheme of industrial and import licences has been allowed to be turned to the advantage of the industrial and commercial interests they were designed to control. The richer industrialists having better 'connections' and better access, have got away with the lion's share in the bureaucratic allocations of the licences thus pre-empting capacity creation and sheltering oligopolistic profits.[21]

Even when the big houses created unlicensed capacities they were never punished but in many cases actually rewarded by subsequent 'regularization' of such illegally created capacities. Government financial power through the term-lending institutions (with the right to convert debt into equity) was never really exercised, and real managerial control was left in the hands of private monopoly houses. Instead, the government became a risk-absorber of the last resort, a place for the private sector to dump its sick units. In recent years, the avenues of big business growth have been further cleared.

The small-scale industrial sector has not been ignored. It has grown substantially and its linkages, through subcontracting and ancillarization, with the big private sector companies have become stronger. The number of products whose production was to be reserved exclusively for the small-scale sector grew from 46 in 1967 to 844 by August, 1981. Over 350 products are purchased by the government exclusively from the small-scale sector. The principal socio-political significance of state support for this sector has been its weakening effect on trade unionism as well as the avenues it provides for upward mobility to members of the urban petty bourgeoisie and to a lesser extent the rural rich.

The other main proprietary class is the agrarian bourgeoisie or rich farmer class, which is numerically far more important than the industrial bourgeoisie. Land reforms, like the Zamindari Abolition and Tenancy Acts of the fifties, helped promote the rise of this class. Its members have been the main beneficiaries (much more so than their more numerous allies, the family farmers) of government agricultural policies providing institutionalized credit and liberal and subsidized inputs of various kinds (fertilizers, seeds, water, electricity, and so on); they have also benefitted from ever-escalating procurement or 'floor' prices which have been well above average costs of production since the mid sixties for wheat and since the mid seventies for rice.[22]

If size of landholdings is used as a criterion for classification, then, according to Bardhan, roughly 19 per cent of the rural agricultural

(handwritten marginal note: current? figures?)

population, accounting for 60 per cent of cultivated area and 53 per cent of crop output (in 1975), could be considered as belonging to the rich-farmer category[23] (see Table 3). A classification based more strictly on labour hiring would probably reduce this class to 14–15 per cent of agricultural households.

Bardhan's third proprietary class is made up of the 'professionals', by which he appears to mean the public bureaucracy (civilian and military), which he stretches to include public-sector white-collar workers.[24] But to justify calling this a *proprietary* class, Bardhan is forced to introduce a notion of 'cultural capital'. The privileged access of this class to education and technical skills is said to give them an extra 'rent' income related to scarcity. This they are able to multiply through corruption stemming from their manipulation of a vast array of public controls over private industry and trade. Having introduced the criterion of cultural capital there is no logical reason why this proprietary class should not be further extended to include the intelligentsia and the professions *outside* the public sector. This is, in fact, what Rudra does, endorsing the notion of cultural capital but using as his principal criterion of classification the notion that the third class in the dominant coalition includes all those who do not produce but nevertheless share in the surplus appropriated and disposed of by the other two proprietary classes, the industrial and agrarian bourgeoisies. Rudra's approach, as André Beteille has argued, paves the way for incorporation of even public-sector manual workers in the third 'ruling class'.[25]

Bardhan, in making a case for his 'professionals' to be considered part of the dominant coalition, focuses entirely on the professionals of the public bureaucracy. This clearly stems from the importance he attaches to the physical occupancy of positions in the state structures, both in the central services and in the states. It is this that is supposed to give them the class power which they are then able to turn to their benefit. Indeed, his efforts at substantiating his hypothesis rely on the 'benefit' argument, for example, citing evidence of the rising real incomes of government employees and their assured employment.[26] The fact of rising middle-class prosperity, of this group's vested interest in maintaining this prosperity, or even of the state's constant concern to succour this stratum can by no means clinch the issue. The urban petty bourgeoisie constitute the crucial mass social base for the industrial bourgeoisie and a vital part of the economic base and market for both the industrial and agrarian bourgeoisies. The very pattern of capitalist development and industrialization pursued and promoted by the Indian state was geared to meeting the needs (actual and fostered) of a minority of the total population. There is no mystery, therefore, about its rising incomes. If on the supply side the Indian state has had to promote and develop a class of producers–owners, and even involve itself directly in production, it has also had to promote and develop on the demand side a broadening social category of reasonably well-off consumers, thus creating minimum conditions for an internal dynamic of growth. But can or should the class and social power of 'producers' (in the bourgeois sense) and consumers be approximated, let alone equated?

What class power do these professionals enjoy and how do they exercise it? How do they influence state decision-making with respect to the whole gamut of domestic preoccupations – from industry to agriculture to commerce to state expenditure in non-developmental areas? Their interests appear to be more linked to the expansion and consolidation of educational and administrative functions and presumably to further nationalization than to technological, agricultural or industrial progress. This class as a whole has no unifying interests apart from wanting to increase its incomes, preserve employment, and extend job prospects.[27]

According to Bardhan, in the principal conflict within the dominant coalition, the public-sector professionals line up with the industrial bourgeoisie against the rich farmer. Furthermore, he argues that there is a secondary conflict between these professionals and the industrial bourgeoisie which is focused on the licence-permit-quota raj, the system of government controls over private-sector investment and production.

The tension between the industrial and agrarian bourgeoisies has focused on the issue of terms of trade between agriculture and industry. The evidence available on this issue is not conclusive since the choice of base year for measurement can lead to substantial variation of outcomes. There is some agreement, however, that net barter terms of trade, having been roughly stable till the mid sixties then moving against industry till the mid seventies, began to shift against agriculture, even if the net income terms of trade have not shifted in the same way. Disaggregation of agricultural products into consumption or wage goods (mainly food) and into raw materials (agro-inputs into industry) and of industrial products into consumption goods and industrial inputs into agriculture suggest that where farmers have really lost out (though by how much is not clear) is as buyers of both industrial inputs and consumption goods and as sellers of raw materials, rather than as sellers of wage goods. The biggest beneficiaries have been the urban producers, both on the output and input side. Urban consumers have benefitted from state subsidization of foodgrains, which have kept prices lower than they otherwise would have been.

But is this the result of pressure from public-sector professionals or of the state elite's desire to restrain urban inflation in order to maintain social and political stability and to its general sensitivity to the urban constituency as a whole, the 'middle class', whether employed in the public sector or not? There is simply no justification for seeing this policy as a specific response to some presumed pressure of the public-sector professionals. The policy of food subsidization is a long-standing one and was never initiated as a simple response to the needs of the professional class. Their attitude to what the rich-farmer lobby calls the rural versus urban (or Bharat versus India) conflict has been one of indifference. It is the agrarian bourgeoisie which has every interest in drawing the battle lines along an exaggerated city versus countryside divide, both because it benefits most from government attempts to 'rectify' the terms of trade (or at least prevent them from getting significantly worse) and because this is the best way for it to secure the necessary cross-class and cross-sectional mobilization in the countryside that is vital to its political and social strength. The rich-farmer lobby wants to win over a maximum of the family farmers and neutralize a minimum of the poor peasantry and the landless. Anything more is a bonus.

The secondary conflict between the professionals and the industrial bourgeoisie postulated by Bardhan and others assumes that this 'class' as a whole benefits through corruption and other private favours from a regime of state controls. This is broadly correct. Corruption has been sufficiently institutionalized in government administration and in the nationalized financial and industrial units that it flows down to even manual and blue-collar employees (so why not include them?). But the crucial point is that responsibility for institutionalized corruption lies at the upper layers of the administrative hierarchy. Those lower down may be silent if willing partners in preserving a system of controls but they possess no leverage in deciding whether this system is to be continued, deepened or weakened. It is the state elite that has the power to take decisions on this as on the whole range of industrial, agricultural and other policies. This state elite, which can be further subdivided into its political and bureaucratic components, is not susceptible to pressure from below, which is in any case negligible with regard to general issues of sectoral or national interest. Its horizontal linkages to the dominant classes outside the state apparatuses but within the ruling coalition are incomparably more important than any downward linkages it has to lower-level state employees.

Bardhan is not unaware of the great disparity in power between the upper and lower ranks of his professional class. He calls the former the state elite but confines it rather too narrowly to the political leadership when it should include the upper echelons of the permanent civilian and military bureaucracy. The latter do not merely implement decisions taken by the former, as he seems to imply, but play a crucial role in determining the range of options examined and influencing final choices.

The apex of the state bureaucracy can be said to include both the political and the non-political appointees in the state apparatuses.

As for including white-collar workers in the public bureaucracy – that is, those below the non-unionized managerial cadre – their power to block implementation is limited and rarely exercised. The central argument for nevertheless including them as members of the proprietary class ignores critical questions. What proportion of 'class' power do they wield? Is this proportion significant? The argument rests on the fact that they share in the multiplication of incomes arising from disbursements by the main beneficiaries of the decisions that are implemented.

The 'neta-babu class' is neither a class nor is its magnitude anywhere near the figure of 16 million that was once calculated by Prof. Raj Krishna.[28] Had this really been the case there would be no adequate explanation for the ease with which the post-1980 Mrs Gandhi government and the Rajiv government endorsed and carried out programmes of liberalization. In fact there was a broad consensus within the apex of the state bureaucracy as well as among the ideologists outside government (senior journalists, professional economists, and so on) in favour of both liberalization and a reduction in the economic role of the state. No ideological battle on this was ever really joined because there was no underlying material conflict between professionals and the industrial bourgeoisie. If the liberalization programme has been implemented cautiously, this is not because of subterranean resistance from a bureaucratic class, stretching down to unionized white-collar workers, responding to threats to their livelihood from the erosion of a bloated system of administrative controls, but because significant sections of the state elite along with important sections of the industrial bourgeoisie are themselves concerned that liberalization should not proceed too far too fast.

Conflicts within the dominant coalition should in theory be refracted in struggles within the state apparatuses and as such should leave significant traces on state policies and in particular the state budget, its principal financial mechanism for reproducing itself and expanding its power. The fiscal crisis of the state is thus always a social crisis and Bardhan is fully justified in seeking evidence of intra-coalition conflicts through a disaggregated analysis of the state budget and the factors behind the government's growing fiscal deficit. But this must always be done with due care. When it is not possible to specify the particular mediations through which a particular class has succeeded in securing a greater allocation of resources for itself, it is necessary to be doubly cautious.

The fact that state expenditure on public administration and defence has progressively risen does not necessarily mean nor even plausibly suggest that a bureaucratic class exists or that it is part of the dominant coalition. Many analysts have made much of the higher than average growth rates of expenditure in this area. Patnaik has also emphasized this, though with the economic rather than sociological intention of showing that Indian growth has been too strongly skewed towards the services sector and fuelled to a great extent by non-plan expenditures.[29]

The budget deficit has been growing steadily. The main expenditure is on defence, public debt interest payments, and subsidies on food and fertilizers. Subsidies have grown fastest at over 40 per cent per annum over the last few years. Tax collection is inelastic. There is no question of taxing rural wealth or incomes. In keeping with its policy of encouraging corporate private-sector growth and pleasing the urban middle-class consumer, direct taxes as a proportion of total revenue collection have been declining. Indirect taxes bear a heavy burden. The overall result has been a growing fiscal gap covered by deficit financing and market borrowings. Behind this fiscal crisis lies government pandering to the industrial bourgeoisie, the rural rich, the urban middle-class consumer and the defence establishment. Where then does the 'bureaucratic class' come into the picture, especially when the orientation of the present government is to cut budgetary support to the public sector and generally reduce its role in the economy?

The 'professionals' cannot be held responsible for the importance given to defence. The continued allocation of significant resources to defence is not a function of the pressure of the 'public bureaucracy' as a whole, let alone Rudra's 'intelligentsia', but of the general vision of the future held by the state elite (which includes the top echelons of the defence services) and its larger political and military ambitions. Revealingly, defence expenditure remains something of a sacred cow, subject to only the faintest and most occasional criticisms.

As for the progressive increase in value added in public administration and defence, a recent study shows this to have been significantly overestimated, as also for the services sector as a whole. Original estimates showed value added (for public administration and defence) in the sixties and seventies to be 7.9 per cent per annum rising to 12.1 per cent per annum in the eighties (up to 1985–86). Revised estimates following a different and more accurate method of computation show value added in the eighties at 6.5 per cent per annum. Transport, banking and insurance have shown growth rates in value added significantly higher than administration and defence, and communications has shown comparable rates of growth in the eighties. The services sector is now believed to have grown at 5.7 per cent per annum in the eighties instead of the earlier 7.4 per cent per annum computation.[30] The growth acceleration in the primary and secondary sectors in the eighties has been sharper than in services. The service sub-sectors most closely connected to the commodity producing sectors have had relatively faster growth. Given that state autonomy is greatest in the sphere of allocation rather than production, why, if the 'bureaucratic class' exists, has it not done better for itself in the eighties?

Political elites must be distinguished from bureaucratic elites at both the central and state levels. Bureaucratic elites at the centre are far less susceptible to the pressure of the agrarian bourgeoisie than their counterparts in the states or the political elites in both centre and states. In the states the more localized the bureaucracy, the more subordinated it is to the power of the rural rich. The industrial bourgeoisie clearly exercises greater authority on the bureaucracy at the centre and a reasonable counterweight on the bureaucracy in the regional metropolises. The political elites at the centre and in the states suffer the strongest of dual pressures from both the industrial and agrarian bourgeoisies. These elites, constituting the apex of the bureaucracy with all its internal factionalism, are the crucial forums within the state where the intra-coalition conflicts are fought out. Detailed study of these elites, their factions, their relationships to the numerous class organizations and to the movements of the rural and urban bourgeoisie are likely to provide important clues about the transmission and selection mechanisms that link class power and state power.

Democratic politics favours the agrarian bourgeoisie whose powers of popular mobilization cannot be matched by its industrial counterpart. Against this, the very logic of capitalist development ensures that the industrial bourgeoisie will remain the strongest class even as the social and political challenge of the rich farmer grows. Capitalist development means progressive industrialization. There is no getting away from this. The needs of industry and the service sector become more important. Their relative weight grows. Expanded reproduction becomes *their* expanded reproduction. The government's turn to liberalization had everything to do with Indian industry and very little to do with agriculture. At the same time it must be remembered that the increased attention paid to agriculture from the third plan onwards did reflect the growing importance of the agrarian bourgeoisie.

But the dominant coalition need not be a permanent fixture. For all the sharpness of the present conflict between agrarian and industrial bourgeoisies, it remains a struggle about the terms of accommodation within the 'first', prospering India, as distinct from a 'second', where tragic levels of backwardness and poverty persist. The dominant coalition could give way in time to a more conventional ruling-class alliance or even a bloc. After all, by the year 2000 the agricultural sector might at best contribute only a quarter of total output, though the rural and peasant population will remain large both absolutely and relatively. The struggle of the agrarian bourgeoisie exists in two phases. At present the rich farmer must secure assurances that the state will do everything it can to give it secure and growing surpluses. But it is the second phase that is decisive for this bourgeoisie's future. The capitalist farmer *family* must be able to make the transition to becoming the farmer capitalist *family*. This is not just a question of progressive industrialization and commercialization of agricultural production and marketing. It is above all a question of the rich farmer family having sufficient scope to invest its surpluses in industry and trade, to traverse the worlds of town and country with near-equal facility, confidence and profitability. These phases are not distinctly demarcated in either time or space. For many a rich farmer family in Punjab the transition has already been made, while for many more the inability to invest accumulating surpluses in a productive manner is a growing frustration which has not a little to do with Punjab's social and political crisis. If in the medium term the state aims mainly to manage this basic conflict within the dominant coalition, its more fundamental challenge is to resolve it.

The sheer size of this agrarian bourgeoisie, the weaknesses of the tendencies towards social polarization in rural areas, the absence of any process of cumulative land consolidation, the limited time-span available, all combine to make this task of class integration an endeavour without historical precedent or parallel.[31] If such a process gathers adequate momentum it will ultimately reflect itself in a shift or extension of agrarian demands. In the fifties and sixties the central issues were land reform (this much but no further), compulsory procurement of foodgrains and the Damocles sword of taxation on agricultural property and incomes. The pressure then was directed primarily at state governments. From the late sixties onwards, the main issues have been output and input prices and cost subsidies, with the pressure directed mainly at the centre. The state governments remain the foci of agrarian mobilization not only on such issues as debt cancellation but also because they are seen as important avenues for pressuring the centre on issues where the latter has final decision-making powers.

Class Relations and Economic Performance

Has the preservation of a bourgeois democratic system helped or hindered economic growth? The experiences of Brazil during its 'miracle years' and the 'gang of four' in East Asia might tempt one to opt for the latter. But economic development has taken place under such historically varied political conditions that it is not possible to venture with confidence any such general conclusion. Authoritarian political structures can in the short run lead to greater extraction of surplus value but in the longer term produce declining worker productivity through various forms of covert resistance of which work apathy is but one manifestation. In the Indian context, it might be argued that the fiscal crisis would not be so severe or might even be absent if there had been no democracy, since the kulak lobby among others would be prevented from pressing its case for greater subsidies.

However, the consequences of shackling the kulaks might have been just as detrimental to the economy, giving rise to insufficient agricultural production, inflated pricing of wage goods, higher levels of food imports, more serious foreign exchange problems, and so on. It makes little sense to engage in historical might-have-beens. It is more fruitful to accept the reality of a functioning democracy and focus instead on how the shifting relationship of forces between classes seem to have been reflected in corresponding shifts of emphasis in government policies and shifting patterns of economic development. The principal components whose inter-relationships need to be investigated are state capital, private industrial capital, the rich farmer and his rural petty-bourgeois ally, the urban petty bourgeoisie, and the working class.

But before this, there is an issue which can be more easily disposed of – the relationship between political stability and economic performance. Frankly, it is difficult to see any determinate relationship at the aggregate level. The period 1947 to the mid sixties was one of relative political stability corresponding to the period of the first three five-year plans. This was also the period when the industrial infrastructure was laid down, when the 'green revolution' in agriculture was initiated and when overall economic performance was reasonable, if modest. Politically, the period since then has been one of endemic instability. But in economic performance this period can be divided into two phases. From the mid sixties to the mid seventies there was a deceleration in overall growth, particularly marked in the industrial sector. But from the mid seventies there has been a noticeable pick-up, with average growth rates in the eighties superior to even the first two plan periods.

Only at a more disaggregated level of economic and political evaluation can any meaningful determinations be established. Thus, the two periods of serious inflation (1965–67 and 1973–74) were also the two periods of intense political turmoil. The first saw growing electoral disillusionment with Congress (witness the 1967 election results), the emergence of organized dissidence in almost every state Congress unit, and later the first break-up of the Congress. The second saw the anti-price rise movement, Nav Nirman movement and J.P. movement (named after the leader Jaya Prakash), the 1974 railway strike, followed by the Emergency. It is impossible to believe that economic factors like inflation, declining food production (in the crisis years of the sixties), the increasing inability to absorb all the educated unemployed (early seventies) had nothing to do with the growing social and political unrest of these years.

Even in the post-Emergency years of better overall economic performance, variations in regional growth, inequities of income and wealth distribution, persistence of high unemployment have all promoted specific political and social mobilizations, such as the textile strike and the revival of Naxalite activity in Bihar and the forest regions of central India. In other cases, such as the Punjab crisis and the kulak movements of north, west and southern India, it is the problems of growing prosperity that have promoted turmoil.

During the first two plan periods, (1951–55 and 1956–60) state policies reflected both the relative unity and freedom of the state elite and the constraints imposed by the propertied classes of town and country. Their pressure on the state was expressed partly in what it did and in what it did not do. Thus in agriculture, the Congress (not without some infighting) gave up the idea of radical institutional changes in the countryside, such as collectivization, major land redistribution in favour of the poor, heavy taxation of the rural rich, and so on. The community development programmes were subverted to benefit the better-off. The Panchayati Raj became a major tool for institutionalizing the power of the rural elite.

The Industrial Policy Resolutions of 1948 and 1956 went further than the private sector had hoped in matters of ownership and management. The state pursued its own course in trying to establish control over the commanding heights of the economy. But it also reassured private capital through its policies and behaviour that it need feel no fear of expropriation and that every effort would be made to nurse the private sector through a healthier adolescence and adulthood.

By the early sixties the growing social and political weight of the agrarian bourgeoisie had begun to be felt in the Congress and there was a sharp jump up between the second and third plans in allocation for the agricultural sector. Between the first and second plans total outlay on agriculture/irrigation had fallen from 34.6 per cent to 17.5 per cent. The attention to agriculture has been sustained in subsequent plans; both state and private industrial capital agreed that public outlay (rather than rising agricultural incomes) was the only way to create adequate aggregate demand and to provide the wherewithal for constructing core industries.

By the end of the third plan (1961–65), import-substituting state capitalism had done its job and come closer to exhausting its possibilities. Between 1951 and 1969 there was a 300 per cent increase in the index of industrial production, comprising a 70 per cent rise in the consumer goods industry, a 400 per cent rise in output in the intermediate goods sector and a 1,000 per cent increase in the capital goods sector. The last two sectors, which accounted for less than a third of value added in large industry in 1951, accounted in the mid sixties for two-thirds of value added in large industry.[32] After a three-year hiatus, the fourth five-year plan (FYP) was launched (1969–73) and represented no significant change from the previous strategy emphasizing self-reliance, promoting new technologies in agriculture and coddling the private sector.

The most important economic measure of this period, one which had a decisive impact on the subsequent development of the economy, has still not been adequately analysed – the 1969 nationalization of the fourteen largest commercial banks. In retrospect this measure, along with the setting up of government controlled financial institutions – such as the Industrial Finance Corporation, the Industrial Development Bank and Industrial Credit and Investment Corporation – can be seen to have established a crucial financial infrastructure for systematic capitalist development in the country. At the time of nationalization there were 10,000 bank branches and bank deposits valued at roughly Rs 6,000 crores. Today there are over 55,000 branches and deposits total Rs 129,000 crores plus. In the present climate the decibel level of the voices calling for privatization of public-sector companies and for reducing the state's role in the economy is rising. But the calls do not extend to the nationalized banking system or to the term-lending institutions. Nor will there be any such calls before the end of this century. The nationalized financial system mobilized domestic resources and organized their disbursement for productive investments over a scale and with an efficiency which the private banking system could never have come close to matching.

But at the time neither the industrial nor agrarian bourgeoisie wanted it. Indeed, Mrs Gandhi's move to nationalize the banks helped precipitate the first split in the Congress. The existence of state autonomy was the prerequisite for carrying out the measure in the face of class hostility. But it is not clear that the state elite saw the move as in the general interest of the dominant classes (though this might have been the case). The government justified the measure as a way of equalizing the benefits of growth and providing opportunities to smallholders in the countryside, and to small capital in the cities, as well as providing the financial means to fund basic needs programmes for the poorest sections of society.

The conjunctural economic crisis of 1965–68 and the political turmoil it helped to unleash (in the late sixties the Indian polity moved from relative stability to endemic instability) put more pressure on the

Congress wing under Mrs Gandhi to go ahead with the nationalizations than is perhaps acknowledged. Certainly, one immediate effect was to greatly expand job opportunities for the urban petty bourgeoisie and white-collar workers. The actual relationship of class forces in India's capitalist economy ensured that, once the nationalized financial institutions were established, they worked to further strengthen the position of the dominant classes, particularly the industrial bourgeoisie.

In the seventies and eighties the state has had to play a careful balancing act. Even while mediating tensions within the dominant coalition it has sought to broadly satisfy all segments of the industrial bourgeoisie, big and small, while also keeping the urban petty bourgeoisie and middle class relatively content. Bardhan and others are perfectly correct to stress that this has led to a proliferation of subsidies and transfer payments in various guises – for example, programmes for helping the poor where massive 'leakages' benefit others too.[33] A rough balance has now been established between the claims of major sector groups. Therefore relative plan allocations should not be expected to change significantly, even with a change of government. This was dramatically illustrated by the Janata accession to power in 1977, followed by Mrs Gandhi's return in 1980.[34] But such constancy of government behaviour also assumes that class pressures do not let up, that the intra-coalition relationship of forces does not shift dramatically (this is never purely an economic matter) and that the balances established in the last two decades carry on into the nineties.

Growth and Backwardness

How well has the Indian economy performed? The image of India as a nation of mass poverty is not unjustified. But fulfilment of basic needs of the mass of its population is in a sense an odd standard for judging a capitalist economy's performance. The test of a 'successful' capitalism is not whether it eliminates poverty or not, but whether it lays the foundation for the reproduction of capital on an ever-expanding scale. In this light, India's performance can either be judged in relation to its potential, compared over different time periods since 1947, or contrasted internationally. The first of these approaches is fraught with difficulties. It has necessarily to abstract to some degree from the living play of class forces or make simplifying assumptions that are bound to be sharply disputed. One example of this, discussed earlier, is the question of whether an authoritarian state would not have assured a better performance. The last two approaches seem methodologically soundest or at least safest, though references to the gap between reality and potential can hardly be avoided when discussing the weaknesses of India's socio-economic structure.

India is a backward capitalist country having a number of economic and sociological features characteristic of the poorer third world countries. But in terms of its fundamental economic structure and its dynamic of growth, it is much closer to the weaker of the advanced capitalist countries. In the forty-one years since independence its quantitative and qualitative achievements have been undoubtedly impressive. In 1950 consumer goods accounted for almost 75 per cent of industrial output. By 1976 basic, capital and intermediate goods accounted for over 70 per cent of total industrial output (see Table 4). As can be seen by adding up the first two groups (basic and capital goods) it was in the second and third FYPs (1956–60 and 1961–65) that the essential foundations of India's industrial structure were established. The relative strength of basic and capital goods sectors combined rose after that but much more slowly and have, since then, more or less stabilized.

By the early seventies India had achieved near total self-sufficiency in the standard modern capital goods required by domestic industry, though by the best international standards the technology was often outdated. India produced its own machine tools, chemical equipment, mechanical machinery, heavy and other electrical equipments, transport equipment, professional and scientific equipment, basic metals and alloys. It also had its own steel and power plants, while developing its all-important railway network, the most extensive in the world. Its coal reserves are also among the largest but ash content is high and substantial amounts of coking coal are imported.[35]

Most of this production was located in the public sector whose contribution to total GDP reached 15 per cent in 1970 and is around 25 per cent today. As far as gross domestic capital formation is concerned, the state's contribution is even more important, accounting for 50–60 per cent of the total in most years. The seventh plan leaves more space for private-sector investment by bringing down the public sector's contribution from 53 per cent to 48 per cent, but it is highly doubtful if this will be realized.

State capitalism, then, is and will remain central to the whole economic structure. What is more, probably no other developing country has such an array of public controls over the private industrial sector, controls which have only begun to be streamlined in the last decade following Mrs Gandhi's return to office in 1980. The growing criticism about the stifling effect of these controls on the private sector and therefore on overall industrial growth is broadly correct. The Indian economy has reached a stage of capitalist maturity where private capital must more and more take the lead, with the state seeking increasingly to play a supportive (if still preponderant) role. There is a solid consensus on this both inside and outside the government which is reflected in the near complete abandonment of earlier pretences to pursuing a socialist pattern of development.

But this criticism ignores or minimizes the historical role that these state controls have played. Many controls may have been ill thought out or on balance detrimental. But overall the specific form taken by Indian state capitalism (licence-permit-quota raj and all) did establish a basic 'macro-efficiency' at the expense of serious 'micro-inefficiencies'.[36] Three features, in particular, need to be mentioned: self-reliance; low inflation growth; the widening base for Indian entrepreneurship, that is, the possibility for smaller capitals to emerge and flourish alongside big capital, which was also able to achieve a greater measure of concentration and centralization.

The private industrial sector has grown and diversified. In 1947 the twenty largest firms owned 25 per cent of total private corporate assets. Today they own 40 per cent. Corporate investment is rising steadily as private firms tap more financial resources from the capital market as well as government credit institutions. In 1987 corporate investment was Rs 6,171 crores. In 1988 it should be close to the Rs 7,500-crores mark.[37] The capital market – which accounted for 1 per cent of domestic savings as recently as 1981 – now accounts for 5 per cent. Though limited, this relative shift away from government-controlled credit agencies does give the corporate sector more leverage vis-à-vis the state.

Meanwhile, the share of the small-scale sector in total industrial production has steadily risen since the second FYP, surpassing 40 per cent in 1976 and reaching almost 50 per cent in 1984–85. This sector is responsible for one-fourth (Rs 2,350 crores) of the country's exports. If the estimates of the seventh FYP prove roughly accurate, by 1990 this sector will produce an output worth over Rs 80,000 crores and exports worth more than Rs 4,100 crores as well as employing 11.9 million people.[38]

A recent study of small-scale registered units suggests that, contrary to popular perception, profitability (that is, profits after tax as a percentage of net worth) is higher in this sector than in the corporate sector. It also appears that, within the small-scale sector, smaller units use capital more efficiently than bigger units. However, the inequality in asset holdings favours the latter – 0.27 per cent of units are estimated to own 9 per cent of total plant and machinery.[39] So even within the small-scale sector there seems to be an inverse relationship between size and profitability. This is not as improbable as it might first appear. There is a tendency for small units to substitute capital for labour and use it more intensively. They often use unpaid family labour; they certainly exploit paid labour more ruthlessly. The relatively greater profitability of the small-scale sector vis-à-vis the corporate sector is the consequence of greater efficiency in its use of capital, greater capacity to exploit labour through both low wage costs and higher workloads, and various fiscal and other concessions from the government.[40]

No wonder then that professionals seem to be going into small-scale entrepreneurship and that the big corporate companies are themselves setting up smaller production units – that is, decentralizing production while centralizing marketing and purchasing operations. The small-scale sector is, by this reckoning, a high-productivity, high-profit, low-wage area of operation. But however valid this generalization is for manufacturing activities, it is unlikely to be so for village and cottage industries. Other factors also indicate a less sanguine picture for the small-scale sector. Out of more than 1.3 million registered units, some 5 per cent to 8 per cent are 'sick' units, many perhaps beyond resuscitation. Employment absorption, while obviously better than in the corporate sector (where there has been an absolute decline in recent years), is not as great as once thought and only just exceeds the overall 2.5 per cent per annum growth rate of the labour force. In fact, it is the bigger, less profitable units in the small-scale sector which provide both somewhat higher wages and a greater volume of employment. Clearly, where worker numbers and potential for solidarity are greater, exploitation is less brutal.

Ancillarization and subcontracting by larger firms have undoubtedly grown. Only 2 per cent of all units register themselves as ancillaries, but this is misleading in three ways. First, a much greater percentage are actually functioning as ancillaries or being subcontracted but are not registered as such. Second, there is growing subcontracting and ancillarization within the small-scale sector itself. Third, the ancillarized units account for a disproportionately higher contribution to total value added in this sector. Thus, handlooms may be 12 per cent of all units but they contribute in value added only a 1.5 per cent share, while auto ancillaries are less than 1 per cent of all units but contribute in value added an 8 per cent share. The modern manufacturing sub-sectors are most important. Indeed, eight areas – rubber, plastic, petroleum and coal products; chemicals and chemical products; non-metallic mineral products; basic metals and alloy industries; metal products and parts; machinery and machine tools; electrical machinery, transport equipment and parts – are estimated to contribute almost 58 per cent of total value.[41]

Thus, there is no serious conflict of interest between big and small capital – as long as the state continues to play its regulating and refereeing role, which it shows every intention of doing. Furthermore, it seems clear that a large part of the dynamism in Indian industry is located in registered and unregistered small-scale units. We have here a phenomenon somewhat similar to that of Italy, which in recent years has done well in comparison to other advanced countries, partly as a result of the productivity and expansion of smaller business in its northern region.

The decline in average industrial growth rates in the mid sixties led to a number of projections which now appear to have been excessively pessimistic. There was indeed a distinct downturn in industrial growth overall after the mid sixties. Between 1956–57 and 1965–66 it was 7 per cent per annum. Afterwards it fell to 5.5 per cent per annum. The deceleration was apparently sharpest in the heavy industries which earlier had achieved sectorally faster growth. Among the tardily developing sectors, only consumer durables did not experience a further retardation in growth after the mid sixties. But much of the problem is due to periodization. While it was undeniable that there was a slowdown between the mid sixties and the mid seventies, the pick-up after that was missed in many statistical tabulations which averaged out figures from 1965 to the early eighties.

The reasons for both the downturn and the upturn remain the subject of much dispute. The most influential school of thought with perhaps the best hearing in government circles held that the fault lay basically on the supply side, though it also accepted that the slow rise in agricultural incomes did depress demand for industrial goods. The biggest culprit was said to be the fall in public investment in infrastructure, which reduced demand for products of heavy industry, but, more important, created damaging bottlenecks in power and railway freight traffic. What was needed therefore was to raise investment in infrastructure (but not public investment levels overall) and streamline cumbersome and restrictive government regulatory policies which were preventing the healthy winds of domestic competition from blowing through the economy.[42] The basic assumption was that efficiency of factor use in the organized sector of manufacturing industry was declining (and declining even more steeply in the public sector) and that this was reflected in very high capital–output ratios, despite rising investment in fixed capital in the public sector even after the mid seventies.[43]

Bardhan argued the same point in a different way. He said that excessive subsidies amounting to Rs 15 billion in 1980–81, or half of gross capital formation in that year, was an indication of the enormous waste of resources forced upon the state by its efforts to manage intra-coalition tension and that one consequence was declining public investment in infrastructure.[44]

There were some who reacted against this analysis and its pro-liberalization policy implications. K.N. Raj argued that the assumption of declining factor productivity was either not justified or greatly exaggerated and warned against the erosion of self-reliance, especially in the capital goods sector.[45]

Sudipto Mundle, in perhaps the most perceptive of all responses to the prophets of stagnation, carefully showed that on the supply side a major reorganization of the structure of industrial output was taking place whereby the more modern and faster growing sub-sectors in each overall industrial sector (basic, capital, intermediate, and consumer goods) were increasing their relative weights.[46] At some point this upward pressure would reach a critical point, pulling up the overall growth rate in industry – assuming, of course, that there would be no sharp decline in the level of demand or any shift away from the emerging pattern of demand with which this change in the structural pattern of industrial supply was obviously associated.[47] These modern sub-sectors include heavy chemicals, electricity generation, and aluminium (basic); motor vehicles and machine production (capital); synthetic fibres and petroleum products (intermediate); and electrical appliances and pharmaceuticals (consumer goods). On the input side, there was an equally clear shift from primary-based inputs, such as mining/quarrying and agricultural raw materials, to metal-based and secondary inputs. That is to say, a longer chain of backward linkages was emerging. Industry was becoming the best customer for industry and the agricultural sector's capacity to act as a brake on industrial production was declining. This was confirmed by the limited impact which the grave drought in 1987–88 had on industry in general.

To the extent that this reorganization of industry and the economy meant that the coefficient of energy needs for industry would rise, then, clearly, power and infrastructure constraints could be damaging. Mundle thus implicity recognized the importance of public-sector investment in infrastructure but situated it in an overall economic perspective which provided a more balanced and coherent understanding of the developing dynamic of the Indian economy. Indeed, public-sector investment did pick up from 1976 onwards, but not at such a rate that it could be the key variable explaining the acceleration in industrial and overall GDP growth which became so marked in the eighties.[48]

This puzzle is solved if one puts the supply side picture drawn by Mundle together with the demand side now being sketched by more and more economists, including many who were earlier pessimistic about prospects in the eighties. Rising middle-class consumption, especially in consumer durables, has provided the necessary pull. The weight of consumer durables in industrial production today is 8.5 to 9 per cent, a dramatic advance from the mid seventies. This is not surprising. Where most bourgeois economists exaggerated the deficiencies on the supply side, most radical economists exaggerated the deficiencies on the demand side by giving undue emphasis to the problems posed by the low purchasing power enjoyed by the masses (mostly rural) – the latter do not in fact constitute the principal buyers of India's industrial output. This point can be further elaborated.

Between 1965 and 1986 the share of agriculture in GDP fell from 46 per cent to 32 per cent but in the same period its share in the workforce only went down from 73 per cent to 70 per cent. Meanwhile, industry's share of GDP went up from 22 per cent to 29 per cent but its share of the workforce went up only from 12 per cent to 13 per cent. Similarly the share in GDP of the tertiary sector went up from 31 per cent to 39 per cent while its share of the workforce went up from 15 per cent to 17 per cent (see Tables 5 and 6a). Thus the increases in production in the industrial and services sector have been shared out among a relatively smaller proportion of the workforce. The average per capita income in 1986–87 was Rs 3,000 per annum. In industry it was around Rs 6,500 per annum and for the top 15–20 per cent in industry it was obviously proportionately greater. In fact, the top 10 per cent in industry enjoy average per capita incomes of around Rs 22,000 per annum.[49] The top decile of the population accounts for around 34 per cent of the national income; the top two deciles for around 49 per cent (Table 6b). Clearly there is a very sizeable domestic market for Indian capitalism.

Another aspect that must be taken into consideration is the 'black economy'. This is not unique to India but its size – conservatively estimated at 40–50 per cent of the recorded economy (and growing) – is almost certainly significantly larger than in other industrializing countries, such as Brazil, South Korea, and Mexico, if only because of the array of Indian government controls. It is also much bigger than any equivalent 'black' or 'grey' economy in China.[50] In India, this black economy is closely integrated with the 'white economy'. Black savings flow into the capital market and into bank deposits (with few questions asked), thus providing resources for investment.[51]

Unrecorded, that is, 'black' output, can sometimes originate from the organized industrial sector; it is output which is simply not disclosed. This undisclosed output is generally thought to be greater than reported 'non-production' from fictitious firms conjured into existence to help owners/managers claim certain fiscal benefits or conceal from the taxman the siphoning off of undisclosed monies. Both under-recording and reported non-production are widespread phenomena. Even though the government makes an estimate of production by unregistered units, the sheer size of the black economy, and the fact that it will grow alongside the rest of the economy, means that a great deal of production and services (and therefore, incomes, savings and investments) is missing from the national accounts. Even allowing for such unproductive black activities as real estate speculation, gold hoarding and smuggling, it is not at all unreasonable to assume that actual total production of the economy is underestimated. The overall capital–output (and incremental) ratios in the black economy are bound to be lower than the ratios in the recorded sector by virtue of the absence of heavily capital-intensive industries and of stifling, time-consuming regulations. The degree of underestimation of total output is a matter of speculation, but it may not be farfetched to assume that the real growth rate in GDP could be perhaps half a per centage point higher than official figures indicate.[52]

To be sure, the existence of the black economy also means the inequality in distribution of urban incomes is greater than that indicated by official figures. Since this is largely an urban phenomenon, its effect on the Gini coefficient for calculating overall inequalities in income distribution is probably negligible. Poverty and employment estimates are also carried out independently and are thus not affected by the size of the black economy.

Though the weight of the agricultural sector is declining, it continues to have great importance for the economy both because the majority of the workforce depends upon it and because of its linkages with industry. It provides wage goods (of which the most important is food) and agro-raw materials. On the demand side, agricultural incomes provide an important market for industrial products.

The post-green revolution rate of growth in agriculture of 2.7 per cent per annum is not significantly different from that between 1947 and the mid sixties, but it is highly respectable considering that the earlier period of growth was extensive while the second period was based on higher productivities of land and labour. It is also highly respectable when compared to the average growth rate in agriculture between 1900 and 1950 of 0.5 per cent per annum or to the performance of the advanced capitalist countries in which long-term agricultural growth (after substantial early industrialization) rarely exceeded 2.0 per cent per annum. Of course, in the post-colonial era, a number of third-world countries have had long-term agricultural growth rates even higher than those in India. India's steady growth has been achieved through the systematic capitalization of Indian agriculture, through the extension of capitalist relations of production and through the expanding use of capitalist means of production. There are, of course, enormous regional variations, various ways in which the pre-capitalist forms of the labour process are subsumed under the rule of capital, and great difficulty in the sociological characterization of the Indian peasantry because differentiation has not been on clear-cut capitalist lines.[53]

Nonetheless, the accomplishments are real. Out of a geographical area of 329 million hectares, India has a cultivable area of 186 million and net sown area of 143 million. Gross cropped area is 175 million hectares.[54] Major and minor irrigation schemes have covered at least 60 million hectares of net sown area. However, minor schemes involving spot storage are basically dependent on the rains. The maximum limit for coverage by major and medium schemes is not more and probably slightly less than 55 million hectares. Dependent on the USA for food supplies in the mid sixties, India now produces enough food theoretically to feed its population and keep a small stock for storage. In terms of total output it ranks first in the production of tea and groundnuts, second in rice (paddy) and butter/ghee, third in cotton yarn, milk and tobacco, and in the top five in wheat, cotton lint, potatoes and sugar.[55] Application of fertilizers and nutrients reached 8.4 million tons in 1984–85, compared to 770,000 tons in 1964–65 when the green revolution was just beginning. This is an average of 46 kilograms per hectare, which is still one third of average international levels. The seventh plan envisages that by 1990 some 13.5 to 14 million tons of nutrients will be used (though this may be over-optimistic). High-yielding seed varieties covered 56 million hectares in 1984–85. This is expected to go up to 70 million hectares by 1990; pesticide consumption is expected to rise from 50,000 tons to 75,000 tons in the same period, while irrigated area is expected to expand to 71.3 million hectares by 1990.[56]

What then are the principal features of India's socio-economic backwardness? One of them has received earlier mention – the problems confronting transformation of kulaks into industrialist families as much as farming ones. The industrial bourgeoisie also remains seriously dependent on the state, particularly in respect of finance and working capital. Furthermore, the process of concentration and centralization of capital has been slow, despite the ability of many big monopoly houses to turn government regulations to their advantage. Expanding ownership of assets does not reflect itself adequately in the construction of large factory units which can take advantage of major economies of scale. Even in the public sector, political pressures lead all too often to the construction of a number of regional public-sector units without due regard to minimizing the costs of associated downstream and upstream activities where a lesser number of better located and larger units would obviously be more economically efficient.

The relative weakness of medium capital in India suggests that the 'natural' processes of accumulation and growth and the crowding out of less productive competitors are being artificially restricted. According to I.J. Ahluwahlia, 'In India, apart from reservation, there are substantial financial and fiscal incentives provided to small-scale enterprises. These *rent takers / + intermediate / backward Hindu mass.*

incentives have tended to result in the strong resistance of small units to growing medium-sized in the normal course and in the fragmentation of big ones into small.'[57]

There also exist huge opportunities for making profits in the unproductive activities of trading, hoarding and rent. Thus social groups such as urban traders, middlemen, real-estate speculators, rentiers and smugglers have been able to thrive. Even the industrialist will diversify his investment capital into a variety of non-industrial activities in order to spread and thus lower his risks. There has been no accurate quantification of the social groups involved solely or primarily in such activities, but a not unreasonable estimate might be over fifty million (including dependants), of which traders form the single largest component. By and large they are self-employed and tend to come largely from the intermediate or backward castes which constitute the Hindu majority.

Many who have underplayed India's industrial achievements have suggested that tertiary sector growth has had an undue share of relative growth. This gives a misleading picture of the actual health of the economy. In fact, a good case can be made that the services sector has not grown fast enough.[58] Of course, this can only be a meaningful statement if the performance of its sub-sectors is looked at carefully. In 1986 the size of the tertiary sector in India was 39 per cent. This was lower than in all its major competitors in the developing world (barring Nigeria and non-capitalist China) and far lower than in the advanced capitalist countries, which ranged from a low of 55 per cent to a high of 67 per cent.[59]

As Ahluwahlia has correctly pointed out, three areas in particular require dramatic improvement: construction, transport and communications.[60] After food, the second basic need is shelter. The absence of sufficient demand is a major reason for the low growth rate of 3.5 per cent per annum for construction in the eighties. The railways need substantial improvement while road networks are not only extremely poor for a country of India's size but also very badly maintained. This has serious repercussions for the potential growth of road freight traffic and for any expanded output of heavy and light vehicles. While the government has invited the private sector to make investments in this field, the latter have, not surprisingly, failed to respond seriously. As for communications, there is some recognition that this is a field of top priority in which low-energy using electronics development must lead the way.

While the existence of mass poverty does not prevent the cumulative reproduction of capital, it does constitute a block which widens or at least sustains the gap between actual and potential output. It also has significant effects on specific sectors of the economy, such as construction. Rural poverty creates a serious disequilibrium problem in the food and labour markets. The demand for labour is lower than the actual supply. In the product market, output is less than the maximum because effective demand is curtailed by the inadequate incomes of the rural poor who are either unemployed or in low-productivity employment. A substantially higher growth rate in agriculture is possible and can be a major stimulus for growth, as it has been in China since 1978, or can compensate for a relative decline in industrial growth rates, as in South Korea during the eighties (see Table 7). The impact in India would be akin to China since here agriculture constitutes a 'reserve' area for overall expansion. Rising real incomes of the rural poor (whose demand for foodstuffs is highly elastic) would also help to solve a central dilemma facing the state in the form of pressure from the kulaks. In contrast to progressively escalating procurement, issue and market prices, flexible prices – that is, downward moving prices in periods of good supply – can raise the living standards of the poor, reduce pressure on the urban consumer and still mean higher total incomes for the rural rich since more output could be purchased by the rural poor. For the state it would mean substantially lower food subsidies and thus greater resources for investment elsewhere. In capitalist terms this would be a more rational arrangement.[61]

Two other weaknesses need to be mentioned. It is often noted that conscious insulation of the Indian economy has exacted a price, in the form of a relatively high-cost economy. This general assessment can be accepted, but with due caution. Revised estimates indicate that real levels of domestic savings were not as high as originally thought. The gross savings per centage was thought to have gone from single figures in the first years of independence to a peak of 24 per cent in 1978–79 and to have remained above 20 per cent through the eighties. The figures have now to be scaled downwards, which suggests that investment rates also have to be scaled downwards and, therefore, that capital–output ratios (and inefficiencies) were not as great as originally assumed.[62] Even the accepted capital–output ratios and the incremental capital–output ratios, high though they were, could not be considered exceptional by the standards of most developing countries.

Similarly, there appears to be something of an ideological dimension to the wolf-cries of gross inefficiency. Among those who have been pushing hardest for opening up the Indian economy are to be found many who go too far in criticizing India's import-substituting path of self-reliance. In fact, over a whole range of manufactured goods, India is by no means an inefficient producer (see Table 8). Of course, the comparison between India and the USA in terms of purchasing power parity does not take into consideration the quality factor. But purchasing power parities also reflect indirect taxes, which are higher in India, so the latter's comparative efficiency tends to be underestimated, particularly for items like fridges, beer, televisions and household appliances.[63]

It is safe to say that Indian industry is not as uncompetitive or as inefficient as widely thought. Of course there are areas of terrible inefficiency, for example, steel, where Indian prices are 50 per cent higher than world prices (the result of outdated technologies). And the problems posed by a high-cost economy and relative inefficiency cannot be wished away, even allowing for exaggerated fears. It may be some consolation that the Indian buyer of Indian goods gets pretty reasonable value for money, or that Indian products are better than those of many other countries. But if leading third world competitors and other industrializing countries are more efficient, then Indian capitalism will lose out in exports. It can maintain a sheltered domestic market but if factor productivity does not rise fast enough India's international ranking will not improve in the long-run. The policy conclusion that seems to have been drawn is that selective technology upgrading in the capital goods sector, through a cautious opening up of the economy, is vital, but that it must not be allowed to jeopardize India's broadly self-reliant posture.[64]

India's particular pattern of development has so far been premised on the construction of its own capital goods sector. How then is it now going to cope with what is becoming a major world technology transition – the 'electronics revolution' – whose implications for the reorganization of the international division of labour are still unclear?

This brings us to one of the central aspects of India's relative technological backwardness. It is not only the most fervent enthusiasts who believe that the electronics sector will in the future play the role presently assigned to the capital goods sector. It will be the most important source of new skills and innovations which, through their cumulative application, will substantially transform economies and societies. If Indian self-reliance is to be sustained in the future will India not have to develop a strong semi-conductor base of its own? And how can it go about doing this?

The Indian government is sufficiently aware of the importance of 'hi-tech' that it has developed a comprehensive approach to the promotion of electronics production and use.[65] To increase demand for consumer electronics and computers it has cut excise duties, cutting tariffs for import of principal components from 65 per cent to 25 per cent and eliminating import duties for a wide range of computers. It is encouraging foreign investment (up to 40 per cent) in areas like colour television, computers and telecommunications and in areas where local research and development is poor. Production of large integrated circuits, digital watches, VCRs, and microwave ovens is to be undertaken by the public sector or by the private sector with the help of government subsidies. The state has also set up the Centre for Development of Telematics (CDoT) for developing indigenous digital electronic switching systems. There has also been an attempt to get the latest state-of-the-art computing technologies from the USA. Without doubt, the electronics sector has been the focus of many of the hopes aroused by liberalization.

Between 1978 and 1983 growth in this sector was 19 per cent per annum but this is not high by international standards. Since 1984–85 it has been substantially faster. There was 39 per cent growth in 1984, 41 per cent in 1985 and 30 per cent in 1986. The production of consumer electronics has outpaced that of industrial electronics and components.[66] Seventh plan output and investment targets are highly ambitious and may not be met. Despite India's reservoir of technical skills there is a shortage of electronics engineers and software specialists. Three thousand mini- and micro-computers were produced in 1984, 20,000 in 1986 and hopefully 100,000 in 1990. But most of this input is simply assembling knocked-down imported kits. Therefore the government has given incentives to select foreign companies to make mainframe computers and joint ventures have been encouraged to promote technology transfer.

There is a conscious attempt to build an indigenous base for semi-conductor and integrated circuit manufacturing. There are twenty semi-conductor plants; and India is now self-sufficient in the production of very large-scale integrated circuits. But despite rapid growth, the base is still weak and production is at relatively high cost. The Economic Intelligence Unit assessment is that

> the electronics sector will undoubtedly achieve exceptionally rapid growth, but some way short of the annual 40% rate envisaged in the plan. There will be serious bottlenecks of manpower and investment resources possibly leading to a substantial and growing import demand for electronic capital goods and components. There will also be demand limitations due to market saturation in consumer goods; and serious difficulties which have not yet been fully anticipated in integrating electronics into industry and services. As a result of these obstacles the growth of the industry as a whole is more likely to be closer to the 20–25 per cent band, half the plan estimates.[67]

Warning Signals

Can the acceleration in the Indian growth rate be maintained? If India has broken away from the 'Hindu rate of growth' – that is, low-level equilibrium – is it on the verge of a breakthrough, an 'Indian miracle' akin to the Brazilian performance of the seventies or that of South Korea over an even longer period? There are sound reasons for rejecting such a scenario and even for a measure of caution about whether the near 5 per cent average growth rate of the eighties (and of the fifth, sixth and the as yet uncompleted seventh plan) can be maintained in the nineties. A deceleration, to between 4 and 5 per cent, or closer to 4 per cent cannot be ruled out.

In the coming period, the Indian economy is likely to face two constraints – the threat of inflation and the problem of a worsening balance of payments position. Inflation is the lesser danger. Though government deficits have been rising, only the most diehard monetarist would see this as the principal source of inflation in so large and complex an economy as India's. The present trend of a slow upward creeping of prices, however, is unlikely to be reversed.

Much the more serious problem is the rising debt. India's total foreign debt is currently around $48 billion, which for a country of India's size and resources is manageable. But the warning signals are there. The debt service cost has crossed the danger mark of 20 per cent of foreign exchange earnings and is close to 27 per cent today. The state's sensitivity to the aspirations and expectations of the rich farmers, the industrial bourgeoisie and the urban middle class makes it difficult to reverse its current expansionary policies, at least in the short term. The eighth plan will be larger not smaller than the seventh. The state will do its best to avoid choking off the rising incomes of the middle class or its growing consumption demand, which has been a significant factor in promoting the upturn in industrial and overall growth rates. Many of the things in demand, such as modern consumer durables, have a growing import content. Furthermore, selective technology imports are seen as vital for modernizing the industrial base. The deteriorating balance of payments problem can obviously be met by exporting more or importing less. Significantly raising exports would be the best solution, reducing the pressure on the balance of payments, enabling higher levels of imports of needed technology and further stimulating the consumption-led recovery of recent years. But the possibilities are frankly uncertain and a sharp formal devaluation of the rupee in place of creeping de facto devaluation can safely be ruled out, not only because of fears of fuelling domestic inflation but also because price elasticities for Indian exports may not be sufficiently great.[68] Exports, after all, have to grow substantially faster than imports to rectify the existing imbalance.

Reducing imports would seem to offer better prospects. If technology imports are to remain untouched there have to be compensatory reductions in other purchases, especially of bulk imports. The principal bulk imports are (in order of importance) crude oil and oil products, chemical fertilizers and raw materials, edible oils, finished steel and alloys. The first three items provide some scope for reduction, provided domestic production in each case takes a significant leap forward. Much depends, therefore, on whether there will be a major oil strike in the next five years which can decisively reduce import needs. In the absence of such a strike, Indian self-sufficiency in oil production will fall from 75 per cent in 1984–85 to 64 per cent by 1990.[69] Exploitation of India's considerable gas potential could partially fill the gap. Total proven reserves are over 900 million cubic metres but much of it is currently wasted/flared. Fertilizer plants are being built to use this gas, as is a major 1,700-kilometre gas pipeline project. But though the pipeline is being built rapidly the fertilizer plants are not. In the short term, at least, it is not clear whether or not India can reduce its fertilizer imports. Domestic production of edible oils, however, could improve considerably, providing some breathing space.

If bulk imports do not fall sufficiently and if they are not to squeeze out imports of capital goods then, to make up the gap, the centre can provide incentives for non-resident Indians, encourage the entry of private foreign capital, or borrow from commercial sources or from the IMF. The last is perhaps the least likely. What is most likely is that the government will promote exports through subsidies and try to attract wealthy Non-Resident Indian (NRI) investors from the USA and UK to compensate for the levelling off of remittances by working-class NRIs, mainly from the Gulf countries. If it has to, it will probably buy time by borrowing more from international commercial sources. If in spite of all efforts the balance of payments position gets significantly worse in the nineties, then the state might well prefer to impose serious restrictions on imports and risk deflating the economy rather than allow self-reliance to be decisively undermined.

Industrial/Financial Capital: Domestic and Foreign

State capital dwarfs private domestic capital which in turn is far more important than foreign capital. Of the top fifty companies (ranked according to total capital employed) only seven belong to the indigenous private sector of which only two make it to the top twenty and only one to the top ten (see Table 14). Slightly over 1,000 public sector companies have almost four times as much paid up capital as that of over 170,000 non-government companies (see Table 15). It is true the Indian state has no alternative but to promote the indigenous industrial bourgeoisie. In the seventh plan, for the first time ever, the public sector refrained from setting up new projects in manufacturing. It is in this sense that the leading role (though not the dominant role) has been handed over to the private sector which has also for the first time been invited to invest in domains like power and energy generation that were earlier monopolized by the public sector. Privatization of certain public-sector companies is also a trend that is likely to gather force in the decade to come. Nevertheless, the indigenous industrial bourgeoisie's relationship to the apex of the state bureaucracy will remain, for a long time to come, essentially that of supplicant. Even the figures in Tables 14 and 15 do not give an accurate picture of the real economic relationship of forces between private and public. In asset terms the public sector is at least five times larger.

The Ministry of Finance controls the five most important financial institutions in the country: the Industrial Development Bank of India (IDBI), the Industrial Credit and Investment Corporation of India (ICICI), the Unit Trust of India (UTI), the Life Insurance Corporation of India (LIC) and the Industrial Finance Corporation (IFC). Though their exact portfolio holdings are kept a secret, it is widely accepted that the first four institutions hold over 50 per cent of the corporate sector's total equity. The UTI with over Rs 10,800 crores investible funds is the single most important influence on the stock exchange. The IDBI and the ICICI are the main lending agencies to industry and in the first nine months of 1989 they disbursed funds totalling Rs 4,469 crores – or almost as much as the yearly sales of all the companies controlled by the Birlas, the country's premier monopoly house.

What is more, the convertibility clause which allows the term-lending institutions to convert loans into equity if they are over Rs 5 crores is like a Sword of Damocles perpetually hanging over the heads of the borrowing companies, even though it is rarely used. These financial institutions play the key role in inter-corporate wars by helping (at government behest) one monopoly house or another to benefit at the expense of the rest through mergers and acquisitions. The remarkably rapid expansion of Reliance, currently the third largest business house in terms of gross sales, is in no small measure the result of its excellent connections with government and the ruling party.

There is really no way that foreign companies can hope to achieve the same kind of favoured relationship that the indigenous bourgeoisie as a whole, and certain sections of it in particular, have with the government. The Indian state's fundamental commitment is to the extension of its own power and authority and therefore to that of the Indian bourgeoisie. The indigenous corporate sector has a far greater weight in the Indian economy than foreign capital. The latter has two components – branches of foreign companies operating in India and foreign-controlled (possessing more than 40 per cent of equity) Indian subsidiaries of multi-nationals. These are also called foreign-controlled rupee companies.

The number of foreign branches stood at 510 in 1974–75, fell to 300 by 1980–81 – through closures and transfer of undertakings to Indian companies largely in response to strict foreign exchange regulations (the Foreign Exchange Regulation Act or FERA) – and then began a climb upwards to 414 by the end of 1988 (see Table 16). This was due to the sharp increase in the setting up of liaison and representation offices. After 1974 the Indian government disallowed further setting up of foreign branches except for financial, primarily banking, and tea companies (see also Table 17). According to Table 17, of the 183 branches for which balance sheets are available and which had total assets by 1986–87 of Rs 6,332 crores, the 19 branches of foreign banks accounted for Rs 6,048.68 crores or over 95 per cent of the value of all assets. Average assets for the bank branches was Rs 318.35 crores while average assets of the remaining 164 foreign companies was a paltry Rs 1.73 crores. Within the overall financial structure in India, foreign banks constitute a quite insignificant part in respect of total deposits/loans and contribution to the economy. But they are far and away the most profitable sector of the banking industry, accounting for a strikingly high proportion of total banking profits. Thus in 1987 of the Rs 280 crores profit made by all banks, the foreign banks accounted for Rs 80 crores. They will continue to cream off a great deal in the area of export–import international dealings.

The other component of foreign capital – the Indian subsidiaries of foreign companies – is rather more important. As can be seen from Table 18 it is not to be found anywhere in the commanding heights of the economy and its spread of activity is not to be compared with that of Indian capital. How significant then is the weight of this 'imperialist bourgeoisie' vis-à-vis the Indian bourgeoisie? Here a comparison will be made only with the Indian upper bourgeoisie as represented by the 574 companies registered under the Monopolies and Restrictive Trade Practices (MRTP) Act. As of 1986–87 the total assets of the Indian subsidiaries amounted to Rs 2,782 crores compared to Rs 40,276 crores for the 574 large MRTP companies. The total number of large private-sector companies for 1986–87 was 2,422, with assets totalling Rs 70,699 crores. Thus average asset holdings of the Indian upper bourgeoisie (574 companies) at Rs 70.27 crores is substantially greater than that of the Indian subsidiaries of multi-nationals at Rs 39.2 crores at the end of 1986–87. For the top 86 corporate giants the baseline in asset holdings was Rs 105.7 crores, stretching to an upper limit of Rs 2,002.7 crores. The rate of growth of assets of the top Indian giants has also been substantially faster than that of the subsidiaries of multi-nationals, so the gap between the two is growing wider, for example, 10 per cent for the former between 1985–86 and 1986–87 and 4.74 per cent for the latter in the same period.[70]

But again multi-national activity is highly profitable and does constitute a very significant drain on scarce foreign exchange resources. It can and has been argued that provided there is a quid pro quo in respect of provision of needed technology this is not too bad. But the essential point is that where the multi-national shoe pinches most is in foreign exchange. A look at company finance studies for dividends repatriated by foreign-controlled rupee companies reveals the following: in 1984–85 dividend repatriation amounted to Rs 78 crores; in 1985–86 it was Rs 75 crores; in 1986–87 it was Rs 85 crores; and in 1987–88 dividend repatriation came to Rs 92 crores. To this last figure add profits repatriated by branches of foreign companies in 1987–88 of approximately Rs 8 to 9 crores. A rough estimate of the *visible* outflow in that year would be around Rs 100 crores. But invisible repatriation through transfer pricing would be anything between three and five times this. An annual outflow of Rs 600 crores in foreign exchange is very considerable indeed considering that the net outflow of the total corporate sector (domestic and private) in 1987–88 was around Rs 900 crores.

Apart from the foreign exchange squeeze the other area of growing concern is the rising trend of foreign equity participation, especially in process and manufacturing. But even allowing for these legitimate reservations, the basic hierarchy of power – state capital, domestic private capital and *then* foreign capital – within the Indian economy is clearly going to remain unchanged as the country enters the next century.

International Comparisons

How has India performed compared to other 'high flyers' in the developing world? A distinction should be made between Indian performance relative to other capitalist countries and relative to China. The latter comparison carries special systemic implications, in that it contrasts the performance of capitalist and non-capitalist paths of development. Tables 2, 5, 6 and 7 provide a reasonable data base for a macro-survey. In the eighties, India's industrial, manufacturing and overall performance was bettered only by China and South Korea. What is interesting is that the weight of machinery and transport equipment plus chemicals output in India is greater than for any other country in the tables. India's low inflation rate since 1965 and its debt-service percentage (of GNP) is bettered only by China. Its inequality of distribution is substantially

less than that of Brazil or Mexico, which means that though Brazil
has a per capita income six times that of India, the bottom 40 per cent
of Brazil's population have a mean income less than twice as large as
India's lowest 40 per cent. Had Brazil been able to keep up its 'miracle'
it would have surged far ahead of India in total GDP and challenged
China's supremacy in the developing world. But the sharp downturn of
the eighties has allowed India to catch up, and if allowance is made for
the relatively greater size of the black economy in India, it probably has
a real GDP slightly in excess of Brazil's.

India's general performance weakens the World Bank/IMF's argument
that strong outward orientation is the best prescription for cumulative
growth in the developing capitalist countries. Of the major developing
countries only South Korea has managed to come out of the debt trap
(it is now a net creditor) and reduce its inflation rates to reasonable
proportions. Of the strongly outward-oriented countries only the East
Asian 'gang of four' have prospered consistently. Of these, Singapore
and Hong Kong are city states with no rural hinterland or problems of
linkages between agriculture and industry, and the scale of Taiwan's
economy holds no real lessons for much larger ones.

India's per capita income and life expectancy, however, are among
the lowest in the world and greatly inferior to those in other major
industrializing countries of the third world (barring Nigeria). China,
with only a slightly higher per capita income, would undoubtedly fare
much better than India on a Physical Quality of Life Index (PQLI)
because of its greater equality of distribution of income and wealth, and
its substantially superior life-expectancy and literacy rates. Since 1949,
by most major quantitative indices, China has done better than India.

How much better? The unreliability of Chinese data has posed a
problem. In the seventies, in the wake of the Sino–US entente there
was considerable willingness to accept Chinese data at face value. The
Joint Economic Committee of the US Congress estimated that growth
rates for China and India between 1957 and 1965 were roughly equal at
3.6 per cent per annum. But this was later pushed up for China to 3.9
per cent and then to 5.5 per cent per annum. The World Bank estimates
have also fluctuated. It first stated that China's per capita income grew
at twice India's rate for the period 1957–79, or 2.7 per cent to 1.4 per
cent per annum, and gave total figures of $256 in 1979 for China and
$190 for India. This was later revised downwards in the early eighties
and by 1980 China was said to have reached $290 compared to India's
$240. In 1955 both were said to have a per capita income of $160. But
in the latest World Bank report, China's per capita income in 1986 was
at $300 – only $10 higher than India's – but per capita income between
1965 and 1986 was stated to have risen at nearly thrice the Indian rate

in the same period – 5.1 per cent per annum as compared to 1.8 per cent per annum.

Amartya Sen, perhaps the most internationally renowned of all Indian economists, has strongly disputed World Bank data. He argues that if the 5 per cent per capita rate for China is accepted then this would suggest a gap of nearly $100 in 1960 between the two countries in India's favour, which is presumably ridiculous.[71] Sen believes that Chinese and Indian growth rates are roughly comparable up to the end of the seventies but that China has done far better in the realm of distribution so that it has had greater success in eliminating endemic deprivation or permanent malnutrition. Also, China's average caloric intake per day is 2,620 compared to 2,126 in India. Against this, China had approximately 30 million famine deaths in the terrible 'Great Leap Forward' years of 1958–61.

Sen's analysis tends to lean too much in India's favour. China started out in 1949 with a significantly lower industrial and capital base than did India in 1947. It had much higher man–land ratios and productivity per acre, so potentials for further productivity increases and growth in agriculture were also lower. That it should have matched Indian agricultural growth rates on a cultivated land area 40 per cent smaller even before the late seventies (when China made a dramatic leap forward in agricultural growth) is remarkable in itself. From 1978 onwards even Sen will concede that there is simply no comparison; Chinese growth has far outstripped that of India in agriculture, industry, manufacturing and even in services, though given the non-capitalist structure of the Chinese economy this sector does not play the same quantitative and qualitative role as in India. Furthermore, China has accomplished this with a long-term inflation rate (even allowing for high levels of disguised inflation in recent years) which is still better than that of a low-inflation country like India. It is also more self-reliant and has a superior debt position. In areas of direct export competition with India, for example, cotton textiles, Chinese quality is at least as good, if not better, than Indian. Poverty exists in China and there is some indication that the post-1978 liberalization has worsened it. But the World Bank estimate of 15 per cent below the poverty line in China is much better than the official Indian estimate of 37 per cent, widely considered an underestimate. Though in both countries the overwhelming majority live in the countryside and this is unlikely to change much for some considerable time, China has done much better in providing jobs. Both in absolute and relative terms it has lower levels of unemployment and underemployment. The welfare net for the average Chinese family has also reflected itself in a lower rate of growth in both population and labour force.

India and China, for reasons of history, size, resources and approximate economic parity at the time of independence and liberation respectively, have correctly been seen as exemplary models of the virtues and weaknesses of two different systems and paths of development. They are eminently suited for both inter-nation and inter-system comparison. Examining the evidence, it is difficult to see how one can avoid the conclusion that the Chinese road to socialism, for all its detours, hiatuses, political drawbacks and indeed, its highly 'unsocialist' features, has nevertheless had a far more impressive economic record than the Indian road to capitalism.

Sen has two cautionary comments on the Chinese experience. He points out that since the 1978 liberalization in China, which greatly accelerated growth, there has been a disturbing deterioration in life expectancy and infant mortality rates, especially affecting females (see Table 9, 10 and 11). Public health services in China, once internationally acclaimed, have also deteriorated. He is clearly right in pointing out some of the social costs of turning to the market and of putting economic growth ahead of all other considerations. To this can be added the growing consensus that if the economic boom is not yet over, it will be less strong in the coming period than it has been in the decade since 1978. The tragic events of June 1989 have exposed some of the real problems in China's attempt to combine bureaucratic planning with the market. They will reinforce the turn towards decelerating the pace of the economic liberalization first initiated in mid 1987. Most of the productivity gains of Deng's NEP came through higher work intensity in agriculture where the family plot was again made the primary unit of production. These gains in productivity cannot be sustained at the same level in the nineties. In industry, the Chinese mix of planning and market has had less impressive results.

Sri Lanka was also adversely affected after its IMF-inspired turn of the seventies, when one of the most impressive welfare systems in any third world capitalist country was dismantled. But though these negative developments constitute a powerful indictment of the pursuit of market-led growth at the expense of public provision of welfare, nobody assumes that the deterioration in life expectancy, mortality and literacy rates will be at such a pace that the Chinese PQLI will come down to anywhere near the Indian level. The gap is too wide and the essential scaffolding of the Chinese socio-economic system too firmly in place for this to happen.

What about those 30 million famine deaths? Sen has been very cautious in limiting himself to one inference that can easily be supported. The free flow of information in a more democratic political system would make the chances of such a major catastrophe occurring very remote. In the early stages of such a development, public clamour would very likely force a reversal of policies leading to so many deaths. It is certainly true that in a system where private property in the major means of production have been expropriated, state policies both good and bad have a much more powerful impact than otherwise. But unless one believes that political authoritarianism is an *inherent* adjunct of a socialist planned economy, and that comparable disastrous experiences will therefore be repeated under this system, it can be plausibly argued that the Chinese performance would have been even more impressive were it not for the all too avoidable excesses of post-1949 Maoism. The substantial variety of political regimes in the socialist world, from Cuba to Nicaragua to Yugoslavia to Gorbachev's glasnost in the USSR, indicate a much more complex relationship between economy and polity in socialist societies than most Western defenders of capitalism and bourgeois democracy have been willing to concede.

Poverty and Employment

The proportion living below the poverty line varies from year to year, depending not only on fluctuations in food production but also on its regional distribution. This makes it difficult to establish any clear cut trend.[72] Perhaps the most optimistically rational generalization is that the proportion of poor is either stagnant or declining, but so slowly that the absolute numbers of poor are increasing. By the year 2000, the number of poor is likely to exceed the total population at the time of independence.[73]

Unemployment is not the same as underemployment or low-productivity employment. The poor exceed by a large margin the total of unemployed and underemployed. To remove poverty it is necessary to increase the rural poor's on- and off-farm productivity or else place them in productive employment elsewhere. But a balance has to be struck. Excessively high productivity in agriculture will act against employment. There has to be a labour-intensive strategy of development which exploits the value of appropriate technologies. In rural India there is clearly a strong association between the incidence of poverty and the rate of unemployment for wage-dependent households. The correlation is weak for self-employed households. But the number of self-employed poor (for example, poor peasants and rural artisans) is as large as the number of wage-dependent poor. The overall effect of the new technologies on agriculture or employment absorption has been limited. Unless it can substantially raise off-farm employment opportunities it cannot prevent rising poverty. Capitalist agriculture involves both labour-using and labour-saving technologies. In the first category come such activities as irrigation and drainage, planting of high yielding seeds and fertilizer use, multiple cropping and rotation. Examples of the second are farm mechanization of irrigation, weeding, threshing, ploughing and harvesting, as well as improvement of traditional farm implements. While the new technology seems to reduce seasonal fluctuation in employment it appears to have no significant effect on related off-farm activities.[74] This is very important because non-farm rural activity, which had grown to employ one fifth of the total rural labour force by 1981, is (along with agricultural activity and the urban informal and services sector) one of the three key areas where labour has to be absorbed.

By 1990 the total workforce is estimated to reach around 345 million and is likely to grow annually by an average of 5 million. Seventh-plan calculations are that from a base of 187 million standard person years (SYP) in 1984–85, another 40 million SYPs will have been generated by 1990. Since total unemployment is calculated as 47 million SYPs, this will leave a backlog of 7 million to be taken care of by future plans.[75] In the light of existing data about sector-wise employment absorption this is absurdly optimistic. Agriculture is expected to take up 45 per cent or 18 million SYPs, manufacturing, mining and quarrying around 17 per cent, leaving sectors like transport, communications and housing and infrastructure industries and services to absorb 13 per cent or roughly 5 million SYPs. Other service sub-sectors will absorb nearly 10 million SYPs or about 25 per cent.

A number of studies have convincingly shown that if agriculture is to absorb more labour, two conditions have to be met in the short term: redistribution of rural assets, that is, fundamental land reform; and lower food prices, that is, real market-determined prices.[76] The class power of the kulak has ruled out both these possibilities. The long-term solution requires rapid absorption of labour in non-agricultural activities, either in rural or urban areas. Industry, whether big or small, cannot take up the slack, which leaves the unorganized sector. The workforce here rose at 3.5 per cent per annum between 1970–71 and 1983–84.

Urbanization is progressing at a very slow rate and migration into even the big cities is not more than the international average of 3 per cent per annum of the metropolitan population. Relatively limited job opportunities reduce the pull of urban areas. Rising off-farm rural employment is dependent on the level of demand for locally produced non-agricultural goods and services, on the level of local demand for agricultural products and services and on the location, scale and technology of the activities catering to these demands. The interplay of these processes leads to an employment absorption rate which just keeps pace with the growth rate of the labour force – a low-level equilibrium situation.

Employment then is the Achilles heel of Indian economic development. It guarantees that poverty will remain a terrible reality as the nation enters the twenty-first century. It is a powerful indictment of Indian capitalism – which does not mean that it cannot be effaced from the minds of the dominant classes, the state elite and the defenders of the system. The government economist who has his career in mind knows which direction to take. He will concentrate on finance and taxation or foreign trade and investment studies, not on labour economics. The poor, the unemployed and the semi-employed somehow survive. As long as their voices are not heard they will remain forgotten and ignored.[77]

Ecological Dangers[78]

The air in Indian cities is polluted from vehicles, factories and plants. There is serious water pollution from human and industrial wastes. Only 8 out of 3,119 towns and cities have full sewage facilities; 209 have partial facilities. Worse, the country's whole river system has been seriously polluted. But the land and its resources have been the biggest victims of ecological devastation. Class relations in the countryside, poverty and population pressure, green revolution strategies for agricultural development, a state committed to supporting the rural rich, commercial ravaging of the country's forest wealth, and an exceptional human–cattle ratio of 2:1 (compared to 10:1 in China) have all combined to cause ecological exhaustion and degradation.[79] India's 'food bowls' are located in what P. Bidwai calls the 'prime-watersheds of half-a-dozen river systems'.[80] Elsewhere, land is in various stages of desertification; vast areas of Gujarat, Kerala, Maharashtra, Karnataka, Tamil Nadu, as well as parts of Himachal Pradesh, eastern Uttar Pradesh, north Bihar, Orissa, central and western Madhya Pradesh and the Rayalaseema and Telengana districts of Andhra Pradesh are all becoming arid.

According to Bidwai, two-thirds of the country faces 'biological' drought, that is, depletion of soil micro-organisms which help retain moisture and fertility. The major dams so favoured by central and state governments impoverish the bulk of the watershed in order to store water in tiny pockets which benefit the well-off peasantry. Besides disrupting the natural watershed, these projects are also responsible for salinating or water-logging some 13 million hectares of sown land. At the turn of the century one third of the country was forested; now less than 11 per cent is forested today. Both droughts and floods have become more frequent and more severe. The area subject to floods has risen from 20 million hectares to 40 million.[81]

In the first phase of agricultural development after independence extensive farming patterns meant growing pressure on grazing lands. Ploughing meant more bullock power. In the absence of land reforms the poor encroached on village common lands as well as deforesting areas to bring them under the plough or make an extra pittance from cutting trees for exploitative forest contractors. This practice has, of course, gathered momentum with the passage of time. Now, in the absence of institutional changes and provision of alternative mechanisms for meeting fuel, food and fodder needs, the ravaging of forests by the poor continues. In addition, 70 per cent of rural and 40 per cent of urban needs are still met by firewood, so it is not only the rural poor who have promoted deforestation. In fact, they have played much the lesser role in deforestation than the contractors and the timber businesses. Drought recurrence and deforestation are locked in a vicious circle, since in times of drought the pressure to earn some income through the sale of forest produce becomes much greater.

Today there is a vital need for planned afforestation in ecologically vulnerable areas such as hill slopes and catchment areas for ponds, reservoirs, and so on. Commercial tree farming is not the answer and in any case benefits the well-off who alone can afford to undertake such capital-intensive activities.[82] Can community or cooperative forms of forest farming be an answer? The Chinese have encouraged afforestation through incentives within the framework of socialized control. Forest cover in China has apparently risen from 8.6 per cent of land mass in 1949 to 12.6 per cent by the mid eighties. Since China faces even greater problems with respect to land–man ratios, its experience is illuminating. Equitable land reforms reduced poverty and pressure on grazing lands. In the absence of private contractors and private markets commercial deforestation was not feasible. Afforestation was encouraged by giving rural communities a stake in it.

> On the basis of the new policy framework, barren hills and water-logged land owned by collectives have been allotted to peasants for tree-planting on a private basis with right to sell the produce, or transfer half-mature trees for money and to inherit the trees. . . . According to some estimates more than half the rural population in China derives income from working part-time in forestry.[83]

Even if the Indian state cannot go so far it can try on a limited scale to do away with the most pernicious aspects of the forest contractor system, offer remunerative prices for minor forest produce and tree-planting, and provide basic inputs, including credit for temporary consumption needs.

By raising yields, the green revolution has perhaps reduced the pressure on forests. Bullock power has been partially replaced by tractors; the by-products of crop outputs as well as fodder production have promoted something of a milk revolution, for example in Punjab. Animal husbandry has been developed and dependence on fuel wood for many households has declined. But here another kind of eco-degradation has taken place through the progressive chemicalization of the soil from fertilizer and pesticide applications. Crop husbandry has replaced land husbandry. In many areas rich farmers have been allowed to sink private tube-wells which have dangerously lowered the water-table.

Since per-hectare application of fertilizers and pesticides is much below international standards, the dangers of degradation may seem more potential than real. However, eco-systems are not uniform and standardized farming practices can have highly variable effects. The effects of monoculture, such as foodgrain production, can be devastating over time and only now are the negative side-effects of dwarf varieties and the ecological virtues of traditional leafier and longer-stem crops becoming better known. Overall fodder shortage is the result of the shift to dwarf varieties. N.S. Randhawa, director general of the Indian Council of Agricultural Research, which did so much to promote the green revolution strategy, has warned of the suicidal direction of agricultural growth in Punjab. In some areas, for every kilo of grain harvested, thirty-six kilos of topsoil are lost which can only be replaced by nature after decades.[84]

Science alone is not the answer to these growing ecological problems, though bio-technology and genetic breeding can offer some new solutions by adapting crops to more efficient use of water and nutrients.[85] But science has to be integrated into a set of social and technical practices which reorganize class relations in a more egalitarian fashion and which do not rely primarily on high-energy, high-input agriculture to increase production. Seventy per cent of cultivated land in India will remain rain fed. This is where the challenge has to be met, both socially and technologically.

Ideology and Economics: An Indian Thatcherism?

Thatcherism in the West is a response to the failure of the Fordist model of accumulation through mass production, mass consumption and mass employment. Thatcherism in India is the response to the failure of a larger and somewhat more generous Nehruvian vision of populist welfarism and liberal democracy where both mass prosperity and popular power would systematically expand.

There are, of course, profound differences between the two Thatcherisms in ideological sweep and their bases of social and political support. In India, it is a construct of intellectuals and ideologues inside and outside the government. It serves different functions from the British or even the East Asian 'gang of four' variety, as could be anticipated in a case where the state continues to play such a dominant role. Indian Thatcherites do not say an outright no to planning; they say yes to somewhat less planning. But there are also certain things in common. If the state is to be rolled back from the economy (to a greater or lesser degree) it must also be rolled *into* society to police the losers. Both Thatcherisms aim at creating a privileged nation which lives in constant (but, hopefully, always manageable) tension with a less privileged one. The one-nation economic ideal of Keynesianism or Nehruvian socialism is gone. In the West the two-nation model has the privileged citizen or affluent worker on one side and at least a social security state to take care of the others. In India there is only the state sans 'social security'.

The essence of this Indian Thatcherism is that it legitimizes the promotion of more differentiated production and distribution of almost everything – from tangible consumable commodities to health, education, transport and housing – while simultaneously reducing the importance, in word and deed, of transfer payments (organized by the state) from the rich to the poor as a means of financing collective provision of essential goods and services. But the 'two nations' of India have to be connected in some positive way. This is what the 'trickle-down' thesis attempts to do in theory at least. It legitimizes the growing unconcern in an increasingly hedonist middle class and Americanized upper elite about the 'other India'. More specifically, it reassures intellectuals that high agricultural and industrial growth will resolve the problem, that class collaboration rather than institutional reform is enough. The problem is not that the trickle-down thesis is necessarily wrong but that the trickle-down mechanisms have to be clearly located and made to work, not just left to the invisible hand of the market. Nor are the trickle-down mechanisms any substitute for the more effective 'trickle-up' mechanisms which are basic to a radical programme for transformation centring on provision of massive and immediate benefits to the poorest.

Sometime in the middle or late seventies the age of ideological innocence began to draw to a close. The ideology of the mixed economy and of a 'socialist pattern of society' became increasingly meaningless, out of kilter with the basic dynamic of the economy. This dynamic was bringing together the two blades of the scissors – expanding supply of those goods demanded by the pattern and level of middle-class consumption. But the ideological vacuum created by the demise of Nehruvian socialism has yet to be properly filled and the Indian version of Thatcherism is just one passing contender. In the East Asian, newly industrializing countries, Thatcherism can be used to justify the maintenance of a strongly outward-oriented pattern of development; in India it has different functions. It is used by believers to promote a shift from a strongly inward-oriented to a moderately inward-oriented pattern of growth. A much smaller proportion of admirers would go so far as to advocate a moderately outward-oriented pattern of development for India.[86] The Thatcherite bandwagon in India thus carries a fairly diverse range of passengers. That has been its strength. They may not agree on precisely what Indian Thatcherism consists of, but they are agreed on more liberalization, more scope for private capital and more freedom for market forces, and they have found a valuable reference point and a useful, if borrowed, codeword for encapsulating these and other commonly agreed themes.

The post-Mao reforms in China, most notably Deng Xiaoping's decision to liberalize the economy in the late seventies, has had an ideological impact on the Indian elite which should not be underestimated. This has been dramatically reinforced by the terrible political repression unleashed against the Chinese masses in June 1989. Gorbachev's perestroika has also helped to spread this new mood, which has become an elite consensus. Rather perversely, these developments have been read as a vindication of India's capitalist path of development. Having been told for so long even by the West that the Chinese performance on all counts was so much better, the Indian elite, with a real sense of relief and gratification, feels able to respond with renewed self-confidence. The Indian record of sustaining bourgeois democracy and overcoming the Emergency seems in many ways better than the Maoist excesses of the Cultural Revolution and Deng's Bloody Sunday and its aftermath. And if the Indian economy has not done quite as well as the Chinese, it has nevertheless performed reasonably. And is there not a trade-off between potentially higher growth rates and authoritarianism? Even China's post-1978 'leap forward' can with some stretching of the imagination be turned into evidence of not only the limited virtues of a limited use of the market mechanism, but somehow of the unlimited virtues of capitalism itself.[87]

By any objective set of standards, capitalism, as a *world* system has been a devasting failure. The successes of the 'gang of four' are feeble entries on the credit side of the ledger when counted against the reality of capitalism's workings in south and West Asia, Africa and Latin America. One can at least comprehend if not share a view which argues that, dismal though capitalism's record is in the last quarter of this century, it is still to be preferred to the more dismal showing of actually existing socialism. But the utterly irrational glorifications of Reaganism and Thatcherism are incomprehensible.

The smug complacency of the Indian version is deeply disturbing. But it is not altogether inexplicable. It is entirely appropriate that the growing hedonism and self-centredness of the Indian elite should be accompanied by an involution of the intellect, a containment of its moral concerns and its imaginative responses. *Indian* capitalism works – who cares about evaluating the merits of capitalism globally? The new emphasis on liberalization is a self-conscious challenge only to the *economic* insulation of India. It demands no other broadening of vision.

The appeal of socialism within the Indian intelligentsia has withered faster than anyone might have imagined at the beginning of the decade. But it is far from dead or dying. The existence of poverty, of glaring inequalities, of powerful social eruptions by the oppressed, and of mass communist parties, albeit reformist, prevents any such tidy tying-up of ideological loose ends. Thatcherism has been the master deceiver. It has been loudest when proclaiming the burial of a socialist corpse which is not there. Its attraction for a large part of the Indian elite has little to do with its inner coherence, which is little understood and of minimal concern to its admirers in the subcontinent. It has filled a temporary need. The need is temporary because, in general, Indian self-reliance extends also to the ideological domain. Nehruvian socialism is dead. The need for an indigenous successor remains. But the search will come to an end, sooner rather than later.

Notes

1. The autonomy of India's economy and polity is essentially the creation of the state, not of the Indian bourgeoisie. On its own this bourgeoisie could never have succeeded in achieving what clearly was (in hindsight) its general interest – a substantially self-reliant and relatively insulated economic system. Nevertheless, as the 1944 Bombay Plan drawn up by the most important representatives of India's big business showed, monopoly capital was well aware that the state had to take a leading role in (a) developing the necessary infrastructure and (b) providing a sheltered market for domestic capital.

2. E. Mandel, 'Semicolonial Countries and Semi-Industrialized Dependent Countries' in *New International*, Autumn 1985.

3. For an excellent general survey of capitalist economic development in India since independence see A. Mukherjee and M. Mukherjee, 'Imperialism and Growth of Indian Capitalism in the Twentieth Century' in *Economic and Political Weekly*, (*EPW*) 12 March 1988. They reach a similar conclusion about the exceptional autonomy of the Indian economy and the irrelevance of foreign capital as a social force in the basic class relationships of the Indian social formation. Some of the statistical evidence presented is taken from this article. However, the Mukherjees do include a broad section of the 'middle class' in their 'ruling coalition'.

A vivid example of the left's aggravated fears of dependency was the 1981 IMF loan of $5 billion SDRs, the biggest such loan in its history. Twenty-three prominent left economists collectively condemned the terms of the loan arguing that it would lead to a fatal dependency when in fact the USA was opposed because the terms were too 'soft'. India went in for the loan on its own terms and not because it was compelled to do so. After receiving $3.9 billion in instalments it cancelled the agreement in May 1984, not needing to go in for the last tranche.

4. Also Table 18, pp. 256–7, *World Development Report*: 1988, Oxford University Press, New York.

5. R.B. Lall, *Multinationals from the Third World*, OUP, Oxford 1986. These flows to and from India are really rather small. Hong Kong is the third world leader with an equity stock in the early eighties of close to $2 billion. Less than half of this is from Chinese firms; the rest is from expatriate British companies based in Hong Kong. The overseas investments are concentrated mainly in Southeast Asia and are in textiles, plastics, and consumer electronics. Brazil follows with roughly $1 billion in overseas direct investments. Singapore ranks third, but technically its foreign investments are mainly relocation activities of multi-nationals in Singapore. South Korea, Taiwan, Mexico and Argentina had in this period each invested between $50 and $100 million. Indian investments had the widest geographical spread, encompassing west and east Africa, the Middle East, South and Southeast Asia, and even Europe and the USA. 80% of equity stock held by Indian firms abroad was in manufacturing concerns.

In 1988 an estimated Rs 210 crores will flow into India. This is a significant increase from seven or eight years ago. But to put matters into perspective, estimated overseas investment into China in 1988 is likely to be Rs 2,800 crores. See *India Today*, 31 December 1988, p. 122.

6. A. and M. Mukherjee, 'Imperialism'.

7. Between 1980 and 1986, India's average annual growth rate in GDP of nearly 5% was bettered by only the following countries in the non-socialist world: Pakistan, Botswana, Cameroon, People's Republic of Congo, South Korea, Oman, Jordan, Hong Kong and Singapore. *World Development Report 1988*, Table 2, pp. 224–5.

8. In the crisis years of the mid sixties, there was a very significant increase in India's external financial and food dependence. At the time of the third plan (1961–66) foreign aid constituted 28% of plan investment. This fell to 10.6% in the sixth plan (1981–85).

9. The 1984 Hussain Committee Report (commissioned by the Indian government) clearly stated that the need was not to give up import substitution but to make it more efficient. The liberalization should be for capital and intermediate goods. Where technology import was not through purchase but involved equity participation then old forms of government screening must apply. Most liberalization was in the OGL ('on general licence') categories which are not competitive with domestic industry. Since importers must apply to government for foreign exchange, there remains an inbuilt mechanism for checking excessive imports. See S. Kathuria, 'The New Trade Strategy', *EPW*, 21–28 December 1985.

10. T. Skocpol, 'State and Revolution: Old Regimes and Revolutionary Crisis', in *Theory and Society*, January–March 1979.

11. H. Alavi, 'The State in Post-Colonial Societies', *New Left Review* 74.

12. M. Kalecki, 'Social and Economic Aspects of Intermediate Regimes' in his *Socialism and the Mixed Economy: Selected Essays*, OUP, Oxford 1972. According to Kalecki, where the national bourgeoisie was weak an intermediate regime could be established. Such a regime would be characterized by unimpressive agricultural growth and inflation, while foreign credits would be of great importance. Without strong external pressure from foreign capital for the restoration of 'normal' capitalist rule by big business (and imperialism behind it), the intermediate regime could enjoy remarkable stability.

13. If the top two deciles – or approximately 160 million people – are taken as the effective market for industrialization, then apart from China the total populations of only three other countries exceed it – Indonesia (barely), the USA and the USSR.

14. For industrial capital's superior and regular, if behind the scenes, access to government, and its efforts to get its way, see S.A. Kochanek, *Business and Politics in*

India, University of California Press, Berkeley 1974. According to Kochanek, business is the best-organized interest group in the country and the only one with day-to-day contact with government.

15. The various writings of Claus Offe during the seventies in the Marxist theoretical journal *Kapitalistate*, and his more recent works like *Contradictions in the Welfare State*, Hutchinson & Co., London 1984 have been particularly important. Also James O'Connor, *The Fiscal Crisis of the State*, St Martins Press, New York 1973.

16. P. Bardhan, *The Political Economy of Development in India*, OUP, Oxford 1984.

17. A. Rudra, 'Emergence of the Intelligentsia as a Ruling Class in India', in *EPW*, 21 January 1989.

18. T. Skocpol, 'State and Revolution', and *States and Social Revolutions*, Cambridge University Press, Cambridge 1979.

19. 'The state elite that inherited the power at the time of independence enjoyed enormous prestige and a sufficiently unified sense of ideological purpose about the desirability of using state intervention to promote national economic development; it redirected and restructured the economy, and in the process exerted great pressure on the proprietary classes. This led to considerable complexity and fluidity in the composition of the proprietary classes and their relationship with the state.' P. Bardhan, *Political Economy*, p. 38.

How relative then was the 'relative autonomy' of the Indian state at independence? Or how possible was it for the Indian state to exercise its 'potential autonomy'? When a sizeable bourgeois class exists, as it did at the time of independence, then the pursuit of any genuine socialist alternative necessarily means the expropriation and economic decimation of this bourgeois class. There is no half-way 'mixed economy' house of 'Indian socialism' or 'third world socialism'. When the state refuses to consider, let alone carry out such an expropriation then the option of pursuing genuine socialism is foreclosed. This is not to say that the tasks of political expropriation of the bourgeoisie and its economic expropriation have to be synchronized. But the first has to take place and invariably involves a revolutionary dismantlement of the previous state structure.

While much has been made of the post-independence autonomy of the Indian state from the dominant classes, the Congress played an exceptionally important role in anchoring and stabilizing the Indian state. Given the class supports of the Congress, its history of multi-class mobilization and cross-class collaboration, the political and social perspectives of its leadership explicitly ruled out before 1947 any possibility of revolutionary destruction of the colonial state (as in Vietnam), or economic expropriation of the bourgeoisie thereafter. If only by default, it could go nowhere else but along the path of capitalist development. Once the capitalist class is allowed to exist, it imposes two basic constraints on the economy – class control of land, and private investment in industry. Both must be decisively undermined, and not just 'relativized' by the growth of state capital, if a fundamentally non-capitalist pattern of economic development is to emerge.

20. C. Offe called it the state's allocative and productive policies respectively.

21. P. Bardhan, *Political Economy*, pp. 40–41.

22. Ibid.

23. Bardhan's cut-off is 4.05 hectares or roughly 10 acres. L.J. and S.H. Rudolph, *In Pursuit of Lakshmi: The Political Economy of the Indian State*, Orient Longman, Bombay 1988, make 15 acres their cut-off point (see their Table 40, p. 336), thereby expanding the size of their 'bullock capitalist' or family farmer category. According to the 1971 census, the average size of holdings above 10 acres was close to 24 acres (see L.J. and S.H. Rudolph, Table B-3, p. 410). Ten acres seems a reasonable cut-off point because most farmers holding between 10 and 15 acres can safely be assumed to be accumulating surpluses in most years, using more mechanized inputs and reducing their own labour to more supervisory functions. Also, better-off farmers are more likely to hide their true wealth from data collectors so the size of this class is almost certainly underestimated and that of the 'middle' peasantry overestimated, though the discrepancy may not be more than a few percentage points.

24. Bardhan has since clarified that he refers to the same social category as does Rudra, both inside and outside the bureaucracy. But he is uneasy with the term 'intelligentsia'. P.

Bardhan, 'The Dominant Class', in *EPW*, 21 January 1989, p. 155.

25. A. Beteille. 'Are the Intelligentsia a Ruling Class?' in *EPW*, 21 January 1989. Rudra's approach is more Weberian than Marxist though he tries to centre his taxonomy on the concept of contradiction. Marx did not get around to presenting his final definitive explanation of class as promised in Vol. III of *Capital*. But Geoffrey de Ste Croix (*The Class Struggle in the Ancient Greek World*, Duckworth, London 1981, pp. 43–4 and 'Class in Marx's Conception of History, Ancient and Modern' in *New Left Review*, July–August 1984) is surely right in arguing that the overwhelming weight of evidence in Marx's writings clearly points to the centrality of the concept of *exploitation* and not merely contradiction in his concept of class, that is, the appropriation and disposition of the fruits of surplus labour. This exploitation can be direct and individual or indirect and collective (for example, state taxation) but it must be present if classes are to be defined at either end of the relation in properly Marxist terms. Social groups which do not fit easily – namely the modern middle class or the peasantry – obviously create extremely difficult problems of classification. They can be forced into one existing class or the other, theorized in non-Marxist terms as a new class (which is what Rudra does) or allowed to exist in their complexity as 'contradictory locations within exploitation relations' which is what Erik O. Wright has argued for (*Classes*, Verso, London 1985) and which is probably the best solution available at the moment. It then remains to evaluate the 'objective' or 'fundamental' long-term 'interest' of the occupants of these contradictory locations through a concrete investigation of their specific circumstances.

What is wrong with Rudra's approach is not that it is non-Marxist but that by forcing this broad social group with its many differentiations into the mould of a single class and, furthermore, pushing it into the ruling coalition as itself a 'ruling class' he grossly and misleadingly simplifies reality and greatly confuses the political task of class and social differentiation. This differentiation is ultimately undertaken not as an academic exercise but with the purpose of identifying those classes and social groups and alliances which have the deepest interests in fighting for radical change whatever the level of their objective awareness, which can change quite dramatically. Marx recognized the complexity of the middle stratum and thereby termed it a 'vacillating class', that is, one site of the fight for hegemony. Moreover, this stratum could not by virtue of its inherent vacillation be the leader in social transformation.

Rudra accepts that his intelligentsia is indeed a vacillating class which in part or whole can swing to the side of revolution. For this very reason he insists that it has had to be incorporated in the dominant coalition. In short, you have a ruling class which plays the pivotal role in sustaining exploitative class rule but which has no *inflexible* interest in the permanent preservation of capitalism. Where the other two classes are part of the ruling coalition because of their non-vacillating commitment to preserving exploitation, the intelligentsia is there because of its vacillation. It has not only been co-opted, it has also become the leader. At bottom, Rudra's analysis is the logical consequence of a trajectory which assigns less and less importance to classical Marxist perspectives concerning the central role of the working class. The intellectual has become the prime mover of history in India.

26. The professionals should presumably have a vested interest in maintaining their scarcity value, by preventing the spread of education, particularly higher education. There are many reasons for the dismal failure of literacy to expand fast enough and for the problems the Indian education system faces. But it is very difficult to see in this the result of a collective and conscious 'middle-class conspiracy'. It could be more plausibly argued that middle-class pressure has led to an improperly planned expansion of higher education; this has devalued degrees even as it has raised degree requirements for the lower levels of middle-class occupations and thus promoted the semi-proletarianization of sections of the educated middle classes.

Between 1960–61 and 1984–85 the real incomes of public-sector workers more than doubled while the real incomes of workers in the organized private sector rose by 60%. What conclusions can plausibly be drawn from this? That public-sector workers are part of the dominant coalition? Or that the state's role as model employer (from which it now wishes to withdraw), the degree and scale (often national) of unionization, and the strategic importance of public-sector industries and nationalized services in the overall economy, all combine to give these workers a *class* strength and potential (their strike action being far more dislocating in its effects than similar action in the private sector) which, unsurprisingly, is reflected in higher growth of real incomes?

27. Annual rate of absorption in the public sector taken as a whole has shown a steady decline from 3.4% in 1971 to 2.4% in 1986. While the trend in central and state government sectors, though declining overall, has tended to fluctuate from one year to the next, the decline has been sharpest and with least fluctuation in the quasi-government sector which includes the public sector industries. The rate of growth of this so-called bureaucratic class is barely keeping pace with the rate of growth of the labour force as a whole. With pressures for cutting down the role of the state in the economy growing, it is extremely unlikely that this trend will be reversed. See *Statistical Outline of India: 1988–89*, Tata Press, Bombay, June 1988, p. 135.

28. The late Prof. Raj Krishna, a member of the Planning Commission under Janata rule, was one of the earliest advocates of liberalization as a way of undermining the 'neta-babu class' which he identified as the major social force blocking such economic rationalization. R. Krishna, 'Economic Outlook for India', in J. Roach (ed.), *India 2000: The Next Fifteen Years*, Riverdale Press, 1986.

29. P. Patnaik, 'Recent Growth Experience of the Indian Economy' in *EPW*, Annual No., May 1987. See also C.P. Chandrasekhar, 'Aspects of Growth and Structural Change in Indian Industry' in *EPW*, Annual No., spring 1989.

30. I.J. Ahluwahlia, 'The Services Sector: An Analysis' in *Economic Times*, 11 and 12 January 1989. Ahluwahlia has suggested after her examination of earlier methodology that pre-1980s figures (for which there are no revised estimates) were almost certainly overestimates while the revised figures may tend to underestimate the true figure. But she suggests that there is no justification for assuming a marked acceleration in expenditure over the last decade.

31. D. Thorner, *The Shaping of Modern India*, Allied Publishers, Bombay 1980. Thorner's 'steel-grey revolution' – as distinct from the much touted 'green revolution' – was a reference to this process of transition. But the kind of off-farm activities controlled by kulaks that he was describing – tea shops, brick kilns, flour mills, etc., even sugar production through cooperatives – are only the earliest stages. Ameliorating and then eliminating the tension between agrarian and industrial bourgeoisies requires much more. Most such activities are too narrowly confined to and dependent upon rural prosperity and incomes. The aspiring farmer capitalist family must be able to enter fields of production where agro-raw materials constitute a lesser and lesser proportion of total value added in production. That is, there should emerge a closer and closer integration of the farmer capitalist family in the (lengthening) chain of industrial production.

R. Sau, 'A Theory of Underdeveloped Capitalism: The Case of India' in *EPW*, 27 August 1988, is among the few leftists who have stressed the importance of this transition for the future political economy of India. He is frankly sceptical that there can be a successful transition. More recently, Bardhan has suggested that the intercoalition tension between urban and rural bourgeois might well decline. P. Bardhan, *EPW*, 21 January, 1989.

It is in Punjab, the most advanced kulak state, that there has been a foretaste of the kind of demands that could be raised on a larger scale in the future. The Akali Dal, the class party of the Jat peasantry, especially its richest layer, has time and again, even when out of office, stressed the importance of further industrialization of Punjab. The demand here is for public sector heavy industry which could then create sufficient backward and forward linkages for smaller-scale investments absorbing farmer surpluses. There is, of course, a communal aspect in that at present urban industry and trade in Punjab is dominated by Hindus, and opportunities for aspiring Sikh entrepreneurs from both urban and rural areas are felt to be blocked.

32. A. Vaidyanathan, 'The Indian Economy Since Independence 1947–70', in *The Cambridge Economic History of India*, Orient Longman, Bombay 1984.

33. In 1986 the government released its Long Term Fiscal Policy (LTFP) paper. This defined the problem clearly. The way to resolve it was also clear, if not spelt out – it

depended on the government's political will in the face of class and social constraints. If it will not raise direct taxes or tax the rural rich, then, apart from raising administered prices, it must reduce its outlays. If it cannot do so to the extent required it must resort to market borrowings and deficit financing. Deficits rose steadily from Rs 1,417 crores in 1983–84 to Rs 8,265 crores in 1986–87. In the sixties, government's market borrowings were less than Rs 100 crores. In 1986–87 they reached Rs 6,350 crores. This is a strategy of marking time, of holding the fort as best it can – that is, no strategy at all. See C.P. Chandrasekhar, 'Aspects of Growth'.

34. When Mrs Gandhi's Congress was restored to authority in 1980 it was thought that the absence of a Charan Singh-like kulak component within it might lead to a significantly lower emphasis on agriculture. Raj Krishna, 'The Budget and the Plan' in *Indian Express*, 7 August 1980, put things in perspective. He pointed out that 'successive governments keep repeating the same pattern, while announcing new priorities. The allocations for 1980–81 provide a striking illustration of this continuity . . . the share of agriculture and irrigation in outlays rising from 24.4% (Janata rule) to 24.8% in the current year (Congress rule), and in the provision for large industry, power and transport from 56.6%k to 56.8% . . . for small industry has been reduced from 2.3% to 2.0% and the provision for social services, research etc. from 16.7% to 16.4% . . . sectoral shares in investment have remained more or less the same for the last quarter of a century.'

35. See M.R. Bhagavan, 'Indian Industrialization and the Key Role of the Capital Goods Sector' in *Journal of Contemporary Asia*, Vol. 15, No. 3, 1985.

36. See V. Joshi and I.M.D. Little, 'India's Macro-Economic Policies' in *EPW*, 28 February 1987.

37. R.H. Patil and R. Pendharkar, 'Corporate Investment in 1988: A Forecast', *EPW*, 27 August 1988. Corporate investment is gross capital expenditure of all private and joint sector companies given assistance by government financial institutions.

38. R.K. Vepa, 'Small Industry Development', *EPW*, 29 August 1987.

39. H. Nagaraj, 'Some Aspects of Small-Scale Industries in India', *EPW*, 12 and 19 October 1988. Nagaraj's conclusions are based on a survey of nearly 850 registered small-scale units receiving bank credit.

40. Ibid.

41. Ibid.

42. The most systematic and forceful representation of this case – diagnosis and prescription – was by Isher J. Ahluwahlia, *Industrial Growth in India: Stagnation Since the Mid-Sixties*, OUP, Oxford 1985. I.J. Ahluwahlia is research professor at the Centre for Policy Research in New Delhi. Her husband, Montek Singh Ahluwahlia, was subsequently appointed chief economic adviser to the government.

43. Between 1965–66 and 1974–75 gross fixed capital formation fell from 8.5% of GDP to 6.1% and then rose to 9.4% in 1979–80 and 11.3% in 1982–83. In actual fact the prices for capital goods rose faster than the average rate of inflation, so allowing for properly deflated prices, the rise was only from 6.1% in 1974–75 to 8.6% in 1982–83. See K.N. Raj, 'New Economic Policy', his V.T. Krishnamachari Memorial lecture, Institute of Economic Growth, New Delhi, 20 November 1985.

44. P. Bardhan, *Political Economy*, p. 62.

45. K.N. Raj, 'New Economic Policy'. Raj pointed out that the exact cause of the decline in factor productivity could not be ascertained. The figure of 1.3% per annum decline over two decades was absurdly high and was in large measure a distortion resulting from a relatively faster rise in prices of inputs such as power and transport or from supply bottlenecks. Nor did the computations take account of the black economy or of the phenomenon of profit siphoning through transfer pricing/dummy firms. He also cited other studies (by Brahmananda and Golder) showing rising factor productivity in the fifties and sixties. His main concern was that such 'exaggerated' fears should not lead to excessive or over-hasty import liberalization.

46. S. Mundle, 'Growth, Disparity and Capital Reorganization in the Indian Economy', *EPW*, Annual No., 1981.

47. Y.K. Alagh, 'Policy, Growth and Structural Change in Indian Industry', *EPW*, Annual No., May 1987. Alagh's analysis confirmed the prescience of Mundle's conclusions

arrived at six years earlier. The overall growth rate in industry since 1976 was 7% per annum. Industries which grew at 10% or more per annum contributed 9% of total production during the 1970–83 period as a whole, but contributed 15% of the total during 1980–83. Those sectors which grew at a rate between 5% and 10% contributed 37.5% for the full 13 years, but at 34.2% for the years 1980–83. The fast-growing states (industrially) were Gujarat, Haryana, Tamil Nadu, Maharashtra, Karnataka. Per capita value added in the factory sector was higher in these states than the all-India average.

48. P. Patnaik, 'Recent Growth Experience'.

49. I am grateful to Krishna Raj, editor, *Economic and Political Weekly*, for these figures.

50. P. Gupta and S. Gupta, 'Estimates of Unreported Economy in India' *EPW*, 15 May 1982. They say that by 1978, the black economy was probably around 49% of official GNP.

51. S. Aiyar, 'Benefits of the Black Economy', in *Indian Express*, 25 February 1985.

52. Ibid.

53. A more detailed class analysis of the countryside and the prospects for rural class struggle and mobilization will be taken up in Chapter 5.

54. N. Bandyopadhyaya, 'Story of Land Reforms in India' in A.K. Bagchi (ed.), *Economy, Society and Polity*, OUP, Oxford 1988.

55. *Statistical Outline of India, 1988–89*, pp. 16–17.

56. Economist Intelligence Unit (EIU) Report, *India to 1990*, revised edn, January 1988, p. 143.

57. I.J. Ahluwahlia, *Industrial Growth in India*, p. 160.

58. I.J. Ahluwahlia, 'The Services Sector', *Economic Times*, 11 and 12 January 1989.

59. *World Development Report 1988*, Table 3, pp. 226–7.

60. I.J. Ahluwahlia, 'The Services Sector'.

61. No doubt the agrarian bourgeoisie would resist such natural market determination of prices and press for government intervention along well-established lines. But once established and allowed to operate for a time, the government would be better able to resist such pressure even if there is no certainty that it would not succumb.

62. In the first four FYPs the capital output ratio varied between 2.6 and 3.2. But in the sixth and seventh plans they doubled to 6.25. These are original (unrevised) estimates. See V.M. Dandekar, 'Indian Economy Since Independence', *EPW*, 2–9 January 1988.

63. See N.K. Chandra, 'Modernization for Export-Oriented Growth', *EPW*, 19 July 1986. Table 8 gives a comparison for the late seventies when the official exchange rate was Rs 8.38 to the US dollar. Since then there has been a substantial devaluation of the rupee to roughly double that figure against the dollar. But given the fact that most of the items are not import-intensive in their production, India's relative efficiency vis-à-vis the USA has very likely increased over time. The 42 listed items were part of a full batch of 76 items of which 44 were cheaper than the official exchange rate against the dollar.

64. According to a front page report by A. Sen Gupta in the *Times of India*, 2 January 1989, Rajiv Gandhi, the most pro-Western Prime Minister the country has ever had, came out strongly against those advisers who, in a high-level internal policy discussion, were against attempting to raise the level of domestic savings and were for linking all sectors of the Indian economy to international pricing. Refusal to raise domestic savings implies greater reliance on external borrowings as and when required.

65. EIU Report, pp. 45 and 105–10. Most of what follows draws heavily on this report.

66. Ibid., pp. 106–7. See Tables 7.10 and 7.11.

67. Ibid. p. 110.

68. Since 1975 there has been a de facto depreciation which reached 15% in 1987 and is now closer to 20%. See also M. Shroff, 'Sand is Not Where Our Heads Should Be', *Economic Times*, 21 August 1986.

69. EIU Report, p. 124.

70. See *Company News and Notes*, Dept of Company Affairs, October 1988, Table IV, p. 3; and 'Private Sector Giants' in *Economic Times*, Mid-Week Review, Bombay,

3 November 1988.

71. A. Varshney, 'Political Economy of Slow Growth in India', *EPW*, 1 September 1984. This was a report on an international discussion in New Delhi to which a number of American and Indian scholars had been invited. The seminar was centred on P. Bardhan's *Political Economy of Development in India*, and the chief participant was Amartya Sen. Bardhan was also present. See also T.N. Srinivasan and P.K. Bardhan (eds), *Rural Poverty in South Asia*, OUP, Oxford 1988, and A. Sen, 'Food for Thought and Survival', in *Economic Times*, January 1989, for a recent restatement of his views.

72. The National Council for Applied Economic Research (NCAER), which is the only organization to collect information on both incomes and household expenditures, suggests that there has been a slight decline from 44% below the poverty line in 1972–73 to 40% in 1975–76. Two papers written in 1978 for the World Bank by M.S. Ahluwahlia have been much cited in this context: 'Rural Poverty and Agricultural Performance in India' in *Journal of Development Studies*, April 1978; and 'Rural Poverty in India: 1956/57 to 1973/74', in *India: Occasional Papers*, World Bank Staff Working Paper No. 279. M.S. Ahluwahlia concludes that there is no evidence whatsoever for arguing that there was a rising trend in the incidence of poverty since the sixties. Nor did he believe that there was conclusive evidence of a declining trend up to the early seventies, though such a trend may have emerged since then.

A. Saith, using the same data but including a price variable, concludes that there was a rising poverty ratio over time. See his 'Production, Prices and Poverty in Rural India', in *Journal of Development Studies*, January 1981.

73. The late Dharm Narain, economist and former member of the government-appointed Agricultural Prices Commission, formulated a hypothesis which now seems to be gathering broader support. He argued that changes in poverty levels were directly related to *nominal* increases in the prices of wage goods produced in the agricultural sector – that is, inflation worsens the position of the poor regardless of the general level of real incomes. In fact, as A. Sen has pointed out, the indirectly 'beneficial' effects of rising prices on rural incomes is less than the direct 'negative' effects of inflation on the poor. Nor do these two effects cancel each other out in the longer term since they may well work on two separate social groups. See the essays in Honour of Dharm Narain, J.W. Mellor and G.M. Desai (eds), *Agricultural Change and Rural Poverty*, OUP, Oxford 1986.

74. This is the conclusion reached by, among others, R. Basant in 'Agricultural Technology and Employment in India', *EPW*, 8 August 1987.

75. EIU Report, p. 63.

76. See J.W. Mellor and G.M. Desai, *Agricultural Change*.

77. This does not apply to the educated unemployed whose voices are heard. The largest portion belong to the backward castes and constitute some of the major battalions of the caste army that is mobilized in support of extending the reservations systems in government employment. The educated job-seekers were an estimated 16.5 million at the beginning of 1987; of these 9.5 million were matriculates, 4.1 million undergraduates, and 2.9 million graduates and above. See *Statistical Outline of India, 1988–1989*, p. 141.

78. I am grateful to Arun Kumar, Centre for Social Studies, Surat, Gujarat, for his comments on this section.

79. S. Hadden, 'Environmental Protection and Economic Development in India', in J. Roach (ed.), *India 2000*.

80. From P. Bidwai, 'Indian Agriculture in Crisis', *Times of India*, 20 and 22 February 1988.

81. S. Hadden, 'Environmental Protection'.

82. The National Wasteland and Development Board was created to promote reclamation of wastelands. But its accent on privatization is promoting the decline of community forestry practices and encouraging their replacement by monoculture industrial/commercial forests.

83. Quoted in C.H. Hanumantha Rao, 'Agricultural Development and Ecological Degradation', in *EPW*, 24–31 December 1988. This is a useful recent study.

84. From P. Bidwai, 'Indian Agriculture'.

85. E.C. Wolf, *Beyond the Green Revolution; New Approaches for Third World*

Agriculture, Worldwatch Paper 73, October 1986.

86. For a lucid critique of the World Bank claim that outward orientation is a proven success, see G. Sen, 'Industrialization and Foreign Trade', *EPW*, 13 February 1988. Apart from the 'gang of four', outward orientation has failed. Nor have the 'strongly outward-oriented' (SO) and 'moderately outward-oriented' (MO) countries done better overall than the 'strongly inward-oriented' (SI) and 'moderately inward-oriented' (MI) countries. According to Sen, the MI countries as a group have lower inflation, higher savings and higher growth rates for the 1973–85 period than the MO countries taken as a group.

87. For an excellent discussion of the 'socialist economies' see C. Samary, *Plan, Market and Democracy: The Experience of the So-called Socialist Countries*, IIRE Pub., Amsterdam 1988. Samary carefully distinguishes between those economies where bureaucratic centralism is still dominant, where the market mechanism has been given a qualitatively more important role in overall reproduction, and 'market socialism', a more 'advanced' stage in the use of the market. China is still in the first system and it is far from certain that it will move to the second.

2

Crisis of Bourgeois Leadership

India faces a basic paradox. On the one hand there is endemic political instability. A crisis of bourgeois leadership has persisted since the mid seventies. On the other hand, the larger bourgeois democratic framework has shown remarkable durability since 1947. Outside the advanced capitalist democracies, among post-colonial countries, this durability has been quite exceptional. Both instability and durability mark the present conjuncture and will almost certainly continue to mark the evolution of the country's political system up to, and probably beyond, the turn of the century.

Those who have lost sight of the system's inherent strength have time and again predicted a collapse or atrophy of basic structures and processes only to be proved repeatedly wrong.[1] Yet the record of upheaval and political turmoil in India over the last two decades easily bears comparison with and may exceed the record of any other country. India's democracy has been a violent one. Every conceivable kind of conflict has taken place – short of revolutionary crisis and attempted seizure of power, at one end of the spectrum, or a military coup d'état, at the other.

There have been direct and militant struggles in conscious pursuit of class aims – for example, the Naxalite upsurge of 1967–72; the historic railway strike of 1974; the 77-day public sector strike in Bangalore in 1981 involving 125,000 workers; the year-long strike by over 200,000 textile workers in Bombay in 1982; the all-India teachers' strike in 1987; and the militant struggles by the rural oppressed which in some cases have reached the pitch of armed clashes with landlords or the state authorities. There have been confrontations where the explicit objective of struggle was related to caste rather than class discrimination. But many of these could be considered class actions of a kind since basic oppressed and oppressor classes were ranged against each other. There have also been caste struggles launched by both lower and middle castes against higher castes aimed at extending or maintaining present caste reservations.

At another level there have been conflicts between the central state authority, representing the general interests of the ruling-class coalition, and an agrarian bourgeoisie seeking to extend its political influence in general and to alter in its favour the relationship of forces within the ruling-class coalition, to tip the balance towards itself and away from the industrial bourgeoisie. These efforts have taken direct and indirect forms. Rich farmers and their rural allies have agitated and rallied against the centre and against state governments for changes in agricultural policy. More indirectly their pressure has been expressed through factional tussles within ruling parties in the states and through the ongoing conflicts between the centre and the opposition-ruled states, in which the latter seek greater autonomy and devolution of central powers.

There have been regional multi-class movements on issues such as ethnic imbalances in population, cultural and economic discrimination, local political and economic grievances (for example, price rises and corruption), in all of which the urban petty bourgeoisie and students have played a leading role. Such was the case in the 1972–73 Nav Nirman agitation in Gujarat, the J.P. Movement of 1974–75, the Assam agitation of the early eighties. Even seemingly non-class communal clashes have often had a significant class source in that the urban petty bourgeoisie of one religious community felt threatened by the upward mobility of aspiring artisans and traders from another community. This is not to say that all conflicts can or should be reduced to some core scheme of antagonistic class relations and struggles. Rather, it is simply to stress that many, though not all, 'non-class' and 'multi-class' or 'sectoral' conflicts do contain significant and specific class aspirations which should not be ignored because of the 'broader' character of these conflicts and which, indeed, go some way towards explaining how they emerged in the first place.

There are also the explicitly political manoeuvrings and agitations within the bourgeois political arena. Both the opposition parties and the Congress seek to discredit each other in the eyes of the electorate – witness, for example, the anti-corruption campaigns of the opposition, and the Congress efforts to unseat state governments ruled by opposition parties on the grounds of alleged failures and misconduct. There have been powerful secessionist movements in the northeast and more recently in Punjab. The Punjab problem is closely allied to the issue of communalism and its exacerbation has led to growing alienation between Sikhs and Hindus, the assassination of Mrs Gandhi, a communal holocaust in its wake, continuing terrorist attacks on innocent civilians both Hindu and Sikh, and to state-sponsored repression as an ineffectual rejoinder to terrorism.

Why has such persistent political unrest not led to total chaos? The bafflement is best captured by the phrase 'functional anarchy' coined by the American economist and former ambassador to India, J.K. Galbraith. It is a term of descriptive rather than analytical merit. The Indian state has been able to cope with, if not always resolve, these numerous conflicts without resorting to a decisive authoritarian involution (barring the Emergency interlude in 1975–77). This is in large part due to the 'limited' scope of many of these conflicts (relative to the continental scale of the country) and to the fact that most of the upheavals which have caused endemic instability have not been between the fundamental classes of Indian society – between the industrial and rural proletariat on the one hand and the industrial and agrarian bourgeoisie on the other. The backward character of Indian capitalism has not led to the kind of social polarization, either in town or countryside, which would have progressively reduced the importance of the intermediate classes as a buffer. Indeed, the importance in Indian politics of the intermediate classes – the agrarian petty bourgeoisie, the urban professionals, traders, service-sector self-employed – has grown substantially. Furthermore, the intensity and scale of fundamental class eruptions has not been so great that the state was unable to cope. It has had the capacity to wait out agitations like the textile and teachers' strikes, or to respond successfully with ruthless repression, as in the Naxalite rebellion and the railway strike.

The mainstream Stalinist left (Communist Party of India and Communist Party of India (Marxist) – CPI and CPM respectively) and the Maoists of the Marxist-Leninist (ML) movement have all failed to come to theoretical grips with the complex and paradoxical nature of the Indian polity. They have been fatally handicapped by their refusal to recognize the bourgeois democratic nature of class domination. Such a recognition would, of course, only be the starting point of analysis. Liberal-pluralist political scientists both in India and among America's India-watchers have had no such handicap and have consequently developed a sophisticated understanding of the specificities of Indian democracy.[2] But their vision is circumscribed by a refusal to assign much relevance, let alone centrality, to the class configurations in which the Indian political order is embedded. The socio-economic environment is not ignored but remains peripheral to their analytical framework, which in true liberal-pluralist tradition focuses on the inadequacy of political institutions in coping with the growing 'overload' on the structures of the state and the political system generally.

This overload is the result of growing disparity between the expectations of and claims made on government (and on other structures) by a variety of interest groups (which in India are exceptionally diverse) and the capacity of the political system to manage or mediate conflicts arising from greater interest-group articulation and pressure. These rising expectations and pressures are themselves the result of growing mass political participation, that is, the 'successful' functioning of the democratic order with its party competition, electoral contests at various levels, plurality of associations, free media, and so on.[3] Insofar as liberal-pluralists acknowledge that a process of crystallization of various classes is taking place in India, however haltingly, it is seen as affecting the state from the 'outside', through the demands it generates on the system and its accentuation of the overload problem. All class struggle, in their view, is Weberian and related to a competitive conflict for greater access to resources. It is not, as Marxists would have it, a manifestation of inherent exploitation in the existing relations of production.

The state is both a mediator of and a participant in this competitive struggle for power and allocation of resources. It cannot be otherwise since, for the liberal-pluralists, the state is wholly autonomous, looks to national and corporate interests and has no class character even if it does sometimes show a specific class bias.

It is obvious that this conceptual framework has real explanatory power and appeal, all the more so in India because of the significant autonomy of an 'overdeveloped' state and of the Congress party from the dominant classes.[4] But this framework excludes or renders peripheral certain fundamental questions which, Marxists insist, must be explored. Who benefits and who suffers in the existing system and how? What kind of social and political relations are reproduced and how? What role does the state play in this reproductive system? Is the system and the state necessarily exploitative and oppressive? If so, how is this exploitation and oppression to be eradicated and not merely meliorated? Thus, it becomes vital to look into the class-sources of conflicts and at the class-effects of attempted solutions or responses to the 'overload' problem; to examine the effectiveness of the institutional forms and ideological norms of democratic rule; and to lay bare the changing geometry of social forces underpinning the system.

India has not experienced a classical bourgeois revolution. What then are the social and political foundations of the emergence and continuation of India's bourgeois democracy? The rise of the most developed industrial bourgeoisie in any colonial country may have been a necessary condition for the emergence of democracy. But it was not a sufficient one. The two other social forces crucial to the emergence of bourgeois democracy and for its maintenance after 1947 have been the petty and agrarian bourgeoisies. Before 1947 the urban middle class played a disproportionately important role. After 1947 the agrarian bourgeoisie and the rural petty bourgeoisie have progressively come into their own as factors of decisive importance.

Goran Therborn has argued that among the internal factors most responsible for the rise of democracy, the three most important have been: (a) the strength of the labour movement; (b) the independent strength of the agrarian petty bourgeoisie and small bourgeoisie land-owners; and (c) divisions within the ruling class (or power) bloc.[5] Barrington Moore has stressed as preconditions for the emergence of democracy: (a) weakening of the landed aristocracy; and (b) absence of an aristocratic–bourgeois alliance against workers and peasants.[6]

Both Moore's conditions seem to pertain in the case of colonial India. The landed elite was gravely weakened by its close affiliation and identification with the British colonial masters, while the burgeoning industrial bourgeoisie saw its economic ambitions and interests thwarted by the preservation of colonialism, hence its long-term and fundamental opposition to the metropolitan bourgeoisie's domination in India. But Moore's conditions by themselves cannot adequately explain the Indian case. While Therborn's perspective, with important modifications, may prove fruitful for dissecting the evolution of the democratic order after independence, it offers little help in understanding how it emerged from the colonial incubus.

The Historical Specificity of Indian Bourgeois Democracy

The exceptional nature of the Indian experience has strong historical roots in the specificities of British colonial rule, the National Movement and the character of Congress. Here we will do no more than indicate the most salient aspects of this complex inheritance. After the 1857 Mutiny, the British gave up their attempt to overthrow the princely states and, wherever possible, began to forge an alliance on terms that were usually favourable to themselves. At the same time, in areas under their direct rule, the colonial authorities supported and advanced the zamindari system of parasitic landlordism. These two orientations prevented any alliance between the landed elite and the rising industrial bourgeoisie and, along with the growing penetration of British culture, certainly helped push the Indian bourgeoisie towards ideas of political democracy.

Given the diversity of the huge subcontinent, Britain could never confidently rely upon the threat or practice of coercion to assure stable rule, but had to institutionalize at least a passive form of consent on the part of the colonized layers with which it came into direct contact. The authorities established a uniform legal code and a hierarchial judicial structure spanning most of the country. This superseded customary laws, which had varied from locality to locality, and destroyed the power of the village, caste or religious community to enforce codes of behaviour. For all its discriminatory legislation in favour of Europeans and other whites, the British legal system sanctified and strengthened the bourgeois-democratic principle of equality before the law as interpreted by an independent judiciary.

From the 1850s the British administration was also the chief agency for the spread of modern education in India. This was no doubt motivated by the need to turn out educated Indians in sufficient numbers to man the lower and middle rungs of the administrative services. But once started, the process took on its own dynamic – relayed by private foreign missionaries and progressive Indians – and in no other colony did there develop such a large stratum of urban professionals steeped for the most part in the values of bourgeois liberalism. This educated middle-class elite, which provided all the leaders of the National Movement, came to oppose British rule in the name of the most advanced bourgeois democracy, represented by Britain itself. Similarly, a variety of religious and socio-religious reform movements invoked the principles of European liberalism in order to modernize and invigorate a Hindu social life that was weighed down by stultifying traditions and religiously inspired sanctions of an often thoroughly backward nature.

The state machinery which established unification evolved over time in accordance with various acts of the British parliament. However, a contradiction made itself felt between this 'constitutionalist' approach and the fact that the colonial government was answerable not to Indians but to a sovereign Westminster. The National Movement, given the ideological orientation of its leadership, became a movement to extend democratic rights and to make existing structures more accessible to Indians – hence the call for administrative reforms, Indianization of services, a constitution along the lines of the self-governing dominions, and so on. So deep was the influence of liberal values that the Congress and other mass organizations based their own internal structures on elective principles, respect for majority decisions, democratic committees, and so on.

The Urban Classes, the Rural Elite and the National Movement

In his essays on German fascism, Trotsky emphasized the significance of the petty bourgeoisie as the mass base of the industrial bourgeoisie, and

lower middle class
hindu nationalism
+ aggression

showed how its self-consciousness played a crucial role in determining the form of bourgeois rule. This insight has particular resonance in the Indian context, where the petty bourgeoisie was a leading actor in the National Movement and in the moulding of its typical conciousness. A section of the leadership with its base in the lower middle class was much more strongly inclined to a cultural, Hindu definition of bourgeois nationalism and in favour of a more aggressively agitational approach. But in its political demands it followed the more Westernized liberals in never venturing outside the framework of bourgeois-democratic aspirations. The rise of Gandhi significantly ameliorated the tension between these two streams.

The strength of the philosophical tradition in Hinduism meant that materialist philosophy had a limited attraction for the Indian intelligentsia in the first two decades of this century and a correspondingly reduced influence on the course of the nationalist struggle. This was reinforced by the fact that the emergence of the National Movement preceded by many years the Russian Revolution and the advent in the twenties of an organized, if strongly economist and localist, working-class movement. The industrial bourgeoisie, which started to grow rapidly in strength and self-confidence from the turn of the century, saw its economic interests seriously fettered by colonialism, and its opposition to British rule was both genuine and consistent. But its leading spokesmen, G.D. Birla and P.T. Tandon, were acutely aware of the need to prevent the national struggle from exceeding the bounds of class order, and the self-limiting character of the Congress programme was eminently suited to this end. From 1920 the Gandhi-dominated Congress succeeded in establishing a controlled paternalist relationship with its mass peasant base, thus ensuring its loyalty to the bourgeois-nationalist project of the indigenous capitalist class and effectively countering the possibility that the emergent working class would seal an alliance of its own with the peasantry. Admittedly, there were in any case powerful obstacles to such an alliance. Despite the substantial industrialization that followed the First World War, the urban working class was comparatively weak and the class relationship of forces, unlike that of pre-revolutionary Russia, was tilted towards the bourgeoisie. Indeed, the working class did not succeed in firmly establishing an independent political expression until the growth of the Communist Party in the 1930s, and even then the perspectives and policies of the Stalinist Comintern hardly helped the problems to be overcome. For most of the colonial period the working class remained peripheral to the National Movement and never mounted a serious challenge for hegemony within it. Thus, the Indian bourgeoisie, because of its relative independence from metropolitan capital and the

industrial bourgeoisie + its ties to colonialists

indigenous landed elite, and because of its large degree of insulation from domestic working-class pressure, could firmly commit itself to the revolutionary project of creating an independent bourgeois-democratic nation-state.

The pre-independence Congress has been characterized with some justification as both a class party of the bourgeoisie and a multi-class movement. But it would perhaps be even more accurate to call it an umbrella or patchwork quilt of various social movements, an aggregation of classes and interest groups loosely united by a common desire for independence, which was seen by all of them as essential for achieving their own particularist goals. Only a pluralist, democratic system responsive to such a multiplicity of pressures had a chance of gaining acceptance from the various currents within the Congress. Moreover, insofar as the central political aim, independence, was to be achieved through an 'escalating series of compromises' culminating in the formal transfer of full power, the strategic line of advance of the National Movement inevitably assigned a very important status to parliamentary activity. The Government of India Act (1935), promising provincial autonomy for India, was probably the decisive turning point. The Gandhi-led Congress preferred cooperation with this Act to Nehru's alternative of a struggle for the immediate establishment of a Constituent Assembly. In so doing it made clear that independence would only be achieved through cooperation with Whitehall and the existing legislatures.

In the 1936 elections, Congress scored massive victories in seven provinces. Though decisive power was still vested in the provincial governors appointed by the centre, and in the civil service, the Congress administrations did have a measure of authority, a fact which no doubt helped to explain why Congress reneged on an earlier promise not to take up office. Public response to these Congress administrations was overwhelming. The ordinary poor were able to identify, for the first time, with their own administration, while the landowning proprietary classes/castes joined the Congress en masse in search of power and patronage.

From a membership of 600,000 in 1936 the Congress reached 3 million in 1938 and 5 million in 1939. After war-time travails (harassment and arrests during the Quit India Movement) primary membership rose from 5.5 million in 1945–46 to around 11 million in 1949–50.[7] But the most significant point is that from the mid thirties onwards the nexus between the Congress and the dominant landowning castes solidified to such an extent that there was no way the Congress could ever act against the fundamental interests of the rural elite. While the Congress retained its umbrella-like and multi-class character up to and beyond independence, its class bias in favour of the rural rich became more pronounced.

The prolonged character of the struggle of the Indian National Movement, bearing comparison with the struggles in Vietnam and China, involved a gradual hegemonization by the Congress which by 1947 had become a kind of parallel government or government-in-waiting. It had been able constantly to test and develop a complex and sophisticated organization, with an established hierarchy of leaders most of whom had gained some measure of authority from their participation in the movement. This prior consolidation explains why there were no serious administrative upheavals when the transfer of power finally took place. Inherited from the old colonial state was a neutral and Indianized civil service and a professional military. The decisive weight of the Congress and its immense prestige meant that the bureaucratic-military apparatuses were discouraged from developing the exaggerated sense of self-importance which proved so significant in Pakistan. From the beginning they were to remain strictly subordinated to civilian authority embodied by the Congress.

Pakistan: A Contrasting Legacy

Some of the specificities of the Indian experience may perhaps best be grasped by a comparison with the other inheritor of the Raj: Pakistan. In fact the class structure in the two components was already quite different at the time of partition; the industrial bourgeoisie was primarily Hindu or Parsi, while pre-capitalist relations dominated in the regions that became Pakistan. In the west the landed elite or tribal chiefs were pre-eminent and parasitic; in the east the mainly Hindu zamindars fled across the border to India, so that a large part of the land was redistributed among peasant smallholders supporting a small rural elite and an urban petty bourgeoisie of traders, functionaries and professionals. In neither west nor East Pakistan was there a capitalist class worthy of the name. 'No bourgeoisie, no bourgeois democracy' is surely a formula of general applicability.

The Pakistani state had to create an industrial and commercial bourgeoisie by organizing an industrialization programme around a tiny core of Gujarati-speaking Muslim immigrant businessmen in the west. Not only was an authoritarian form of the state best suited to pump out a surplus for accumulation at the necessarily high rate, but any genuinely democratic form of rule was excluded by the geographical separation of the ruling class in western Pakistan from the eastern Bengalis, who constituted 60 per cent of the country's total population.[8] At its very infancy the tension of the unresolved national question left its mark on the Pakistani state.

Even the legacy of the National Movement was not a shared one. Muslims came into the anti-colonial struggle much later. For a variety of reasons the majority of the Muslim middle class gravitated towards the Muslim League, which was also the principal political vehicle of the Muslim landed aristocracy. The League was a very different formation from the Congress. Even its middle-class base, lacking a common liberal ethos – indeed looking to the British for much of the colonial period as the protector of its minority interests – was united only in its desire for an independent Pakistan in which its fortunes would be secured by the absence of secular competition from non-Muslims. Within a few years of the formation of Pakistan, however, the Muslim League collapsed as this heterogeneous middle class became further differentiated in the scramble for upward mobility through the new state machinery.

If Congress was the most crucial legacy of the colonial period for independent India, its counterpart in Pakistan was the military-bureaucratic oligarchy. Indeed, the nascent Pakistani bourgeoisie was so dependent on the bureaucracy that, unlike the landed elite, it was unable to create a political party of its own or to co-opt one of the existing parties as its principal political vehicle. Although the early Ayub and Yahya Khan regimes operated through carefully controlled civilian apparatuses and were not total military dictatorships in the sense that the Zia regime was, real administrative power rested with a bureaucracy which had a unitary structure of its own. At its apex was the Secretary General to the government of Pakistan, who presided over a 'super-cabinet' of secretaries of ministries which displaced the party-mandated cabinet of the traditional parliamentary system.[9]

It took the emergence of a new layer of white-collar workers and urban professionals, the growth of powerful tensions and inequalities within a ruthless, outward-oriented capitalism, the trauma of national dismemberment in 1971 and the subsequent disillusionment with the army to create the preconditions for the rule of Zulfikar Bhutto's Pakistan People's Party (PPP). This brief interregnum could not and did not last. The PPP could not resolve its own internal contradiction. A radical section of the petty bourgeoisie pulled in one direction while the landowning and industrial elite pulled in another. For all his rhetoric, Bhutto rapidly aligned himself with the latter and with the oil-rich West Asian states that demanded, and easily secured, the ideological price of a half-baked Islamicization. This further eroded the PPP's declared commitment to democratic norms.

Most dangerous of all for Bhutto was his failure to tackle the national question adequately. In Baluchistan and the North-West

Frontier Province the PPP was extremely weak; a real commitment to democratic functioning would have required it to share power with the dominant regional parties within a federal framework. Bhutto rejected this alternative, in part because of his dependence on the landlord–industrialist nexus of Punjab and Sind. He then had to resort to coercion and therefore to the army, whose status and power he helped rehabilitate.[10] The final price was soon to be paid in the coup of General Zia-ul-Haq, whose rule lasted till the transition to 'guided democracy' in November 1988. A much changed PPP, now under the leadership of Bhutto's daughter, Benazir, currently heads the government.

Rise and Decline of One-party Dominance

Up to the mid sixties, the Congress was the central political institution supporting the democratic order. Rajni Kothari, followed by Anglo-American liberal scholars, did path-breaking work in mapping the contours of what has come to be called the 'Congress System' or 'One Party Dominance System'.[11]

> A huge, hierarchically structured party, broadly rooted throughout the countryside, apparently provided the mechanism whereby a plurality of elites, sub-elites and groups could both voice their claims and attempt to realize them. At the same time, the Congress could adequately mediate and settle these multiple and often conflicting claims. If necessary the Congress High Command would intervene to seal the final bargain. The post-independence Congress was the biggest vehicle for political patronage the world has ever known.[12]

Central resources were under the control of the Congress leadership at the top, which disbursed them to Congress-controlled state governments, while local government structures also dominated by the Congress – for example, the Panchayati Raj network – distributed resources to intended and unintended beneficiaries. What is more, access to jobs in a rapidly expanding bureaucracy at national, state and local levels was often most easily secured via the Congress, especially lower down.

Kothari and others have argued that the Congress was also more than this. Ideas and ideologies mattered. Factions organized around different ideological positions were tolerated in a centrist party of broad consensus. This did not mean that opposition parties outside the Congress were consigned to the political wilderness and rendered impotent till an election victory. They could and did exercise significant influence on policies – but *through* the Congress in alliance with the internal factions closest to them. There existed a 'margin of pressure' in this 'Congress system' which ensured flexibility of response and, therefore, stability.

But at best this applied to the upper echelons of decision-making in regard to centre-inspired policies concerning industry and commerce. At the lower levels the ascendancy of the rural rich soon became complete and unchallengeable. Zamindari abolition in 1955 finished off the system of parasitic landlordism but did not involve the expropriation of the majority of landlords. What the Zamindari Abolition and Tenancy Acts, passed in various states in the fifties, did do was to facilitate the growth of a powerful class of rich capitalist farmers comprising former landlords, rich peasants and ex-tenants. They also shifted power from a small layer of upper castes to a much larger stratum of intermediate castes.

When a section of the top leadership (for example, Nehru) flirted with the formation of agrarian cooperatives, they were ignored. When, in the late fifties, Nehru tried to push the idea seriously within the party, he was defeated with ease. Similarly, the various land ceiling acts passed from 1961 onwards which would have challenged the rising class of capitalist farmers were never seriously implemented. By the early sixties there was a broad consensus that the way to transform the agricultural situation was not through institutional measures aimed at redistribution of assets, but through the application of green revolution techniques and development of infrastructure: expanding irrigation, building dams, developing seed farms, spreading the use of electrified water pumps and fertilizers, providing greater access to credit and other material and financial inputs, and so on.[13]

This hold of the rural rich over much of the Congress organization below the central apex is a matter of great importance; it has often been noted but repeatedly minimized by liberal-pluralists, partly because it raises uncomfortable suspicions that the Congress may not have been as class neutral or amorphous as they thought. Sudipta Kaviraj, a Marxist, has been among the few political scientists writing on the Congress who has insisted that a dominant coalition of the industrial bourgeoisie, rich peasantry, and a state elite of professionals operated through the 'one-party dominance system' to impose structural constraints on policy choices and implementation.[14]

But the larger, more fundamental question concerns the nature of the relationship between this evolving agrarian bourgeoisie and the Indian democratic order, and also its relationship with the Congress. What effect, for example, did the growing power of the agrarian bourgeoisie have on the organization of the Congress? How was its evolution connected to the 'de-institutionalization' of the Congress? It is this collapse of the old Congress that constitutes the origin of the current crisis of bourgeois political leadership.

Advanced bourgeois democracies have been characterized by the late arrival of universal suffrage. Typically, full extension of the franchise has occurred when there was already a substantial degree of industrialization and urbanization. The weight of the industrial bourgeoisie was, if not overwhelming, decisively greater than that of its agrarian counterpart. It was the hegemonic class in the ruling class alliance, if there was one, or else some fraction of a single bourgeois ruling class hegemonizing other fractions in the power bloc. There existed a strong, urban working class with a powerful interest in preserving and extending bourgeois democratic norms. Moreover, in the older, advanced democracies, a bourgeois democratic ethos was institutionalized over a prolonged historical period in the various fortifications of civil society.

None of this applied to India. Universal suffrage arrived at an early stage of industrialization when urbanization was limited, the industrial bourgeoisie was still relatively weak and the agrarian bourgeoisie was far from insignificant. It was the state that organized 'forced march' industrialization. The urban working class was comparatively small and weak. The tussle between the agrarian and industrial bourgeoisies in the ruling coalition was more intense and more balanced than in the advanced democracies. There is a problem of comparison here since the twin processes of political and economic evolution have been much more strongly combined and telescoped in the case of the more recent industrializing countries. Here, in consequence of this more hurried and complex rhythm of development, the state was more autonomous from the two bourgeoisies.

Since India had (and has) an underdeveloped civil society, the state structures and the ruling Congress party had to shoulder even greater responsibility for organizing the acceptability of any form of bourgeois rule, be it democratic or otherwise. However, the Congress at its middle and lower reaches was dominated by a landed elite itself in the process of crystallizing into a rich farmer class of mass proportions. According to Table 3 some 19 per cent of rural households having ten or more acres account for more than 60 per cent of the total land area. Below them, some 25 to 30 per cent of other rural households constitute roughly an agrarian petty bourgeoisie having family sized farms (four to ten acres) which are run primarily through exploitation of family labour.[15] A majority of such households have strong aspirations to move upwards – though only a smaller proportion have the potential to succeed. They constitute a wide base of support for the rich peasantry whose hegemony and leadership in struggles for common economic demands is being increasingly accepted. What is more, this collective category of around 40 per cent of rural households enjoys a broad caste homogeneity, belonging for the most part to the closely clustered intermediate

rich peasantry

castes. At a micro-level and for micro-issues, such as marriage and commensality, it is the jati and its rules that are important. For broader macro-issues requiring wider mobilization, broader caste aggregates of these jatis become more important and more acceptable. Two farming households belonging to different jatis may not intermarry but they will combine to fight for common class demands. The sheer numerical strength of the rich farmers and their rural petty-bourgeois allies, as well as their growing class and caste consciousness, has made them the most important strategic beneficiaries of universal suffrage.

It is impossible to avoid concluding that the rich peasantry has imposed (and will continue to impose) a decisive stamp on Indian bourgeois democracy. It has had a vested interest in sustaining a system of elections and of voting procedures at various levels, and in strengthening a democratic-federalist system of power sharing. It was responsible for institutionalizing Congress electoral support up to the mid sixties, and subsequently for helping to de-institutionalize it. It resorts increasingly to extra-parliamentary mass agitations even as its influence in state assemblies, state governments and regional parties grows. It fights the industrial bourgeoisie for a greater share of centrally allocated resources but has no fundamental opposition to the extension of industry. Indeed, it seeks to benefit from the growing integration of town and country, industry and agriculture, and to enter the expanding small-scale industrial sector, whether agro-based or not.[16] Along with their petty-bourgeois allies, the rich farmers oppose the mores of the urban middle class and extol the virtues of farming life, though they are certainly not immune to the consumerist culture that dominates much of urban middle-class life. This rural bloc accuses the centre and the state governments of being biased in favour of urban India but seeks places for its non-farming members in the state bureaucracies, where its influence has grown steadily.

A rural capitalist farming family today may have some children in the services, own small shops or tiny businesses.

After independence rich peasants, landlords and the emerging capitalist farmers began to invest on a wider scale, rather than simply consuming surpluses. The establishment of tiny transport companies, tea shops, small flour mills, brick kilns were all part of this process. Some move into trade in direct competition with previous merchant classes/castes. With the establishment of cooperative sugar factories the new kulaks fought the domination of urban industrialists and merchants and in the process transformed some of their wealth into accumulation in India's second biggest industry. The spread of rural education with the establishment of numerous societies running schools and colleges has also been largely their work.[17]

Therborn's framework refers to a single industrial class with its fractions and not to a ruling coalition of industrial and agrarian bourgeoisies, but his observations are relevant here. 'Capitalist relations of production tend to create an internally competing peacefully disunited ruling class.' In the specific conditions of India, peaceable disunity could well describe the relationship between the agrarian and industrial bourgeoisies, though rather more emphasis should be given to the latter term than the former. Therborn also points out that 'the development of capitalism has usually stimulated the expansion of petty commodity production, before tending to destroy it. Thus the commercialization of agriculture transformed a self-subsistent peasantry into an agrarian petty bourgeoisie with interests of its own.'[18]

In India, a sizeable agrarian bourgeoisie hegemonizing a significant part of an even larger rural petty bourgeoisie has emerged. However, the backwardness and lateness of Indian capitalist development means that the general tendency for the agrarian petty bourgeoisie to be squeezed out of existence through a process of polarization is weak. The sheer size of this petty bourgeois layer makes this extinction virtually impossible. Only a proportion can graduate to the ranks of the rich peasantry and hire labour. At the other pole, there is no empirical evidence of relatively increasing semi-proletarianization or proletarianization.[19] A sizeable yeoman-like peasantry will remain.

Within the dominant class coalition, the *economic* strength of the industrial bourgeoisie is growing. Agricultural production accounts for a steadily declining proportion of total GNP. But the absolute contribution of agricultural production is still very significant. The overall growth rate and even the growth rate of the industrial sector is still influenced by that of the agricultural sector. A prospering rural elite is one of the principal sources for expanding the domestic market for manufactures. In the absence of rapid urbanization and adequate growth of opportunities in industry, the agricultural sector must absorb a large part of the surplus labour. Furthermore, despite the disadvantages in its economic relationship to the industrial bourgeoisie, the rich peasantry enjoys a growing social and political importance vis-à-vis the industrial bourgeoisie. The third plan marked a shift in the allocation of resources towards agriculture. Subsequent plans have roughly maintained its proportions. Another marked increase in the proportion allocated to agriculture in the forthcoming eighth five-year plan would clinch the case for the growing authority of the agrarian bourgeoisie.

Its political power is in large part the consequence of the functioning of a democratic system. During the Emergency the response of the industrial bourgeoisie was at best ambivalent. On balance it may well have favoured it. Certainly, many top industrialists spoke out in support of it in a manner which did not suggest that they were motivated only by a fear of stepping out of line. In contrast, the most powerfully organized sector of the country's agrarian bourgeoisie, in the northwest of the country, expressed strong and consistent hostility through its leading political representative, Charan Singh of the then Bharatiya Kranti Dal, the most important peasant party.

Before independence the Congress was a political movement, a social reform movement dedicated to Gandhian class conciliation and, logically enough, constructive work. It was also a bourgeois party promoting strongly the interests of the dominant bourgeoisies. After independence only the last characteristic survived. At the top, there was still a dedicated group of leaders committed to the establishment of a populist welfare society embodied in the ideology of 'Congress socialism'. At lower levels, this 'socialism' only meant that rural elites should have access to state resources. James Manor has cast an admiring yet cynical eye over the functioning of the Congress.[20] He has described it as a gigantic system of 'transactional linkages', a mechanism for the distribution of spoils in return for electoral support and organizational loyalty. 'The main integrating ideas were opportunism, self-aggrandisement, the impulse to enter patron–client relationships and to forge deals via the mutual pursuit of the main chance.' The ingredients of patriotic sacrifice and nation-building rapidly disappeared from the party's ideological glue.

An increasingly assertive rural elite used traditional caste/kinship/ patron–client links to organize electoral support for the Congress. Through this process state-level 'party bosses' arose. By the time of Nehru's death in 1964, power had already shifted from the central leaders to these party bosses and the state units. The passing away of an older generation of Congress leaders also took its toll. New bosses like Pratap Singh Kairon, Bakshi Ghulam Mohammed, Biju Patnaik and Kamaraj Nadar were men of a different creed, relatively uninterested in ideology and less concerned than their predecessors with preserving liberal values or liberal norms of functioning.[21]

Moreover, two parallel processes were taking place which decisively altered the character of the Congress. The functioning of the democratic process over time politicized more and more sections of society, including Dalits and tribals. Along with secret balloting, this progressively under-mined and weakened the vote banks system, thereby rendering the 'transactional linkages' of the Congress increasingly without purpose. The heart of the Congress system in the countryside was dealt a fatal blow. 'De-patronization' did not take place everywhere, nor did vote banks disappear altogether. Even today, the Congress must operate through local notables enjoying a sizeable local following or able to organize it through vertical linkages of various kinds. But at a certain point the vote bank system could no longer be relied on. If Congress was to retain electoral dominance it would have to devise a new strategy. According to Frankel, 'Clientelist politics had broken down not only in urban constituencies but also in rural areas.'[22]

The second crucial factor was the frustration of the growing agrarian bourgeoisie. While the Panchayati Raj system was being established during the fifties and the state and local bureaucracies were growing, the rural rich had opportunities to expand their capacities and increase their access to resources through Congress control of the Panchayati Raj network, which rapidly began to call the shots in local government bureaucracies. For a time, this satisfied aspirations for more power and wealth. By the mid sixties these avenues were exhausted. The Congress could provide no other. Where now could this layer turn to aggrandize itself?

In terms of the 'overload' thesis, a more crystallized class formation – the rich peasantry – not only made more demands on the system but was willing to organize pressure in ways not amenable to incorporation in the traditional bargaining networks within Congress, which was, in any case, breaking up organizationally. The upper peasantry began to look for alternative structures and mechanisms through which to assert its authority. In the mid sixties, for the first time, there was a series of major defections from the Congress. Splinter groups emerged in every state. In the Hindi heartland, Charan Singh's Samyukta Vidhayak Dal (SVD), the first significant independent class formation of the peasantry, emerged and came to power in Uttar Pradesh in the 1967 elections. In these elections, the Congress suffered dramatic reverses, conceding power to opposition forces for the first time in a number of states.

Liberal-pluralists have never given sufficient weight to the rise of kulaks in their explanations of how Congress de-institutionalization took place or why political instability persists. Giving explanatory primacy to the rise of a class would not sit easily in a framework of analysis which insists on downgrading the importance of class politics. In addition, both the sources and solutions to the dilemma of prolonged instability and the crisis of leadership are thought to be found in an analysis of political institutions and their capacities/incapacities to handle the 'overload' of rising expectations from all sections of society. The liberal-pluralists have thus assumed that the rise of the kulak lobby does not make it *functionally* different from the subordinate classes/castes. The former is different only in that it voices more demands more loudly and presses for their realization more aggressively. But even within the terms of the liberal-pluralist model such an assimilation of roles is probably not justified. Part of the objection is that the subordinate classes/castes have not been able to articulate grievances effectively, and have become even less able to do so since the de-institutionalization of the Congress. Political institutions like parties and parliament/assemblies have, on balance, become less able or concerned to articulate the demands of the oppressed classes/castes. The latter have had to seek new and hopefully more effective channels of expression, but with little success. This has led to a higher frequency of outbreaks and struggles from below, not because there is a greater gap between claims articulated within the arena of 'normal' bourgeois politics and the capacities for redressing them, but simply because their grievances are not even heard short of violence. Their expectations may well have grown but their opportunities to voice and press their claims institutionally have been reduced. There are few class-specific institutions for demand articulation and the oppressed classes are less able to press their claims within existing multi-class institutions, such as 'centrist' parties like Congress, Janata or even in parties of the mainstream left.[23] The ensuing frustration could then be channelled into non-class, communal, regional, caste directions through organizations based on these identities.

If this is true, even in part, then the infrequency of class-conscious mobilizations cannot be taken as an accurate barometer of the potential for mobilization along class lines. It would also suggest that even greater responsibility be placed on the agrarian bourgeoisie and its allies for the overload problem. The reluctance of non-Marxists to see the *class* role and power of the rich peasantry could be related to their hopes that stabilization of the political system can be achieved through the re-establishment of a 'one-party dominance system', either by a refurbished Congress or some new Congress-like national and centrist formation. In such a view, the argument that the rise of the agrarian bourgeoisie makes this impossible would clearly not be acceptable. Indeed, it would probably be argued that the rise of peasant power reinforces centrist politics in India and enhances the prospects of constructing a stable centrist party.[24]

After the Nehru Era

Lal Bahadur Shastri, Nehru's successor, was a man much more in tune with the aspirations of the agricultural elite. He was also seen by state party bosses as more amenable to pressure. But in response to the growing organizational disarray in the Congress, he strengthened the Prime Minister's secretariat, thus insulating the Prime Minister from party pressure. Many analysts have blamed Mrs Gandhi's centralizing manoeuvres for fatally weakening and 'de-institutionalizing' the Congress. But though her political predilection was for more personalized control, and though she has to shoulder some of the responsibility for accelerating the process of 'de-institutionalization', the charge is basically unfair. The Congress had already begun to break up before her time.

It would thus be incorrect to regard Mrs Gandhi's style of functioning as the fundamental cause of the 1969 crisis, when she precipitated a split on the question of the party's presidential nominee. In a sense her rise may be compared to that of the Labour left in the UK in the early eighties. It was essentially the decline of Labourism that explained the latter's advance, not the other way around. Similarly, it was the decline of the old Congress that explained the rise of Mrs Gandhi and not, as her opponents and critics have argued, the other way around.

In setting out to establish a new kind of Congress party, Indira Gandhi addressed herself to two tasks: to reassert the authority of the High Command; and to define more clearly the party's social base.[25] The Nehru Congress had always relied on the support of the 'core minorities' – the Scheduled Castes and Tribes (some 22 per cent of the population, now around 110 million and 45 million respectively) and the Muslims (now about 90 million or 12 to 13 per cent) – which tended to vote for it en bloc. After the 1967 elections, when Congress rule was overturned in a number of states as a result of the growing power of the intermediate castes, Mrs Gandhi turned much more consciously to these minorities and to the 'forward' castes threatened by the same intermediate groups. She also made subsequent attempts to woo the kulaks, their rural allies and urban traders – the caste Hindu vote – but in comparison this remained an unstable source of support. The electoral configuration may have been sufficient to allow Mrs Gandhi and the new Congress to take over at the centre. What it could not do was assure her an easy passage in office.

The Other Institutions

Other structures of Indian bourgeois democracy – such as the legislatures, the judiciary, the press, the administrative bureaucracy and the coercive apparatuses – were generally based on imported models. Their implantation was weak in comparison with the Congress's. They have survived now for some forty years and this fact alone has given them substantial roots in Indian society. But if the early post-independence harmony was conducive to their consolidation, the subsequent period of turbulence has promoted processes of decay which in turn have reinforced this turbulence.

The legislatures, with no parliamentary tradition to speak of, were critically dependent on the Congress leadership for establishing such a 'tradition' as well as general norms for the relationship between the legislature and the executive. The old leadership, particularly Nehru, was acutely aware of this problem, of the fragility of the legislatures and of the need to strengthen legislative checks on an executive which could be easily tempted to ignore such weak bodies. Nehru spent more time in parliament and paid more attention to the issue of the executive's accountability to the legislature on a day-to-day basis than any of his successors. He did much to establish a routine of sorts but, after his death, the legislatures rapidly degenerated into rubber stamps for executive directives at both state and central level. Serious debate is virtually non-existent, and the watch-dog role of parliamentary committees has been downgraded as members lose the necessary skills and commitment. Political power is an important and easy route to economic wealth and upward mobility. This is because of the enormous power of the state in national economic activity and the relative weakness of class vis-à-vis state power. In the USA the opposite route is more frequently traversed.[26] Politics attracts a new breed of legislators and career politicians. Members of Parliament (MPs) and Members of the Legislative Assemblies (MLAs) enjoy perks significant for a country like India, such as allowances of various kinds, housing, telephones, medical care, travel facilities, and so on. They use these not only for themselves but for relatives and friends. More importantly, their position affords them ample opportunities to amass wealth through corruption and misuse of power and authority.

The Union Legislature comprises the President and two houses. The lower house is the House of the People (Lok Sabha) and the upper is the Rajya Sabha (Council of States). The Rajya Sabha can have no more than 250 members of which 12 are selected by the President as representatives in the fields of literature, science, art and social science. The remainder are elected by the members of the state legislative assemblies on the basis of proportional representation. The Lok Sabha can have a maximum of 552 members. To be an MP a person must be an Indian citizen and, for the Rajya Sabha, not less than 30 years old and in the Lok Sabha not less than 25 years old. Legislation requires the assent of both houses, except for money bills where the lower house prevails.

The legislatures in the states comprise the governor and a single, directly elected assembly. In Bihar, Jammu and Kashmir, Karnataka, Maharashtra and Uttar Pradesh there is also an upper house known as the legislative council. This has not less than 40 members and no more than one third of the numbers in the legislative assembly of that state. One third of the numbers of the legislative council are elected by the MLAs from outside its ranks; another third by members of municipalities, district boards and other local authorities; one twelfth by teachers and another twelfth by registered graduates. The remainder are nominated by the governor on the basis of their record in the arts, sciences or social service. The legislative assembly, which cannot have less than 60 or more than 500 MLAs, is elected on the basis of geographical constituencies.

The social composition of legislatures in the Lok Sabha has changed. The proportion of professionals has declined. The only occupational group to have shown a substantial rise is, as might be expected, the agriculturalists, whose proportion of the Lok Sabha went up from 22 per cent to 38 per cent between 1952 and 1984.[27] In the state assemblies the percentage of agriculturalists is significantly higher. The disarray is also far greater in these assemblies, reaching a nadir in Bihar, widely acknowledged as the most lawless, badly run and backward state in the Union. Between 1967 and 1981, the Bihar government practised an enormous fraud on the people by promulgating some 256 ordinances through executive fiat between assembly sessions.[28]

The much vaunted 'steel frame' or civilian bureaucracy bequeathed by British colonialism has been rightly credited with maintaining substantial administrative cohesion in the country. What was bequeathed was both an organization with well-codified rules and a substantial cadre of highly educated and competent 'generalists' in the higher civil services of which the Indian Civil Service (later the Indian Administrative Service) formed the core. The Congress accepted the principle of civil-servant 'neutrality' and thereby eliminated the stigma of having faithfully served British interests. This paved the way for a smooth transition. The 'steel frame' was left in place.

A stable and capable bureaucracy is by itself no guarantee of democratic political rule, as Pakistan's experience shows. But in India, given the authority of the Congress and the prolonged history of a popular nationalist movement, the civilian bureaucracy was from the beginning conscious of its moral subordination to the Congress and willingly accepted Congress pre-eminence.

Up to the mid sixties, Congress dominance and the broad consensus regarding national goals and values meant that the non-partisan loyalty of the civil service was never tested. A self-confident bureaucracy and a self-confident Congress could establish an appropriate modus vivendi in which the unspoken constraints on both sides were as important as formal divisions of authority and responsibility.[29]

Destabilizing and demoralizing political interference – favouritism in promotions, penalizing transfers, vitiation of normal procedures/operations through corruption – led to a gradual erosion whose cumulative trajectory took a qualitative leap in the state bureaucracies after the 1967 assembly elections. Since then neither the Congress nor the opposition can count on a permanent tenure. The temptation to bend state bureaucracies to partisan purposes has proved irresistible and the effects of constant interference are now all too evident.

At the centre a somewhat different dynamic has been at work. The collapse of the old Congress meant that the top leadership, for example, Mrs Gandhi, had to compensate for the party's organizational decline by relying more on the top civilian administration. This led to greater pressures for a more committed and partisan bureaucracy. If these pressures have led to greater political interference and demoralization in the ranks, they have also led to greater authority and power for a large number of top bureaucrats. These bureaucrats have been willing accomplices in the practices which have weakened the independence and professionalism of the civil service as a whole. Since at this national level there is no stable pattern of party alternation, the occasional efforts to enhance the bureaucrat's independence and prestige (for example, the 1986 pay commission raising pay and perks) have not had the desired effect.

The common dilemma of the ruling parties (Congress or Janata) is their lack of a properly functioning organizational structure and the existence of severe internal wrangling. They have had to buy the temporary support of activists. To do this they have sought to extend their control over the central and state bureaucracies. What is remarkable is that, despite these trends and the institutionalization of corruption, the civilian bureaucracy remains a reasonably effective instrument, impressively so in comparison to other third world bureaucracies. This can be attributed to the continuing quality of the higher civil services which play a crucial binding role and to the pressures of federalism. Reproduction of this quality is largely ensured through well-established recruitment and training mechanisms which impart to selected candidates the appropriate ethos and sense of superior social status. In the federal set-up, the all-India services are the vital arteries of administration. Politicians cannot have the same expertise as experienced bureaucrats. Indeed, where ministers are themselves more able and experienced, they are more likely to value this bureaucratic expertise and encourage official criticisms of party policies. The Indian 'steel frame' shows signs of rusting and weakened links but it remains an imposing construction.

In his *The Crisis of the Indian Legal System*, Upendra Baxi alleged that the political elite of the country had not 'internalized the value of legalism'.[30] When everyday politics is one of manipulation and abuse of power, when corruption is accepted as necessary for getting things done, when the politics of protest is most likely to get its way, then the law is seen, above all, as a means of legitimizing power grabbing and sharing.

Technically, the Indian constitution, one of the most liberal documents of its kind, allows the courts to play an almost equal role with the executive and legislature in building a welfare state. With the legislature incapable of providing any serious check on the executive, the conflict between the latter and the judiciary has come to the fore since the late sixties. In 1973 a compromise of sorts was established. The Supreme Court was empowered to decide on the basic structure of the constitution, which could not be tampered with.[31] But at the same time the Court acknowledged that in certain areas the executive could override fundamental rights in the interests of social transformation. In practice the top levels of the judiciary (the judges of the Supreme Court and High Courts) were by and large prepared to go to considerable lengths to let the executive have its way. During the Emergency the behaviour of most Supreme Court judges was subservient in the extreme. The relationship of forces between the Court and executive so favoured the latter that in time any capacity of the Court (through powers of judicial review) to challenge the executive would have been done away with. The 1977 electoral repudiation of the Emergency gave the judiciary an unexpected reprieve, helped restore its authority and gave it the power and spirit once again to act as a check on executive abuses.

In the post-Emergency period judicial activism took on new scope and meaning. As if in reaction to earlier supineness, Supreme Court judges (such as K. Iyer and P.N. Bhagwati) who had promoted the accretion of executive power under Mrs Gandhi now became the foremost advocates of citizen interests against state arbitrariness. Furthermore, through Public Interest Litigation (PIL) the Supreme Court took it upon itself to play a socially transformative role. PIL was to be the cutting edge of a judiciary committed to the social goals which the executive had earlier claimed as its motivating ideals.

However, the capacity of judicial activism and creative application of constitutional directives to subvert the legal system for radical ends is limited. Some of the euphoria over PIL has worn off. PIL will obtain favourable decisions where the petitioners belong to the most disorganized sections of the oppressed – but not where they belong to its more organized and explicitly radicalized sectors. Most supporters of judicial activism see it as a way of preserving the traditional principles of a liberal-democratic order rather than as a means to radical ends. In short, there is considerable judicial self-restraint, reinforced by the executive's power to appoint and transfer judges.[32]

For the press, the Emergency marked a watershed. Then, with few exceptions, neither the English-language nor the vernacular press

acquitted itself honourably. Subsequent attempts at generalizing censorship through the 1982 Bihar Press Bill and the 1988 Anti-Defamation
Bill met with much stronger resistance in which the English-language
press played the leading role. It has an influence much greater than its
vote-catching ability or the size of its readership. It is this legitimizing
function of the press and not its vote-catching role that is important to
the government and to the other aspiring political parties. The vernacular
press with its limited resources has to feed off its more affluent and better
equipped English-language brethren. This reinforces the latter's leading
role in fixing the terms of public discourse. Its political importance
should therefore not be underestimated. The corruption issue (witness
Bofors and other defence deals) badly damaged the Rajiv government's
credibility and helped the emergence of Vishwanath Pratap Singh as a
national rival for leadership – and a great deal of the credit must go
to sections of the press which played a vanguard role in uncovering
scandals.[33] But what this press cannot do is reduce political instability.
In fact, by personalizing and simplifying complex political issues it has
tended to promote a politics of image which undermines the legitimacy
of one set of rulers while promoting the illusion that simply by changing
them for another, 'better' set, the instability problem will be resolved.

Television, of course, simplifies issues even more. In general, Indian
television promotes the values and ideology of the urban elite. What
is still not clear is the extent to which television can or will influence
electoral politics. It could be said that the increasingly plebiscitary
character of Indian national politics would tend to promote media-based
mobilization at the expense of traditional organizational methods. But
clearly the former is still nowhere near as important as it is in
the fully urbanized and culturally less diverse Western democracies.
Furthermore, as long as Doordarshan TV and All India Radio are
denied autonomy, media-based politics cannot become a generalized
phenomenon because exposure of the opposition parties, their leaders
and their programmes is substantially restricted. The Indian public may
be illiterate but it is nonetheless bound to be seriously sceptical of the
one-sided political messages of controlled programming.

Perhaps most disturbing of all to the Indian state are the problems
that have beset the coercive apparatuses, in particular the police.[34]
There are some fifteen paramilitary units controlled by the central
ministries comprising around 750,000 men. The most important such
units are the Border Security Force (BSF) with over 100,000 men, the
Central Reserve Police Force (CRPF) which is the major riot control
force, the Railway Protection Force (RPF), Central Industries Security
Forces (CISF), Defence Security Corps (DSC), Assam Rifles, and the
Indo-Tibetan Border Force. They are often poorly trained, poorly paid

and work in bad conditions. Unlike the civic police these paramilitaries are insulated from the public and do not enjoy the benefits of corruption which can act as a safety-valve. But they have been used with ever greater frequency to help curb outbreaks of civic violence. There is both political interference in promotions and misuse of junior personnel by seniors in a hierarchical structure that faithfully reflects the colonial military tradition. In fact the whole of the police force is still based on the 1861 Police Act. In 1979 the CRPF and CISF went on strike.

The rest of the police are controlled by the state governments and divided into the armed wing or provincial armed constabulary and the civic police armed only with lathis (long wooden sticks). The armed constabulary comprises 250,000 out of around 800,000 policemen and officers in all. They too suffer from bad pay and conditions, a military culture and isolation from the public. The civic police in everyday touch with the public suffer brutalizing work conditions. While there has been little democratization or modernization of the police, their politicization has been enormous. Constables, who make up over ninety per cent of the force, suffer from particularly low levels of pay and training, have limited promotion opportunities and poor ancillary support. They have been denied effective rights of association and adequate channels for the articulation of demands. Political factions within ruling parties at state level have not hesitated to utilize police organizations for their own benefit. In the rural areas, the extension of the Panchayati Raj system has greatly contributed to the politicization of village administration and the misuse of policemen by the dominant castes and classes in the countryside. Political interference in postings, transfers and promotions are now an established fact of police life. In metropolitan areas the criminalization of politics and the politicization of crime (top smugglers and mafia dons are beyond the law's reach) have played havoc with the anti-crime functions of the police, dramatically enhanced corruption within its ranks and seriously lowered its self-image.

Police agitation and strikes now have a history of more than thirty years. Not a single major metropolis has been spared – with the 1982 Bombay police strike constituting a zenith of sorts. The army had to be called in to restore order after three days of bloody repression against police and textile workers who forged a practical alliance on the streets.

The kind of reforms that are required to transform the police service are well known. They would involve revamping the pay and promotion structures, vastly improving work conditions, democratizing internal functioning (and stopping the abuse of power by seniors), reorganizing responsibilities to increase the scope for initiative from below, reducing the excessive powers currently enjoyed by sub-inspectors and police superintendents, upgrading training and educational qualifications at all levels, introducing greater levels of specialization, professionalization and autonomy. The apex Indian Police Service (IPS) would have to be strengthened. The erosion of democratic rights, the increased use of repressive apparatuses, the greater role given to the intelligence agencies in the last two decades are all undisputed facts of Indian political life. Until such time as the construction of a depoliticized and highly professional police force is considered vital for preserving the bourgeois order, present patterns are likely to continue.

The fact is that political leaders in the states, the agrarian bourgeoisie and even the senior civil service (the IAS) do not stand to gain from changing the present character of the police services. Politicians and the rural elite much prefer the present state of affairs – a weak democracy – to the alternatives of a strong democracy or its complete absence; in both cases the civilian bureaucracy and the police would be better organized and less amenable to manipulation by the run-of-the-mill politician or local notable. In any event, the IAS would oppose any attempt to upgrade the IPS to an equivalent level of prestige and authority. A paradox of sorts emerges. The drift to a more authoritarian democracy is evident; recourse to repression more frequent. But there is little or no attempt to enhance the prestige and professionalism of the principal internal instrument on which this authoritarian drift must, in practice, rest. This is because this drift is not a planned strategy controlled by the centre, but the result of a series of ad hoc responses to various accumulating pressures by a harassed and beleaguered executive.

The military is a different proposition. It is a truly national institution, as reflected in the regionally varied composition of its officer cadre and in its fighting units, which are usually organized in regionally homogeneous units. There is growing politicization since the army is being called in to do more internal policing as a result of the growing scale and violence of riots and other disturbances which the demoralized police feel less and less equipped to handle. The army has also been involved in prolonged counter-insurgency activity in the northeast and more recently in Punjab. Moreover, the changing composition of its officer cadre involves more recruits from lower-middle-class and 'humbler' backgrounds than in the past. The families they come from are more likely to be buffeted by the winds of economic adversity and they cannot be so easily insulated from the general problems of the public. Recent hikes in pay and allowances have only partially countered the appeal of other elite occupations in civilian life which enjoy greater status and prestige.

But the military remains easily the least politicized and most profes-sional of the major institutions, more so than the civilian bureaucracy. Its deliberately cultivated lifestyle of mess and club life, special facilities, and so on, does insulate it substantially from the rest of the population.

There is also a conscious effort to limit interchange between Indian military officers and their foreign counterparts. In order to strengthen its ultimate authority the civilian government promotes inter-services parity *and* separation, which works to the detriment of the army, much the largest of the military services. Chairmanship of the joint chiefs of staff committee, for example, is held in rotation among the heads of the three services. Though there have been instances of political interference with the seniority rule at the highest levels of promotion even these cases for the most part were not considered to have fallen outside the acceptable limits of political discretion.

On the whole if a bourgeois democratic regime is to survive it must be confident that the military will remain aloof from the inter-bourgeois conflicts of civilian life. It must not be called in to act as final arbiter in such conflicts. Yet this is what Jayaprakash Narayan, leader of the Bihar movement, did in 1974–75, when he called on the army to intervene to oust Mrs Gandhi. For her, this was an unacceptable breach in the rules governing political conflicts between the ruling party and the opposition. In her eyes it justified the declaration of Emergency to 'save the country from chaos and total breakdown', though, of course, she had other motivations. That such a call was made testified to the weakness of Indian bourgeois democracy, but that it had no impact testified to its underlying strengths. Indeed, it should be remembered that the military played no role in bringing about the Emergency, in sustaining it during 1975–77, or in bringing it to an end. The one experience of generalized authoritarian rule in post-independence India did not involve any direct participation by the military. Nor is there evidence that the military exercised significant influence, even indirectly, on Congress policies during this period.

The Mid Sixties Onwards

A number of commentators have correctly pointed to the rise of plebiscitary politics in the wake of the 'de-institutionalization' of the Congress.[35] As argued earlier, among the key factors responsible for this were the crystallization of an agrarian bourgeoisie in a large part of the Hindi heartland whose path to aggrandizement was blocked within the old Congress and the decline of this Congress as a reliable vote-getting machine. The politics that emerged was plebiscitary in a number of senses. Lok Sabha elections were increasingly centred on a simple message which could appeal to a broad cross-section of the electorate and became, in effect, single-issue referenda. In 1971 it was Garibi Hatao; in 1977 Emergency Hatao; in 1980 Janata Hatao; in 1984

Desh Bachao; and in 1989 the election turned into a contest between a 'clean' opposition versus a 'corrupt' government, with V.P. Singh the new 'Mr Clean' of Indian politics.

Individual leadership appeal became far more important than party structure (which had decayed terribly anyway) for obtaining votes. The legitimacy of a party and its structures was supplanted by an altogether more unstable and inherently ephemeral legitimacy of individuals. Those critics who attribute Congress decay and the rise of plebiscitary politics to Mrs Gandhi will have to explain why other political parties aspiring to central rule (barring the cadre-based Communist parties and the Jan Sangh/BJP (Bharatiya Janata Party)) have also become essentially plebiscitary and substantially de-institutionalized.

All Rajiv Gandhi's early efforts and rhetoric notwithstanding, the Congress under him remains in a state of decay. Other rival bourgeois parties are also crucially dependent on the public appeal of their principal leader, be it the Janata under Ramkrishna Hegde or the Jan Morcha, totally centred on its leading personality, V. P. Singh. Even the most cohesive and structured class party of the north Indian peasantry, the Lok Dal, has split after the death of its unifying leader, Charan Singh. The Lok Dal, even if united, could never on its own be a national alternative. It is revealing that the two Lok Dals and other rump parties which have split off from parent organizations have followed the Congress pattern of suffixing their names with the initials of their leaders. Plebiscitary politics clearly outlives Mrs Gandhi herself.

This is a phenomenon whose origin and persistence cannot be adequately explained by reference solely or even primarily to Mrs Gandhi's political style. In the 1969 Congress split, for example, the Congress (0), dominated by the 'syndicate' of powerful state bosses, carried with it around forty per cent of the undivided Congress's organized strength. But this wing withered away rapidly. Its only real claim to national pre-eminence and leadership in the uneasy Janata coalition rested on the national and historical stature of Morarji Desai.

Plebiscitary politics is less important in state assembly elections. At this level, it is more possible to construct reliable – or at least less unreliable – vote-gathering electoral machines. Party control over state government is more pronounced, better structured, and more coordinated with the general agrarian class and caste power structures. The politics of patronage has greater scope and efficacy. But as 'wave' effects in the 1977 and 1980 elections have shown, a plebiscitary appeal is not without significant impact even here. Had general and assembly elections not been delinked in 1971, the plebiscitary character of state-level politics would have been even more pronounced, though a variety of opposition parties would probably continue to enjoy significant and electorally decisive regional appeal.

The electoral arithmetic required to secure victory at the national level is different from that required in the states. Here, the dominant agricultural classes and castes are more important and have to be wooed more assiduously. A sizeable part of the middle castes has to be won over even by parties which do not focus their regional appeal on them. At the all-India level the cross-class and cross-caste appeal needed to secure a pluralist majority has to be much wider, especially in the crucial Hindi belt where the relative size of core minorities (Scheduled Castes, Scheduled Tribes and Muslims) is substantial in key states. Clearly defined programmes or too close an identification with any single class, set of castes or broadly homogeneous group is a handicap. Since the growing self-consciousness and aggressiveness of the agrarian bourgeoisie and its rural petty-bourgeois allies puts pressure on all parties to make just such an identification, there is a real dilemma for all aspiring parties seeking power through a centrist appeal. These parties must try and woo the intermediate castes and classes of countryside and town and yet not alienate the castes and classes above and below them. They must also seek a mandate from an increasingly sophisticated electorate which is quite cynical about party programmes and promises. This clearly promotes a plebiscitary approach where the essential electoral choice is simply and starkly put. This does not mean an end to ideological platforms but it does mean greater eclecticism and less consistency. Congress socialism was the populist message of Mrs Gandhi after 1969 when she sought consciously to solidify the traditional support of the core minorities and when she had to rely on CPI support for her minority government till the 1971 elections. Her son then flirted with the idea that pragmatic technologism might be the best way to construct a broad ideological consensus. In the end he relied on the simple electoral appeal of 'national unity under siege' in the 1984 elections (see Table 13).

Since the mid sixties voting by the core minorities has become more volatile and less loyal to the Congress. But the intermediate castes in the north (even allowing for some support for the Congress) emerged as the single largest bloc consistently opposing the Congress. Charan Singh was able to unify this bloc behind himself and a single party. But after his death it split. Peasant castes in the north, for example the caste following of Mohinder Singh Tikait, or in other parts of the country, such as Sharad Joshi's movement in Maharashtra, have now made it clear that they will not align themselves permanently with *any* political party and that they will pursue agitational as well as electoral methods to get their way.

The great political virtue of Mrs Gandhi was that in the latter half of the sixties – a period of severe political and economic crisis – she was able to weather the decisive decline of the 'Congress system' and rapidly find a new way to retain the Congress party's national stature and electoral viability. Her style prefigured the general political style of the seventies and eighties. But the huge majorities that her Congress and the Janata were later to secure did not make more effective governance possible nor were they indications of the development of stable political bases. Ironically, these majorities reflected the fundamental instability of the system and the organizational weaknesses and lack of electoral consolidation of the parties concerned.

The history of Mrs Gandhi's leadership of the Congress in the late sixties – of the 1969 split, of the emergence of a new, ascendant Congress under her tutelage, of the rapid decline in Congress credibility, of the imposition of Emergency rule, and of her 1977 debacle – has been amply and ably documented by numerous writers. Whatever the immediate triggers for the declaration of Emergency, it should also be seen as the probable outcome of deeper, longer-term forces and as an attempt to resolve the deeply rooted crisis of political instability and re-establish firm bourgeois leadership by changing the form of bourgeois political rule from a weak and crisis-ridden democracy to a cautiously generalized form of constitutionally sanctioned authoritarianism. Mrs Gandhi possibly saw this as a prelude to the establishment of a 'guided democracy' with significant resemblances to the Bonapartism of early Gaullist rule in the French Fifth Republic. Indeed, talk of instituting a presidential system along French lines first surfaced during the Emergency when some of Mrs Gandhi's ministers sought to promote a controlled public debate on the issue. In calling for elections, which she thought she would win, in 1977, Mrs Gandhi was probably seeking popular legitimacy for further steps towards the fulfilment of some such project. Whatever her intentions (and these remain unclear) her massive defeat restored the bourgeois democratic framework and made clear that generalized authoritarian rule was no answer to the central question of how to restore long-term stability. Indeed, it only made matters worse.

The Janata interlude provided mainly negative lessons. It confirmed that a stable two-party competitive system was still a far-off proposition. It also suggested that any centrist formation which contained within it a coherently organized peasant party representing dominant agrarian interests would be bound to break up as this component sought to establish hegemony within the party. This was the essential conflict underlying the fight for leadership between Charan Singh and Morarji Desai, with the Jan Sangh, the other strong caste- and class-based party, throwing its weight behind the latter.

Once again, liberal-pluralist analysts have downplayed the role of the agrarian bourgeoisie and preferred to assign responsibility for the Janata break-up to the personal rivalries between ageing egotistical and overambitious leaders.[36] Yet it should be obvious that any future Janata-like attempt at forming a national alternative to the Congress by incorporating a strong class party of the middle and upper north Indian peasantry, even if it comes to power, will in all probability meet the same fate of rapid disintegration. The logic of plebiscitary politics implies that the leadership of any bourgeois party or coalition aspiring to national power cannot be identified too strongly with the sectoral interests of any particular class or caste segment, no matter how strong or important that particular component may be. The agrarian bourgeoisie, for all its growing strength, has yet to solve the problem of how to establish its political hegemony at the centre.

The Indira Congress and the Gandhi Cult

After Mrs Gandhi's fall in 1977, and the subsequent split in 1978, she continued to plot a strategy for political revival which was crucially dependent on her own appeal. Although the Election Commission ruled that only her party – and none of the rivals, Congress (C), (S), (J), and so on – could claim the historic title of Indian National Congress, she preferred to retain the name Congress (I) in order to underline the break in continuity. Nonetheless, one of her persistent problems was assuring a foundation for her all-India party that would be more stable than her own much-publicized charisma.

Given her undisputed stature as the only cement and national asset of the party, no faction or individual in the Congress (I) dared to challenge her openly, nor did they need to. While paying formal obeisance in the most cringeing manner, in practice they could simply bypass or ignore her directives. For although Mrs Gandhi possessed powers of ultimate sanction and discipline and could dismiss chief ministers at will, it was impossible for her to intervene directly at every level of the party. Factionalism flourished as never before as the spoils of power became the paramount objective of political activity. The absence of a cohesive structure also meant that there were no buffers between herself and local discontents within the party.

It was not the economic or social programme of the Congress (I) that distinguished it from the coalition of its bourgeois opponents. Admittedly, the Janata's bias in favour of the 'intermediate castes' and rural kulaks was more pronounced, but it was not markedly so.[37] At a more general level, there had emerged an ideological consensus about the unambiguously capitalist nature of the Indian economy. The days of fanfares for the 'mixed economy' were definitely over now that the infra-structure of state-sponsored core industries had been established. Today, the various parties may differ in emphasis, but they share a basic economic perspective. The essential goals are to encourage market forces and increase the relative strength of the private sector; to restrict the power of the unions; to promote greater production for the market by the kulaks through higher procurement prices, lower input charges, and credit support for agricultural mechanization, capitalization and commercialization; to reduce corporate taxation; to foster the growth of the share market; to maintain important sections of the public sector while modernizing and perhaps privatizing certain other parts; to provide higher remuneration for the managerial and technical professions; and to limit the growth of the black economy while learning to live with it.[38]

Intuitively, if not analytically, Mrs Gandhi had grasped the essence of the politics of the new order. Assuring the longer-term survival of the Congress as a national entity required a person of similar stature as an eventual successor. No effort was spared to build up the cult of Mrs Gandhi's sons, first Sanjay and then Rajiv. Yet this too proved no answer to the larger question of assuring political stability and an enduring Congress appeal.

Disillusionment with the Rajiv Congress

Large sections of Indian society, particularly the urban middle class and the industrial bourgeoisie, vested great hopes in the rise of Rajiv Gandhi. Though Mrs Gandhi had already moved a long way to accommodate their interests in her economic policies during the Emergency and after her return to power in 1980 (her election manifesto of that year made no reference to socialism), she was still encumbered by her past. Rajiv Gandhi had no such handicap. He was perceived as an outstanding representative of the new India, of the rising middle class and of the modernizing and aggressively ambitious private sector fettered by the chains of state controls. His 'Mr Clean' image was consciously cultivated; he was seen as a leader who would apply the modernizing broom to the political arena itself and strengthen the bourgeois democratic system by attacking corruption and patronage, re-institutionalizing the Congress, halting the erosion of other institutions and promoting healthy two-party competition in the states and more stable and norm-guided competition between the Congress and opposition forces at the centre.[39]

Such an enormous range of expectations was bound to lead to disillusionment. The fact that this burden was imposed in the first place indicates the extent to which intellectuals and India-watchers are still prisoners of a Huntingtonian equilibrium model of politics. It also reflects their unwillingness to recognize that the Indian political system is in irreversible transition to a new order whose topography has still to be properly surveyed.

All Rajiv Gandhi's efforts at institutionalizing a stable competitive party system and at re-institutionalizing the Congress were to no avail. In the early part of his term, many of his more discerning sympathizers considered his record a mixed one. Thus, the Rudolphs felt that though many of his policies before 1984 'could not easily be distinguished from the de-institutionalizing actions of Indira and Sanjay Gandhi', his later 'conduct took a different turn. The party remained centralized and subject to its leader's managerial ideology and professional style, but it was less subject than it had been under Indira Gandhi to arbitrary tests of loyalty that dissolve institutional commitment and procedural regularity.' In the light of what has happened since the authors would no doubt present a more gloomy and pessimistic assessment of the Rajiv government. But liberal pluralists must ask why they were taken in, as it were, why they believed 'collegiality, institutional autonomy and decentralization seemed to have a better chance than they had had in a decade.'[40]

Hopes turned into widespread disillusionment with almost bewildering speed. His staunch supporters in the independent media become his vociferous critics.[41] The Congress is more disorganized than ever. Rajiv Gandhi as prime minister and party president centralized more power than ever before in his hands and in those of his close coterie. The problems of the civilian bureaucracy are as serious as ever. Opposition goodwill to the Rajiv Congress quickly dissipated and their hostility to him became as strong as it was to Mrs Gandhi. By mid 1987, just two and a half years after the 'new era of Indian politics' was ushered in, one crisis after another was rocking the government. What emerged was a partial crisis of political but not social relations. This partial crisis was not the result of a class groundswell from below but of the shifting tensions within the ruling coalition, or, even more narrowly, of conflicts within and between the ruling political institutions of civil bureaucracy, political executive, judiciary and party. Endemic instability necessarily implies a recurring series of conjunctural crises whose intensity and duration varies, and whose causes are specific combinations of the general and the immediate. These conjunctural upheavals do undermine in a certain way the legitimacy of the system, but are prevented from becoming deeper and more enduring by the fact that those social forces and their political representatives which have an objective interest in the overthrow of the system are simply nowhere near powerful enough to take advantage of these periodically recurring opportunities to widen the breaches in bourgeois hegemony and push popular anger in a radical direction.

It is not surprising that the conjunctural crises should so often be connected to the periodic accumulations of tensions within the Congress. The latter was, for all its handicaps, the 'ruling' and 'unifying' party. But where was its ruling and unifying ideology? By mid 1987 an acute conjunctural crisis had emerged, one of whose essential components was a constitutional conflict between president and prime minister (it was alleged that the former was conspiring to dismiss the latter in the context of the corruption scandals surrounding defence deals and the possibility of those close to or within the Gandhi family being involved in them).[42] Coupled to this were the surfacing of serious inter-corporate rivalry in which the administration was alleged to have played favourites, the failure of the Congress in the West Bengal and Kerala state elections, the inability of the Congress regime to deal adequately with persisting domestic and external problems (of which the most notable were Punjab and Sri Lanka), the growth of inner-party discontent as the old guard fought Rajiv's new men, the rise of V.P. Singh as a national figure and possible alternative to Rajiv Gandhi, and, above all, the problem of corruption in the government, which became the focal point of the crisis.[43]

One of the effects of the Rajiv government's right-wing acceleration in economic policy was to increase corruption in the private sector as earlier obstacles to corporate growth were removed. The opening up of the economy to capital from abroad also promoted tie-ups between indigenous capital and multi-nationals, on one hand, and non-resident Indian companies/investors (NRIs), on the other. However, government deregulation has only been partial. In the transition from what has been called the 'neta-babu raj' to a 'freer economy', government domination over business has given way to a somewhat more participatory relationship. The interface between government and business has not narrowed and therefore corruption and favouritism do not disappear. But an ideological dilemma surfaces. In the neta-babu raj, corruption is in the order of things. It is unremarkable. In the freer economy of enhanced competition, the market is supposed to be a neutral arbiter in the struggle for success and government is expected to be non-partisan.

Thus, the freer economy has to have new ideological standards more strongly felt and proclaimed. It is no coincidence whatsoever that the coming of the Rajiv era with its accelerated economic turn to the market was accompanied by a new rhetoric of cleaning up government, business and the interface between the two. When the reality fell short of the aggressively asserted ideals, the embarrassment was that much greater.

The same could be said of the Rajiv government's attempt to clean up political fund-raising by making company donations legal and bringing it above ground. Since this was accompanied by a campaign to clean up Indian big business – a populist campaign guided by V.P. Singh as Rajiv Gandhi's finance minister – the Congress had to rely much more on NRI contributions in return for promoting NRI influence in the Indian economy and on kickbacks on major international civilian and military deals.[44] Rajiv Gandhi's clean-up campaign did not and could not eliminate political dirty deals. These were written into the anti-corruption campaign. Only their area of operation was displaced. But what this anti-corruption drive and Rajiv Gandhi's 'Mr Clean' image did do was make subsequent disillusionment and loss of credibility that much more acute.

The same could be said of the campaign against domestic business. Given present structures and the economic need to respect, indeed enhance, so-called business confidence, there had to be a limit to such operations. These were meant to improve the government's popular image – and increase its tax revenues through more honest returns from business as a quid pro quo for corporate tax liberalization. When V.P. Singh went beyond these limits and pursued his clean-up campaign against indigenous capitalists with excessive zeal (because of personal political ambitions), he was shifted to the defence ministry where he promptly played a role in raising uncomfortable queries regarding a submarine deal with a West German firm. His expulsion from the Congress was as fated as his subsequent effort to build himself a national image as the new and genuine 'Mr Clean' of Indian politics.[45]

Within the Congress, Rajiv Gandhi's managerial approach to party organization and stewardship helped to create serious rank-and-file discontent. His has been a much more aloof and remote style of functioning than his mother's. As his policy failures mounted, as his vote-getting appeal in assembly elections weakened, discontent sharpened. But since the structural weakness of the Congress invests great authority in its national figurehead/leader, and because a viable national alternative to which loyalties could be confidently shifted did not emerge, party factionalism rarely went beyond certain self-imposed boundaries. This factionalism operated mainly as a challenge to Rajiv Gandhi's chief ministerial appointees and their supporters in the Congress-ruled states.

It is in this context that the emergence of V.P. Singh became so important. Merely besmirching Rajiv Gandhi's political credentials through use of the Bofors scandal revelations would not on its own have made his position so difficult or the credibility crisis of the Congress so severe. Under the pressure of these events, Rajiv Gandhi backtracked and patched up many of his differences with the old guard. In the run-up to the general elections, V.P. Singh was able to translate his personal popularity into support for the new political formation, the Janata Dal, which he heads. This too is and must be a 'centrist' force, eschewing too close an identification with either the cadre-based left – the Communists – or the right – the BJP. The *general* programme of such a formation cannot be and has not been much different from that of the Congress.

In the summer of 1989 Rajiv Gandhi seemed to have found his key electoral plank: 'Power to the People'. This was the message embodied in his much-touted schemes for strengthening Panchayati Raj and for devolution of power through promoting local decision-making bodies in the cities. Local government is structured as follows. In major cities there are corporations headed by elected mayors. Administration of the city is exercised by an elected general council, standing committees and the municipal commissioner or chief executive. Smaller towns elect councils which in turn elect a president. These municipal councils usually function through various committees with delegated powers and responsibilities.

The Panchayati Raj system introduced in 1959 is a three-tier structure of local self-government at the village, block and district levels. All states are free to make changes in the structure to suit local conditions. All Panchayati Raj bodies are linked up, with special representation given to backward castes, Dalits, women and cooperative societies.

The Panchayati Raj was the key. By promising more proportionate representation on the panchayats for women and Dalits, Rajiv Gandhi was, typically, trying to make a multi-class, multi-caste, centrist appeal. The overall effect of his measures would have been to further shift the rural relationship of forces in favour of kulaks, though it also would have provided a greater dribble of benefits for the poor.

The Crisis of Legitimacy

Any discussion of this issue has to distinguish two levels. The first is that of the general relationship between the bourgeois democratic state and the economy and between this state and society in India. The second is that of the particular governing authority and of aspirants to that authority, that is, the political parties and the competitive party system as it exists. Obviously these two levels – the system and its sub-systems – are interconnected, and there are carry-over effects between them. For the first two decades after 1947, the Congress sub-system played a vital role in legitimizing democratic rule as a whole. However, the intensity of the legitimation crisis is different at these two levels, being much more acute at the second. Were this not the case it would not be possible to perceive or understand the central paradox of the Indian polity – an enduring crisis of leadership combined with the overall durability of the bourgeois democratic framework.

The great strength of bourgeois democracy is that it establishes a mode of legitimacy which has more to do with the general principles (elections, representation and mandate) by which political authority is secured than with the substance of that authority, that is, what it actually does, the class content of its policies, and so on. It does this by allowing and encouraging (within limits) popular participation in the political system within a framework of rules, rights, structures and processes which must be broadly respected by both rulers and ruled. In advanced democracies this framework determining acceptable and unacceptable forms of political behaviour has an organic strength arising from its long historical evolution and implantation. Both class formation and class structures of domination in these societies are advanced. The dominant classes are politically and ideologically homogeneous and their hegemony over the subordinate classes is firmly secured through the more advanced institutions of civil society.

In India, where the dominant classes are more heterogeneous and conflicts within the ruling coalition sharper, these classes are generally much weaker in relation to an over-developed state. The latter has to take greater responsibility for securing broad acceptance for the existing political system. What the state does in a weak democracy like India would seem, in a sense, to have a much more direct bearing on the problem of legitimacy than would be the case in an advanced democracy. If, following Habermas, one accepts that the advanced democracies suffer permanent problems of legitimacy related to the indissoluble tension between a solidly entrenched capitalist mode of production (the requirements of accumulation/reproduction) and a strong bourgeois democracy (which generalizes, articulates and expands needs and demands much more effectively than any other form of bourgeois rule), one might easily conclude that the tension between a weak capitalism and a weak democracy, as in India, should be that much greater.[46] Where state welfarism is weak, should not legitimation problems be more acute? Having already pointed out the relative decay of state institutions, the inescapable question would seem to be why the crisis of legitimacy of bourgeois democracy in India is not *greater*. What is it that contains or mitigates this crisis?

According to Bardhan, the survival of democracy is the passive consequence of contradictory pulls within a loose, large 'dominant coalition', most notably between a state elite of professionals and the industrial bourgeoisie, and more importantly, between the state elite and industrial bourgeoisie on one side and the agrarian bourgeoisie on the other.[47] He also points to the management and fiscal crisis of the state, concluding that this has promoted a 'crisis of political legitimacy' wherein the hold of the dominant coalition over the subordinate classes has significantly weakened. To be sure, the management failure of the executive, the breakdown of Congress 'bargaining federalism' and the fiscal crisis are well recognized features.[48] But Bardhan's inference that democracy exists almost by default and his optimism regarding the growing strength of the oppressed would seem to be unjustifiable simplifications.

The political system has secured a substantial measure of loyalty from both the most powerful classes/groups and from the masses. The decline of the Congress and the alternation of governments in the states have actually helped to distinguish government from party in popular perceptions. It would also be dangerous to underestimate the impact that forty years of various forms of popular participation at various levels – from elections to national campaigns to local mobilizations – have had in legitimizing the democratic system. No other arrangement could possibly have coped as effectively with such a segmentary, loose-knit society and culture as India's. The Emergency was, again, a powerful negative lesson. It was unacceptable to the agrarian bourgeoisie, to the intermediate castes, and to the oppressed classes/castes in north, east, west and central India. Its relatively greater acceptability in the south had much to do with its more limited practical impact there, in which social and political relations were largely undisturbed. Movements and struggles in the south, for all their regional impact, have rarely seriously challenged central authority.

Ironically, some of the very factors responsible for the weakness of Indian democracy have also helped to diffuse the challenges to it. To attach importance to the problems of political legitimacy is to attach importance to political life – to assume the large spread and considerable cohesiveness of the political community. The legitimation crisis in advanced democracies forces the system's defenders and its defending mechanisms to find ways of privatizing public preoccupations, loyalties and activities and channelling them away from mass political participation. Democracy with its formal commitment to equality must constantly find ways of masking and mystifying the reality of inequality and hierarchy.

In contrast, Indian society has always endorsed the principle of hierarchy and provided numerous mechanisms for ensuring its acceptability. According to A. Nandy, 'Indian culture traditionally applied the concept of hierarchy to more aspects of life than did many other cultures.'[49] A bourgeois political order is in this context just another hierarchical system which can be accepted and can coexist with others.

Moreover, the sphere of privatized behaviour is given enormous importance in Indian life. In fact, the traditional concept of power is power over self, that is, self-control and regulation of instincts and desires. The idea of uniform codes of behaviour acceptable to all is fundamentally at variance with the dharmic idea of different ethics for different spheres of life and for different social groupings. In India, the normative order of a modern political system sits on a more traditional value system sustaining a more compartmentalized existential order. The supreme wielder of power may be expected to live by high moral standards, but politics itself is assigned low levels of respect as a less important part of human existence. Thus, the cultural characteristics which facilitated prolonged Mughal and British rule persisted after 1947 and helped the establishment of a new 'Delhi Durbar'.

But the political community is growing and politics is invading more and more spheres of existence. There is a living tension between traditional and modern value systems which makes the task of generating an ideological consensus that much more complex. The integrating symbolisms that must be promoted to legitimize and strengthen the existing political order are likely to be cultural–religious as well as political–rational. It is perhaps here that the issue of Hindu nationalism can best be situated. There are powerful objective forces at work promoting Hindu nationalism; political parties are inevitably tempted to pander to it and consciously adopt it as part of their ideological appeal.

India is a nation-in-the-making in that the nation that does exist is in a process of consolidation. The economic processes of national integration are powerful, well-established, uni-directional and continuous. The political processes of integration are less secure, subject to greater pressures and challenges, and their progress has been halting. Striking the right balance of devolution and centralization of powers is always a matter of dispute and is constantly affected by the changing relationships between the centre and the states. The danger of balkanization remains remote, but the kind of broad cultural–ideological consensus that could stabilize a national political order has yet to be constructed.

There is also a Hindu community-in-the-making. This is still only to a limited extent a political community; it is much more a cultural and ideological phenomenon. The material driving forces of this cultural expansionism are the intermediate castes of rural and urban India. Assertion of their Hindu identity is the form taken by their aspirations for higher social status and for a cultural upward mobility in keeping with their upward economic and political mobility. Hindu cultural nationalism is the offspring of the long flirtation between these two entities-in-the-making, their intertwined development.

It is difficult to see why any mainstream, bourgeois party aspiring to power in New Delhi would avoid some identification with this cultural nationalism. As it is, the Congress has long suffered from the absence of a positive ideology which can attract the widest possible support. Rajiv Gandhi's technocratic pragmatism and eulogization of the market have obvious limits in a backward society like India. Given Congress's traditional support among the core minorities, its promotion of Hindu nationalism would have to be controlled and modulated. But this has always been a component of traditional Congress ideology along with Western-inspired liberal secularism, populist welfarism or 'socialism' and a conscious appeal to Muslim orthodoxy. It will be no surprise, therefore, if the relative weight of the Hindu nationalist component in Congress ideology were now to increase at the expense of its secular and 'socialist' components, even if these will still sometimes be invoked. Some of the other parties less hampered by Congress traditions may go further in accommodating themselves to this cultural nationalism. It cannot provide a complete answer to the legitimation crisis faced by all of these parties, including the Congress, but it does seem to them an important part of the answer.

The prolonged Congress dominance at the centre would have undermined the legitimacy of the competitive party system more than it has were it not for the compensatory role of federalism.[50]

Since the 1967 elections, Congress control in many states has been the exception rather than the rule. Newer formations have had the opportunity to enter state assemblies, win municipal elections and play an influential role as a sizeable component of ruling or opposition coalitions. In a few states, such as Kerala, West Bengal and Tamil Nadu, a reasonably stable system of alternation between parties or coalitions, in which the Congress usually features as a key partner on one side, has emerged. Elsewhere there has been at least a temporary rupture in Congress dominance by a party or coalition which in the end proved unable to survive. In the states, voter preferences have been more stable. Election outcomes have reflected the fact that a *majority* of the Indian electorate has never supported the Congress. Were it not for this safety valve and for the fact that in practice there has been significant decentralization of power, the opposition would have been more strongly inclined to challenge the legitimacy of existing democratic arrangements. Its strength, however, does remain institutionally under-represented at the national level. It should be noted that, with the exception of Punjab, the assertion of a Pan-Indian Hindu identity does not contradict the simultaneous assertion of a stronger regional identity. Growing Hindu nationalism and growing federalism are perfectly compatible trends.

A System in Transition

We are now in a better position to trace the process of systemic transition and to point out those characteristics which are likely to become more important and give a special stamp to the new variant of bourgeois democracy that is crystallizing in India. This is taking place through a kind of laboured forward movement; it should not be taken to imply the imminent arrival of a finished product with the sharply defined and permanent properties of an entity resting in a state of equilibrium.

The four most important political characteristics of this emerging variant of bourgeois democracy are: (1) the continuation of plebiscitary politics at the national level; (2) the growth and partial consolidation of Hindu nationalism; (3) growing federalism and decentralization of power; (4) a more 'authoritarian' democracy.

The class forces and social segments which are likely to expand their relative political power are the agrarian bourgeoisie, petty bourgeoisie and the urban middle class, comprising the self-employed, small businessmen and traders and the professional salariat. The agrarian petty bourgeoisie's economic prospects are largely linked to those of the agrarian bourgeoisie, whose hegemony it will therefore increasingly accept. Though the industrial bourgeoisie's economic pre-eminence will remain, and though in normal circumstances it is the single most important and best organized group acting on and through the state, it lacks the mobilizational capacities of either the agrarian bourgeoisie/petty bourgeoisie or the urban middle class. Nor does it have sufficient hegemony over the latter, which is considerably differentiated. Its relative economic weight will increase. But its basic problem is how to translate this into a *commensurate* political status and authority. The agrarian bourgeoisie, by contrast, enjoys a political strength disproportionately greater than its economic importance, which is, of course, by no means insignificant. How the class coalition between the industrial and agricultural bourgeoisies will be handled so as to minimize disunity and conflict will be one of the central (and more difficult) tasks of state management.

If the emergence of plebiscitary politics has eroded the difference between the Congress and the opposition, what reason is there to believe that Congress successes in Lok Sabha elections will continue? Are we moving towards a post-Congress future? The first question is more easily answered. The supplanting of the Congress by a comparable centrist, coalitional alternative in New Delhi is a distinct possibility. It would require substantial (if temporary) opposition unity behind a credible national leader; electoral alliances/arrangements with the major non-Congress parties outside the 'centrist' coalition and thus the avoidance of multi-cornered contests which split up the majoritarian non-Congress vote. What is equally certain is that such an alternative, even it it came to power, would face the same problems of instability and be equally inadequate at coping with them.

The greatest electoral asset of the Congress, built up over decades, has been the relative stability of its support from the core minorities. 'Relative' is the operative word. There has been growing volatility in Scheduled Castes and Muslim support, though not in support by Scheduled Tribes. A sizeable section of Dalits and Muslims have supported other parties in Lok Sabha elections in the past and can do so in the future, thereby facilitating victory for alternative formations in 'wave' elections. But no other national party (besides the Congress) has been able to count so strongly or for so long on the faithfulness of a large part of the Dalits and Muslims. This is an historically accumulated source of strength which even an inept Congress cannot easily squander nor another party easily garner. This makes the Congress more capable of sustaining itself as a national party, weathering splits in the wake of election defeat and re-emerging as a major contender – once it appears to have at least temporarily resolved the problem of procuring a 'charismatic' leader. The Congress, then, will continue to be very much around even if not always in power.

The growth of Hindu nationalism, Hindu communalism and, indeed, communalisms of all kinds has been seen by the left, in particular, as a portent of emerging Hindu fascism or a Hindu state. The dangers of Hindu nationalism will be dealt with later. For the present it is necessary to point out how exaggerated are these fears. While a Hindu state necessarily means Hindu nationalism, Hindu nationalism does not necessarily mean a Hindu state. The spread of Hindu nationalist appeal and the adoption of a modulated cultural nationalism by mainstream bourgeois parties are not incompatible with the preservation of the broad structures of bourgeois democracy. This phenomenon can be more faithfully seen as the system's response to its own crisis of legitimacy. But it is a response which makes the existence of non-Hindu minorities, especially the poorer strata of such minorities, significantly more insecure. In the case of Sikhs and Punjab it could reinforce the thrust towards Khalistan. Elsewhere, the deteriorating relations between Hindus and other minorities, and even between caste Hindus and Dalits, and the more frequent outbreaks of communal violence must be matters of the deepest concern in their own right. But it is not Hindu fascism or the Hindu state that must be the focus of present and future concerns but the rise of Hindu nationalism, along with other religious fundamentalisms, and communalism.

The centrifugal pulls in Indian society have led to the growth of a number of regional movements aiming at political and cultural autonomy in various degrees and forms. The left has tended to perceive this as a manifestation of a 'nationalities problem'. This characterization has obscured rather than clarified matters. It has fostered a bookish approach in which reality has been fitted to pre-existing theories and concepts; what is needed is investigation of the applicability of these theories and concepts and then utilization of them to explain reality. What is at issue is the dialectic of centralization and decentralization, involving for the most part a redefinition of centre–state relations and, to a lesser extent, the question of whether or not to concede a degree of territorial–political autonomy to certain ethnic groups, for example, Jharkhand, Gorkhaland. Neither of these two dimensions of the dialectic threatens the territorial unity of the country, nor its bourgeois democratic form. If anything, further decentralization would probably invest it with greater legitimacy and durability. The overall trend is, at any rate, in favour of further decentralization, not the least because of growing power of the agrarian bourgeoisie and the state's need to accommodate its aspirations. Only in the northeast (where secessionist forces have been seriously weakened) and more recently in Punjab and Kashmir have centrifugal pulls seriously posed the issue of territorial secession.

The progressive erosion of civil liberties, the extension of repressive legislation on the statute books has been the unsurprising response of the state to endemic instability, the rise of various oppositional movements, and the ever greater recourse to extra-parliamentary forms of protest. After all, one obvious way to ease the 'overload' problem is to reduce demands through discipline, through repression. But the essential feature of these repressive measures is that they are aimed mainly at eroding the rights of association and collective struggle. The attacks on voting procedures and representation rights are less fierce and more temporary. Moreover, this trend of repression falls well short of the imposition of any system of generalized authoritarian rule. Nor is such a system likely to emerge as the result, for example, of some gradual cumulative process of democratic erosion. What has happened is that the government has armed itself as best as it could wherever it has had to play a 'fire-fighting' role. Since the size and frequency of 'brush fires' is growing, the drift towards what may be called a more authoritarian democracy has continued apace. But any balanced evaluation of future trends and outcomes in India will require equal emphasis on both the noun and the adjective.

Notes

1. H.A. Gould, 'Apperception of Doom in Indian Political Analysis', in P. Wallace (ed.), *Region and Nation in India*, Oxford and IBH, Bombay 1985, pp. 287–97.

2. A representative sample would be in L.I. and S.H. Rudolph, *In Pursuit of Lakshmi*, Orient Longman, Bombay 1988; 'Party Decay and Political Crisis in India', J. Manor, in *The Washington Quarterly*, summer 1981; Robert Hardgrave Jnr, *India Under Pressure*, Westview, Boulder 1984; S.A. Kochanek, 'Mrs Gandhi's Pyramid: The New Congress', in H.C. Hart, (ed.), *Indira Gandhi's India*, Westview, Boulder 1976; R. Kothari, *Democratic Polity and Social Change in India*, Allied Publishers, Bombay 1975; D.L. Sheth 'Social Basis of the Political Crisis', in *Seminar*, January 1982; P. Brass, 'National Power and Local Politics in India', in *Modern Asian Studies*, February 1984; R. Joshi and R.K. Hebsur, 'Introduction' in *Congress in Indian Politics: A Centenary Perspective*, ISBN, 1987; M. Weiner 'Party Bureaucracy and Institutions', in J. Mellor (ed.), in *India: A Rising Middle Power*, Westview, Boulder 1981.

3. See the classic *Political Order in Changing Societies* by S.P. Huntington, Yale University Press, 1968 and for an important critique Claus Offe, *Contradictions of the Welfare State*, Hutchinson and Co., London 1984.

4. For the original presentation of the thesis of an 'over-developed' post-colonial state, see H. Alavi, 'The State In Post-colonial Societies,' in *New Left Review* 74.

5. G. Therborn, 'The Role of Capital and the Rise of Democracy', in *New Left Review* 103, May–June 1977, pp. 23–4.

6. Barrington Moore Jnr, *Social Origins of Dictatorship and Democracy*, Penguin University Books, Harmondsworth 1966, p. 431.

7. F. Frankel, *India's Political Economy* 1947–77, OUP, Oxford 1978, pp. 53–70; and D. Thorner, *The Shaping of Modern India*, Allied Publishers, Bombay 1980, p. 70.

8. Tariq Ali, *Can Pakistan Survive?*, Penguin Harmondsworth 1983, p. 41.

9. H. Alavi, 'Class and State', p. 75, in H. Gardezi and J. Rashid (eds), *Pakistan: The Roots of Dictatorship*, Zed, London 1983.

10. T. Ali, *Can Pakistan Survive?*, p. 123.

11. R. Kothari, 'The Congress System in India', *Asian Survey*, 1964, p. 1170.

12. J. Manor, 'Party Decay', p. 26.

13. F. Frankel, *India's Political Economy*, p. 240 and G. Omvedt, 'Capitalist Agriculture and Rural Classes in India', *Bulletin of Concerned Asian Scholars*, July–August 1983.

14. S. Kaviraj, 'Indira Gandhi and Indian Politics', *Economic and Political Weekly*, 20–27 September 1986, p. 1698.

15. P. Bardhan, *The Political Economy of Development in India*, OUP, Oxford 1984, p. 46.

16. This is D. Thorner's 'steel-grey revolution'. *The Shaping of Modern India*, Allied Publishers, Bombay 1980. See Chapters 10 & 11.

17. From G. Omvedt, 'Capitalist Agriculture', p. 42.

18. G. Therborn, 'The Role of Capital', p. 31.

19. L.I. and S.H. Rudolph, *In Pursuit of Lakshmi*, p. 335–54.

20. J. Manor, 'The Dynamics of Political Integration and Disintegration', in A.T. Wilson and D. Dalton (eds), *The States of South Asia*, Vikas, New Delhi 1982, pp. 101–5.

21. E.N. Mangat Rai, *Patterns of Administrative Development in Independent India*, Athlone Press, London 1976, Chapters 7 & 8.

22. F. Frankel, *India's Political Economy*.

23. Such a situation would naturally reflect itself in more volatile voting behaviour by the lower classes/castes. One caveat can be entered: reservation quotas for government jobs and places in government-sponsored educational institutions has created a layer from Dalit and tribal communities who do get somewhat incorporated into the 'normal' structures and processes of politics. Their grievances are heard. They also provide limited ventilation of grievances from lower down, and partially channel deeper discontents by their less fortunate brethren into 'safer' streams of political behaviour. To the extent this layer can

grow – both in absolute terms and relative to the rest of the Dalit/tribal populations – they act as a social safety valve. But the bitterness, violence and frequency of caste and tribal conflicts with upper castes and non-tribals suggests that the gulf between these 'middle class' layers and the bulk below them is growing. Furthermore, even these layers find themselves increasingly on the defensive from the thrusting pressures of, especially, the intermediate castes.

24. L.I. and S.H. Rudolph, *In Pursuit of Lakshmi*. See especially Chapters 1 and 13.

25. Congress's 'High Command' comprises its chief executive body, the Working Committee, the Parliamentary Board which supervises the activities of the Congress legislative parties in the states and also forms the core of the Central Election Committee, which selects Congress candidates for the Lok Sabha and Assembly elections. See S. Kochanek, 'Mrs Gandhi's Pyramid', p. 95.

26. R. Krishna, 'Economic Outlook for India' in Roach (ed.), *India 2000: The Next 15 Years*, Riverdale Press, 1986.

27. S. Kashyap, 'The Eighth Lok Sabha: A Profile of its Members', in *Indian and Foreign Review*, 31 May 1985.

28. D.C. Wadhwa, *Promulgation of Ordinances: A Fraud in the Constitution of India*, Orient Longman, Bombay 1983, was the first and best account of this chicanery.

29. On the evolution of the Indian bureaucracy there are a number of competent surveys. See E.N. Mangat Rai, *Patterns of Administrative Development*; S.K. Ray, *Indian Bureaucracy At Crossroads*, Sterling Publications, New Delhi 1979; D.C. Potter, *India's Political Administrators 1919–1983*, Clarendon Press, Oxford 1986; B.B. Misra, *Government and Bureaucracy in India, 1947–1976*, OUP, Oxford 1986.

30. U. Baxi, *The Crisis of the Indian Legal System*, Vikas, New Delhi 1982, p. 7.

31. See, the *Keshavanda Bharati* case, 1973, reaffirmed in the *Minerva Mills* case, 1980. For a useful discussion of the issue see A.G. Noorani, 'The Supreme Court on Constitutional Amendments', in A.G. Noorani (ed.), *Public Law in India*, Vikas, New Delhi 1981.

32. I. Jaising, 'The Transfer of Judges', in *The Lawyers*, April 1988, p. 8.

33. *India Today*, 15 May 1987, pp. 30–45.

34. See collection of articles in *Seminar*, on 'Using the Army', No. 308, April 1985. Also S.P. Cohen, 'The Military', in H.C. Hart (ed.), *Indira Gandhi's India*, Westview, Boulder 1976; P. Karat, 'The Structure and Role of the Armed Forces', in K.M. Kurian (ed.), *India – State and Society*, Orient Longman, Bombay 1975; P.D. Sharma, *Indian Politics*, Research Co., Delhi 1977 and *Police Polity and People in India*, Uppal Publishing Co, New Delhi 1981; S. Sen, *Police Today*, Ashish Publication House, 1986; R. Hardgrave, *India Under Pressure*; U. Baxi, *The Crisis of the Indian Legal System*; D. Bayley, 'The Police and Political Order in India' in *Asian Survey*, April 1983.

35. L.I. and S.H. Rudolph, *In Pursuit of Lakshmi*, Chapter 4; P. Wallace, 'Plebiscitary Politics in India's 1980 Parliamentary Elections', in *Asian Survey* 6, June 1980, pp. 619–25.

36. L.I. and S.H. Rudolph, *In Pursuit of Lakshmi*, pp. 172–7.

37. See Chapter 1, note 34.

38. See *India Today*, 15 September 1983.

39. This programme of unexceptional and mostly unattainable populist demands served as the ideological framework for Rajiv Gandhi's new forces whose trademark was 'competence' and 'professional working methods'.

40. L.I. and S.H. Rudolph, *In Pursuit of Lakshmi*, p. 158.

41. The most remarkable volte-face was by Arun Shourie, editor of *Indian Express*.

42. See *India Today*, 15 April 1988 for an inside story on this subject, pp. 72–80.

43. *Illustrated Weekly*, 22–29 August 1987. S. Kottary, 'Guilty?', pp. 8–17.

44. A good account of the imperatives of party funding can be found in S.A. Kochanek, 'Briefcase Politics in India', *Asian Survey* 12, December 1987, pp. 1278–1301.

45. *Illustrated Weekly*, 5–11 July 1987, G. Fernandes 'In Murky Waters', pp. 16 and 17.

46. J. Habermas, *Legitimation Crises*, Beacon Press, Boston 1975; also J. Sensat Jnr, *Habermas and Marxism*, Sage Publications, London 1979; C. Offe, *Contradictions of the Welfare State*.

47. P. Bardhan, *Political Economy*, pp. 54–9.

48. The Indian fiscal crisis is directly related to the needs of the private sector of industry, the agrarian bourgeoisie, the urban middle class and the defence sector all demanding fiscal benefits. As Bardhan and others have pointed out, the result of these pressures has been the proliferation of subsidies, the fastest growing of all main heads of expenditure, the other two being defence and public debt interest. Of subsidies, those for food and fertilizers have grown most, by over 40% per annum over the last three years (though the fertilizer burden on the exchequer is exaggerated since the government has high administrative prices for feedstock into fertilizer companies). Important are also the subsidies on electricity/water charges and the expenses in extending bank credits (frequent debt write-offs) to the rural sector. Thus pandering to the agrarian bourgeoisie is one of the main reasons for the fiscal crisis. Land, the most widely distributed asset for 500 million people, bears practically no tax, progressive or otherwise either in the form of asset-wealth tax or on its income/revenue. Since the end of the seventies, the government's budgetary fiscal gap has grown progressively to 8%–9% of GDP on revenue account. For detailed quantification of the fiscal crisis, see J.A. Bernard, 'A Maturation Crisis in India', in *Asian Survey* 4, April 1987, pp. 408–26.

49. A. Nandy, *At the Edge of Psychology*, OUP, Oxford 1980, p. 54. Nandy has numerous perceptive insights concerning the interrelations between politics and culture and the role Indian intellectuals have played in trying to integrate the alien (politics) with the indigenous (culture). His romanticization of tradition need not be shared. See his Chapter 3, 'The Making and Unmaking of Political Cultures in India'.

50. For two interesting discussions which conclude that a de facto decentralization of power (to the benefit of the system) has taken place and is the present trend, see P. Brass, 'National Power and Local Politics in India', and R. Chatterjee', 'Democracy and Opposition in India', *Economic and Political Weekly*, 23 April 1988.

At the central level the chances of institutionalizing some form of regular coalitional rule, as in Italy, must also be judged as remote. Such a system assumes the existence of four or five stable, even if small, political parties with coherent and distinguishable programmes and fixed social bases with which governmental partnerships can be brokered.

3

Centre–State Relations, Nationalism and Nationalities

Nationalism has been a veritable minefield for a Marxism which has yet to develop the conceptual aids needed to traverse such explosive terrain. It is increasingly accepted as a truism that there is no proper Marxist theory of nationalism. This would suggest that the arguments and conclusions found in the classical texts be applied with extreme caution to present-day India. Stalin's attempt to theorize the 'national question' has only made matters worse.[1] Lenin, however, provided an essentially pragmatic but principled approach which did help communists *politically* to orient themselves towards the national movements of his time.[2]

But his views were so strongly shaped by the Russian experience and the immediate circumstances of Tsarist rule, as well as the rebellion against it, that he himself would have been surprised at the way his insights have been subsequently transmogrified into a kind of Marxist key for unlocking the riddle of the national question. Not only have Lenin's analyses and prescriptions been illegitimately extended but the national question itself has come to mean something quite different from what it was taken to mean in Lenin's time.[3]

It was then understood to refer to the emergence of 'nations' in the context of the decline of dynastic absolutist empires in Europe or to the rise of national liberation movements in the periphery earlier conquered by imperialism – movements which sought to establish independent and sovereign nation-states no longer under the direct control of oppressor nations. The territorial boundaries of these new post-colonial nation-states were in almost all cases virtually congruent with the administrative boundaries established by colonialism–imperialism.[4]

Lenin saw the rise of nationalism as a transient political phenomenon more than counter-balanced by the concurrent trend towards internationalization of economic, political and cultural life. This is why he never bothered to provide explicit definitions of such concepts as nation, nationality and nationalism or to clarify the distinctions between them. But the basic thrust of his thinking was to see these as economic and political phenomena – the result of the centralizing tendencies of capitalist modernization. His thinking was less biased towards the cultural than Stalin's. More important, it was much more subtle, flexible and, above all, politically sensitive. However, there is no convincing evidence that he opposed the basic methodology and framework adopted by Stalin in his famous critique of the Austro-Marxists.[5]

Indian Marxists and the National Question

This methodology has dominated the thinking of the Indian left on the 'national' or 'nationality question'. This 'question' now refers essentially to the internal political arrangements of an Indian Union comprising a number of linguistic-territorial state units and confronted with a variety of regional pressures – and not to a 'nation's' external political dependence on an imperial power. Even when they entertain strong reservations about Stalin's excessive rigidity or schematism, Indian Marxists (whether affiliated to a party or not) have generally adopted some kind of check-list of objective criteria whereby a nation or nationality, however embryonic or immature, could be said to exist.[6] Some check-lists even allow for the presence of the subjective factor of 'national consciousness' as one element (however important) among others.

There is a broad division among Indian Marxists between those who argue that India is a multi-national state and those who insist that it is a multi-nationality state where nationality formation precedes nation formation and does not necessarily lead to the latter.[7] Within this second group there are differences on whether India is a nascent nation or nation-in-the-making or whether it is already a nation-state.[8] In the former category there are also differences, some analyses being more sophisticated than others. At its crudest there is an uncritical and unqualified transposition of Stalinist and Leninist maxims according to which India, by definition, cannot be a nation. It is therefore a multi-national state. Most Maoist groups in India take this view.

After the inauguration of the first stage of a popular democratic revolution in a two-stage schema of revolution, a 'Union of Peoples' Republic' will be established along the lines of the USSR. In this union each nation-republic – state unit – would have the right to secede or to unite with a neighbouring nation-republic. There would be a co-ordinating centre to oversee the voluntary unity of these republics. The class basis for the existence of such nation-republics is, of course, the existence of various regional bourgeoisies. It cannot be otherwise since the emergence of nations, according to classical Marxism, is indissolubly linked to the rise of the bourgeoisie.[9]

In more sophisticated accounts there is recognition of the existence of a dual consciousness, of a pan-Indian identity as well as of regional, linguistic-based nationalisms. The National Movement is said to have fostered and promoted both types of identity. Moreover, behind these regional nationality/national movements are not distinct regional bourgeoisies but different sections of the working class and peasantry with specific democratic aspirations. In general, demands for greater state autonomy should be supported because it is said to enhance democracy. However, a distinction should apparently be made between regional claims or movements backed by the oppressed classes and those backed by oppressor classes. This divergence reveals itself largely through the nature of the opposition parties leading these movements or in the character of the party in government in the state unit. Thus states led by the CPI (Communist Party of India) or CPM (Communist Party of India (Marxist)) express, by definition, the aspirations of the working class and oppressed peasantry, just as bourgeois parties in the states represent the interests of segments of the ruling class. However, there can be practical unity between the CPI/CPM and non-Congress state governments in the struggle for more state autonomy. While there are oppressed nationalities there is no oppressor nationality since the Indian bourgeoisie is 'supra-national' in character. Proponents of such a view see 'national crystallization' as virtually synonymous with 'nationality crystallization' and would argue that there are nations/nationalities in the subcontinent at different levels of maturity.[10]

Much of the debate on the national question in India has got bogged down in a terminological morass of competing definitions which produce no higher synthesis. The great diversity in classification and definition of such concepts as nation, nationality, nationalism and nation-state is the result of the larger theoretical maze that surrounds all thinking on this issue, bourgeois or Marxist. This maze has grown out of the sheer complexity of the subject. Different analysts can thus choose to develop their views from quite different starting points. These viewpoints, despite their different points of methodological departure, all reflect attempts to chart a way out, and each of these has specific strengths and weaknesses.[11]

The Dual Dimension

Broadly speaking, it can be said that nationalism is about politics or power; it is about culture, and about the immensely complex relationship between the two. The nation can be conceived of as cultural entity or as political fact. The state, of course, is always a legal and political entity. However, the nation as cultural fact and the state need not be indivisible or symbiotically bound together. One can exist without or before the other. But when the nation becomes a political fact it expresses itself in just such a symbiosis – the nation-state.

Gellner says, 'It is nationalism that engenders nations and not the other way around'; this can be interpreted in two senses.[12] Nationalism as a cultural process precedes and induces the formation of a nation as a cultural fact. Alternatively, nationalism as a cultural process and/or a political movement precedes and induces the formation of a nation as political fact.

Thus nationalism can refer to the 'idea of the nation' – the beginnings of a national identity or consciousness which then spreads. This is a subjective definition which, however, has strong objective foundations both cultural and non-cultural, for example, capitalist modernization, growth of communications, erosion of traditional identities, emergence of new forms of cultural representation, and so on. Or nationalism can refer to a specific political doctrine or movement which has the achievement or use of state power as its goal. Corresponding to these two senses, nationality too can be perceived as either a cultural process both anterior and posterior to the emergence of the nation as a cultural event or as the legal–political attribute (citizenship) of the nation as a political entity, the nation-state.

A cultural nationalism can thus be seen as both prior to and capable of existing independently of political nationalism, for example, Jewish nationalism or black nationalism in the USA. But it is the ubiquity and *political* significance of nationalism that gives this phenomenon its importance in the contemporary world. What gives value and purpose to the investigation of cultural nationalism, then, is its ultimate connection to a political movement or a political event, namely the dated formation of a nation-state.

A cultural perception of nationalism can take as its point of analytical departure either the fact of common consciousness or identity or the existence of a cluster of identity marks, such as script, language, ethnic/racial similarity, and so on.[13] Although the latter may be responsible for the former, it need not be, given the modular character of the 'idea of the nation'.[14] Benedict Anderson has provided an impressive case for choosing the former as one's starting point; all the more so in the Indian case because nationalist consciousness was initially an intellectual import, though its subsequent consolidation and extension into a popular consciousness and ideology owed much to the absorption of indigenous cultural symbols, ideas and values, and to the impact of the

National Movement itself.[15] Nationalist ideology and political movement developed in a reciprocal relationship.

Here nationalism, even nationality and the nation itself, are perceived above all as states of mind or acts of consciousness. As Kohn has said, a 'Nationality is formed by the decision to form a nationality.'[16] Usually such factors as territory, language, tradition, religion and state play a part in the genesis and consolidation of such a consciousness. But they need not and most certainly do not do so in any immutable combination. Individually, none of these factors is indispensable. Kohn also correctly stresses the crucial linkage between culture and politics, when he argues that nationalism is a state of mind striving towards a political fact – that is, the transformation of the nation as cultural entity, *lodged above all in consciousness*, into a political entity, the nation-state.[17]

With these distinctions in mind it becomes possible to chart more accurately the course of nationalism in India from the first stirrings of national identity among a section of colonized intellectuals faced with their own identity crisis but able to avail themselves of existing, alternative 'nationalist' models of self-perception to the development of a nationalist ideology which had no choice but to appropriate, however selectively, indigenous cultural symbols and values.[18] In this perspective India is both a nation-state in the political sense (dating from 15 August 1947) and in a cultural sense very much a nation-in-the-making (understood here as a process of consolidation, not genesis). This nation-in-the-making seeks a stronger cultural–emotional foundation for a pan-Indian identity which obviously cannot be based simply on regional or linguistic characteristics, but is no less real for that.

Nationalism understood not as cultural process but as a synonym for a national political movement can have as its aim independence, unity or merger with some other independent nation-state, or nation-building. In the last case it might be better thought of not as a political movement but as the ideology of an existing nation-state apparatus, that is, a government-sponsored nationalism in which both popular elements from below and manipulative ones from above are likely to be present. In contrast Breuilly has defined nationalism more loosely as a political movement of opposition which can have either separation, merger or reform of state power as its objective.[19] Such a definition would encourage the tendency to describe as 'nationalist movements' even those internal political movements which merely seek concessions from the centre or varying degrees of political autonomy. It would be far better to follow Lenin and append a less confusing label to such movements.

False Characterizations

It should be obvious from the above that I would reject any characterization of India as a 'multi-national' state. India is very much a nation-state which in the classical Marxist sense has 'solved' the 'national question'.[20] The establishment of a minimum national unity and independence – that is, resolving the national question – is not congruent with resolving the nationalities question, which even post-capitalist regimes like Yugoslavia and the USSR (let alone capitalist Spain) have not satisfactorily resolved. What confronts the bourgeoisie and the class-state of India is the problem of nation-building or national integration. When discussing India liberal political scientists (who are obviously committed to preserving the essentials of the present order) revealingly avoid the use of terms like 'nationality', preferring instead such terms as ethnic and linguistic 'pluralism', 'minority problems', and so on.[21] But is India then a union of nationalities or a multi-nationality nation-state?

Anderson's powerful insight that the nation/nationality is an 'imagined community', one among other 'imagined communities', suggests that the use of the term nationality can easily mislead.[22] There can be communities in-the-making as well as in-the-dying. Using the term is dangerous because it involuntarily links one level of community imagining with another level with which it has no necessary connection.[23] It promotes a simplistically and erroneously linear vision of community and identity formation. There are 'imagined communities' based on more local, more geographically compact identities which may or may not give rise to political movements in which the common consciousness acts as a political resource. There are also 'imagined communities', of which the nation is surely one, which are based on larger, more diffused, enveloping identities. These various 'imagined communities' coexist and interact with each other. If there is nationalism and internationalism (which is not a *popular* imagined community) there is also casteism and communalism as as well as the various regional/linguistic identities/communities. The latter are more appropriately termed *subnational*. This term is used here simply as a way of referring to movements or levels of community imagining which are smaller in scope than the national and larger than the highly localized, such as family, kinship, or village.

Since there is no intrinsic reason why such sub-national identities or movements should graduate to a broader level where the identities or demands are of a national character, there seems no reason why they should be perceived of as nations-in-embryo or immature nationalities existing in some early stage of national identity formation. In fact, sub-national identities are often of as recent vintage as the national identities they are supposed to oppose.[24] In the Indian case they often post-date the emergence of national identity and are linked to the problems thrown up by the nation-state's attempt to promote national integration. In other words, they are explicitly linked to the post-independence phase of capitalist development. They should not be seen as the inevitable maturation of a long, semi-dormant historical process, a maturation which is supposed to have been merely hastened (but not created) by post-independence developments.[25]

Some lower-level identities, however, clearly existed prior to 1947. Indeed, the National Movement built upon and promoted these lower-level identities.[26] National identity did not substitute for them but grew alongside them. This suggests not only that there is no *necessary* opposition between many sub-national identities and the national identity, but that the levels of development of these sub-national identities and of national identity formation can share a common mechanism of development, for example, the emergence of both a pan-Indian identity and regional linguistic identities through National Movement politics. This makes it all the more illegitimate to collapse these sub-national identities within the cocoon of nationalism. Clearly, the use of the term 'sub-nationality' would also be unjustified and misleading.

Sub-national Identities

The sub-national movements have either sought a more decisive say in the centre, more local say through greater federalism and regional autonomy, or greater access to centrally organized (and sometimes, state organized) distribution of resources. Very rarely has the issue of complete independence been posed, even as a subordinate theme, by such movements. Where this issue has been centrally posed, as in Nagaland and Mizoram, the movements in question were clearly not sub-national – though in the course of absorption by a much more powerful Indian nation-state, they may become so.[27]

To the extent that a popular movement of opposition to Indian absorption exists in these cases there should be no problem in deciding one's political orientation. Lenin's dictum on the right to self-determination for an oppressed nation/nationality holds, the oppressor nationality in this case being the *Indian* nationality and the chauvinism that has to be opposed being 'great Indian chauvinism'. Such an orientation is demanded by the guiding principles of consistent political democracy and the struggle for socialism. But it would be more difficult to justify such a position of support to Naga and Mizo self-determination, particularly in the case of Nagaland, if nationalism/nationality was not perceived of as a collective 'state of mind striving after a political fact' but as an entity identified as a result of a peopled territory fulfilling a formal set of criteria as to what constitutes a nationality or nation. It is not therefore surprising that the CPI and CPM, given their methodological approach to the national question, should have endorsed, though critically, the state's denial of Naga independence.

If nationalism/nationality is a collective state of mind, then it is enough that a significant number of people in a community feel that they belong to or want to have a nation. No maximum or minimum percentage of adherents can be rigidly laid down.[28] Clearly, Khalistan's supporters do not come anywhere near reaching this critical but necessarily vague benchmark. So there is no justification for describing Khalistan as a nationalist movement or sentiment. But even if it were to reach such a stage it does not follow that Communists would have to support its right to self-determination, a commitment that is contingent on an assessment of the movement's democratic credentials, that is, its aims, methods, motivations, the social forces behind it, and on an overall historical evaluation of the oppressed character of the community represented by the movement. Thus, though it was legitimate to talk of a Muslim nationalism (in the sense of a political movement) before partition, it was not legitimate to support the formation of an intrinsically undemocratic confessional state (as the CPI did) based on the false principle that Muslims as Muslims were an oppressed community or nationality. By doing so the CPI legitimized the programmatically communal Muslim League.

However, various sub-national communities in India have had, besides their particular characteristics (of which the most important is surely the existence or absence of a movement consciously promoting a sense of cultural–emotional solidarity for specific political purposes), a number of general characteristics in common. Among these are a language which may or may not have a written script, an increasingly powerful agrarian bourgeoisie which because of the federal division of the Indian polity operates most effectively within the state unit, a frustrated urban middle class and/or student community, a sense of relative economic deprivation which may or may not correspond (but usually does) to the real regional inequities of uneven capitalist development, a non-Congress regional party in or contending for power, and so on.[29] When these factors come together they do so in very specific combinations which cannot be precisely repeated elsewhere.

But the fact that such common elements do play an obvious role in starting off or sustaining regional movements of various kinds has encouraged Indian leftists to view the issue within a larger theoretical schema of supposedly traditional Marxist provenance. The result has

been a false conceptualization of the problem in India, its misrepresenta-
tion as a 'national' or 'nationality' question. Not surprisingly, there have
emerged a number of theoretico-political viewpoints each claiming to be
the correct Marxist position on the issue.

Regionalism in India

What then are the important problems and issues posed? Do they
require Marxists to take particular political positions? Are these to
be determined on a concrete case-to-case basis or are there general
guidelines that can serve to orient Indian Marxists? One matter can be
disposed of straight away. There is virtually no chance of balkanization of
the country. Whatever the centrifugal forces, the boundaries of the post-
colonial nation-states have everywhere proved remarkably enduring.
In over forty years the solitary example of a completely successful
secessionist struggle and the subsequent creation of a new nation-
state has been Bangladesh. By its very exceptionalism it serves as
a salutary reminder that the post-war nation-states, even where they
seem most fragile, as in Africa or South and West Asia, have powerful
underlying sources of cohesion and durability which are all too often
grossly underestimated.

Secessionism is an issue in India in Nagaland in the northeast (where
it is under control), in Punjab and Kashmir. The nationalist struggle in
Nagaland is a low-intensity insurgency whose protagonists are unable
to translate broad sympathy from a war-wearied Naga population into
a qualitatively higher level of mass or even guerrilla struggle. In
addition, the Indian government's carrot-and-stick policy of pouring in
development funds and consolidating a Naga elite while at the same time
carrying out sustained and brutal repression has been largely successful
in reducing the political aspirations of more and more Nagas from
independence to autonomy and centre-sponsored development within
the Indian Union. The Mizo struggle for secession (and merger with
areas across the Burmese border) in the seventies was led by the Mizo
National Front (MNF) and its armed wing the Mizo National Army
(MNA) under Laldenga. The MNF finally settled for autonomy within
the Indian Union with no serious damage to its popular base. The Naga
question could meet a similar fate.

Khalistani secessionism has an altogether more dangerous potential.
Punjab is the granary of India. It is strategically located on the border
with Pakistan and close to the Hindi heartland. The struggle for Khalistan
has taken the form of planned terrorist attacks rather than rural- or
urban-based guerrilla warfare. Such terrorism, aimed mainly at 'soft',

that is, civilian, targets, is both a reflection of military weakness and
lack of popular support from ordinary Sikhs. But it does ensure high
visibility and constant publicity for the cause and in this way achieves
a more destabilizing effect.

Mixed up as it is with the communal (religious) question, the Punjab
problem carries within it the implicit threat of a communal holocaust.
For all these reasons it constitutes the single most serious problem
currently facing the country. But secessionism is not the solution. Nor
is it feasible – given the enormous power of the Indian state and its
determination to hold on to Punjab whatever the cost. The communal
aspect is central, though any resolution of the crisis will obviously have
to address itself to the question of how much autonomy from the centre
Punjab should enjoy. The Punjab problem therefore has to be discussed
separately.

The central problem that confronts the Indian state and the ruling
coalition has to do with the processes of nation-building and national
integration in the face of a variety of regional movements and pressures.
Such regional pulls are on the rise. A major aspect of the problem of
regionalism (though certainly not its only dimension) is the dialectic of
centralization and decentralization between the centre and the states,
the appropriate pattern of devolution of power.[30]

The general factors behind the growth of regionalist tendencies
towards greater decentralization are the cultural and linguistic diversity
of India, the inevitable unevenness of capitalist economic development,
the growing strength of the agrarian bourgeoisie and the intermediate
classes (the rural and urban petty bourgeoisie), and such political features
as the growing electoral strength of opposition parties and the decline of
the Congress.

Sub-state and State-wide Struggles

Regional problems can be classified in two ways. There are those
regional pressures and sub-national movements whose area of operation
coincides with the federal territorial division of the Union into different
states. In this category can be grouped the centre–state and inter-
state conflicts, that is, those tensions or struggles in which the state
government is the leading or directing agency.

Then there are the sub-state pressures and movements directed against
a state government or the centre or both. Almost all regional movements
combine popular grievances from below with elements of manipulation
from above. Thus, for example, the agrarian bourgeoisie or a section
of the intermediate classes (students or urban professionals) know they

will benefit disproportionately from the success of a mass movement in which all classes participate with their separate as well as collective expectations. Or the leadership of a regional movement seeks to institutionalize its own political authority and through this eventually accumulate wealth and become part of the regional economic elite. Whatever the motivations of the political or class leadership, such movements tend to be most powerful when economic and cultural grievances are fused.[31] However, the emergence of Telugu Desam in Andhra Pradesh suggests that regional patriotism can also be fuelled by reference to political discrimination by the centre.

The sub-state struggles are generally more populist in character and tend to take the form of a movement. For this same reason they tend to be temporally as well as spatially limited – that is, the movement folds up or fades away as a result of failure or partial or complete success. In the case of prolonged movements which show no signs of dying out even after years, these too have fluctuating intensities related to the natural ebb and flow of movement politics, for example, the Jharkhand Movement. Such sub-state movements usually aim either at attaining power at the state level (this was the implicit thrust of the Assam Agitation) or at achieving some degree of political autonomy like statehood or 'autonomous' council status (Gorkhaland). The Assam Movement was wrongly characterized as a 'sons of the soil' movement. This demand was raised but it was a tactical not a strategic feature of the movement.

Such autonomy is seen as a vital pre-condition for economic advance and cultural preservation by the community in question. A significant proportion of such movements are based in the tribal regions of the northeast and the plains; and it is likely that as tribal consciousness and expectations grow there will be more such movements.[32] On the whole it can be said that the historical experience of 'cultural politics' at the state and sub-state level have helped to deepen regional identities.[33]

In contrast, the centre–state tussle is generally more institutionalized in character, rarely populist or agitational in form, and quite constant in rhythm. The linguistic reorganization of states took place in 1956.[34] There were, of course, movements and pressures which remained unsatisfied by this reorganization and which eventually led to the break-up of the old Assam state in the northeast and the formation of Punjab-Haryana and Maharashtra-Gujarat. Then there is the issue of linguistic minorities within individual states. If these minorities share the language of the members of another state and these states are contiguous, this can lead to a demand for merger. If this is not the case or if there is no extra-state linguistic affinity (as in Gorkhaland) then the demand for some special status may arise.

Finally, there is the issue of Hindi as an official language and of how it is to be spread – for example, the 'three language formula'.[35] The centre seems to have learnt its lesson from the anti-Hindi uproar in the south, especially in Tamil Nadu, some decades back when Tamil secessionism could have become an issue. That would have been a clear example of the potential of linguistic regional identity to become a linguistic-based nationalism. The centre is now careful to avoid any suggestion that Hindi might be imposed. The best policy for New Delhi is not to have a policy at all – and it seems to realize this. The three language formula is merely a face-saver for a non-policy and is a dead letter for all practical purposes. Hindi will no longer be imposed anywhere. But left to itself its use will almost certainly grow. Regional languages will also grow and increasingly become the language of instruction and administration in their respective states, without displacing English whose use will also grow and which in reality is the real link language of politics and commerce in the country.[36]

In short, centre–state conflicts and inter-state tensions are now primarily focused on economic and political not cultural issues. The single most important class force behind these conflicts is the agrarian bourgeoisie, supported by the rural petty bourgeoisie, of the states in question. Significant sections of the urban petty bourgeoisie in each state also benefit from greater decentralization of power, greater industrialization and investment of resources organized either directly by the centre or by the state government being given a greater share of central resources. At the end of 1977, state governments employed 5.2 million people compared to 3.1 million employed by the central government, 2 million by local government and 6.2 million by large-scale industry. State and local employment accounted for 50 per cent of total public employment in India and the rate of growth of employment was fastest in the state government sector.[37] State-based linguistic exclusivity obviously favours the middle classes in each state.

The major combatants in the centre–state tug-of-war on the state's side are the agrarian bourgeoisie and the regional opposition party, especially when it governs the state. These parties have regional bases of support and seek to institutionalize their authority accordingly. The principal areas of dispute regarding federal devolution concern: the balance of legislative powers belonging to the centre and states respectively; the role of the governors; the answerability of senior bureaucrats in the state administration; central control over industrial/monetary/commercial/energy policies; the planning system; and most important of all the share-out of financial powers and resources between the centre and the states.

It is noticeable that centre–state tensions are sharper outside the Hindi heartland. This is because the party that dominates the centre almost always rules in the key heartland states. Moreover, the Hindi heartland states enjoy a greater linguistic and cultural unity. Inter-state tensions must not be forgotten, though. These are an unavoidable adjunct to centre–state conflict since states have to compete with each other for greater specific allocations or investments even if they agree that the absolute and proportionate share of all the states together should be greater than it has been. Differential allocations are rationalized on the basis of the respective sizes of state populations but this hardly satisfies everyone. Some states make relatively greater contributions to the centre's pool of resources – for example Punjab Haryana's contributions to the centre's programme of food procurement – and resent the fact that they are not commensurately rewarded. All states have their own backward regions clamouring for development. In short, inter-state tensions are an inevitable by-product of uneven capitalist development. There are also inter-state migrations of labour which have given rise to 'sons of the soil' movements for restricting employment to local state residents. Since the agrarian bourgeoisie generally welcomes migrant rural labour, which helps to push wage-rates down, it is not surprising that the most important 'sons of the soil' movements have been urban-based. The most powerful such movements have been launched by chauvinist organizations like the Shiv Sena in Bombay, Maharashtra, and the Kannada Chaluvaligars in Bangalore, Karnataka. Similar movements could grow in Orissa, West Bengal and Gujarat.[38] The existence of these tensions, plus the facts that regional parties compete for extra-regional power and that the agrarian bourgeoisie's interests are much more regionally demarcated than those of the industrial bourgeoisie, gives alliances between regional parties an ad hoc and temporary character.

State Autonomy and the Centre

The arena of contest between the centre and the states can be broadly divided into the spheres of political and economic decentralization. States want more powers to legislate on issues concerning them. This means an extension of the list of subjects falling under state purview and an abridgement of the concurrent list of subjects which come under both central and state purview. They also want residuary powers (those not explicitly vested in the central, concurrent or state lists) to be held by them and not, as at present, by the centre. It is through the governor's recommendation that President's Rule is imposed by the centre on a state. Opposition-ruled state governments therefore want to have a greater say in the appointment/nomination of governors. The governor can also adversely affect state legislation by forwarding bills passed in the state assembly to the president. At the moment, bureaucrats appointed by the centre to state administrations are answerable ultimately to the former, which is particularly galling to many opposition-ruled states. The CPM, for example, has demanded separate recruitment and control of state-level and central and all-India level bureaucrats. It also wants to abolish the present system whereby cadres of the all-India services are seconded to the state administrations.[39]

With regard to economic issues, the states want more freedom from interference and control over state plans by the central planning commission, to which state plans have to be compulsorily submitted. They also want more licensing powers concerning industry, commerce, energy projects, and so on. But at the heart of the centre–state dispute is the financial relationship. The states are unhappy with their share of the taxes and levies collected by the centre, with central monopoly of certain elastic sources of revenue such as income, capital, company and wealth taxes and most excise and export duties, and with their own dependency on the centre for discretionary loans and grants. The states would like the statutory component of compulsory disbursement by the centre to increase substantially.

It is not that the states do not have the powers to collect certain kinds of taxes and levies. They can impose new and higher taxes on land and agricultural income, estate and succession duties on agricultural property, tax on buildings, sales tax, restrictive excises, electricity and entertainment duties, taxes on advertisements, vehicles, professions and trade. But if state governments are to get substantial increases in revenue from these sources it would mean attacking the wealth of the agrarian bourgeoisie and risking the alienation of the urban middle class, something which all states, whether opposition- or Congress-ruled, are loth to do. They prefer to shift blame for their budget squeeze on to the centre and to press constantly for ever more resources which they can distribute to appease a wide multi-class social (and electoral) base as well as those specific interests organized in inner-party factions.

There has been a continuous debate on whether the basic trend over the last couple of decades has been towards greater federalism and devolution of power or towards greater centralization and reinforcement of the unitary character of the Indian state.[40] A constitutionalist investigation can provide at best a static picture of limited comparative value.[41] Thus an examination of the constitutions of the USA, Switzerland, Canada and India might suggest that India was far more unitary in character. Its upper house, the Rajya Sabha, in which the states have representation, is far weaker than the American Senate. The Indian constitution, unlike the others, has no formal commitment to the equality of all the federating units. But this only indicates the different histories behind the formation of these nation-states. Unlike the USA, India's federation was not formed through a periodically expanding union of states which existed prior to the final establishment of an independent and composite nation-state as we know it today. Here, the principle of federal division was applied *after* the formation of India as a nation-state.

It is the *dynamic* at work that is important, and a constitutionalist approach cannot adequately reflect this. The centre–state relationship is one of constant struggle and shifting balance, although an overall trend can be discerned. In fact, a survey of the constitution would misleadingly suggest that the centre has become more powerful because of the numerous additional amendments allowing it to intervene through various repressive measures. The much more frequent use of President's Rule to dismiss state governments is taken by some as evidence of greater centralization of authority. But it is more plausibly interpreted (note the frequency with which it has been resorted to) as a frustrated and inadequate response to persistent regional pulls on a weakened centre. After the de-institutionalization of the Congress and the rise of regional parties, the Congress-ruled centre had fewer and weaker non-governmental structures to cope with such centrifugal forces and thus resorted more frequently to repression.

There are other indicators. At the state level, the regional languages are becoming more important in administration, education and in the print media. The greatest number of newspapers and periodicals are in the regional languages, then in Hindi, followed by English. State dependence on central allocations has not increased proportionately while there has been a relative shift in central allocations from the discretionary to the statutory and a corresponding shift in importance from the planning commission to the finance commission.[42] The delinkage between Lok Sabha and assembly elections works against the centre and has helped to institutionalize the coexistence of different parties at the centre and in the states. In 1952 the combined opposition to the Congress in the Lok Sabha elections was 29.57 per cent. This rose to 42.39 per cent in 1980, although it fell back to around 30 per cent in 1984. The overall trend of rising electoral support for opposition parties is even more pronounced in assembly elections.[43] The very fact that the Sarkaria Commission was appointed in June 1983 to inquire into the centre–state relationship and to evaluate state grievances is itself an indication of how the centre has had to take more serious account of state pressures. Only a few copies of the full report have been made available and the official summary is said to be slightly biased in favour of the centre in its presentation.[44] Nevertheless, even according to the summary, the Sarkaria Commission conceded ground to the states in almost all the areas of contestation. It made 247 recommendations. It suggested that residual powers (barring taxation) should be vested in the states, that there should be a 'firm convention' whereby the centre confers with states before enacting legislation on subjects in the concurrent list, that governors be appointed only in consultation with the chief ministers of the states, and that governors not be eligible (by way of reward for services rendered to the centre) for other public posts (barring vice-presidency) or other governorships at the end of their term in office. The frequent imposition of President's Rule was criticized and an amendment to Article 356 suggested whereby the reasons for such imposition would always have to be fully and publicly presented, which is not the case now. On the key issue of finances the Commission suggested various ways of increasing the state share of centrally collected taxes and recommended that greater weight be given to the states in the deliberations of the planning commission.

Whatever reservations the centre might have, it cannot completely ignore the Sarkaria Commission recommendations. Furthermore, the struggle for further devolution will continue whatever the scale of concessions, minor or major. In this respect, the setting up of the Sarkaria Commission itself was an important precedent adding legitimacy to the efforts of the states. Even the Panchayati Raj proposal of Rajiv Gandhi represented a specifically Congress-based attempt to strengthen its hold nationally through decentralization and through an offer of more institutionalized power to kulaks in particular.

No Disintegration

Increasing decentralization does not mean that the forces of disintegration are growing. It implies new forms of integration and reorganization of the structures of power within India's bourgeois democratic set-up. Just as greater regionalism can be the consequence of greater capitalist economic integration of India, greater overall integration can be the result of greater decentralization of powers, all of which reinforces that special paradox of political instability within a larger bourgeois democratic durability. The sources of this larger unity and coherence are socio-cultural as well as political and economic, governmental as well as non-governmental, the result of negative as well as positive factors. There is a progressive broadening and deepening of the all-India market and the growth of communications and transport systems. Besides the pan-Indian character of the Indian bourgeoisie, there is also the pan-Indian and mobile character of the urban managerial and professional middle class and a mobile petty bourgeois trading community. Not to be underestimated is the strength of Indian administrative, legal, political and coercive institutions. The first three have hierarchically organized structures which provide connections between the local–regional–national levels, while the military is among the most national of all institutions in its composition.[45]

The regular emergence of regional parties (even if some fade away) and party alternation in the states has done two things. It has given democratic legitimacy and therefore an element of durability to a system which would otherwise have faced more severe strains, given the long domination of the Congress at the centre. It has also provided a social safety valve in that new political elites have been able to follow the route of political power to economic wealth, thereby joining but not displacing existing regional economic elites. For historical reasons it is often the case that local linguistic communities, such as the Maharashtrians and Assamese, are not strongly or even proportionately represented in the urban centres of industrial capital. These avenues of upward economic mobility via regional politics promote the growth and consolidation of a more cosmopolitan industrial/bourgeois class and, therefore, greater integration.

Nor can the growth of a national consciousness and identity be denied. It is here that the question of Hindu nationalism most strongly asserts itself. The features making for political–economic unity are of relatively recent provenance. But the South Asian subcontinent has a sociocultural unity-in-diversity spanning some four thousand years which owes not a little to Hinduism, however vaguely the phenomenon is defined or understood by its own adherents.

Among the negative factors strengthening centripetal pulls is the relative weakness of each individual state compared to the centre and the difficulties involved in stabilizing and not merely initiating alliances between different parties for extra-regional political purposes. Even within a single state, solidarity on the mass level is weakened by a number of factors. State solidarities would tend to rely strongly on 'vertical' identities and patterns of mobilization, such as language.[46] After the linguistic division of states this kind of mobilization has become much more difficult. Furthermore, the existence of tribal, religious, Dalit and sometimes sizeable linguistic minorities within a state also weakens the possibility of consolidating state-wide solidarities. In fact, some of these minorities look to the centre for support against the domination of the majority communities in their state of residence.

What Must Marxists Do?

What conclusions are to be drawn about regionalism and what orientation must Indian Marxists have to this phenomenon? For the Indian state as vanguard defender of the bourgeois order, regional pressures in the overwhelming majority of cases are ultimately manageable. It is essentially a question of reaching the appropriate compromise or final settlement. This is usually a function of the political relationship of forces between a regional agitation at or near its peak and a centre invariably beleaguered by a host of different pressures. It is also sometimes a function of the flexibility shown by both sides and their willingness to shift from original positions to reach acceptable compromise solutions. The centre–state tussle is, by contrast, an ongoing affair.

What should the Marxist position and programme be regarding this problem of regionalism in India which has successfully masqueraded as the 'national question'? There is no real substitute for a concrete analysis of the concrete situation. To support a sub-national tribal movement against oppression and exploitation is one thing; to support a 'sons of the soil' movement is quite another. But the rich legacy of Marxist thought and practice does provide certain guidelines.[47] In general, socialists should support all efforts to rectify regional economic imbalances, to deepen political democracy and make its application more consistent. Marxists would also make every effort to promote integration and to break down the barriers separating people, particularly the working classes. This general principle would entail respect for the *equality* of all languages and cultures. It would mean rejecting privileges for any particular ethnic group while safeguarding the interests of minorities, whether linguistic, religious, tribal or caste.[48] In India this implies the adoption of a policy of 'positive discrimination' or 'affirmative action' for Scheduled Castes and Scheduled Tribes.

In a multi-lingual and multi-cultural society like India, to respect the equality of all languages and cultures inevitably raises the issue of what educational policy to follow and what language of instruction to adopt. The Leninist perspective here is quite apt. While there should be the greatest possible homogeneity in the content of the educational syllabi, the medium of instruction will vary according to the dominant language of the region. Furthermore, due allowance will have to be made for the addition to the common syllabi of various subjects which may be locally relevant, including locally spoken languages.[49]

With respect to regional movements and pressures, a distinction has to be drawn between the centre–state tussle and other kinds of state-based or sub-state pressures. Demands for 'state reservation' of one kind or the other – such as 'sons of the soil' or Assam-type movements against an influx of 'foreigners' – would in general be opposed, even allowing for recognition of the fact that real cultural–ethnic discriminations and imbalances are a factor promoting such movements. But it is not a fixed rule. The problem of preserving the political status of indigenous tribes in Sikkim or in some states in the northeast through some kind of political quota cannot be wished away completely.

The sub-state tribal movements for autonomy should in general be supported because these are invariably the result of non-tribal exploitation and displacement of indigenous tribals. Other minority movements are best assessed individually. In view of the multi-class base of such movements, the manipulative role played by elites or dominant classes and the specific forms of struggles adopted, even if support was extended to the movement it would rarely be uncritical and might sometimes even be conditional.

The general Marxist bias towards encouragement of centralization and integration respects the complexity of this process and its dialectical nature, and recognizes that if centralization is to be effective and stable it must be *democratic* and not bureaucratic.[50] Minorities in struggle always claim to be oppressed. But this claim must in each case be historically evaluated and this evaluation is but one input among others into a complex set of criteria on which the adoption of a position will be based. Contingent factors or circumstances may have to be taken into account – for example, if the nation were under military siege – which might necessitate a temporary rejection of demands that would otherwise be endorsed.

The centre–state issue – and the concomitant problem of an appropriate devolution of powers – is an altogether different affair. The commitment to consistent democracy means that the repressive powers of the centre and the laws and constitutional amendments sanctioning these powers should be opposed by socialists.[51] This is common ground among the opposition-ruled state governments, opposition parties and revolutionary socialists. But this does not mean that socialists must sanction such powers in the hands of opposition-ruled states either. They are not for transference of such powers to the state governments, but for their abolition. Nor is there common ground on rearrangement of legislative, financial and planning powers. It is a fundamental mistake for Marxists to take any position on these matters either in support of the centre or of the states. They cannot accept the argument that greater resources in the hands of the bourgeois opposition parties in the states – or even in the hands of the reformist Communist parties – will necessarily lead to a shift in control over resources (and therefore of class power) in favour of the regional oppressed. In fact, given the close connection between regional parties and the rural kulaks and intermediate classes any such fundamental shift in the relationship of class forces is ruled out, especially as even the CPI and CPM are forging closer relations with the kulaks and their rural allies.

Nor is it an objective of revolutionary socialists to establish the most appropriate distribution of federal powers within a bourgeois democratic system; they seek instead its replacement with a socialist democratic system of governance through revolutionary struggle and victory. The particular patterns of devolution which might promote and strengthen the process of socialist democracy cannot be established beforehand within the confines of bourgeois society but must by their very nature be post-revolutionary creations. Only the experiences of a successful revolutionary struggle will throw up the various political units and sub-units – for example, territorially organized 'soviets', industry-wide producer associations, new forms of electoral representation and popular assemblies – on which a socialist devolution of powers will have to rest. Similarly, the pattern of financial and planning possibilities will be related to the particular mix of economic units and mechanisms that will then emerge, such as cooperatives, collectives, the market, centralized and decentralized forms of planning for different kinds of productive activity and products.

All this is very different from the types of federal devolution possible in a bourgeois democratic set-up. Socialist devolution requires a decisive rupture from existing structures of bourgeois federalism. It cannot emerge as a result of a gradual transformation of the latter. What is more, federal devolution in India is based primarily on the relationship of forces *within* the ruling coalition. The CPM's attempt to distinguish its claims for state autonomy from those of other bourgeois parties, insisting that it represents quite different class interests, is essentially spurious. True, the mainstream Communist parties are workers' parties. But they are workers' parties pursuing bourgeois politics; they have no serious commitment to bringing about revolutionary change. They are becoming more and more multi-class in character and increasingly concerned to sustain this broad, multi-class appeal by pursuing methods of class conciliation rather than class struggle. Their strategy is to give something to everybody, not to subtract resources and power from the rich and dominant classes and add them to the poor and oppressed classes. Otherwise the CPM, for example, would have used the powers it already has to heavily tax rural kulaks and transfer substantial benefits to the poor. It prefers, however, to demand a rising share of centrally collected revenue with which to disburse patronage.

The mainstream Communist parties, especially the more powerful CPM, are still basically regional forces. They are also undergoing a steady process of social democratization. They believe in a two-stage schema whereby the immediate goal is to establish a people's or national democracy and the struggle for a socialist revolution is postponed to an indefinite future. This schema fits in comfortably with a political strategy that is electoralist, gradualist and constitutionalist. They seek a growing space for themselves within the bourgeois democratic system. They therefore attach great importance to the struggle for favourable amendments to the bourgeois constitution and make no attempt to question or undermine its legitimacy.

One can see why it becomes so important for this Communist mainstream to characterize the existing linguistic division of states as a division reflecting the existence of different nations or nationalities. By doing this they hope to cloak their pursuit of quite narrow and unsocialist aims in a mantle of ideological respectability, to justify their regional and reformist political orientation in the name of a Marxist concern with the 'nationality question'. Such an abuse of Marxism's theoretical and political traditions must be exposed, not endorsed.

Notes

1. J.V. Stalin, *Marxism and the National Question*, Progress Publishers, Moscow 1971.

2. V.I. Lenin, 'The Right of Nations to Self-Determination', in V.I. Lenin, *Questions of National Policy and Proletarian Internationalism*, Progress Publishers, Moscow 1970. This volume includes all Lenin's major writings on the subject.

3. For Lenin a 'national movement' did not necessarily raise the demand for independence but it did have to have a *clear tendency* towards political independence.

4. The rise of 'nationalist' consciousness in the struggle against Tsarist Russification and the emergence of 'nationalist' rebellions against Tsarist rule in the course of the 1917 February and October revolutions fully justified Lenin's view that Tsarist Russia was a multi-national empire breaking up. If a stable, Socialist Republic encompassing the huge territorial expanse of the former empire was to be constructed it could only be done through a recognition of and respect for the reality of national oppressions.

It was necessary, therefore, to adopt a political approach which respected their right to self-determination, that is, secession. This principle was subordinated to the more important principle of defending and promoting the interests of proletarian unity and socialism. But Lenin saw no conflict between this advocacy of political democracy and socialist unity. If the unity of the Socialist Republic was to be strong it had to be based on a union of its constituent parts/nations which was *voluntary*. The freedom to unite, however, necessarily implied the freedom to secede. The assumption that democratic principles and socialist needs would broadly coincide was to be severely tested only after the October Revolution. See R. Conquest, *Soviet Nationalities Policy in Practice*, Bodley Head, London 1967, Chapters 2 and 3.

In the Indian subcontinent before the British arrival there was no equivalent of Russification, nor the emergence of the idea of the nation, though some prominent Marxists like E.M.S. Namboodripad, the CPM general secretary, have argued otherwise. (See E.M.S. Namboodripad, 'The Indian National Question' in *Nationality Question in India*, TDSS Publications, Pune, 1987). More common has been the view that nationalism is a modern phenomenon attendant on the emergence of capitalism. Therefore, various linguistic based nationalisms or nationalities are said to have emerged during the period of British rule, and the National Movement against it.

But what should be made clear is that the National Movement in India was an anti-colonial liberation movement fundamentally different from the nationalisms operating in Russia. There is no justification for considering India a 'multi-national empire' or such an empire-in-the-making either during the period of Mughal rule or under the British raj. Neither Lenin's characterization of Russia nor his analyses or prescriptions for those nationalisms should be transported to this altogether different context.

Lenin recognized two kinds of nationalisms with quite different relationships to the ultimate formation of a nation-state. India fell into his second category, but there have been more than just these two kinds of nationalisms in history (see Ben Anderson, *Imagined Communities*, Verso, London 1983, Chapters 3, 4, 5, 6, and 7. This is easily the single most impressive and original contribution to the subject presently available.)

5. See Lenin's own endorsement of Stalin's efforts in V.I. Lenin, *Collected Works*, Vol. 24, Progress Publishers, Moscow 1964, p. 223. Also I. Deutscher, *Stalin*, Penguin, Harmondsworth 1972, pp. 126 and 131. A generation of Trotskyists have also been sidetracked into undeserved complacency by Trotsky's exaggerated veneration for Lenin's contribution. L. Trotsky, *History of the Russian Revolution*. Sphere, London, 1967, Vol. 3, p. 62. 'Whatever may be the further destiny of the Soviet Union . . . the national policy of Lenin will find its place among the eternal treasures of mankind.' See also M. Lowy, 'Marxists and the National Question' in *New Left Review* 96, April–May, 1976.

6. One exception is Nirmal Sengupta who makes just this criticism in his paper, 'Nationality Question in the Present Epoch' which was presented at an all-India seminar on the nationality question at Hyderabad, Andhra Pradesh in August 1981. (See pp. 165–8 of *Nationality Question in India*.) While he prefers a subjective definition – 'A Nationality emerges if the people decide to emerge as so' – he confines himself to a critique of the 'objective' approach rather than constructing a superior alternative.

He does make a telling point in respect of the so-called regional or local bourgeoisies. In regional movements which demand industrialization by the centre, he asks how 'local' bourgeoisies, even assuming that they exist, can raise such a demand when they themselves must be the bearers of such industrialization. He concludes, therefore, that it is the middle class and proletariat which are the social classes behind such movements. Sengupta forgets, however, that an agrarian bourgeoisie and petty bourgeoisie can raise such a demand since kulaks and aspiring kulaks benefit directly and indirectly from the industrialization of agriculture and the growing integration of industry and agriculture. See D. Thorner, *The Shaping of Modern India*, Allied Publishers, Bombay 1980, pp. 228–37 and 249–53, and G. Omvedt, 'Capitalist Agriculture and Rural Classes in India', p. 42, in *Bulletin for Concerned Asian Scholars*, July-August, 1983.

7. See the collection of papers by well-known Indian Marxists and theorists in *Nationality Question in India*.

8. See in particular, the contributions in ibid. by A. Guha, 'The Indian National Question', pp. 26–7, 48–9 and 53; and 'Nationalism: Pan-Indian and Regional in a Historical Perspective', pp. 231–2; G. Omvedt, 'Marxist Theory and Nationalism', pp. 81 and 89; also I. Habib, 'Emergence of Nationalities in India', p. 20. Guha has striven hard to develop a conceptual–theoretical framework. He is perceptively sensitive to the fact of a pan-Indian nationalism or national identity based on a variety of sources. This is his India as a 'composite nation' or 'great nationalism' as distinct from the 'little nationalisms' of regional 'nationalities'. Guha's problem is that he is not prepared to allow his insights to escape from the prison of Stalinist rigidities. Thus he considers that Stalin came closest to providing the best starting point; that India has not solved the national question and is not a bourgeois democracy. It is supposedly ruled by a landlord–bourgeois combine. His relationship between nationality and nation is mechanical and incorrect. The first is said to correspond to an earlier stage of politico-economic development.

There is thus a curious mix in Guha. At times he shows a real sensitivity to the complexity of the issue and seems to recognize the paramountcy of the subjective factor of common feeling however it may be derived from variable 'clusters of identity marks'. But always he is prevented from further fruitful exploration by fidelity to Stalinist political and theoretical schemas.

9. A representative example would be R. Krishna Murthy, 'Indian Democratic Revolution: National Question', a paper presented at the Hyderabad seminar, 1981. Published in *Nationality Question in India*, p. 163.

10. See J. Alam, 'Dialectics of Capitalist Transformation and National Crystallization', pp. 165–8; and his 'Class Political and National Dimensions of the State Autonomy Movements in India', pp. 224–5, TDSS Publishers, Pune 1987.

11. J. Breuilly in his review article, 'Reflections on Nationalism', in *Philosophy of the Social Sciences*, Vol. 15, 1985, pp. 74 and 75, stresses that for all those who would relate nationalism to modernity (which is of course capitalist) there could be four possible points of departure, each of which would then shape subsequent theory in its own way. One can begin with: (a) changes in social structures; (b) changes in social consciousness; (c) changes in political structure; or (d) changes in political consciousness. A 'primordial' approach would tend to be culturally biased, while an 'instrumentalist' approach would tend to be politically biased.

A striking indigenous example of political confusion is how the Maharashtra and Gujarat units of the undivided CPI in the fifties were at loggerheads on the issue of the division of the old Bombay state into Maharashtra and Gujarat.

12. E. Gellner, *Nations and Nationalism*, Basil Blackwell, Oxford 1983, p. 55.

13. Breuilly, 'Reflections on Nationalism', p. 70, makes a similar distinction between a 'cultural community' understood as a set of relationships and 'cultural community' understood as a collective common consciousness.

14. B. Anderson, *Imagined Communities: Reflections on the Origins and Spread of Nationalism*, p. 14.

15. P. Chatterjee, *Nationalist Thought in the Colonial World*, Zed Books, London 1987. Chatterjee provides a particularly interesting account of this process. But surprisingly he is less than fair in his criticism of Anderson for supposedly over-emphasizing the 'foreign' element. As the subtitle of Anderson's book indicates, he has confined himself to certain 'reflections on the origin and spread' of the 'idea of the nation' leaving it to others to flesh out the processes whereby nationalist thought in a particular country deepens and graduates to becoming a fully fledged but 'specific' and 'original' ideology, pp. 19–22.

But Chatterjee correctly stresses the much closer connection between the development of national identity and national ideology in the 'new' nations like India. This point is also ably made by H. Seton-Watson, *Nations and States*, Methuen, London 1977. According to Seton-Watson, the key difference between 'old' and 'new' nationalisms was that the leaders of the former had no idea that they were engaged in forming nations, pp. 6–13.

16. H. Kohn, *The Idea of Nationalism*, Macmillan, New York 1944, p. 15.

17. Ibid., p. 19.

18. See P. Chatterjee, *Nationalist Thought*, and G. Omvedt, 'Capitalist Agriculture'.

19. J. Breuilly, *Nationalism and the State*, Manchester University Press, Manchester 1985, pp. 12–18.

20. For a competent survey of the idea and views of the most famous Marxists and Marxist currents that addressed themselves to the phenomenon of nationalism and the national question, see R. Munck, *The Difficult Dialogue*, OUP, Oxford, 1986.

21. See among others I. Narain, 'Cultural Pluralism, National Integration and Democracy in India', in K.R. Bombwall, *National Power and State Autonomy*, Meenakshi Prakashan, Meem 1977; P. Brass (ed.), *Ethnic Groups and the State*, Croom Helm, London 1985; J. Manor, 'The Dynamics of Political Integration and Disintegration', in A.J. Wilson and D. Dalton (eds), *The States of South Asia*, Vikas, New Delhi 1982; M. Weiner, 'India's Minorities', in J. Roach (ed.), *India 2000; The Next Fifteen Years*, Riverdale, 1986.

22. B. Anderson, *Imagined Communities*, Chapter 1, p. 15.

23. Indian Marxists would do well to heed the warning of H.B. Davis, *Towards A Marxist Theory of Nationalism*, Monthly Review Press, New York, 1978, p. 13: 'This is not to say that Communists in a country such as India should spend their time trying to build up linguistic groups into nationalities. This procedure can be justified in Marxist terms, when, and only when it is a contribution to freeing such groups from exploitation

and domination by other cultural groups.' Frankly his secondary, provisional statement is also no justification for indulging in such nomenclatural licence.

24. J. Breuilly, *Nationalism and the State*, p. 223.

25. Whatever its supposed historic roots, there would have been no Gorkhaland agitation if independent India had not opted for a federalism based on linguistic reorganization in 1956. Note, moreover, that the leaders of the Gorkhaland agitation are seeking to assert an identity as *Indian* Gorkhas as distinct from Nepali Gorkhas; this would hardly have been possible if India and an Indian nationality/identity had not first come into existence.

According to Geertz, the discontent of 'primordial' groupings in independent nation-states can be connected to: (a) the new sense of 'political suffocation' that arises when a nation-state is formed with new, nationally organized institutions of civil power and influence; and (b) the fact that these 'primordial' groups and their members are not so isolated from their own governments/centre of power/civil state as they were from the more remote colonial regime. There are, therefore, likely to be more clashes of identity where formerly there was accommodation, and greater demands for the preservation of some of these 'primordial' identities and boundaries.

In short, though 'primordial' groups and loyalties are traditional and pre-date even colonial rule, 'primordial' *discontent*, and, therefore, movements based on these frustrations, are very often only the result of independence and subsequent efforts at nation-building. The task of the new state then is not to eliminate these loyalties and movements but to domesticate them. See C. Geertz, 'The Integrative Revolution', in C. Geertz (ed.), *Old Societies and New States*, Amerind Publishing Co., New Delhi 1971, pp. 114–28 and 139–53.

26. The British administered through multi-lingual provinces in which there were linguistic movements led by the middle classes. In 1931 the concept of linguistic states was adopted in the Congress party's Declaration of Rights. Even earlier the Congress's internal structure had been organized along these lines. The 1945–46 Congress manifesto promised linguistic division of states wherever possible.

27. Nationalities are not fixed. They can disappear or merge into another nationality, in this case the *Indian* nationality. See H. Kohn, *The Idea of Nationalism*, p. 13.

28. H. Seton-Watson, *Nations and States*.

29. The 1956 States Reorganization Act made the states the basic arena for political clashes especially in view of the considerable and real powers that state governments have.

30. The meaning of the term 'national question' has now been stretched to cover the problems of regionalism. Once a regional group is defined as a nationality then the Leninist prescription of the right to self-determination can be blindly applied since it has the right to define its own political future in any way it likes, up to secession, provided it is 'oppressed'.

There is a real danger that such loose usage of the term nationality for what is really a minority group, even if oppressed, can foster an excessively facile, schematic and uncritical approach to a movement which then substitutes for the more difficult task of making a 'concrete analysis of the concrete situation'.

31. R. Hardgrave Jnr, 'The Northeast, Punjab and Regionalization of Indian Politics', in *Asian Survey*, November 1983, p. 1171.

32. This is certainly the conclusion drawn by M. Weiner, 'Indian Minorities', in J. Roach (ed.), *India 2000*.

33. R. Hardgrave Jnr, 'The Northeast', p. 1171.

34. In certain cases, e.g. Maharashtra, Punjab, the demand for a linguistic division had behind it a very well organized kulak and middle-caste character. These states were formed some time after the original division in 1956 took place, when these kulaks were also relatively stronger. See P.C. Mathur, 'Regionalism in India', in Ramankant (ed.), *Regionalism in South India*, Aalekh Publishers Jaipur, 1983, pp. 10–12.

Even elsewhere, other considerations besides linguistic homogeneity have played a big part in the redrawing of state boundaries. So in the northeast (Nagaland, Meghalaya, Manipur, Tripura, and Arunachal Pradesh) ethnic and economic factors were very important; in Haryana and Punjab, religious considerations came into play; division within the Hindi belt (Bihar, Uttar Pradesh, Madhya Pradesh, and Rajasthan) had to do with issues of history, politics and problems of integrating the former princely states. See I. Narain, 'Cultural Pluralism' in K.R. Bombwall, *National Power and State Autonomy*, pp. 187–9.

According to the 1961 census of the Central Institute of Indian Language (CIIL), India had 197 languages (not dialects) broken up as follows: Indo-Aryan 98, Austric 21, Dravidian 26, Tibeto-Chinese 52. The 1971 census showed that there were 22 languages spoken by more than 1½ million people. These covered 93% or 548 million people out of the population then. Clearly, nothing could be more absurd than to make a fetish of language division or make each language group into a nationality whether 'mature' or 'immature'.

35. According to this formula, the states will have in their educational institutions English, the regional mother tongue and a third language not of that region. This was seen as a non-coercive way of promoting the use of Hindi, which was the single most widely used Indian language.

36. For a sober and convincing appraisal in this regard see R.D. King, 'The Language Issue Revisited', in J. Roach (ed.), *India 2000*.

37. P. Brass, 'Pluralism, Regionalism and Decentralizing Tendencies in Contemporary Indian Politics', p. 230, in Wilson & Dalton (eds), *The States of South Asia*, Vikas, New Delhi 1982.

38. One of the more detailed studies of such movements is M. Weiner, *Sons of the Soil*, Princeton University, Press, 1978. The probability is much higher in Gujarat than in Orissa or West Bengal.

39. An official CPM statement listing all its basic demands with respect to state autonomy can be found in S. Sahani (ed.), *Centre–State Relations*, Vikas, New Delhi 1984, pp. 26–32.

40. India divides 800 million people into 25 units while the USA divides 230 million people into 50 units. From this one might easily infer that the USA is a much more federal society. But a number of writers on Indian federalism have quoted approvingly from one of the first studies on administration in India by P. Appleby, *Public Administration in India: Report of a Survey*, Govt of India publication, New Delhi 1953. Appleby writes . . . 'no other large and important government . . . is so dependent as India on theoretically subordinated but actually rather distinct units responsible to a different political control, for so much of the administration of what are recognized as national programs of great importance to the nation.'

K.R. Bombwall (*National Power*) argues that there has been a shift from 'dominant federalism' to 'cooperative federalism'. P. Brass 'Pluralism', pp. 224–5, has suggested that differences in assessment are connected to the vantage point chosen. Those who look mainly at the planning commission, finance commission and at the use of President's Rule tend to see on balance a movement towards centralization and a corresponding decline in state autonomy. Those who look mainly at the Congress tend to be more divided in their conclusions. While those who look at state party systems or at language policy tend to see greater regionalism and state autonomy. Brass himself believes there has been greater decentralization.

Most intellectuals in or close to the mainstream Communist parties, not surprisingly, believe there has been greater centralization and a relative decline in state autonomy. But even they allow for fluctuations and perceive the 1967–71 period and the post-1977 period when Congress lost power in many states as occasions when the states gained some ground.

41. W.S. Livingstone, *Federalism and Constitutional Change*, Cassell London 1956, p. 21. 'The essence of federalism lies not in constitutional or institutional structure but in society itself.'

42. P. Brass, 'Pluralism', p. 229–37; also Tables 1 to 4.

43. R. Chatterjee, 'Democracy and Opposition in India', *Economic and Political Weekly*, 23 April, 1988, pp. 843–7. However, in making his case for greater federalism and for better 'institutional' representation for the opposition parties whose strength is

'politico-environmental', he tends to overdraw the dangers of failure in this regard, thus underestimating the sources of durability in the system overall.

44. Official summary of the 'Report of the Sarkaria Commission on Centre–State Relations' issued by the Press Information Bureau (PIB), Govt of India, New Delhi, 30 January 1988.

45. R. Hardgrave Jnr, *India Under Pressure*, Westview, Boulder 1984. This is a particularly clear-headed account of the sources of what Hardgrave considers to be quite remarkable 'regime stability'.

46. This point has been forcefully made by the renowned sociologist, M.N. Srinivas, who stresses that caste is the most powerful of the 'horizontal' identities.

47. See, in particular, V.I. Lenin, *Questions of National Policy and Proletarian Internationalism*, Progress Publishers, Moscow 1970.

48. Ibid., pp. 32–7.

49. Ibid., pp. 37–43. One useful reform that a post-revolutionary government might adopt is the promotion of a single common script, for example, the Roman script, in *addition* to and not at the expense of any existing script. Such a common script would facilitate transliteration of one language to another and thereby promote greater familiarity among Indians with the diverse richness of their literary and cultural traditions. The learning of such a common script should not, of course, be imposed on any region or community. If the Chinese experience is anything to go by, such a reform will progress slowly at best.

50. Ibid., pp. 37–40.

51. The constitutional sanction for such repressive action is contained in Articles 356 and 357.

4

Communalism and Hindu Nationalism

The rise of communal tensions and the post-independence growth of various communalisms have posed serious problems for those nationalist historians who perceived the Congress as an essentially secular force (albeit with communal elements) and the National Movement itself as secular in its fundamental thrust. Communalism in its extreme manifestation – the communal riot – has become commonplace. At one time this term referred only to Hindu–Muslim violence but it now has to be extended to cover Hindu–Christian and Hindu–Sikh clashes. Nonetheless, the overwhelming majority of these riots still involve primarily Hindus and Muslims. The frequency with which they break out has risen dramatically in recent decades. According to official sources, the numbers killed and injured annually have risen markedly over time.[1]

The dismantling of the colonial state (which, it is widely agreed, deliberately promoted communal divisions), its replacement by an independent secular state, and the finality of partition were all expected to lay the foundations for a continuous *decline* in communal tensions and strife. But, particularly from the early sixties onwards, these expectations were progressively belied. However, if there are discontinuities in the character of the communalism of the pre- and post-independence periods there are also important continuities. At the very least, free India's failure to overcome communalism should inspire a re-examination of widespread conceptions regarding the secular character of the National Movement and of the Congress, the secularity of the Indian state, the presumed antinomy between communalism and nationalism, the supposed incompatibility between stable bourgeois democracy and low levels of secularization.

Much of the confusion arises because of the paradigmatic elevation of European history. The manner in which nations and democratic political systems emerged in the West has been taken as an ideal type by which to gauge the nature of the relationships between that famous triad of secularization, nationhood and political democracy.

Anderson has pointed out that eighteenth-century Europe saw both the dawn of nationalism and the dusk of religious modes of thought, and that this was taken to imply an intimate relationship between the two processes. The religious community of old had an 'unselfconscious coherence'.[2] Geographical and cultural exploration, the advances of science, capitalist production techniques and relations, developments in the technology of communications, the historicization of human existence – that is, the emergence of a modern historical sensibility – all helped to undermine ontological innocence and erode traditional identities, most notably that of the 'universal' religious community. The importance of secular identities had already been established by the defeat of the church by the state, and the former's declining capacity to regulate social life even outside the political realm; substantial secularization of state and society *preceded* nationhood. In the transition to it there were religious wars, inter-religious and intra-religious sectarian strife, as well as high levels of intolerance towards religious minorities. Secularization in the West was paid for with what Asian intellectuals today could easily describe as religious–communal conflict. In a broad historical sense, Dumont is right in perceiving communalism as an unexceptional characteristic generally marking the transition to nationhood.[3]

But this evaluation, carrying as it does an implicit note of historical reassurance, may deflect attention away from the specificities of the Indian experience. In Europe, the emergence of a national identity became in large measure a replacement for the weakened virtues of religious loyalty. There, the growth of a political community, which eventually became coterminous with the boundaries of the nation-state, compensated for the shrinking space occupied by the 'imagined' religious community. Secularization of the state, civil society and even of personal and family life follows in the wake of industrialization and urbanization, the rise of the capitalist state, and the consolidation of the basic institutions of civil society. Even allowing for substantial national variations, religious hegemony in civil society tends to be systematically replaced by secular-democratic hegemony in which political authority ultimately rests on the non-religious yet stable foundations of the 'consent of the governed'.[4]

Historical Roots of Hindu Nationalism

Nationalism and bourgeois democracy emerged in India in utterly different circumstances. Nationalism as political movement, national identity, and nationalist ideology did not develop in the wake of religious decline. A Hindu religious 'renaissance' was central to the emergence of all three. To illuminate this argument it is necessary to start with pre-British India. In Mughal India (and before), the cellular character of Indian society meant that a high level of religious tolerance at the base was not so much the consequence of intrinsic folk wisdom or some valued attribute of popular religion as of the careful insulation of religious communities and the absence of integration.[5] Communal separateness characterized Hindu–Muslim relations. This was publicly signalled through separate residential quarters as well as distinct modes of dress, behaviour and social organization and routines. Social order and the stability of the village community were maintained because of an easy coexistence which accommodated these separations in an overarching framework of occupational and functional integration which ensured that simple (or slowly expanding) reproduction of agrarian relations and existing life patterns would take place.

Colonial control built upon the existing interfaces in society. The emergence of urban/semi-urban centres of trade and production along with the other accoutrements of colonial modernization transformed the situation. Migrants from villages to towns followed earlier caste and kinship migration patterns, giving rise to homogeneous neighbourhoods which were not, however, integrated within any framework of functional reciprocities. British conquest decisively undermined the power and wealth of the Muslim upper classes who had administrative but not hereditary control over territories; in contrast, the Hindu business and commercial elite prospered through this separation of political power and economic wealth, giving rise over time to significant economic and social disparity between the upper and middle classes of the two communities. Communal distinctions could thus more easily become antagonisms reinforced by inter-elite competition.[6]

Cultural colonialism and modernization clearly created an identity crisis for the Hindu elite and middle classes, pushing them to search for new forms of self-definition. But the centralizing mechanisms of British economic and political power were sufficiently disruptive of society as a whole to give this search for self-identification a wider and more popular base. When the material foundations for the easy coexistence of plural identities and of different communities are weakened, then the individual search for more clearly defined boundaries to the self becomes more urgent, while the willingness to accept hierarchically ordered separateness gets eroded. A loose agglomeration of caste and religious identities gives way to greater self-assertion and competitiveness.[7] If a sharpening of the Hindu–Muslim distinction was one result, another was the elite-led search for an 'essential' Hinduism to replace the earlier mingling of flexible religious sects which constituted the polymorphousness of what can be designated 'classical Hinduism'.

As Romilla Thapar, one of India's outstanding historians, describes it,

> The notion of Hindu community as it is defined today became necessary when there was a competition for political power and access to economic resources between various groups in a colonial situation. There was need to change from a segmental identity to a community which cut across caste, sect and region. This social need also required a reformulation of Hinduism which was attempted in various socio-economic reform movements of the nineteenth century.[8]

The construction of a religious 'tradition' always involves a selection from the past in the light of contemporary needs. In the case of Hinduism, Thapar argues, that upper caste or Brahmanical beliefs and rituals (which were attractive also to the excluded lower castes) came to constitute the core of tradition. This 'Sanskritization', paralleled by 'Islamization', was a mechanism for institutionalizing uniformity in Hinduism (and Islam) in India.

The point of this brief discussion of pre-British and British times is simply to establish that the early stirrings of cultural nationalism had necessarily to be infused with the glow of a redefined and 'reformed' Hinduism and the assertion of a new-found 'Hindu identity'. Furthermore, the pull of this cultural–religious nationalism was so strong that a bourgeois-dominated national political movement could hardly be expected to avoid the temptation of accommodating itself to its dynamic. Gandhiism both legitimized this thrust and ensured that it would not take the extreme form of a political demand for a Hindu state. But in fact the Mahatma, as he came to be popularly (and revealingly) known, made the National Movement a mass movement by substantially Hinduizing it. More precisely, he sought to build a patchwork alliance of existing communities, classes and religious groups by basing himself on their existing states of consciousness.

Indeed, for Gandhi, not only was such an approach expedient, it was also morally incumbent. National identity had to have a religious basis. Even in a multi-religious situation like India this would involve no favouritism because the truth or essence of all religions was the same. If appeal to specific religious loyalties constituted the first stage whereby the masses could be drawn into the National Movement, the second stage of common mass struggle would strip away the inessentials of religiosity, its artificial barriers, and consolidate an overarching national identity all the stronger for being based on 'true' religious belief and commitment. The first part of his strategic perspective was a resounding success; the second a tragic miscalculation. Communal cleavages came to dominate the National Movement era and communalism has come to dominate much of contemporary Indian politics.[9]

Communalism then is Janus-faced. Not in the sense that it is both good and bad – it is always reactionary – but in the sense that it can be just as much a vital agent of nationalism as an enemy of it. Dumont, for all his reluctance to use the term 'Hindu nationalism', was essentially correct in his summation:

> We are led to understand how fundamentally the political action of Tilak and Gandhi was based on an intellectual synthesis that was prepared in the nineteenth century and which is often called neo-Hinduism . . . . Let us only characterize it schematically by saying that it is a synthesis in response to Western challenge which is still more political and social than religious: an integration of the new social and political values within a reformed traditional and at least outwardly religious view; a reaffirmation of supposed Hindu values on a new level. The major fact for us here is that this integration and internationalization of modern Western views which was conscious of being a victorious reaffirmation of traditional Hindu values was a preliminary condition of an active political struggle against foreign domination on the part of Hindus. One is led to speak of 'Hindu Nationalism', an expression which were it not self-contradictory could well describe the common ground between tendencies as different as those of Tilak and Gandhi.[10]

Clearly, the Hindu nationalism of contemporary India has vital historical precedents and foundations.[11]

Most historians are united in locating the social base of Hindu and Muslim communalism in the urban petty bourgeoisie or middle class. In a situation of economic stagnation, colonial patronage and increasing competition within the urban middle classes for government appointments, educational placings, and political positions in legislative councils and municipal bodies, mobilization on explicitly communal lines made sense – especially as it had real effects on the direction of colonial patronage. Organizations with explicit communal programmes such as the Rashtriya Swayamsevak Sangh (RSS), Hindu Mahasabha and Muslim League were based preponderantly on the urban petty bourgeoisie.

But as a general sociological explanation this analysis falters badly. It cannot adequately explain the growth of Hindu nationalism and communalism since the sixties. Even before 1947 what distinguished the Congress from those groups with an explicit Hindu communal outlook was the moderated, controlled and implicit character of its Hindu nationalist appeal, an appeal which existed alongside other ideological themes. This admixture gave it unmatched multi-class, multi-caste and multi-regional appeal. It also enabled it to retain the support of large sections of untouchables and (up to 1937–38) sizeable sections of the Muslim population.

Since independence the most important social force behind the rise of Hindu fundamentalism and Hindu nationalism (the most effective ideology of Hindu communalism) has been the intermediate castes. In class terms the intermediate castes comprise the agrarian bourgeoisie and the rural and urban petty bourgeoisie. This social force does not express itself solely through explicitly communal parties but also through mainstream bourgeois parties, as well as through the regional class parties and organizations of the kulaks. Nor is this assertion of Hindu fundamentalism a reaction to economic and social failures. On the contrary, it is the consciously chosen cultural expression of a social force which has enhanced its authority and which is upwardly mobile on the economic and political fronts.

The intermediate castes are seeking to improve their status by adopting a 'larger' identity commensurate with their developing self-image as major social actors in modern India. Rising prosperity has not reduced competition, social alienation or psychological insecurities among the urban middle class. Hindu fundamentalism, the aggressive assertion of a collective religious identity, may not be equivalent to Hindu communalism, but it is clearly a major factor in its spread and eruption. Within the intermediate castes, the urban petty bourgeoisie still provides the ideological and organizational leadership. But it is the ruralization of Hindu fundamentalism (and its spread into semi-urban layers) that constitutes the new factor of importance for the future of Indian society.

The 'backward' or intermediate castes, especially the rural component, constitute the bulk of the Hindu population. They are in the process of developing a religious coherence based on a common Hindu identity. If there were doubts in the earlier part of this century that there was a Hindu community-in-the-making there must be fewer now, and this is a development of the utmost significance. This popularization–ruralization means that the integrating symbolisms of an increasingly monolithic Hinduism may in some respects depart from Brahmanical traditions. It should be noted, however, that this popularization–ruralization is most impressively visible in the north and west, regions where Brahmanism has traditionally been most strongly rooted.

The essential burden of argument of a previous chapter has been that the agrarian bourgeoisie and petty bourgeoisie have a vital macro-interest in the preservation of the bourgeois democratic system; it is also now argued that they are a driving force behind the desecularization and Hinduization of the Indian polity. Within broad limits there is no incompatibility between the two projects, between the simultaneous existence of a weak (but functioning) democracy and a weak secularity, just as there is no incompatibility (within broad limits) between the maintenance of a stable and strong democracy in the West and increasing racial oppression of a minority of the population.

Legitimization and Integration

The development of a democratic political system in free India comes at a time when civil society is weak and secularization of social life minimal. The contrast with the West is striking. In the Indian context, the unfolding of the democratic process actually retards secularization – since electoral politics follows the path of least resistance, encouraging mobilization on the basis of existing identities and beliefs.[12] For the aspirant to national governance, the broader and less segmented its appeal, the better. The Congress, after the end of the era of one-party dominance, had to mount a constant search for a winning electoral arithmetic. It turned first to the core minorities. With the rise of the intermediate castes and the growing volatility in the voting behaviour of Dalits and Muslims, the Congress party's pitch to Hindu nationalism became more pronounced. It was strikingly visible in 1980 when Mrs Gandhi switched from her previously populist ideology of Congress socialism to a more clearly defined Hindu appeal, which led the RSS to shift much of its support to her even as she criticized the opposition parties, including the Bharatiya Janata Party (BJP).

In a first-past-the-post system there is always a grave disproportion between votes polled and seats obtained. This works against confessional and narrowly caste-based parties at the national level. But it can allow such parties to flourish at the state level. If a modulated Hindu nationalist appeal will increasingly come to characterize Lok Sabha election campaigns and politics, a much more aggressive assertion of communal interests and themes will be found at the level of assembly, municipal and metropolitan elections. It is at these levels that the communalization of politics has already gone furthest, as in Assam, Punjab, Kerala, Maharashtra, Gujarat and Andhra Pradesh.

In the Hindi heartland where Dalits and Muslims are to be found in sizeable proportions and where Congress influence has been dominant, state and sub-state politics have tended to follow the more cautious tempo of a modulated and diffuse Hindu nationalism. But there is no simple correspondence between the degree of communalization of electoral politics and communal rioting – beyond the obvious point that a growth in the former promotes outbreaks of the latter. Thus, in Kerala's assembly-level politics, institutionalization of explicitly communal parties (and alliance-making with them) has gone further than anywhere else. But the frequency and seriousness of communal riots is far less there than in Uttar Pradesh. The politics of communal riots, though related to the larger transformations in politics, ideology and culture at the extra-regional and national levels, have their own specific rhythms and causes – which indeed have been the subject of numerous detailed surveys.[13]

For the ruling classes, Hindu nationalism's contemporary function and promise is twofold and overlapping. It can, if controlled, enhance national integration and it is an attractive, if partial and short- to medium-term answer to the system's problem of legitimacy. To cope with the overload, the state needs to reduce claims on it and to increase its own capacities. Hindu nationalism as a hegemonizing ideology can do both. The system projects it as a 'fundamental value', even without naming it as such, and then promises to protect it, urging supporters to invest greater trust in the state as well as asking them to adopt the patriotic virtue of sacrifice in its cause. Hindu nationalism as a new consensus can partially, if temporarily, bridge some of the basic divisions of Indian society and of the political system. It transcends the urban–rural gap, it is multi-class, multi-caste and pan-Indian in its appeal. It can allow for greater assertion of regional identities without damage to its own claim.

But to approximate to its potential, Hindu nationalism has to be moderate in its tone, restrained in its thrust. It must not be allowed to overwhelm the apparatuses, only to infuse them cautiously with its ethos. A rampant Hindu nationalism would dramatically catalyse the latent unhappiness of the south and east with the political domination of the Hindi belt and of the north Indian Hindi-speaking Hindu. It would be intolerable to a Muslim community whose absolute numbers make it second in size only to Indonesia's. It would exacerbate beyond safety caste conflict with untouchables, tribal repression and communal rioting.

Political aspirants to government in New Delhi may recognize and adjust to the hegemonizing power of such an ideology. But even if they are not sufficiently attuned to the dangers of rabid extremism, they are sensitive to the electoral calculus of the Hindi heartland and the importance of the core minorities. A 'centrist' (in bourgeois terms) party can only win support from north, south, east and west, from the urban and rural petty bourgeoisie as well as from kulaks, while sustaining reasonable levels of Dalit, Muslim and tribal support, if it adopts a moderately Hindu nationalist approach. Aspirants to central power can be counted upon, therefore, to distinguish themselves from the more rabid ideologies and programmes of explicitly Hindu chauvinist formations in much the same manner as mainstream parties of the West seek to distance themselves from the explicitly racist formations to their right even as they bend to the pressures exerted by them.

The Janata experience of 1977–80 suggests that the more plebiscitary the centrist party is in make-up and appeal and the less dependent on tightly organized internal blocks, the better its chances of avoiding break up. The Janata shattered in the end on the rocks of the conflict between Charan Singh's Bharatiya Lok Dal (BLD) and the tightly-knit and more overtly communal BJP-RSS. The BJP (as well as outside actors such as Prime Minister Morarji Desai) did push for anti-conversion laws and a ban on cow slaughter. But this attempt to alter policies associated with the Indian secular state did not finally succeed. It is notable that the kulak component in the Janata coalition rationalized its clash with the BJP in terms of the latter's 'communal' link with the RSS.

Another source of perhaps minor consolation is that the ruling coalition is sufficiently heterogeneous and the conflict between its members sufficiently sharp to ensure that Hindu nationalism has limited value as a unifier. Even though the intermediate castes as a whole are responsible for the growth of this cultural nationalism, powerful differences between the rural and urban components of these castes (sometimes called 'backward') undercut Hindu nationalism's integrative capacities.

Aspirants to national authority can also be counted on to preserve the secularity of the Indian state with at most some adjustments here and there. A neutral state in a context where the weight of Hinduism is so overwhelming cannot be 'neutral' in its impact. Its very impartiality in action or adherence to equal treatment can only reinforce existing trends in the distribution of religious influence. Such a situation is tailor-made for the advance of a *restrained* Hindu nationalism.

The Secular State and Civil Society

Where secularization outside the state realm is weak, there is a responsibility on the state to promote secular influences and practices. On the whole, both by inclination and official policy, the Indian state has refrained from such activity. There are two significant exceptions to this rule. Indian society had no secular law. Most early societies, including those with Roman and Germanic law, institutionalized a system of differential rights and obligations for different social groups. Hindu law or, more aptly, customary right was therefore not unique in enshrining the principle of unequal treatment for similar offences depending on the caste or social status of the offender. But this principle was undoubtedly more systematized and pervasive in Hindu society than elsewhere. This was, of course, incompatible with the bourgeois democratic principle of formal equality before the law. The Indian state after independence moved towards the codification of Hindu personal law so as to make the democratic system meaningful in this vital respect for the majority of its citizens.

Apart from this the government has sought to carry out certain reforms, for example, banning the exclusion of untouchables from temples because Hinduism, lacking an ecclesiastical structure, was unable and unwilling to carry out such self-reform. But these measures, though they exist on paper, are largely absent in practice. Overall, the 'secularity' of the Indian state – which has been described as an admixture of Western concepts of secularism and certain aspects of Indian tradition – does not favour the development of a progressively non-religious state. It is for this reason that many Marxists see the Indian state as non-communal or non-sectarian rather than secular, that is, non-religious.

In what remains one of the most impressive (and earliest) investigations into the relationship between Indian secularism and Hinduism, D.E. Smith has argued that classical Hinduism could encourage the formation of a secular state because of a number of inherent traits. The idea that life could be compartmentalized into the political–secular and the private–religious was, of course, utterly alien to Hinduism's ethos. But its specific challenge to the political realm facilitated a relative separation of religious and political functions. Hinduism, unlike religions with an ecclesiastical structure, did not frontally challenge the state or the political realm. But a 'dialogue of power' between the sacred and secular realms nevertheless existed and Hinduism's influence on the latter was real, if diffuse. Undoubtedly the absence of doctrine and structure meant that classical Hinduism was, relatively speaking, more tolerant, accommodative and absorbent of other faiths, rituals and beliefs.[14] Classical Hinduism spanned the spectrum from atheism to the crudest forms of animism. Such a tradition can be conducive to the formation of a secular state, but it is far less able than Christianity to accommodate itself to the secularization of society itself.

Hindu nationalism is the outcome of a process wherein this classical legacy has undergone historicization, territorialization and dogmatization. As long as the Indian secular state does not seek to seriously challenge the expansion of religious influence outside its domain, the two are capable of comfortable coexistence. Though civil society in India is weak, its institutions are expanding and developing. It is an area of contestation in which secular forces are most definitely not backed by the state. The struggle lies between an expanding and self-confident Hinduism as well as an orthodox Islam engaged in a powerful operation of retrenchment within an inward-looking Muslim community, on the one hand, and, on the other, the secular mechanisms of expanding market relations, modern technology and science, corporate and non-corporate bureaucratization, urbanization, and class divisions and struggles in industry and agriculture.[15]

The refusal of the state to engage in this arena means that secularization is uneven at best and, where it can be said to have advanced, it has done so at a disturbingly slow pace. This holds for such crucial areas of civil society as education, health, recreation, welfare services, the private media, even trade unions and political parties. In the face of this it takes remarkable complacency on the part of Indian secularists to insist that the fundamental need of the hour is to leave civil society and private life alone, strengthen the secular character of the state and supplement it by mass ideological campaigns.

This misplaced preoccupation with the state's secularity leads to a one-sided assessment of the rise of Hindu nationalism and communalism. They are seen as essentially uncontrollable in impact and internal dynamic (when this is still far from being the case) and always and completely antithetical to Indian democracy and nationhood. In fact, as we have seen, it can actually be supportive of democracy and nationhood in its own contradictory way. This support has its negative consequences. It clearly reinforces the slide to a more authoritarian and less healthy democracy. But since when has bourgeois democracy denied itself the flexibility to be more or less authoritarian? However, the growth of Hindu nationalism and communalism is far from being a dangerous prelude to fascism or semi-fascism any more than the rise of racism in the West proved to be the thin end of a fascist or semi-fascist wedge. If anything, such wrongful emphasis helped to shift attention away from the real problem of racism in Western societies to the far more abstract and remote problem of fascism. Similarly, Hindu nationalism and communalism of all kinds are the important issues not the anticipated collapse of Indian bourgeois democracy and its imminent replacement by some species of authoritarian or semi-fascist rule.

Contemporary Dangers

What then are the real and practical dangers of growing Hindu nationalism and Hindu communalism? These are numerous and grave enough in their own right not to need the embellishment of fearful prognostications of fascism or balkanization. The progressive legitimization of Hindu cultural nationalism can only make the minorities more insecure and promote among them a sense of being culturally second-class citizens.

It would be naive not to expect that such popular attitudinal changes among Hindus would lead to an increase in actual and de facto discrimination against minorities, whatever the legal strictures against such discriminatory practices. At the same time it needs to be asserted that elites within the minorities will continue to prosper and be co-opted in society's upper reaches and by the secular state, even if certain new barriers or constraints are felt.

Though pressures for the promulgation of restrictive, pro-Hindu legislation like anti-conversion acts or a ban on cow slaughter are likely to grow, it is by no means certain that such legislation will actually be passed, bearing in mind the moderated character of Hindu nationalism and the state's determination to preserve its secularity. But these growing pressures will themselves be a source of inter-communal tensions, movements and counter-movements. The strengthening of Hindu communalism will also reinforce the thrust towards Khalistan and make it that much easier for the state to adopt and justify acts of repression against Sikhs. In general, communal tensions will be aggravated, with a real likelihood that the frequency and intensity of communal riots will increase.

Hindu fundamentalism can only encourage minority fundamentalisms, which in turn feed the former in a continuing cycle of action and reaction. Of course, minority fundamentalisms and communalisms are not simply a reaction to Hindu fundamentalism or communalism. They have their own independent dynamic. The capacity of Hindu nationalist appeal and communalism to disguise class divisions and obscure class interests is a matter of obvious concern to Marxists and leftists in general. The consolidation of religious demarcations within the oppressed classes can only hamper class mobilization. Finally, the spread of a Hindu religiosity and ethos will indirectly promote certain forms of caste and women's oppression. Its baleful effects are already evident. The linkages between Hindu 'creationism' (revivalism is an inappropriate term since what is involved is an historically new way of defining Hinduism) and the reflorescence of such barbaric practices as sati and sati worship, spurred on by the secular techniques of mass publicity and mass organization, should serve as a warning. Clearly religious sanction can be obtained and mobilized for the preservation and extension of gender oppression and its internalization within Indian womanhood.[16] Religious sanctification does not merely disguise demands and practices which have a fundamentally secular purpose, it also sacralizes them, gives them a meaning and power that shows religion as far more than merely an efficacious tool for generating mass support.[17]

One is struck in recent times by the frequency and persistence with which ideologues and champions of Hinduism refer to its 'inherently' tolerant character and, therefore, to the misapprehensions of the minorities and secularists about its resurgence. This very self-conscious insistence on Hinduism's tolerant nature betokens a profound intolerance, equivalent in its own way to the doctrinally inscribed intolerance of the monotheistic, revelatory religions. Classical Hinduism was tolerant because it was incapable of being self-consciously so. Its very structure (absence of structure) could not allow it to be self-consciously tolerant any more than its diverse practitioners could have a consciousness of being 'Hindu'.

The birth of a *self-conscious* Hindu identity marks the beginning of the process of a Hindu community-in-the-making. Today's self-consciously avowed tolerance masks an implicit arrogance and dismissal of other less historically 'gifted' religions which, by contrast, are 'intolerant' and therefore 'inferior'.[18] True, the classical characteristics of Hinduism and the fragmented character of Indian society may prevent the Hindu community-in-the-making and the Hindu religion's ideology-in-the-making from reaching as *crystallized* a form as other religious communities and ideologies.[19] But these very processes themselves are dangerous, regardless of what destination point they reach or do not reach. Classical Hinduism was unaware of and unconcerned about millions of low-caste conversions to Islam and Christianity. In 1983, the conversion of at most a thousand outcastes to Islam at Meenakshipuram, Tamil Nadu, caused a nationwide uproar. The response to that single incident indicates the vast distance that contemporary Hinduism has travelled from the Hinduism of only a few centuries ago.

Communalism: Some Conceptual Difficulties

What is communalism? Is it a modern phenomenon? Is it a specifically Indian or Asian phenomenon? What is its relationship to secularism and secularization? How is the struggle against communalism linked to the struggle for socialism? On these basic questions there is neither unanimity nor convincing clarity.

The term communalism was first employed by British colonialists to describe what were considered to be basic social characteristics in colonies, such as India and Malaya, where substantial religious minorities existed alongside a religious majority. The colonial use of the term seems to have carried negative connotations of divisiveness, religious bigotry, backwardness and parochialism. As such it provided the useful function of justifying colonial dominance and its 'civilizing mission'. But it was only one way among possible others for colonial administrators and intellectuals to make sense of the complex Indian reality. Its choice must have been inspired to some degree by its innate, if partial plausibility as a viable filter of perception. Perhaps just as important, if not more so, it seemed to correspond to the actual path of colonial expansion and conquest, namely defeat of Mughal rulers, alliances with Hindu princely kingdoms, defeat of Ranjit Singh's Sikh kingdom. It no doubt also served as one useful organizing principle for a general British policy of divide and rule.

Indian nationalists, even as they contested the veracity of the British perception of India's past and of its essential sociological make-up, seem to have shared the British view that communalism was a negative phenomenon and something to be avoided.[20] Where the British saw this as a pre-modern legacy, the nationalists saw it as a post-British potential which had to be prevented from becoming an enduring reality. Communalism, then, could not be just the politicization of religious conflict because that was common enough in ancient and mediaeval world history. According to some, it was rather a process of making political conflict 'religious' in the era of the mass political community – when mass political movements and democratic egalitarian secular ideals emerged which shortened religion's reach and made for the first time the political use of religious ideology and identity illegitimate. It is perhaps this illegitimacy, more than anything else, that constitutes the modernness and negativism of what has come to be called communalism.

In the West, secularization has advanced beyond a critical point and conflicts between religious communities in the name of self-preservation no longer pose a major threat to the body politic or to each other. Even in cases like Northern Ireland, the religious dimension is seen as secondary to what is essentially a nationalist struggle. Whatever the religious imagery, rhetoric or appeal, the ultimate objectives are defined by all sides in clearly secular ' terms – Irish reunification or British union. The call for Khalistan, for example, is different because it is posited as a necessary means to achieving a more basic and ultimate end – the preservation of Sikhs as a distinct religious community. Western intellectuals have felt little need, therefore, to attempt any theorization of a phenomenon apparently so remote from their contemporary situation. In the West, religions and sects have finally learnt to live and let live.

This is obviously not the case in India. The most systematic and sustained attempt to theorize the phenomenon of communalism in India was undoubtedly undertaken by the Marxist historian Bipan Chandra in his *Communalism in Modern India*.[21] This book suffers from numerous weaknesses and the views presented here are generally critical of its most fundamental propositions. But critique is one thing; construction of an alternative theoretical framework another. Chandra's remains a landmark contribution which has helped to raise the level of debate and comprehension of the complex phenomenon of communalism to a significantly higher level. What is at issue is not an academic matter. Any programme to combat communalism is directly tied to its definition and to its perceived connections with secularism and bourgeois democracy.

Chandra's fundamental assertion is that communalism is essentially an ideology. It is an ideology that promotes the 'false consciousness' that a religious community – that is, one united only by a common religious identity – also has common secular (economic, political and social) interests. In his historical survey, Chandra perceives nationalism and communalism as basic opposites. For all his reservations about the 'strong Hindu tinge' of the Congress and about Gandhi's penchant for religious symbolism, Chandra sees the Congress, like the post-1947 Indian state, as fundamentally secular. His definition is interchangeable – it can be used to describe other species of 'false consciousness', like casteism and linguism. This chameleon quality confirms how little his definition has to do with religion.

Although it is no longer fashionable even among Marxists to talk of 'false consciousness', the concept is not without some merit. In capitalist societies or in societies undergoing transition to capitalism, the exploitation and oppression of the working class is an objective fact rooted in the very nature of the economy. This means insecurity of employment, inadequacy of income, oppressive work rhythms and alienation at the workplace. It is perfectly reasonable to talk, therefore, of the objective interests of the working classes in removing this state of affairs. A 'true' class consciousness then is that consciousness appropriate to a recognition of this structural character of capitalist relations. If the subjective interests of the working class do not lead it to develop this appropriate consciousness then this is partly because the complex ways in which social relations are established and subjective identities and interests are formed create compensatory mechanisms as well as barriers to the achievement of class consciousness. 'False consciousness' becomes a shorthand for saying that there is such a thing as objective interests for the working class (which through a different set of arguments are considered to be 'universal interests') and that if these are not self-evident and reflected in the subjective perceptions of this class, it is partly because of certain barriers cultivated and fostered by capitalism and the exploiting classes.

But beyond this, the concept of false consciousness is singularly unhelpful. It cannot help to explain why these barriers exist and why they remain so powerful, which is surely a theoretical prerequisite for overcoming them in practice. In communalism the most important subjective identity is religious identity.

Chandra's approach therefore suffers from a number of serious flaws. He asserts that communalism is the politics of religious identity, but the question or importance of religious identity, its formation and meaning is never incorporated in any sustained way into his analysis.[22] By insisting that religious ideology, as distinct from religious identity, has nothing to do with communalism, he ignores the fact that the central importance of such ideology is not its ethical dimension – its moral dos and don'ts – but its ontological prescriptions, whose basic purpose is to fix and consolidate a *particular* religious identity. In short, to deepen one's understanding of communalism means to deepen one's understanding of the religions in question, the ways in which they fix identities or create loyalties, the very real and material, if psychological and emotional, needs they address and fulfil.[23]

Ignoring these issues leads to underestimation of the power and scope of religious appeal and mobilization. There is, in consequence, a strong tendency to perceive communalism as purely a species of manipulation. Certain social forces or communal leaders representing them have certain secular aims and ambitions and seek to achieve these by manipulation of the lower classes – playing on their religious beliefs and fears. This is, at best, partially correct and raises as many questions as it answers. This approach also encourages the tendency to see communalism as the ideological mask behind which lurk the forces of fascism. Such an ideology cannot be free-floating. It is rooted in the urban petty bourgeoisie, the social base of fascism.

Taken to its extreme, minority communalism is said to mean separation, as in the cases of Khalistan and Pakistan. Majority communalism is said to mean the Hindu state and Hindu fascism. As a worst-case scenario this logic is impeccable. But the failure to see the complex ways in which communalism and bourgeois democracy interact and make use of each other leads to a simultaneous overestimation of the dangers of fascism and an underestimation of the dangers of communalism in its own right.[24]

This definition of communalism as ideology also provides a ready reckoner for ranking communal forces among the various bourgeois parties and organizations. It is the programme and ideologies of these organizations that supposedly determine how communal they are. Thus the Congress may have communal elements and may sometimes engage in communal politics but it is not fundamentally communal, while the BJP-RSS or Akali Dal (AD) is. Alliances with parties like the Congress against the 'truly' communal parties thus become not only permissible but necessary. Such a view simply ignores the fact that the main function (at least for very considerable periods of time) of explicitly communal forces is not to constitute the principal bridgehead through which communalism advances, but to shift the whole political spectrum to the right on the communal issue, making it easier for the mainstream political parties in and out of government to institutionalize or endorse communal practices.[25] The dangers of an emotional ghettoization of Sikhs stem primarily from the attitudes and behaviour of the state and not from the RSS or Vishwa Hindu Parishad (VHP). Similarly, the rabid Hindu chauvinism of these groups makes the modulated Hindu nationalism of the mainstream parties both more possible and more respectable, and it is this modulated nationalism that captures the most ground.

Chandra's definition also carries within it the prescribed solution – the construction and propagation of a 'counter-ideology' of secularism. This is not just one front of the anti-communal battle; it is the central terrain of the whole struggle.[26] A national campaign counterposing unity and secularism to communalism becomes the principal organizational form for such a struggle. While acknowledging that capitalism establishes the social foundations for the growth of communalism and therefore the anti-capitalist struggle does help to defeat communalism, Chandra rejects as dogmatic any assumption that only the overthrow of capitalism will eliminate communalism. Indeed, this attitude or belief, he fears, would tend to postpone the struggle; communalism can and should be defeated in the here and now. In a society with a strong nationalist and democratic ethos, communalism must appear an aberration which will rapidly disappear. Secularism and the defeat of communalism is thus seen as a bourgeois democratic task, capable of being carried out by a strategic alliance of left and secular bourgeois democratic political forces.

There is an obvious tension between insisting that religion per se is not the enemy and advocating secularism as the cure. This is because secularization does mean (however you define it) some kind of attack or restraint on religious power. This tension is usually resolved by a compromise wherein the secular project becomes limited to the state and secularization comes to mean the *separation* of religion and the political domain. It becomes enough to consolidate the secularity of the Indian state and have the state carry out its responsibilities (dare one say it) religiously. The negative function of the state's struggle against communalism is to prevent communal outbreaks through the strict and neutral exercise of its law and order functions, including the use of counter-violence against the violence of communal terrorist groups. The positive function of the state is its promotion of a counter-ideology of secularism.[27]

The Indian state's concept of secularity is strongly influenced by the idea of Sarva Dharma Sambhava or equal treatment of all religions, which remains a bone of contention among liberal secularists inspired by the Western concept of secularism. Equal treatment or the state's role as an active balancer, they say, must give way to complete abstinence. But whatever the differences, this is essentially an in-house debate on how best to define and establish the state's religious impartiality. It assumes that the Indian state can by its actions or non-actions actually be neutral in its impact.[28]

The fallacy of this view has been noted earlier. Furthermore, such a delineation of the problem (and solution) has no place for any dialectical understanding of the relationship between secularization and desecularization: how the very processes of secularization of the state in third world countries whose societies have not undergone an organic and substantial secularization can promote desecularization in civil society. What is involved here is not so much an absolute decline of religious influence and power, but a phenomenon of *displacement* within the apparatuses of the state itself and between state and society.[29] Religious influences on political life are then mediated in other ways. Furthermore, when circumstances change it may become possible for religious forces to assert their influence in state apparatuses or to control them more directly. This is surely the lesson of Iran after the Shah, of the various government-sponsored Islamization programmes and of the growing power of confessional and sectarian parties in the Arab world.

Ultimately, Chandra, though an avowed Marxist, is no different from the liberal secularists in either his diagnosis or prescription for the problem of communalism.[30] Being Marxist for the sake of being Marxist means nothing. But what is disturbing is that Chandra's approach, even when most generously evaluated, suffers from a tragic consistency. His restricted definition of communalism leads to a restricted understanding of the phenomenon and, therefore, to a restricted programme for combating it.

Towards an Alternative Approach[31]

Secularism and communalism (desecularization in religiously plural societies) do stand as powerful opposites in a way that pairings like nationalism–communalism, democracy–communalism do not. To be sure, as ongoing processes in living societies, they also give rise to some remarkable syntheses – the secularization–desecularization dialectic. So to define and explore the meaning of communalism requires some kind of prior definition and exploration of the meaning of secularism.

Historically, there have been two basic ways in which secularism has been defined and understood – either in terms of coexistence or as negation–autonomy. The first believes religion's rightful place is in the private sphere and sees as necessary the absence of religious influence from politics and education in particular. It is, in effect, a rationalization of the fact that, in the West, religion has lost a great deal of social significance. Opinions may differ on what current trends in the West are or will be. But in general it is agreed that there is both a dichotomy and coexistence of the sacred and the secular, the latter enjoying temporal authority and the former spiritual authority derived from its connection with a higher reality to which the temporal is ultimately subordinate.

The second view argues that to be consistently humanist is to centre existence on man and his autonomy and that this requires a comprehensive rejection of the sacred, mythological and transcendent world view, that is, of religion. Secular humanism here has to mean a many-sided process (at both ideological and material levels) involving the progressive decline of religious influence in the economic, political and social life of human beings and even over their private habits and motivations. A Marxist view of secularism sits firmly within this latter tradition.

Unlike the static definition of secularism as a state of affairs – the separation of church and state or religion and politics – this definition is dynamic and involves a number of levels of human existence. It does not draw a strict boundary between the public and private domain or between the state, civil society and personal life. It also implies that secularization must be progressively promoted and extended even in the 'secular' societies of the West. Nor can a Marxist understanding of secularization be satisfied with a unilinear relationship between capitalist modernization and secularization. Capitalism as a mode of production within a social formation does revolutionize the economic level and progressively secularizes it by extending market relations, destroying crucial non-market economic privileges, powers of religious orders, and so on. But there is no general pattern explaining the *overall* process of secularization of different social formations, even if the capitalist mode of production dominates all of them. Specific social formations have specific histories and are marked by specific combinations of the secular and non-secular.[32]

At this juncture one can attempt a provisional and tentative definition of communalism. It can be defined as a process involving competitive desecularization in a religiously plural society – that is, a competitive striving to extend the reach of religion through ideology and control of institutions – which along with non-religious factors helps to harden divisions between different religious communities and increase tensions between them. Note that in this perspective the non-religious is invariably perceived as religious. Furthermore, religious control here is

not merely formal; it permeates institutional functioning. Nor is there
any denial of the fact that communalism has a powerful ideological
dimension. What theoretical merits does such a definition have?

First, it recognizes the importance of religion, religious forces, religious identity and religious competition. The extension of religious
influence even if it is outside the state is recognized as dangerous. The
development of a strong collective religious identity among Hindus,
Sikhs, Muslims and Christians is not a *sufficient* condition for the
growth of communalism but it is seen as a *necessary* one. To understand
communalism one must understand how and why collective religious
identities are expanding and how they interact with each other. At
the same time, this definition does not exclude non-religious factors
but recognizes that they play a major role alongside religious factors.
Only a survey of both the religious and the secular dimension can
help discover the necessary and sufficient conditions for the growth
of communalism.

This broader definition of the problem also implies a broader and
deeper programme of struggle. It is clearly not enough to secularize
the state or promote a secular ideology. Secularization must also go into
the pores of civil society and seek to erode the institutional power of
religion. In a fundamental sense Marxist secularists are anti-religious and
do wish religions progressively to disappear. They do not wish to force
people to give up religion or deny them some private space to express
their religious commitment, but they legitimately contest the influence
of institutionalized and non-institutionalized religion in domains other
than the state.[33]

There are three basic arguments here. First, the great attraction of
religion lies not so much in its ethical and epistemological claims as in
its ontological claim to answer the eternal problems of human existence
– the meaning and purpose of life, cosmic insignificance, and so on. In
contrast, Marxist ontology is, at best, undeveloped. Precisely because
historical materialism focuses primarily on the problems of historical
change it has that much less to offer with respect to the ahistorical,
timeless problems. In brief, Marxism must acknowledge respectfully
the importance of the ontological dilemma. It can reject the religious
resolution of this dilemma but it must accept that, as yet, it can offer no
adequate substitute.

Therefore it is not at the level of faith or spiritual belief that Marxists
must primarily contest religion. To do so in a context where the material
conditions for deep-seated alienation flourish would be to play directly
into the hands of communalists and fundamentalists. And to do so in
deeply religious societies like India would be a recipe for disaster. It is
at the level of economic, political and social needs that socialists must

work. At these levels Marxist socialists must and can refute the claims of religion to provide satisfactory solutions. In short, religion must be attacked not at its strongest but at its weaker points – its inability to address itself to, let alone resolve, the *secular* (economic, political and social) problems of human existence. In the end, this is the best means of eroding religious faith itself.

Secondly, religious identity is among the earliest identities into which the child is socialized. In the subcontinent, the family and the immediate surroundings of childhood constitute for most people a milieu that is saturated by religion and religious-based cultural behaviour, norms and values. This is not mitigated by the existence of any strong, collective, multi-religious working-class cultural milieu and tradition. Capitalist industrialization in India has been too compressed in time to allow for such a development outside small pockets. It would be unmaterialist to imagine that collective religious identities might be easily undermined or *replaced* by other collective identities (class, for example) without some prior construction of an alternative working-class and socialist culture rooted in the everyday existence of the oppressed.

Thirdly, the ontological dilemma which leads to such strong religious identification is surely to a large extent a function of human helplessness, powerlessness and various forms of terrestrial alienation. One can safely expect that the appeal of non-rational or religious 'solutions' to these preoccupations – even the preoccupations themselves – will decline as helplessness, powerlessness, and alienation decrease. It is here that the processes of secularism and socialist transformation become indissolubly linked.

That tradition of liberal humanism which shares the Marxist view of secularism as fundamentally anti-religious cannot, however, follow through the logic of this position. This is because it rejects the socialist alternative and defends bourgeois liberal democracy as the last word in democracy. The existence of the liberal democratic order is premised on the permanent preservation of the distinction between state and civil society because bourgeois democracy, unlike socialist democracy, must forever remain incomplete. It is essentially static. It can have no place for any conception that the state must begin to wither away, that is, to progressively merge into civil society. This sets basic limits on the extent to which human alienation can be diminished – because under this system popular power and direct democracy must be decisively restricted. This leaves some of the key ballasts of religious identification and belief firmly in place.

In the liberal democratic order, the liberalism is, in fact, more important than the democracy because the deepening of democracy is inseparable from deepening egalitarianism at the economic, political

and social levels.[34] The preservation of a liberal order requires: (a) that
the state exist in well-defined contours; (b) that it be interventionist
in, yet apart from, civil society; (c) that it enjoy dominant control of
the political ground no matter what the propagandists for 'political
pluralism' and 'countervailing powers' may wish people to believe;
(d) that nation rather than class be perceived as the crucial collective
category; (e) that unequal property rights in the means of production be
preserved; (f) and that, corresponding to the disjuncture between state
and civil society and between public and private (the two are related
but distinct), the state's capacities and rights to intervene in the latter
must be restrained.

This restrictive conception of democratic possibilities leaves the
atheistic, liberal humanist with two non-exclusive options. The first
is to accept a restrictive definition of the secular project, that is, limit
it to 'cleansing' the political domain. The second is to reconcile hope
and pragmatic accommodation by assuming that the secular processes
operating in capitalist democracies are so strong that religious decline,
though uneven and far from uninterrupted, is nevertheless cumulative
and unstoppable. In short, it is not socialism/socialist democracy and
secularism that are mutually reinforcing but capitalism/bourgeois democracy and secularism. Whatever the validity of such a view regarding
the advanced Western democracies, it is strikingly inappropriate for
India and other third world regions, for example, the Middle Eastern,
Islamic world. Twentieth-century history clearly shows that capitalist
growth is compatible with the preservation, indeed deepening of religious
influence in key areas of state and society.[35]

To even begin the monumental task of making decisive inroads in
the direction of secularism will require the prior establishment of a
dictatorship of the proletariat, of a socialist rupture with capitalism
and bourgeois democracy. Socialist democracy requires the progressive
investment of ever more power in ordinary people, enabling them
collectively to regulate society and carry out a creative and ecologically
respectful transformation of nature. To believe in the possibility of the
complete fulfilment of this project is utopian. But to strive for it, to move
ever forward in that direction, is not. The struggle against communalism
must be integrated with the struggle for socialist transformation and
socialist democracy.

Such a perspective demands a great deal more by way of programme
and activity than just secularizing the nation-state apparatuses or pushing
a secular ideology. It is not so much the expansion of knowledge that
is crucial as the expansion of popular power. In fact, the latter is
the pre-condition for the former. Changes in material relations – the
levelling of economic, political and social powers – are the only way

effectively to generate, on a mass level, the 'scientific temper' that secularists advocate.

What does all this mean for a programme of struggle against communalism today? It means that neither the state nor bourgeois parties committed to capitalism and liberal democracy can be strategic allies in a sustained struggle against communalism and for progressive secularization of the subcontinent. Nor should there be any illusions that communalism will be eradicated within the present framework of capitalist democracy. While struggles for further secularization of the Indian state and its laws and for the propagation of a secular ideology can be endorsed, there are also other responsibilities.[36]

For the left it means integrating the anti-communal dimension in its ongoing activity in unions, among students, women, Dalits, tribals and other oppressed groups. But beyond this, the left and other anti-communal forces must seriously address themselves to the issue of secularization of civil society, which in turn cannot be separated from the question of democratic control of its basic institutions. There are no formulae which can substitute for the painful labours and adjustments of regular grassroots activism. Only a few general propositions will be presented here.

Much of the popularity of communal organizations like the RSS, the Shiv Sena and their Muslim equivalents such as the Jamaat-e-Islami in north India, the various factions of the Muslim League throughout the country and the Majlis-e-Ittihad-ul-Musalmeen in Hyderabad, comes from their effective and organized insertion into the everyday life of urban neighbourhoods. Their ability to mobilize popular communal support is based partly on their capacity to terrorize opponents and protect supporters. It is also partly based on their ability to provide recreational, cultural and genuine welfare services, that is, to meet some of the *secular* needs of its constituencies. There are aspects of such a strategy which can and should be emulated by the left and anti-communal organizations, that is, the construction of 'counter-institutions'.

Confrontation with communal organizations cannot be left merely to those authorities claiming sole legitimacy in the use of force – the state or its local manifestations. Often the local machinery (municipality and police) are under the influence if not control of communalist groups. Even where this is not the case their responses are neither swift nor effective. Alternative sources of defence and principled militant violence against communal violence have to be developed. This is obviously a tricky task (given the extra-legal implications) and requires the most careful preparation as well as the utmost tactical flexibility.

Religious institutional control and influence in such areas as health, education, communication and recreational associations, should be contested – but in a manner which bears certain general principles in mind. One cannot reasonably demand an end to such provision of services by religiously controlled social bodies unless there are alternative non-religious mechanisms for providing them. It is far more sensible to press for a secularization of their functioning and their organs of internal control and for an extension of their services to all sections of the community regardless of caste or religious considerations. Of course, no religion can be singled out for such pressure. It has to be imposed on all. And only those organizations enjoying a measure of local credibility because of their ongoing grassroots activity will be appropriately placed to raise such a demand.

It should be clearly understood that the programme and demands that will be raised will not usually be realizable within the system as it exists; their purpose is mobilization. This is an educational compaign but with a distinct difference. What is involved here is not so much a campaign stressing the abstract virtues of nationalism or secularism, as a series of highly concrete, localized, programme-based agitations which aim to raise consciousness of the practical linkages between secularization and popular power; they demonstrate how basic needs can and should be addressed through mechanisms both secular and democratic in content. There is finally another task: the construction of locally rooted, socialist, secular and working-class culture (in the broadest sense of the term). This too cannot be simply addressed by occasional performances by wandering street theatre or song groups, useful though these are.

Making socialist democracy, socialist activity and socialist culture more real and meaningful is to make secularism and the struggle against communalism more real, meaningful and effective.

The Punjab Tragedy

Punjab differs from other states in the Union in that its creation was only formally connected to the language issue, though the linguistic reorganization of states did set a powerful precedent for the eventual formation of modern Punjab. At the heart of the popular cultural grievance that led to the boundary demarcations of 1966 (which last to this day) was not linguistic but Sikh religious identity, which is why the 'Punjab problem' was not resolved by a new, language-based territorial division. Sikh community identity could at best receive temporary reassurance before feeling besieged by a variety of pressures attending the ongoing processes of capitalist modernization and communalism. The Punjabi Hindu, in sharp contrast to Sikh sentiment, was more likely than not to interpret the formation of the Punjab state as his community's defeat and to see in this his regional subordination to a Sikh majority.

Implicit in the argument of my earlier chapter on the 'nationality question' was that religious rather than linguistic groupings were more powerful candidates for nationhood in the subcontinent.[37] Where regional territorial spaces were marked out as a consequence of linguistic pressures, local movements have largely stopped short of flirting seriously with secessionism. In contrast, the more tenuous incorporation of Kashmir, Punjab, Mizoram and Nagaland has had not a little to do with the fact that the cultural unity of the local groups in question had more to do with religious than with linguistic coherence. Nor is it possible to ignore the importance of the religious–cultural input into the formation of the Indian nation. In recent times the resurgence of Hindu nationalism has not only been compatible with the deepening of regional, language-based identities but has also exercised a powerful contripetal pull.

Punjab is an exception. Here the rise of Hindu nationalism strengthens the centrifugal thrust already encouraged by the deepening of the regional (Sikh-based) identity. Communalism (Hindu and Sikh) and Sikh nationalism became mutually reinforcing in a dialectic whose unrestrained logic is most frighteningly dangerous for Sikhs themselves. What looms on the political horizon is not the break up of north India but the potential tragedies of either state repression of the Sikh masses in Punjab (in the name of the unity and integrity of the country) or the emergence of an Ulster-like situation (with important differences, of course). The Indian state is implacably opposed to the emergence of Khalistan. It will not hesitate to use all its might to prevent it from becoming a reality.

Genesis and Evolution in the Nineteenth Century

Punjab was the last region to come under the sway of the Raj. Here there was no slow or organic anchoring of Western and Christian influences. It all came in a rush in more radical and cruder forms than elsewhere.[38] In pre-partition Punjab Muslims at slightly over 50 per cent constituted a bare majority, Hindus a very large minority comprising 35 per cent and Sikhs making up a little less than 15 per cent, though the boundary line between Hindu and Sikh identity was vague and ill-defined.

The urban, mainly Hindu population of traders, moneylenders, professionals – the middle and lower middle class – forged a common consciousness, striving for upward mobility, but without any coherent ideology, social programme or collective ritual practices that could help them withstand Christian proselytization and carve a permanent place within the British-controlled economy. The Arya Samaj, a reformist current within Hinduism which combined a return to ancient texts (the Vedas) with pursuit of Western science and education (minus their atheistic materialism), proved the best ideological vehicle for the urban trading castes to develop a viable self-image – marking them off not only from the British rulers but also from the Hinduism of the rural poor with whom they had antagonistic social relations.

Reflecting the dispositions of its class base, the Arya Samaj took an aggressive proselytizing turn which brought it into sharp confrontation with Sikhism, which was itself undergoing redefinition in the face of Western Christian pressures.[39] The Singh Sabha was the form taken by reformist Sikhism. It was dominant among the urban Sikh merchant castes and thus fed the intra-class competition between Hindus and Sikhs. The Singh Sabhas sought to distinguish Sikhs from Hindus by identifying Sikhism with the Khalsa or 'Singhism', thereby giving this separation a distinctive physical expression. The politics of communal identity had emerged. It was given sharper edge by British favouritism towards Muslims and Sikhs in recruitment to the colonial administration and armed services.

From the 1870s, massive British investment in canal irrigation in western Punjab soon made the 'canal colonies', as they came to be called, the chief export crop producers, at the expense of the economy of central Punjab. The Land Alienation Act of 1900 divided Punjab's population into agricultural and non-agricultural castes and denied the latter the right to purchase land from the former. This was a conscious attempt to restrain the expansion of the Hindu petty bourgeoisie. Not surprisingly, this class and Arya Samajism soon became part of the anti-colonial National Movement, with significant effects on its ideological development.

The British also imposed restrictions on the canal cultivators (mainly Sikhs and Muslims) so there was an objective basis for an alliance between the rural rich and the Hindu petty bourgeoisie. But this was always an unstable relationship since colonialism could wean away the rural rich through selective concessions. By the turn of the century the political and institutional schism between Hindus and Sikhs had probably reached the point of no return, though at the level of lived relationships the divisions were nowhere near as sharp. Nothing symbolized this schism better than the removal of all Hindu idols from the Golden Temple in 1905.

Hindu, Sikh and, to a lesser extent, Muslim self-assertion, which all came in the wake of the British conquest of Punjab, also led to a revival of Hindi in the Nagari script, Punjabi in the Gurmukhi script and Urdu. This kind of regional linguistic resurgence was, of course, found in other parts of India and was an important aspect of the larger process of pan-Indian nationalism. But in the Punjab, unlike elsewhere, Hindus did not identify themselves with the regional language, Punjabi, but with the Hindu mainstream outside, and therefore with Hindi. The Arya Samaj was an active proponent of this orientation and the seeds for communalizing the language issue were well and truly sown. Hindu opposition to Urdu was never as strong as it was to Punjabi/Gurmukhi.[40]

The Rise of the AD–SGPC Axis

Under the Gandhian leadership of the National Movement, participation was extended through mobilizations on the basis of strong existing identities, which in Punjab meant communal/religious identities. There was a perfect parallel between the Khilafat Agitation (Gandhi's attempt to mobilize Muslims for the nationalist cause by endorsing their pan-Islamic sentiments) and his encouragement of the Sikh Gurdwara Movement of the 1920s, through which the highly self-conscious vanguard of reformist Sikhism sought Khalsa control over Sikh shrines. Since the colonial state had acted as the defender of last resort to those mahants (Hindus) who had controlled the shrines, the National Movement objectively promoted as 'nationalist Sikhs' those asserting their identity and rights against the British. Kapur, in the most comprehensive survey of this period, has rightly called this the decisive period in the formation of Sikh community consciousness and in the institutionalization of Sikh communal polities.[41] This successful agitation resulted in the establishment of the Shiromani Gurdwara Prabandhak Committee (SGPC) which today manages the vast network of Sikh shrines in the north. Elected by the Sikh laity at regular intervals, this body can, with some justification, claim to speak for the community as a whole. It is certainly perceived by vast numbers as having this authority. It subsequently spawned a political wing, the Akali Dal or Akali Party (AD). From 1925 till the time of Jarnail Singh Bhindranwale, Sikh politics has revolved around domination of the AD–SGPC nexus. The AD has always been faction-ridden, reflecting the factional character of intra-Jat family and kinship linkages as well as other social cleavages in the Sikh community. In any case, one faction or another of the AD has always controlled the SGPC. Since the mid sixties, the AD itself has become the principal mouthpiece for the rural Sikh peasant proprietor who is likely to belong to one of the Jat sub-castes. The SGPC is not only the treasury of the Akali Dal (donations from devotees run into crores); it is a major source of employment and patronage; it also provides through its temple network unmatched congregational facilities for politico-religious instruction and exhortation. The leaders of the AD have a religious authority which Sikh leaders in the Congress, Communist or other parties cannot hope to match.

Cumulative Communalization

The AD then is a Sikh party and has a vested interest in the preservation and consolidation of a Sikh community consciousness. Important though this fact is, it remains only one input into the cumulative process of communalization in Punjab. Any synthetic appraisal will have to take in the specific tensions created by green revolution 'prosperity', the parallel growth of Hindu fundamentalism inside and outside Punjab, the political rivalry between the Congress and the AD, and the destructive confrontation between Sikh fundamentalist and state terrorism. Only the barest sketch will be attempted here.

The green revolution made the Sikh Jat peasantry the economically dominant class in Punjab, but without commensurate political authority. While Jat Sikhs are the single largest segment of Punjab's Sikhs, the urban non-Jat Sikhs and the Sikh rural poor (Mazhabi or untouchables) are together almost as large. The AD as the class party of the Jat Sikh peasant proprietor has never been able to rely on the support of these two groups. It has also had to face Congress and Communist rivalry for electoral support among Jats. In short, the electoral–political configuration, not to mention internal factionalism, has denied the AD any prospect of stable governance on its own. Objectively, the AD has had two choices – either to pursue the politics of coalition building and political bargaining with non-Congress parties, including Hindu chauvinists like the BJP, or to seek to expand its base among Sikhs by emphasizing its role as primary guardian of the 'panth' (the Sikh brotherhood/sisterhood), a role in which it can only be convincing if Sikh identity is genuinely felt to be under threat.

These choices are not totally exclusive. From the formation of Punjab state in 1966 to the early eighties the AD pursued both approaches, participating in unstable, non-Congress state government coalitions on three occasions. In recent years it has become totally submerged in the second approach, but this was not inevitable and indeed owes much to factors outside its control. This is best exemplified by an important though generally unremarked fact. Ever since the rise of the Bhindranwale phenomenon (and outlasting his death) the fulcrum of Sikh politics has shifted outside the AD–SGPC axis. Since Bhindranwale's death the various fundamentalist groups lack a clear centre or reference point. Despite this, no faction of the AD is able to reassert a stable authority over the principal Sikh shrine, the Golden Temple, or over Sikh politics as a whole. This has given new space to an array of senior religious functionaries (head priests of the major Sikh shrines) to take on at various occasions the mantle of supreme religio-political authority in a way that has no historical precedent. Factional conflict within the AD is sharper and spans a far wider spectrum of views than ever before, with some Akalis flirting very closely indeed with the extremists ('terrorists'). Fundamentalism, though not any single fundamentalist Sikh militant group, dominates the Sikh political scene in Punjab. How did such a situation emerge?

Capitalist modernization of agriculture brought with it unanticipated social effects. The development of the secondary and tertiary sectors did not keep sufficient pace with the employment needs of the growing layer of educated unemployed, mainly the sons of Jat farmers. Thus the seventies, a period of high prosperity for Punjab, was also a period of high rates of Sikh emigration, either to other parts of India or abroad.[42] At the same time Hindu migrant labour poured in, attracted by prospects of seasonal work in the fields or by jobs in the informal sector (rickshaw pulling, street vending, and so on) which were considered unacceptable to graduates. While the 1985 census shows Sikhs at 60.7 per cent of Punjab's population (not that different from 1971) there was and is a widespread feeling that this does not reflect the true demographic position which, according to a 1984 government press estimate, showed the Sikh population down to 52 per cent of the total. Whatever the true figures, the general feeling among Sikhs was that their numbers were declining. This feeling fed community insecurities already heightened by other developments.

Modernization had encouraged laxity (trimming and cutting of hair and beard) in the observance by Sikh males of the physical norms so central to the Khalsa definition of Sikhism. It also promoted a new culture of conspicuous consumption. Punjab soon acquired the unenviable status of having among the highest per capita consumption of liquor and drugs in the country. For a community whose distinctive physical appearance was seen as vital to its preservation as a non-Hindu identity, the identity crisis was real and growing. Bhindranwale started out as just a religious preacher whose puritanical injunctions and pietistic fervour had made a mark and gained him a limited popularity.[43] But his apocalyptic visions of the dangers facing the Sikh community would never have catapulted him to notoriety were it not for other factors, above all the AD and Congress rivalry and the willingness of both to play the communal card.

For the Congress this did not simply mean posing as the defenders of Hindus. This theme became more marked after Mrs Gandhi's return to power in 1980 and took a qualitative leap forward after the February 1983 metropolitan elections in Delhi, when this stronghold of the BJP-RSS was wrested by the Congress. This would not have been possible without the partial endorsement of the Congress by the RSS. Before that, the Congress, through its Sikh leaders (the former President Zail Singh) and as part of a carefully worked out strategy, sought to weaken the AD by encouraging dissidence from its more extreme and fundamentalist flanks. Thus Bhindranwale was early on encouraged to develop a real public authority as a way of weakening the AD's appeal and ensuring that its electoral base remained fatally fragmented.[44]

The AD was under a variety of internal and external pressures to further communalize its political activity. These pressures took the form of a series of agitations over ostensibly secular demands – the implementation of a 1970 central decision to award Chandigarh (the joint capital of the bordering states of Punjab and Haryana) to Punjab solely and redistribution of the Beas-Sutlej river waters. But by themselves these were not demands that could stir the Sikh population as a whole. The AD had to be both the class party of the Jat peasant proprietor and the defender of the Sikh faith under threat.

The Anandpur Sahib Resolution became something of an official charter for this campaign. There were three versions of this Resolution, the original one formulated in 1973, another in 1978 and the most widely accepted one in 1981, authenticated by Sant Harchand Singh Longowal. The charter itself was not as important as what it symbolized.[45] The general drift towards demands for greater political and economic devolution of power is part and parcel of a wider all-India pattern whose driving force is the greater assertiveness of the agrarian bourgeoisie in its various regional and state-based manifestations, in Punjab the Jat Sikh peasantry. But it is the charter's religious dimension (though it was not a religiously inspired document) that gave it a special character as a semi-secessionist tract quite regardless of its specific demands. It demanded greater autonomy and power not just for a region or class but for a religious community. Hence the persistent ambiguity that has surrounded the Resolution with many of its supporters insisting that no objective appraisal of its contents can justify its depiction as a charter for secession or anything like it.

This, of course, misses the point. The AD had to ride the roller-coaster of a progressively communal campaign where one demand followed another. This does not mean that some of its basic secular demands should not have been conceded, for example, concerning Chandigarh. But at best this could only buy time; it could not decommunalize the situation. The Punjab Accord of mid 1985 between Rajiv Gandhi and Sant Longowal came too late, was not properly implemented and failed to secure even a breathing space. The failure of the Accord was symbolized by the assassination of Sant Longowal by Sikh fundamentalists and the collapse of the Akali ministry in Punjab headed by the 'moderate' Surjit Singh Barnala. In May 1987, President's Rule was imposed. Concessions which earlier had some chance of restoring Sikh politics to its traditional course were bound to be less effective after Operation Bluestar (the storming of the Golden Temple by the army in June 1984), the assassination of Mrs Gandhi and the terrible anti-Sikh riots that followed. These events raised new and deeper grievances, including the demand that the Congress instigators of the 1984 anti-Sikh riots be brought to book. Neither these nor earlier demands were conceded, which has understandably only increased bitterness among Sikhs.

Prior to the decisive year of 1984, the three-year campaign of the AD – which it called the 'Dharm Yud Morcha', a religious–political crusade – had had a tremendous impact in mobilizing Sikhs nationwide (and abroad), an impact heightened by the state's failure to concede seemingly reasonable demands. Sikhs became an even more self-conscious community, broadly backing the AD. The campaign also gave powerful new legitimacy to the fundamentalists, who could not only present themselves as the most devoted and courageous defenders of the Sikh faith, but also as that part of the Sikh vanguard with fewest illusions in the Congress-ruled centre and the greatest wariness of 'Hindu perfidy'. By seeking to capitalize on Hindu fears of both the AD and the fundamentalists, Mrs Gandhi's Congress made matters worse.

Through a combination of processes, Bhindranwale found himself at the hub of Sikh and Punjabi politics. Terrorist attacks on both Hindu and Sikh civilians were shocking. But they should not have been given undue political importance. They were and are an expression of political weakness, of the failure of the fundamentalists to generate real popular support for Khalistan or other extreme aims. Nor did these attacks emanate from a single source – Bhindranwale – who by this time (spring–summer 1984) had taken over the Golden Temple. In a manifestation of its essential political bankruptcy, the centre now turned Bhindranwale into a deus ex machina and made his crushing at all costs the litmus test of the state's own authority. Hence Operation Bluestar – a mistake of gargantuan proportions. Bhindranwale bypassed the AD–SGPC axis and relied instead on support from the All-India Sikh Students Federation (AISSF), supposedly the youth wing of the AD. Together, the Congress-ruled centre and the AD had given Bhindranwale a legitimacy he could never have achieved otherwise.[46]

With the departure of Bhindranwale little has changed. In the post-Bhindranwale period the frequency of terrorist attacks by fundamentalists and the rate of casualties has exceeded past records. The

AD–SGPC is far from restored to its earlier eminence. Even though there is no Bhindranwale-like figure, the fundamentalists and a confusing assortment of religious hangers-on are in the saddle, with the Golden Temple still up for grabs. The reasons are clear. The basic issue in Punjab is not terrorism or Sikh fundamentalism but communalism. The 'moderate' communalism of old AD politics is not the answer, especially in an environment where Sikh separatist consciousness has crossed an emotional and psychological Rubicon, becoming for the first time a deeply defensive minority consciousness. Operation Bluestar and the November 1984 riots were irrevocable turning points. State terrorism (out of the 1,000 killed in Operation Bluestar, 400 were reported to be pilgrims) as a response to fundamentalist terrorism has only succeeded in greatly worsening the situation.[47]

Yet the only strategy which the centre and its well-meaning secular defenders (including the mainstream left) can offer is to insist on a law-and-order approach for the interregnum (which can stretch over an uncertainly long period) until, somehow, the 'moderate' factions of the AD–SGPC nexus are restored to regional authority in Punjab.[48] They maintain this perspective notwithstanding the fact that the general spectrum of AD's factional politics has now expanded to include more extreme groupings. In fact the moderates are less moderate and the extremists more extreme than ever.

In partial acknowledgement that there are broader problems involved in the issue, the centre has made half-hearted statements about the need to further industrialize Punjab.[49] No doubt this was one major reason why New Delhi cleared the controversial Pepsico project – a multi-national collaboration in agro-industry. But Punjab is already the granary of India. It has a major geo-strategic importance since it borders the main invasion routes into and from Pakistan. Large-scale industrialization would therefore only give Punjab even greater objective importance than it already has. It is inconceivable that the centre would tolerate, let alone encourage, such a development given the present turmoil in Punjab and the continuing challenge from the fundamentalists.

What Way Out?

Any permanent way out of the Punjab imbroglio must rest on conscious attempts to build a powerful and genuine anti-communal front which will unreservedly attack both Hindu and Sikh communalism and seek to mobilize ordinary Hindus and Sikhs in and outside Punjab against both state and fundamentalist terrorism. Such a struggle must also be part of a larger social and class struggle.

Some popular mobilizations by the left in Punjab have shown the strengths of the bonds between ordinary Hindus and Sikhs. The Hindu–Sikh relationship is still much closer than the Hindu–Muslim one. The CPI and CPM make the grave mistake of refusing to acknowledge that state terrorism is as dangerous as fundamentalist terrorism. This leads them to search for a secular solution which the centre and the moderates in the AD can help to bring about. This is something like a new, more thoughtful and coherent, Punjab Accord as a prelude to 'political normalization'. This is not at all a convincing perspective. But, unfortunately, it seems to be the lesson the mainstream left has drawn from recent events. Given the enormity of the problem, and the difficulties of constructing an effective anti-communal front, the most likely future scenario is (even allowing for crucial differences between the two situations) something resembling Ulster. There can be a near permanent occupancy of Punjab by central repressive forces. Opposition insurgency can probably sustain itself for a long time to come at a high enough level to rock government authority periodically, even if it cannot displace or destroy it. Thus, the Punjab problem will simmer on.

Notes

1. P.N. Rajgopal, *Communal Violence in India*, Uppal Publishing House, 1987. According to Table I (pp. 16–17), the number of incidents, the numbers killed and injured have all shown rising average trends. Taking years which are not characterized by any exceptional outbreaks, the figures for 1955, 1965, 1975 and 1985 give a good indication of the trend. The number of incidents, killed and injured in each case were respectively 75, 24, 457; 173, 34, 758; 205, 53, 890; and 525, 328, 3665. In 1961, 61 districts were affected by riots; in 1970 this went up to 216 districts. In July 1986 the home minister in parliament said 88 districts were hypersensitive and 98 were sensitive. The states particularly affected by communal conflict are Assam, West Bengal, Bihar, Uttar Pradesh, Gujarat, Madhya Pradesh, Maharashtra, Karnataka, Kerala and Andhra Pradesh. Most riots take place in districts where the Muslim population varies between 15% and 60%. The virus has spread to rural areas which in 1985 accounted for 46% of all reported incidents.
2. B. Anderson, *Imagined Communities*, Verso, London 1983.
3. L. Dumont, 'Nationalism and Communalism' (Appendix D), in *Homo Hierarchicus*, OUP, Oxford 1988, p. 318.
4. B. Wilson, 'Secularisation, Religion in the Modern World', in Sutherland, Houldon, Clarke, Hardy (eds), *The World's Religions*, Routledge, London 1988. In certain countries like Belgium and Holland, Catholicism fought back through 'pillarization' by establishing a cradle-to-grave Catholic controlled environment, i.e. Catholic schools, universities, hospitals, professional associations, insurance schemes, etc. Eventually secular criteria came to dominate the functioning of these institutions. 'Pillarization', according to Wilson, failed.
5. Both S. Krishna, 'Problems of Integration in the Indian Political Community' and R. Kumar, 'Secularization in Multi-Religious Societies', in S.C. Dube and V.N. Basilov

(eds), *Secularization in Multi-Religious Societies*, Concept Publishing Co., New Delhi 1983, stress the cellular character of Indian society where 'tolerance is high and integration is low'.

A contrasting perspective is to be found in A. Nandy, 'An Anti-Secularist Manifesto', in *Seminar* 314, 1985. Nandy has useful insights but suffers from an anti-historical idolization of 'traditional' society and of 'folk religion'. Others more historically and sociologically oriented have stressed that the 'traditional' tolerance of Hindu society was rooted in a certain structure of social relations which could not be sustained forever. Facing breakdown, the 'tolerance' that was associated with it had to come under pressure. In such a view, Gandhi's role in promoting communal cleavages comes in for sharper criticism than Nandy would ever make. His veneration for the 'popular consciousness' of the masses, or 'peripherals' as he calls them, leads him to underestimate the strength of the links between 'zealots' and 'peripherals', the dangers of a singular Hinduism-in-the-making and to a glorification of popular practices which too easily degenerates into semi-apologies for caste and gender oppression.

6. S. Saberwal, 'Elements of Communalism – Part II, in *Mainstream*, 28 March 1981.

7. D. Miller, 'Six Theses on the Question of Religion and Politics in India Today', in *Economic and Political Weekly* (*EPW*), 25 July 1987. Miller correctly recognizes the 'emergence of the entire spectrum of identity politics' during the British Raj, but is disappointingly dismissive of the need for secularism and correspondingly sanguine about the rising strength of collective religious loyalties.

8. R. Thapar, 'Historical Realities', in Ramjilal (ed.), *Communal Problems in India – A Symposium*, K.P.S., Gwalior 1988, pp. 82–3.

9. L. Dumont, *Homo Hierarchicus*, R. Kumar, 'Secularization', and in his *Essays in the Social History of Modern India*, OUP, Oxford 1983; T.N. Madan, 'The Historical Significance of Secularism in India' in Dube and Basilov, *Secularization*, are all in sharp opposition to other historians of the nationalist era like B. Chandra, *Communalism in Modern India*, Vikas, New Delhi 1984, for whom nationalism and communalism constitute basic oppositions.

As a measure of how Congress had failed to secure Muslim loyalty, in 1938 out of a total Congress membership of over 3 million only 100,000 or 3.2% were Muslims.

10. L. Dumont, *Homo Hierarchicus*, pp. 324–5. See also the Introduction in J.W. Bjorkman (ed.), *Fundamentalists, Revivalists and Violence in South Asia*, Manoharlal Publishers, New Delhi 1988. 'It was sheer good fortune plus the adroit political tenacity of Gandhi that Hindu extremists like D.V. Savarkar of the Mahasabha or M.S. Gowalkar of the RSS remained a marginal force throughout the freedom movement.' (p. 15)

11. This is what M.N. Srinivas, *Caste in Modern India and Other Essays*, Asia Publishing House Bombay 1962, has to say about Gandhi's technique. 'India was thought of as "Mother India", *Bharat Mata*, and patriotism was love for one's mother, freeing her from the thraldom of an alien ruler. . . . During the Civil Disobedience Movement, for instance, the resistors (*Satyagrahis*) were garlanded, their faces marked with a *tilak* and *arati*, a solution of turmeric and lime powder kept in a tray . . . Mahatma Gandhi . . . saw God Narayana in the poor (*daridranarayan*), the millennium which he wanted for India was conceived of as *Rama Rajya*, and he shared the Hindu and Jain customs of thought.' (pp. 80–81)

12. R. Thapar, 'Historical Realities': 'In the historical process which we are undergoing at this time, related to industrialization, modernization, the building of a nation-state and other similar experiences, there is a premium on the annulling of segmented, segregated groups and the restructuring of society with larger identities. It is not secularism which brings about the choice of a religious identity which can be used in the game of numbers related to democratic representation and by which groups aspiring to power can manipulate the system.' (p. 85)

13. A.A. Engineer (ed.), *Communal Riots in Post-Independence India*, Orient Longman, Bombay 1984; A.A. Engineer and M. Shakir (ed.), *Communalism in India*, Ajanta, Delhi 1985; I. Ahmed, 'The Political Economy of Communalism in Contemporary India', in *EPW*, 2–9, June 1984; P.R. Rajgopal, *Communal Violence*; G. Krishna, 'Communal Violence in India', Parts I and II in *EPW*, 12–19, January 1985.

14. D.E. Smith, *India as a Secular State*, Princeton University Press, 1963. Smith's views on Hinduism's 'non-political' nature is too unqualified. I am grateful to Romilla Thapar for correction on this point. The term 'dialogue of power' is hers.

15. On the evolution of the Muslim community since 1947, see M. Shakir, *Secularization of Muslim Behaviour*, Minerva, Calcutta 1973; I. Ahmed, 'Secularism and Communalism', in *EPW*, December 1970 and 'The Political Economy of Communalism in Contemporary India', in *EPW*, 2–9, June 1984; G. Krishna, 'Communal Violence'.

16. For a convoluted attempt to condemn the practice of sati while defending the philosophy or idea behind it in ancient India and Hindu mythology, see A. Nandy, 'The Human Factor', in *Illustrated Weekly*, 17 January 1988. In keeping with his general stance, Nandy is both sensitive to the hypocrisies of modern, urban India, and insensitive to the cultural, ideological and material oppression of women in ancient rural India in mythology, tradition and folk culture itself. For effective rebuttals of Nandy's views on sati and sati worship see P. Philipose and T. Setalvad, 'Demystifying Sati', in *Illustrated Weekly*, 13 March 1988; R. Thapar, 'In History', and K. Sangari, 'Perpetuating the Myth', both in *Seminar* 342, February 1988.

17. This point is made with some force in M. Juergensmeyer, 'The Logic of Religious Violence: The Case of Punjab', in *Contributions to Indian Sociology*, January–June 1988.

18. For all its tolerance, classical Hinduism also had grave failings too often minimized by its defenders. The caste system was integral to it and alien to any modern conception of equality and justice. Religious reformers like Gandhi tried to give new meaning to Hinduism by arguing that dharma did not mean fulfilment of caste obligations even while seeking to sustain the integration of caste and religion. Despite attempts of some to situate Gandhi's Hinduism in 'popular' Hinduism, there is in fact a sharp break. The Hinduism of religious reformers like Gandhi, Radhakrishnan, etc., was not the Hinduism of the masses. D.E. Smith, *India as a Secular State*, echoes the views of many when he says, 'In the traditional Hindu society, religion and caste were bound together by the strongest ties of mythology, metaphysics, ethics and ritual. It was only a radically reformulated Hindu religion which frankly accepted modern democratic values which could be separated from social institutions based on inflexible inequality.'

M.N. Srinivas in his 'A Note on Sanskritization and Westernization', in *Far Eastern Quarterly*, Vol. 15, 1956, went as far as saying of popular religion, 'If and when caste disappears, Hinduism will also disappear.' (p. 495)

19. Given Hinduism's multiple sects and pluralist character it might be more accurate to talk of Hindu ideologies-in-the-making. The directions that the various forms of a resurgent and self-redefining Hinduism will take are likely to be diverse and all its points of consummation or crystallization cannot be predicted in advance.

20. G. Pandey, *Nationalism vs. Communalism: The Nationalist Discourse*, unpublished paper, January 1988. Courtesy of the Centre for Social Studies, Surat, Gujarat.

21. B. Chandra, *Communalism in Modern India*. For a sound if unnecessarily polemical critique (Chandra does try to qualify some of his major propositions) see Randhir Singh, 'Theorising Communalism', in *EPW*, 23, July 1988. Singh is particularly scathing about the idealized view of some nationalist historians whom he says take it for granted 'that to speak up for nationalism is ipso facto to be secular and democratic' (p. 1543). He correctly reminds us that nationalism and Hindu communalism are compatible and that Independence was achieved in 1947. To be 'nationalist' today can so easily mean being for the ruling classes. Where Singh falters is in presenting an adequate alternative definition of communalism as the starting point for developing a better paradigm. He also exaggerates the fragility of India's democracy.

22. Contrast this with the views of S. Saberwal, 'Elements of Communalism'. Saberwal is much more sensitive to the question of 'cultural integration', the way in which cultural and religious conceptions are symbolized, and transmitted across generations, i.e. the question of socialization of religious identities in the early pre-reflective years of childhood, and hence in the unconscious.

23. Religious communities do have common secular interests. These are invariably cultural, psychological and emotional, touching 'core' loyalties. To speak of a core

identity does not mean these are immutable or always dominant. But it does emphasize how difficult they can be to erode or push back. When communal tensions become very sharp then as R. Singh ('Theorizing Communalism'), perceptively points out, the very security of life, family and property push people to assert and deepen religious solidarities because this is seen as the only *practical* and *realistic* way to attain some measure of protection and security, both emotional and physical. Religious solidarities become even more meaningful, in turn giving deeper, sacred meaning to the exclusivist demands of the community as formulated by its often communal leaders.

There is a conspicuous unsureness in Chandra's attempt to deal with the relationship between religion and communalism. At one point he comes out strongly against 'religiosity' (as distinct from religion) which he defines peculiarly as the invasion of religion into other spheres of life. So religiosity, which by this definition is automatically anti-secular, is bad while religion is not. But all religions (as world views) seek to permeate other spheres of life besides the private and purely spiritual, the Indic religions even more so than Christianity which was in this respect historically 'tamed'. That is to say, religiosity as Chandra defines it, is *intrinsic* to all religions!

The problem is that there is an obvious connection between the growth of religious fundamentalism and growing communalism. One way of seeing the link is to define it as 'religiosity'. This is, however, only a secondary aspect of fundamentalism. Its main importance lies not in its insistence on extending religion's reach but in the way it insists upon the assertion of a collective religious identity. 'Religiosity' and public festivities are some of the ways in which this collective identity is to be expressed, built and consolidated. In short, fundamentalism is a latent property or potential phase of all religions!

24. In Britain during the seventies, organizations of the predominantly white left adopted a similar approach regarding the relationship between racism and fascism, often to the great irritation of black anti-racist groups.

25. Again, the parallel with the way the National Front in Britain (and now in France?) was perceived is striking. In actual fact it is the Conservative and Labour Parties which must bear the greatest responsibility for institutionalizing racism in Britain, a role facilitated by the pressure of the National Front.

26. It is not out of place, therefore, in Chandra's scheme of things that his book should devote a whole chapter to the writing of history textbooks and the communal treatment of history. Academics thus become among the most important sources of communalism as 'producers' of ideology. So their role in bringing about communal harmony is greatly exaggerated even as their responsibilities in the anti-communal struggle are minimized. What becomes required of them is that, above all else, they fulfil their professional duties honestly and accurately, i.e. provide anti-communal teaching and writing. Since the struggle against communalism becomes divorced from the struggle for socialist transformation, the anti-communal academic is not really required to question his relationship to the working-class and socialist movement or bridge the gap between the worlds of theory and practice.

27. It follows that proponents of such a view would give blanket endorsement to Operation Bluestar and largely uncritical support to the state's 'anti-terrorist' activities in Punjab.

28. The basic foundation of Chandra's view that the Indian state is secular is: (a) that it was the culmination of an essentially secular nationalist movement; and (b) the Indian constitution is secular in its basic provisions.

29. Kemalist and post-Kemalist Turkey, and Iran during and after the Shah provide powerful evidence of this displacement phenomenon.

30. For Marx, secularization did not merely mean freedom of religion but freedom from its tyranny.

31. Many of the ideas presented here were foreshadowed in my earlier article, 'Towards a Marxist Understanding of Secularism: Some Preliminary Speculations', which appeared in *EPW*, 7 March 1987 under the pseudonym S. Khan.

32. The debt to Althusser is obvious.

33. If a section of the church becomes a part of the socialist-democratic project of 'power to the people ' (as in Latin America) then it hardly matters if the impulse to

strengthen popular power is partly religious in inspiration (Liberation Theology). The end result is a *practical* secularization and erosion of institutionalized religious power. In any case, the Latin American experience has little resonance here. Even the 'liberation theology' currents within the Christian churches in India are largely fraudulent and better seen as part of the internal struggle for greater power and authority for the church hierarchy of third world countries. The exceptions are certain priests/nuns – activists in Kerala, and Christian Marxist influence in the Naga struggle for liberation.

34. E.M. Wood, *The Retreat From Class*, Verso, London 1986, pp. 164–6.

35. A thoughtful account of the necessary interconnection between the 'permanent revolution' and secularism in most of the Islamic world is S. Jaber, 'The Resurgence of Islamic Fundamentalism', in *International Marxist Review*, spring 1987.

36. Muslim Personal Law should be scrapped in favour of a uniform civil code. But the agitation against it took a communal colouring because it focused on 'Muslim backwardness' rather than the backwardness and oppressiveness of all religious-based and religious-influenced personal laws vis-à-vis women and children particularly. Such an approach would not single out Muslim Personal Law but attack all religious codes – Hindu, Muslim, Christian, Sikh, Parsi – for their culpability in this regard. It is not Muslim identity that would be the issue but the fundamental rights of women and children regardless of the religious communities they belonged to.

37. The point is well made by R. Melson and H. Wolpe, 'Modernization and the Politics of Communalism', in *American Political Science Review*, December 1970.

38. R.E. Frykenburg, 'Fundamentalism and Revivalism in South Asia', in J.W. Bjorkman (ed.), *Fundamentalists, Revivalists*.

39. For a discussion of the rise of the Arya Samaj and its contribution to the emergence of a Punjabi Hindu identity, see R.G. Fox, 'Urban Class and Communal Consciousness in Colonial Punjab', in *Modern Asian Studies*, July 1984.

40. The written script for Punjabi that was most widely used before independence was Persian. After partition the question of its replacement by either Devnagari or Gurmukhi became central and immediately took on communal political overtones.

41. R.A. Kapur, *Sikh Separatism*, Vikas, New Delhi 1987 is the best account so far of the systematic development of Sikh community identity and of how the AD–SGPC nexus came to dominate Sikh politics. Its weaknesses are those of omission. It has little to say on the role of the Arya Samaj or on the communal politics of the Congress-ruled centre. Implicitly the responsibility for the present communal mess is placed almost overwhelmingly on the AD–SGPC's manipulation of the Sikh 'identity crisis'. There is also the misplaced assumption that what was so in the past – AD–SGPC domination of Sikh politics – would carry on in the future. The fundamentalist phenomenon is not given sufficient focus and there is no attempt at a synthetic socio-economic, political and cultural explanation of the Punjab problem.

42. The green revolution had more of an impact in Punjab than elsewhere because already by the mid sixties Punjab was the one state which had carried out land consolidation and established a strong irrigation base and sound infrastructural facilities in such key areas as power, credit, roads, research, seeds, etc. As the benefits of the green revolution tapered off, basic class tensions between Sikh Jat farmers and urban Hindu traders/creditors also sharpened. These were the two main beneficiaries of the green revolution. The farmers needed the trader/creditor but the financial level at which exchange and loans were organized was very often a bone of contention. The farmer often felt unfairly treated. There was also growing rivalry between aspiring Sikh urban traders (non-Jats) and their much more numerous and powerful Hindu class competitors. These inter- and intra-class tensions were not always articulated as such but too easily took on a communal hue. The acute class conflict between Sikh landless (usually an untouchable or Mazhabi) and the Sikh peasant proprietor or landlord could also be substantially diffused through the appeal to communal solidarity.

43. M. Tully and S. Jacob, *Amritsar: Mrs Gandhi's Last Battle*, Rupa Press, Calcutta 1985.

44. Ibid.

45. It is largely forgotten that during the fifties the Akali Dal passed a resolution

demanding that the centre's role be limited to foreign affairs, defence and communications. See A.S. Narang, *Storm Over Sutlej*, Gitanjali Publishing House, New Delhi 1983, p. 213.

46. Punjab, which has a lower than average unemployment rate compared to other states, has a slightly higher than average rate of educated unemployed, but not significantly higher. What is important is that a very sizeable proportion of these youthful unemployed had the AISSF as their organizational and social magnet. See P. Wallace, 'The Dilemma of Sikh Revivalism', in J.W. Bjorkman (ed.), *Fundamentalists, Revivalists*.

According to one of the very few sample studies of captured 'terrorists' by S. Dang, *Genesis of Terrorism*, Patriot Publishers, New Delhi 1988, almost 50% come from a rich landlord or peasant background. Very few landless are in the 'terrorist' ranks; over 60% are in the 20–30 age range; 75% of the sample had Akali backgrounds (pp. 33–5).

47. P. Wallace, 'The Dilemma of Sikh Revivalism'.

48. The bourgeois perspective enjoying perhaps the widest consensus is one of 'managing communalism' rather than seeking to deracinate it. The idea is to physically capture or eliminate the 'hardcore' Khalistanis and then organize a near permanent Jat Sikh political dominance in Punjab exercised through an AD purged of its 'extremists'. This AD, if it cannot rule alone, will have to seek coalitions either with the Congress or non-Congress forces. This could well be characterized as the 'Kashmir solution', i.e. substantial autonomy and the acceptance of the near permanent regional ascendancy of a communal party.

49. See G.K. Chadha, *The State and Rural Economic Transformation: The Case of Punjab, 1950–85*, Sage Publications, London 1986. 'The Punjab experience clearly suggests that in a federal economic structure there are definite limits to agro-industrialization. The stimulus for industrialization cannot be sustained by agriculture alone, however rapidly it may be growing' (p. 54).

5

Agencies of Change

Indian Communists: From Birth to the Emergency

The general failure of the Indian left to recognize that since independence India has been essentially capitalist (however backward) and bourgeois democratic (however weak in comparison to Western democracies) prevented it from theoretically coming to grips with reality. This failure has a long history. Communists of the National Movement period never grasped the relative strength and autonomy of the Indian bourgeoisie and hence its fundamental conflict of interest with British metropolitan capital. Nor did they ever properly understand the nature of the Congress as both party and movement, or Gandhi's strategy of periodic and escalating compromise as the route to independence.

Overstreet and Windmiller have summed up Communist history in the National Movement era as a series of alternations between anti-capitalism and anti-imperialism.[1] More accurately, the Communists failed to be both anti-capitalist and anti-imperialist in a consistent, principled manner while retaining tactical flexibility. Their oscillating and confused orientation to the Congress meant that Communists either opposed it from the outside as a tool of a weak bourgeoisie subordinate to British capital and the colonial state or gave it uncritical support at times when its character as a mass movement became blatantly obvious.

The late formation of the CPI made it more susceptible to outside – that is, Comintern and British Communist Party – influence.[2] But the inability of Indian Communists to steer the struggle for national liberation in a more revolutionary direction transcending bourgeois nationalism was not the result primarily of Comintern tutelage.[3] The problem was a general failure to comprehend the Indian social formation, its basic class configurations, the character of colonial rule, of the post-independence state, and the character and evolution of the Congress.

177

At the time of independence, Indian Communism was essentially a regional force with significant presence in West Bengal, Kerala, Bihar, Tamil Nadu and Andhra Pradesh. In the eastern part of the last named province, Telengana (in what had been the princely state of Hyderabad), from 1946 to 1952 the CPI led a mass movement of impoverished peasantry which affected 3.5 million people in four districts comprising 44,000 square miles. What began as a struggle against autocratic rule and an agrarian system of brutal semi-feudal exactions degenerated into unpopular rural terrorism largely because Telengana Communists were unable to change perspectives and tactics once Hyderabad acceded to the Indian Union and the newly independent and popularly backed Congress government and its army intervened.[4]

Telengana witnessed an incipient Maoism which had taken root even before Maoism was formulated as a rival world outlook to Moscow's official *weltanschauung*. In 1948 the CPI, under a new general secretary, B. K. Ranadive, adopted what came to be known as the Ranadive Line. Refusing to recognize the reality of political independence, the CPI's central leadership made an ultra-left turn and called for urban insurrection and general strikes against the Nehru government, which retaliated with mass arrests and proscription of CPI activities. In 1951, when independence could no longer be doubted, the CPI repudiated the 'left adventurism' and 'sectarianism' of 1948, paving the way for a positive re-evaluation of the Congress. Throughout the fifties and sixties, Congress nonalignment and promotion of state capitalism (with Soviet and East European help) won at first grudging and eventually enthusiastic CPI support. Soviet theorizations about a 'non-capitalist path of development' in the first stage of the Indian revolutionary process further compounded Communist illusions.[5]

Despite the ineptitude of its political analysis, the CPI grew at all levels during the fifties. Its trade union federation, the AITUC, rose from 422,851 in 1956 to 537,567 in 1958, though it stagnated thereafter. In 1951 the CPI right wing put forward a 'tactical line' emphasizing the importance of electoral participation 'for mobilizing and unifying the democratic forces and exposing the policies and methods of the present government'. This perspective was incorporated in 1958 in the CPI's constitution. The 1957 CPI victory in the Kerala state assembly elections made international headlines: it was the first time a Communist party in the non-Communist world had been elected to power at even a regional or provincial level. This experience was a decisive turning point in the process whereby the CPI became committed to a 'peaceful transition' to power. This orientation was not shaken by Nehru's imposition of President's Rule in Kerala in 1959, when he took advantage of Nair and Christian hostility to the CPI administration's attempt to secularize the state's education system. The CPI's most notable achievement in office was the Agrarian Relations Bill which safeguarded tenant interests in a region which had the most complex system of tenurial relations in India.[6]

The 1964 split was triggered off by the Sino–Soviet conflict but had much more to do with internal factional differences over how best to characterize the Indian state and the Congress, and therefore, how best to move forward. The CPI right believed the Congress represented a nationalist and anti-imperialist bourgeoisie and emphasized the need to unite with its 'progressive' (Nehru) wing against its 'reactionaries' and other reactionary parties like the communal Jan Sangh and the pro-monopoly Swatantra Party and 'feudal' elements (princes and landlords). The CPI left, which split to become the CPM, saw Congress as representing the big bourgeoisie and feudalists collaborating with foreign capital. The CPM was also strongly electoralist but did give greater emphasis to extra-parliamentary mobilizations. It scorned the crude anti-Chinese chauvinism which arose in the wake of the Sino–Indian border conflict of 1962. The Chinese Communists initially welcomed the CPM's formation but in response to the latter's careful aloofness over the Sino–Soviet conflict subsequently shifted support to the CPI(ML) (Marxist-Leninist) movement. The Sino–Soviet conflict and the break up of the Stalinist monolith did, however, help lessen CPM fears of international ostracism.

The CPI had a more realistic awareness of the national and independent character of the Indian state and bourgeoisie. But the CPM analysis did have the dubious merit of allowing it greater freedom to define the 'progressive' section of the bourgeoisie as and when it saw fit – sometimes it was the small bourgeoisie, sometimes the regional bourgeoisie. Thus the theoretical foundations were laid for pragmatic alliances with non-Congress bourgeois parties. Since then, the theorization has disappeared, but the pragmatism remains.

After the split, the CPI emerged as the larger of the two parties, with a broader but thinner spread. The All India Trade Union Congress (AITUC) split in 1970 with the CPM forming the Centre of Indian Trade Unions (CITU). Both Communist parties have had uneasy relations since, often distrusting each other as much as they did the bourgeois parties. They shared power in the sixties in coalition governments in Kerala and West Bengal. In Kerala, the CPI and CPM fell out after two years of cohabitation, with the former continuing to rule through Congress support. In West Bengal, the centre imposed President's Rule on two occasions after 1967 before Congress swept to victory in 1972 on the post-Bangladesh euphoria. The most important legacy of that period was the emergence of the CPM and Congress as the two major forces in

West Bengal politics, with the CPM's base there being stronger among the Hindu Bhadralok and migrants from East Bengal than the urban and rural proletariat.

The Emergency was a shock to both mainstream Communist parties, especially to the CPI because of its support for Congress and the Emergency. Though the CPM, in contrast, opposed the Emergency, it took no serious part in actively resisting it. Underground activity was left to the far left, a wing of the Socialist Party and the right-wing RSS. The end of Emergency forced the CPI to make a dramatic reassessment of the Congress party and, ever since, the CPI majority has been anti-Congress and has joined the CPM in declaring that it is an 'authoritarian, anti-democratic force'.

A Peculiar Trajectory

The trajectory of Indian Communism, especially of its two most important components, the CPI and CPM, is unique. Its basic historical features have been factionalism, split and convergence, but not reunification. This experience has been very different from that of any other major Communist movement in the world. Certain schisms in Communism, for example, within American Communism in the thirties, were obviously related to the inner-party conflicts of the CPSU, the contestation between a classical Marxist world view and a Stalinist-National Communism. But such tensions pre-date the emergence of Indian Communism as an organized force.

But even in comparison with the other large Communist parties of Asia, primarily those of China, Vietnam and Indonesia, one is struck by the absence of even a partially effective fusion of communism and nationalism in India. Such a fusion elsewhere surely presupposed the establishment of a programmatic unity on strategic issues so even if party factions existed their differences would be much more related to tactical issues and less likely therefore to carry over into a split. Once state power had been conquered and the Stalinist symbiosis between party and state established, the tendencies toward schisms within a Communist party would only be resolved through purges. Even those Communist parties (North Korea, Outer Mongolia) which rode to power on the backs of the Soviet state have reproduced the monolithism of their Soviet patron.

It is certainly tempting to postulate that the exceptionalism of the Indian situation both pre-independence (the relative strength and autonomy of the indigenous bourgeoisie, the complex nature of the National Movement and of Congress) and post-independence (backward capitalism, bourgeois democracy) posed exceptionally complex tasks for Indian Communism. A factional dynamic was therefore inherent in Indian Communism to a degree unknown elsewhere.

Certainly, even before the 1964 split, the strength of factional pulls in the CPI compared to other Communist parties is striking. The failure, for various reasons, to establish a strong centre further reinforced those factional pulls and helped to institutionalize them. Another result of this centrifugalism in the CPI was that the central leadership had relatively little knowledge of what was going on in the provincial units, a fact which was constantly lamented in Central Committee reports throughout the fifties. What passed for a central leadership was more a collection of leaders who had little national standing but strong local bases whose relative strength gave them their standing within the party.

The geographical and social heterogeneity of India may have to be given pride of place in explaining the existence of a weak party centre and of the existence and persistence of factionalism in the CPI, later in the CPM, and in Indian Communism in general. But these factors are not sufficient to explain why the bifurcation took place and why, despite the existence of factionalism in today's CPI and CPM, there is not the slightest likelihood of a major schism taking place in the near future in either party.

The 1964 CPI–CPM split did not take place along geographical lines. The regional strongholds of the CPI and CPM were the same, though the latter was the stronger force in Kerala and West Bengal. If the split itself is puzzling, its persistence is even more so, especially in view of the politically and ideologically underdetermined character of the undivided CPI. This last point needs to be qualified. In Andhra, an incipient Maoism did take root early on. This trend, which broke along with the CPM and subsequently became part of the Marxist-Leninist (ML) break from the CPM, did generate a virulent polemical dynamic in which initial divisions were theorized into rival world outlooks.

The 1964 split sprang directly from political and ideological differences and was not the refracted expression of other, more important material (regional, social) differences. These political differences had to do, above all, with the contending evaluations of the Congress and of the class character of the Indian state. From its formation till independence, the CPI's inability to recognize the dual character of Congress meant that the CPI *as a whole* swung from one strategic line to the other, even as factionalism flourished within it. Factional divisions did not harden. Members of one particular faction could and did shift their allegiances to others. After independence, the Congress rapidly lost its character as a movement and emerged more clearly as a class party. It was no longer a question of the CPI as a whole swinging from opposition to support and back, but of the need to clarify a long-term stand vis-à-vis the Congress as a bourgeois party. Factionalism now had to harden. The 1948 Ranadive line divided the CPI on this issue of strategic support for or opposition to the Congress; it is no surprise that the 1964 split at the leadership level broadly coincided with the division that took place at this level so many years before over the Ranadive Line.

In the period between 1964 and 1977 the CPI adopted a position of strategic support to the Congress and the CPM a line of opposition. However, neither party was consistent. In 1967 the CPI was a partner in the SVD ministry in Bihar; in 1969–70 the CPM aligned with the Indira faction in Congress. In this same period the CPM shed its left wing of ML supporters and sympathizers. The end of Emergency in 1977 was a decisive watershed for the CPI. From that point onwards, for the first time, a majority of the post-split CPI adopted a strategic posture of opposition to the Congress. Further facilitating the consequent political convergence of the CPI and CPM was the fact that the CPI shed its right wing (the Dangeites, who continued to call for strategic support for Congress). It was also helped by the CPM's own drift towards Moscow.

Only in the eighties did the CPI and CPM begin talking of merger. It is programmatically impossible to justify any longer their separate existence. In this present context one is forced to conclude that the bureaucratic self-interests of two distinct leadership structures (raising the question of how to share the spoils in a unified command structure) constitute the decisive obstacle to a unification which would substantially improve the prospects for radical advance in India. It is noteworthy that at the Thirteenth Congress of the CPI (held in Bihar in mid March 1986), delegates representing the middle and lower ranks of the party were pressing much more strongly than the top leadership for a merger with the CPM.

The Emergence of Naxalism[7]

The Naxalite movement (1967–72) was a product of many things – the domestic economic downturn of the mid sixties, rising social turbulence, growing rank-and-file discontent within the CPM at its increasingly reformist orientation, the worldwide radicalization of youth, the Sino–Soviet split and the image of China as a radical centre of world revolution, enhanced by a general misreading of the Cultural Revolution.

The ML movement was to pass through a number of phases, starting with a tribal uprising in Naxalbari, West Bengal in 1967 which was eventually crushed. The revolt spread to a number of rural areas in the next three years. The most significant uprising took place in Srikakulam, a tribal area in Andhra Pradesh. This state had a Maoist heritage so it is not surprising that Maoist defections from the CPM were heaviest here. In 1968 out of 16,000 CPM members, 3,000 defected with another 4,000 being highly sympathetic to the ML cause and vacillating in their loyalty. After Andhra, the ML was strongest in West Bengal, but was generally weak elsewhere. In Kerala, Naxalite groups emerged but had limited impact. In Uttar Pradesh, Bihar, Punjab and Kashmir, where the CPM itself was weak, ML defections were, relatively speaking, quite significant. In Kashmir the CPM unit collapsed. But the absolute size of these ML groups was very small except in Bihar where Maoism did attain a minimum level of effectiveness. Many of these initial splinter groups retained their separate identities and programmes to the very end, though by mid 1969 a third Indian Communist party, enjoying Chinese support, the CPI(ML), was formed with Charu Mazumdar as its most charismatic leader. Although the CPI(ML) could be considered a movement as much as a party and although the Mazumdar leadership and line was not universally accepted, the political line associated with – 'annihilation of class enemies' – left a decisive stamp on the whole movement. Nonetheless, there were differences within Naxalism on the question of 'annihilation' and individual terrorism, on whether it was right in the first place to form (under Chinese urging) a new party from above rather than letting it spontaneously evolve through struggles from below, on the bureaucratic character of Mazumdar's rule, and on his dismissal of the importance of mass organizations and struggles.

But what was common to all the ML groups was ultimately more important than the differences. For the ML, the economy was semi-feudal and semi-colonial. The state represented the interests of the big landlords, feudal princes and a bureaucratic comprador bourgeoisie. The permanent crisis of the economy automatically translated itself into a social crisis of pre-revolutionary proportions and into a correspondingly high level of latent revolutionary mass consciousness which only needed to be brought to the surface. Since there was no question of the state being bourgeois democratic, there was no question of there being popular support for it. The strategy of armed struggle and Chinese-style 'liberated areas', with the countryside gradually surrounding the cities, was dutifully applied to India. The main force of the Indian revolution, after all, was the peasantry and the principal contradiction was between the feudal elements and the broad masses.

In Mazumdar's perspective, selective annihilation of class enemies would provide the 'trigger' necessary to unleash the storm, bringing the 'seething' revolutionary temper to the surface. The question of the transitional measures and slogans, including those addressing the land question, that needed to be raised and fought around in order to raise rural consciousness was shelved. There was therefore no need for long-term mass work and mass organizations. The spontaneous fire of the masses and the course of the struggle itself would determine the specific forms of organization needed. An emphasis on secrecy, on the combat group and on violence substituted for patient mass work and systematic politicization of the cadre base. Even those ML groups who were opposed to the Mazumdar thesis and had a mass peasant or tribal base to whose needs they were responsive could not challenge Mazumdar because his tactical line flowed logically enough from a general perspective common to all of them. In April 1970 the centre of gravity of the movement shifted to Calcutta; its modus operandi became urban terrorism. The initial levy of radicalized middle and upper-middle-class students attracted by the immediacy of the ML's revolutionary promise gave way to newer recruits from the ranks of the urban lumpen proletariat. This helped alienate what sympathy there had been for the Maoists among sections of the urban middle classes. The CPM, in power in West Bengal for much of this period, was faced with its moment of truth. It came down heavily against the CPI(ML) which, for all its faults and weaknesses, had categorically rejected the parliamentary reformism of the mainstream left. The CPM had a positive option: to oppose critically the positions of the CPI(ML) and Naxalism in general and emphasize its own more sober recognition that the Indian state did enjoy a measure of popular support and had to be fought in other ways. It was also necessary (though perhaps outside the capacity of the CPM) to point out the inapplicability of the Chinese and Vietnamese path of revolution for India.

In China the central authority and repressive apparatuses were far weaker, and great political strength was derived by the leadership of the Chinese (and Vietnamese) Communist parties from the fusion of the struggles for national and social liberation. The very backwardness and autarkic character of agriculture and the relative weakness of the urban proletariat compared to the oppressed classes of the countryside also helped determine the particular paths of these revolutions. But these conditions were largely absent in India. Capitalist transformation of agriculture was proceeding fast. Agriculture was much more integrated with industry and the urban economy (it is noteworthy that many of the strongest Naxalite bases were to be found among tribals whose economy and culture were much less integrated into the mainstream); and there was a powerful and highly centralized repressive apparatus. The much greater weight of the proletariat (both rural and urban) should have implied giving much greater weight to such proletarian forms of mobilization as strikes and mass demonstrations.[8]

It was necessary, too, that the left in general extend solidarity and critical support to the ML under repression by the bourgeois state. But the CPM did none of this. Determined to establish its credentials as a 'responsible' regional administration and keen on weakening the CPI(ML), which it perceived as a dangerous rival, it attacked Naxalism and repressed the Naxalites. Incidentally, there is little doubt that the CPI and the bourgeois parties were willing to allow a limited and watchful tolerance to Naxalism because it was seen as a force which could curb growing CPM influence. In any case, by 1972 the ML movement had effectively collapsed, due to its basic political weaknesses and external repression.

The legacy of Naxalism today is a complex one. According to a secret government study in 1983, there were some 35–40 groups laying claim to the ML tradition comprising around 35,000 members. Eight ML groups accounted for 75 per cent of this total and Andhra Pradesh, West Bengal and Bihar were their principal bastions, with some advances in the tribal forested regions of Maharashtra, Madhya Pradesh and Orissa. By 1987 official estimates were still around 30,000 and the areas of operation were the same.[9] Certain things have changed. The movement is irrevocably splintered and some groups have gravitated towards an essentially electoralist perspective involving alliances with bourgeois formations. In West Bengal, there are spasmodic efforts at ideological unity between different ML groups which for the most part have lost their elan and become more and more like ossified sects.

Naxalism is most vibrant in Bihar, Andhra Pradesh and the forested regions in central India where it is the cutting edge of class struggle and rebellion by the rural oppressed. A number of important transformations since the heady days of 1967–72 have occurred. Naxalism's appeal to urban intellectuals has declined sharply, as has its reliance on middle-class urban leaders. It has taken root in specific regions of the countryside with local leaders drawn from the most oppressed layers such as tribals, landless labourers and poor peasants. Thus, it was really after 1977 that Naxalism expanded in Madhya Pradesh, the most forested state in India with the highest percentage of tribals (23 per cent of the total population).[10]

Naxalite violence is no longer a strategic device nor even a central offensive tactic. Even those groups which have armed squads avoid confrontations with the police whenever possible and act more as defensive shields for the Naxalite base among tribals and rural poor or as the mailed fist behind exactions and demands made on the oppressor classes, the rich farmers and forest contractors. Violence tends to be a local and specific response to local and specific problems. There has been a definite shift towards 'mass work' and notions of violence or 'liberated zones' have been integrated into concepts of mass activity. 'Liberated zones', for example, no longer mean areas where the Naxalite writ runs unchallenged or where the state dare not tread; instead, they are areas where the Naxalites are so entrenched within the local population that the police are unable to prevent them from operating or expanding their activities.

Ideologically, previous theory is now recognized as inadequate but there is neither clarity nor unity on what to replace it with. The evolution of China and the Communist Party of China (CPC) and the revelations about the Cultural Revolution have dismayed even the staunchest of former Maoists, even if they have not yet undertaken an adequate re-evaluation of the nature of Maoism. Despite ritual obeisance to the idea of an imminent revolution, most groups do not act on this basis but prepare instead for the long haul. Theoretical inadequacies have promoted an involution whose positive aspect is much greater attention to local grievances and more concrete analyses of local class and caste configurations. The negative side is that there is no chance of a broad unity based on a common programme emerging within the ML movement. Different groups responding to different pressures trace independent paths of development.

The Vinod Mishra (VM) group in Bihar was pursuing the Mazumdar thesis of class annihilation till the end of the seventies. When it then shifted to mass activity its front organization, the Indian People's Front (IPF), made dramatic gains. But the group has become a prisoner of the IPF's very success in becoming a formidable force in state politics. The IPF's class definition has become blurred as middle and even richer peasants have joined its ranks and become prominent leaders. It is succumbing to the temptation of making broad cross-class alliances, joining electorally with the non-Congress bourgeois parties and diluting its programme; the VM group itself is now on the verge of abandoning underground activity altogether.

Apart from the VM and IPF, the other big organizations which together constitute the 'Naxalite menace' are the Maoist Communist Centre (MCC), the People's War Group (PWG), the C.P. Reddy Group, Party Unity, and the P. Vasudev Rao Group. They have mass fronts among tribals, poor peasants and students. The PWG has invited the wrath of the centre, especially after its successful kidnap and ransoming of a senior civil servant in early 1988. So far it has been able to defend itself and retain its base despite severe repression. Its test has still to come as the centre prepares to launch a sophisticated police/paramilitary campaign against it. The PWG has also joined forces with the MCC and there is some evidence that it has been able to acquire sophisticated arms (AK-47 rifles) from sympathizers of the Tamil guerrilla groups in Sri Lanka.

The other ML formations, though not involved in armed actions to the same extent as the PWG, have all got strong roots in certain regions. What was said of the original Naxalbari revolt can be said with at least as much force of Naxalism today: '. . . a cobwebbed, discreetly shadowed corner of the country's socio-economic life – the world of the landless labourer and poor peasants fast being reduced to the landless – leapt into life.'[11] For all its vicissitudes, the best of the Naxalite tradition survives as the living embodiment of militant class struggle in the Indian countryside. It is a constant reprimand to those who would dismiss the potential for independent class action and consciousness by the most oppressed sections of rural society, even if its prospects for carrying out a revolutionary overthrow of the Indian state are negligible.

The Mainstream Left Today

The CPM is the most powerful force on the Indian left[12] (see also Table 12). The CPM first came to power in West Bengal during the 1967–72 period when it had to share authority with a bourgeois formation, the Bangla Congress (which later merged into the Congress). The first period of CPM popular front rule was March to November 1967. The Congress with 41 per cent of the votes got 127 seats. The CPM with 18 per cent got 43 seats and the Bangla Congress 34 seats. With support from the CPI (16 seats) and smaller left groups, the first non-Congress ministry was formed. President's Rule was imposed in January 1968 after the Bangla Congress had brought down the ministry a couple of months earlier. In the 1969 elections, after President's Rule was removed, the CPM with 19.6 per cent of the votes secured 80 seats while Congress with 40.4 per cent of votes got only 55 seats. Bangla Congress achieved 33 seats. The second popular front ministry had to face the turbulent politics of Naxalism and President's Rule was again introduced in April 1970 – this time for two years. In the state elections of 1972, Congress riding high on the post-Bangladesh wave of popularity, got 49 per cent of the votes and 216 seats; the CPM vote did rise to 27.5 per cent and it complained with justification of widespread rigging by the Congress. The most significant feature here was the emergence of the CPM and the Congress as the two principal parties of West Bengal.

In the 1977 assembly elections held after the fall of Emergency the Left Front of CPM, CPI and smaller left parties got 224 out of 296 seats, with the CPM itself securing an absolute parliamentary majority (177 seats on

35.5 per cent of the vote). The Congress collected 20 seats on 20 per cent of the vote, but made an impressive comeback in the 1982 assembly elections, obtaining 36 per cent of the votes but only 49 seats. The CPM with 38 per cent of the votes and 174 seats held its ground then, and again in state elections five years later.

Since 1977 the CPM has enjoyed an unbroken spell of governance. This experience has thoroughly bureaucratized its internal structures and completely consolidated the electoral path to power as the only serious strategic perspective of the leadership. But it is not to be compared to Allende's Chilean Socialist Party or to the 'Unidad Popular'. For all their weaknesses, Allende's government and party were profoundly committed to extending the class struggle and to deepening their support among the oppressed through class-based reforms. Their failure lay in neither expecting nor adequately preparing for the decisive polarization within the Chilean state and society that was soon to take place. The CPM has no such commitment. It seeks to consolidate itself as a better manager of regional interests than the Congress. It is hardly a surprise, therefore, that it should have calmly betrayed its early pledges by seeking to encourage greater public and private (including multi-national) investment in West Bengal through a promise of better and more 'stable' industrial relations, that is, through tight controls on the West Bengal labour force.[13] Unlike Allende, whose class support increased between 1970 and 1973, in the last assembly elections the CPM lost in urban, predominantly working-class constituencies to Congress (I) candidates.

The overall trend has been CPM consolidation in rural areas and relative decline in urban centres. The CPM-led Left Front ministry has extended trade-union rights to government employees and to the police, in keeping with its policy of consolidating itself in the state administration. But it has failed to improve management of the urban infrastructure of transport, power, medical services, and so on. Where the CPM has succeeded is in its agrarian programme, which has widened its rural support while avoiding serious class conflict and polarization. A bias in favour of rural kulaks has been reflected both in what it has done and what it has avoided doing, including not indexing the minimum wage for the rural landless nor imposing any agricultural tax to raise resources internally to finance food-for-work programmes and investment in schools in rural and semi-urban areas. Its most important positive achievement was in the 1977–81 period when over 50 per cent of the two million bargadars (sharecroppers) were registered and were thus able to secure legal tenancy rights. But even this programme was brought to a halt when opposition by the rural rich became too strong to be ignored. To be sure, even this record of partial reforms stands out in comparison to the dismal record of bourgeois parties in government in other states. But the fact is that the CPM has not sought to bring about structural changes in the countryside, only to extend its own support across class lines (hence the administration's provision of seeds, fertilizers, and so on to kulaks, as well as funds to all sections of the rural population).

Between 1978 and 1985 the CPM's membership in West Bengal grew from 43,300 to 136,980. In Kerala in this period the CPM grew from 67,500 to 122,071. Clearly, this dramatic growth in West Bengal would not have been possible without the dilution of recruitment standards and an influx of the kind of cadres who could easily leave and join Congress or any other party if it were to come to power in the state.

CPM rule over more than forty million people is obviously not the same as municipal or regional socialism in London or Emilia Romagna (the 'Red' region of Italy). But the contrasts and similarities may be instructive. For one thing, the focus of CPM activity has been the countryside. For another, the CPM does not share Eurocommunist perceptions about 'advanced democracy' as the bridge to socialism, and is not therefore committed to extending grassroots democracy or developing counter-institutions. Its approach is firmly paternalist. One of the first things it did after 1977 was to revive the panchayat system of administration and reinstate panchayat elections. By doing so it sought to resurrect a system through which it could extend its influence largely through collaboration with the existing rural elite.

The one major point of similarity between, say, a PCI regional administration and a CPM state administration, is a common desire to enhance financial autonomy by obtaining greater constitutional powers to raise resources regionally, as well as laying claim to a larger share of central resources. The CPM, faced with the reality of a differentiated peasantry, wishes to maintain the broadest possible multi-class support by expanding expenditure and provision of benefits. This places it in a continuous fiscal conflict vis-à-vis the centre. Perhaps there are parallels here with the PCI in its efforts to broaden its support among workers and the 'new middle class' in Italy through expansive budgetary policies, or with the way Ken Livingstone's Greater London Council sought popular support for Labour in the UK in the early eighties.

At the programmatic level the CPM has no fundamental differences with the CPI, which made the transition to becoming a reformist workers' party wedded to a parliamentary road to power even earlier. The CPM now shares the CPI's pro-Moscow orientation in world politics and differences over what domestic alliances to pursue are not fundamental. Both parties believe in some form of popular frontism at both the electoral and extra-parliamentary level – that is, a 'left and democratic front', or, as the CPM sometimes prefers to call it, a 'left and secular front'. For the CPM in particular, its two principal objectives at the moment are defence of the Left Front regimes of West Bengal and Kerala from destabilization by the centre and restructuring of centre–state relations to give the states greater autonomy, greater power and a bigger share of centrally controlled resources. The need to consolidate its regional base in eastern India (West Bengal) has become all the more acute because of the greater electoral instabilities in Kerala and Tripura, where opposition parties or fronts can more easily oust Left Front rule, and because of its failure to make even a limited breakthrough in the northern Hindi belt.

Why did Communism succeed in West Bengal, Kerala and to a lesser extent Andhra and fail elsewhere? Selig Harrison long ago correctly pointed to a partial explanation – the CPI/CPM took root where it succeeded in becoming the 'political custodian of regional patriotism'.[14] Its defence of regional parochialism has become all the more important given its historic failure to utilize the opportunities it had during the independence struggle to make a national impact and throw up national leaders comparable in stature to Nehru and Gandhi.

In Kerala and Andhra the CPI's hegemonic role in championing early on the cause of Malayalam and Telugu speaking states undoubtedly enhanced its multi-class regional appeal. But where this was not strongly supplemented by policies and actions in support of the lower castes and classes, CPI influence proved more ephemeral. In Andhra, for example, the CPI built its regional appeal through support of the Kammas, one of the two dominant peasant proprietor castes. During the Telengana uprising, the CPI could get away with not confronting the Kamma rich and middle peasants in the fight against feudal landlords. But subsequently it had to pay the price for refusing to confront the principal exploiting classes of the Andhra countryside. The rise of Telugu Desam as the principal custodian of regional parochialism has further weakened the mainstream left in Andhra. In Kerala, by contrast, Communist support among the low caste/low class Ezhavas sustained its authority long after the linguistic division of states was completed. As the experiences of Tamil Nadu, Maharashtra, Karnataka and Gujarat (all outside the Hindi belt) show, a general policy of support for regional linguistic particularism was no guarantee of Communist growth.

West Bengal and Kerala share, in fact, certain crucial and exceptional similarities which go some way to explain why the CPI and CPM could establish themselves there. The systems of social stratification in these two states have historically been far more complex than elsewhere in India. They are also the two most densely populated states in the Union. Kerala had easily the most complicated system of tenurial relations in the subcontinent. The success of the 1957–59 Communist ministry in stabilizing tenancy rights paved the way for growing Ezhava prosperity and greater internal social differentiation. Ironically, growing caste and class mobility, along with increasing communalization, has undermined the status of Congress and the CPI/CPM as the major parties in Kerala and institutionalized coalition politics in the state. In West Bengal, British colonialism through the Permanent Settlement generated numerous strata of landed intermediaries. The social dislocation was further compounded by a number of partitions of the region, several famines and heavy migration from eastern Bengal/Bangladesh.

In both states non-Hindu influences are stronger than anywhere else, mass literacy and education has a long history and educated unemployment a sizeable presence. This has surely been conducive to the acceptance of rational and scientific modes of thinking and to a rebellious orientation. Forty per cent of Kerala's population is Muslim or Christian. Though Hindus are a majority in West Bengal, the majority of Bengalis as a whole are Muslims. What is more, Brahmanical Hinduism in Bengal has had to confront three powerful religious-cultural forces: Buddhism, Islam and Christianity (British cultural influence penetrated earliest and deepest in this part of India). Hindu unorthodoxy and reformism have flourished more here than elsewhere, playing a vital role in the development of a distinctly Bengali culture, literature and ethos.

In the case of West Bengal in particular, regional grievances have long and deep roots. Its relative cultural, economic and political decline is all the more galling in view of its long cultural pre-eminence in the nineteenth and early twentieth centuries and its leadership of the independence struggle till the advent of Gandhi. The centre of gravity of the National Movement then shifted to the north (Delhi), whose political eminence was firmly established. Even the Congress in Bengal was more left-oriented and critical of Gandhi than elsewhere. Gandhi's espousal of Hindi as the unifying language of the National Movement could not but further nourish Bengali resentments. Protest, then, has been a dominant characteristic of Bengali political life – whether expressed in terrorism (Bengal has a strong terrorist tradition), revolutionary rejection of the status quo, or electoral opposition. Communism has been the vehicle of this ideological protest, the means of asserting a distinct cultural and regional identity. Its driving force has been the dislocated, dissatisfied Bhadralok (urban educated middle class).

The cultural–ideological impediments to the spread of a class-based ideology like Marxism in the Hindi belt have still to be fully explored. Some speculations may not be amiss. Outside the Hindi belt regional identity has largely been anti-Hindi but not anti-Hindu. The transformation of Hinduism from a mode of civilization, a set of practices or way of life into a more dogma-based religious ideology (centred on some text like the Bhagavad Gita) has been more difficult here, especially in the south. Hindu nationalism, with its link to Hindi linguistic chauvinism, is not as strong a force as in the north and west. Congress ideology, remarkably, could contain within itself for a long period the diverse strands of populist welfarism, liberal secularism, Muslim orthodoxy (accommodated in the name of this very secularism) and Hindu nationalism. The electoral alliance of core minorities and Brahmins, which was the voting mainstay of the Congress for so long, was in its own way a reflection of this unusual religious–ideological web. The rise of the middle castes and the growth of communalism have altered the relative weights of these component strands. In general it is the Congress, its political offshoots and right-wing formations like the Jan Sangh (BJP) which have dominated the ideological terrain in the Hindi belt. A left clearly committed to struggle with and on behalf of the most oppressed classes and castes has some chance of rupturing and shifting the terrain. A left strategically committed to competitive electoralism and willing, therefore, to pander to the numerically important intermediate castes has little chance of making a breakthrough. At best, a future merger of the CPI and CPM might somewhat improve its prospects in the Hindi belt.

What prevents a reunification of the CPI and CPM, however, is the very practical problem of how to integrate two distinct bureaucratic structures, each with its own separate chain of command – that is, how to share the spoils of office and leadership. Given their general support to the 'nonaligned' foreign policy of the central government, their opposition to the centre is essentially confined to domestic issues where they seek to present themselves as a more democratic alternative. They are subject to the pressures of the same social forces that affect the other parties, in particular the intermediate castes, and the kulaks. Their support within the working class has been unstable. Both the CITU and AITUC have lost ground, relatively speaking, to the trade union federations controlled by the bourgeois parties.[15] In the wake of the Congress (I) wave in the 1984 Lok Sabha elections, the CPI and the CPM were pushed onto the defensive. But though their parliamentary cretinism and movement away from class struggle politics were the main reasons for this setback, it proved to be a limited one, at least in West Bengal.

The CPI and CPM, unlike others, are cadre parties with relatively coherent programmes. This gives them a stability other bourgeois parties (barring the BJP) lack. The Janata Dal can touch electoral peaks unapproached by the mainstream left, but it can also suffer precipitate declines. In opposition (outside of Bengal) the CPI and CPM will have to give greater weight to class struggle methods and extra-parliamentary mobilizational politics. Electoral disillusionment with Rajiv Gandhi's Congress (I) has benefited the CPI and CPM. But it has also exposed the irrelevance of its strategic orientation – the 'left and democratic' or 'left and secular' front. The initiative is now in the hands of the Janata Dal, not the CPM or CPI. The failure of the 'left and democratic' or 'secular' front strategy is reflected in the fact that there is growing disagreement within the CPM (between West Bengal and Kerala units) on just how to orient to the BJP. Since the Janata Dal, rather than the left, is calling the shots and since its main leaders do not share the left's view on the necessity of politically ostracizing the BJP, some CPM leaders (in particular Jyoti Basu, Chief Minister of West Bengal) have argued strongly for a modification of current left policies and practices so as to draw closer to the non-Congress bourgeois opposition.

There are two problems here. First the BJP's openly pro-Hindu ideology puts it outside the pale of the 'left and secular' or 'left and democratic' front perspective. Even indirect accommodation with it would highlight the failure of this central strategic line of the post-Emergency period. Secondly, the CPM came to power in Kerala a couple of years ago by reversing a strategy it had consistently pursued since 1964 – to defeat Congress at all costs. This meant that the CPM was prepared to forge alliances with avowedly confessional parties representing sections of the Christian and Muslim communities in Kerala. On the face of it, the CPM's recent assertion of the need to eschew communal alliances and forge a true 'left and secular' front was a welcome step forward. In reality it represented a subtle accommodation to growing communal feelings among Kerala's Hindu population. Since a shift of just a few percentage points is enough to give victory to either of the two main coalitions contesting the assembly elections, what the CPM-led 'left and secular' front lost in support from the Muslim League and a wing of the Christian Kerala Congress it more than made up for in Hindu support. The anti-communalism of the CPM was correctly perceived as opposition to *minority* communalism (especially since Kerala's Hindu vote is not organized into support for large confessional parties like the BJP-RSS). Confirmation of CPM hypocrisy was provided by its willingness to be part of the Dravîda Munnetra Kazhagam (DMK)-led front in nearby Tamil Nadu, which included the Muslim League. Nevertheless, the CPM's 'new' line of eschewing alliances with confessional parties in Kerala makes it that much more difficult for CPM leaders acting from there to accept any softening of official hostility to the BJP as advocated by the West Bengal leaders of the CPM.

What impact has the Gorbachev phenomenon had on the mainstream left in India? It has clearly caused more problems for the CPM than the

CPI. Neither party accepts the CPSU's bias towards the ruling Congress but the CPSU has learned to live with this difference. It is not in any case a serious problem since the USSR is concerned above all with New Delhi's external orientation, which it perceives as generally positive. In this it is joined by the CPI and CPM which combine domestic opposition to the Congress with support for its general foreign policy orientation of nonalignment as well as its specific stand on Afghanistan, Pakistan's transition to quasi-democracy, the Indo–Sri Lanka Accord, the 'rescue' job in the Maldives, and the steps taken to improve relations with China. (The Chinese Communist Party has also established official relations with both the Indian Communist parties.)

However, Gorbachev's glasnost, his progressive de-Stalinization and his invocation of universal principles rather than class struggle as the guiding light for international behaviour has distressed the CPM. In contrast, the CPI, always closer to Eurocommunist influence and more open in its internal organization, had little difficulty in welcoming Gorbachev's changes. The CPM has taken much longer to endorse the new perspectives emanating from Moscow and this has not been done without sharp and open dissent from certain CPM leaders. Behaving as if class struggle was no longer important is one thing – openly proclaiming as much is another. For the CPM, with its institutionalized hypocrisy, this is most uncomfortable. But it is Gorbachev's de-Stalinization campaign and his efforts to democratize the Communist party that have most perturbed the CPM. These shafts hit sensitive regions of the CPM's self-image and its ideological and organizational premises. What debate there has been in the CPM over the Gorbachev phenomenon has been carefully confined to the top. The CPM has gradually moved towards a reluctant acceptance of the Gorbachev-inspired changes but has been careful to stress that these are measures germane to Soviet society and that different Communist parties must behave as they see best in their differing circumstances. In short, the CPM has sought to defuse the potential impact of these changes by formally endorsing them while also taking a certain distance from them. The alternative options were either to continue criticism or to remain silent. Either way, it would have caused dangerous ferment within the party. This is not to say that dissipation of any ideological unease is now guaranteed. But CPM leaders have clearly decided that the policy they have adopted is the safest course and the one most likely to contain dangerous tremors.

Following the Tiananmen Square massacre of 4 June 1989 and its bloody aftermath in the rest of China, the CPI refused to condemn Beijing but did express 'concern' and 'sadness' at the turn of events. The CPM, in contrast, publicly supported the Deng crackdown. If certain leaders of the CPM, like the West Bengal Chief Minister, Jyoti Basu, have had to distance themselves from this position, it is because much of the CPM rank and file has been even more shaken by events in China than by Gorbachev. In particular, they cannot perceive why the CPM, which has hitherto prided itself on its independence from Beijing, had to toe Deng's line on this occasion.

The first generation of Indian Marxists came through the National Movement. They were radicalized as much by nationalism as by communism. The second generation were inspired by Maoism. Both these generations have either faded or are fast fading away. The present leaderships of the CPI and CPM are, of course, pushing the leading cadres of their youth and student wings into top party positions in order to maintain internal continuity. This is one reason why one should not assume that these will remain completely politically immobile in the future. But a large and self-consciously Marxist layer of young cadres or activists who can sufficiently compensate for generational decline is not visible. A newer, more educated and in some ways more militant working class is confronted by a relatively primitive and static Marxist discourse. The Gorbachev phenomenon is, in part, a response to just this dilemma in the USSR. The full impact of this momentous development and of Bloody Sunday in China on the Indian Communist movement has yet to work itself out.

The New Movements

In the last decade a substantial radicalization of youth took place outside the circles of the traditional left – including the CPI, CPM and CPI(ML). These radicals were activists in small autonomous structures, groups involved in areas like popular science, education programmes, rationalist associations, health, environmental protection (the Bhopal tragedy provided momentum in this area), women's issues, literary movements (in almost all the regional languages), civil liberties, tribal welfare and housing for the poor. Though many of these activists have strong sympathies with Naxalism and in certain cases these groups were consciously formed as fronts for this or that ML group, in the process of the institutionalization and expansion of their activities, they have become ideologically independent and more broad-based in their support, composition, programmes and activities.

Empirical data on the size and spread of these new movements has yet to be collected. Any assessments are therefore merely guesstimates. Of the new social movements, the largest, however, are undoubtedly the popular science groups, with 15,000 to 20,000 activists up and down the country, and the women's movement. The former is particularly strong in Kerala where the Kerala Shastra Sahitya Parishad (KSSP) is a genuine mass movement in which the CPM is, for a change, gaining important influence. The KSSP has thousands of members and even more sympathizers in Kerala. Amongst its activists are all kinds of professionals. It produces numerous pamphlets and journals. Its children's science monthly *Eureka* has a circulation of over 25,000. The KSSP has evolved dramatically since 1962 when it first emerged as a forum for science writers. Initially linked to the Malayalam language movement (thus making science accessible to the people), it developed an organizational structure during 1967–72 and from the early seventies took a decisive turn towards the countryside, organizing rural science forums and encouraging its urban activists to spend their holidays in the villages.

As a natural consequence of such rural immersion the KSSP began to take an increasingly active interest in some of the basic issues of everyday existence epitomized by its new slogan – 'Science for Social Revolution'. The perspective remains as much developmentalist as Marxist; Indian society is seen as divided into a rich minority with high technology and high consumption and a poor majority with low technology and low consumption. Thus the KSSP's main areas of activity are now 'taking science to the people' (this phrase means different things to different currents within the pan-Indian Peoples' Science Movement), encouraging 'appropriate' technology development projects and addressing problems of education, ecology and health.

In November 1978 the first all-India Convention of Peoples' Science Movements was held, followed by a second one in February 1983. Both were hosted by the KSSP and over twenty other groups participated in the second convention. These included the Lok Vidyan Sanghatana (PSM) in Maharashtra, Rajya Vigyan Parishat in Karnataka, Uttarakhand Sangharsh Vahini (Uttar Pradesh), the Kishore Bharati (Madhya Pradesh), Kalpavriksh (New Delhi), Patriotic and People Oriented Science and Technology (Madras), Eastern India Science Club Association (Calcutta).

Broadly two trends can be discerned in the PSMs. The conservative one attempts to confine itself to providing scientific information and analyses to help grassroots mobilization but does not see itself becoming a vehicle of such mobilization. Its principal aim is to disseminate a scientific temper and outlook. A second perspective sees the PSMs as an integral part of the struggle for dramatic social change; the linkages between the social and natural sciences are more strongly stressed or, to put it somewhat differently, 'the man–nature relationship cannot be divorced from the man–man relationship'. Despite a certain woolliness in their formulation of goals and perspectives, a sizeable chunk of this current is influenced by radical and Marxist thought, often of Western origin.

A third current, of much smaller proportion and consequence, appears to pride itself on its 'indigenous' character, arguing for a rejection of scientific thinking derived from Western intellectual traditions. But it is not at all clear what its own definition of a truly popular and Indian concept of 'science for the people' actually is.[16]

The autonomous Women's Movement of India took shape after the mid seventies.[17] In the pre-independence period the Women's Movement was very much a part of the Nationalist Movement. In the roughly three decades following independence there was widespread optimism; it was thought that the lot of women would steadily improve. The government's development perspectives and its often progressive legislation concerning women seemed to promise much. It was the decline of such hopes and the more clearly perceived gap between pious legal enactments and implementation that led to growing disillusionment.

During the sixties large numbers of women had been mobilized within general movements focused on a variety of social issues. Women participated in significant numbers in the Naxalite movement, the urban anti-price rise demonstrations, the student movements and the general struggles of the rural poor, industrial workers and in certain important tribal movements (such as the 'chipko' or 'tree-hugging' anti-deforestation struggle of the seventies in Uttar Pradesh). In the mid seventies major catalysts were added to this general melange of women in ferment. Urban middle-class women were undoubtedly influenced by the literature and example of the Western women's liberation movement. There was also the undoubted impact of the UN-sponsored International Decade of Women (1975–85) which helped legitimize women's issues. The end of the Emergency was like the bursting of a dam. The time was over-ripe for the emergence of a broad women's movement with a specifically feminist focus; all that was needed was a trigger.

It was provided by the now famous Mathura rape case of 1979–80; the issue of violence against women became the spur for the country's first real autonomous women's movement. Three policemen raped a teenage girl in their custody; the Supreme Court reversed a High Court judgement indicting and sentencing the policemen for this crime. The decision sparked an unprecedented furore. Rape as an issue came out of the closet. There were demonstrations throughout the country as well as a prolonged public debate which forced the Supreme Court to review the matter and eventually to support the earlier High Court judgement. The government enacted a new and somewhat harsher anti-rape law. Other forms of violence against women, hitherto confined to the family, became public issues, including alcoholism, wife-beating and dowry death.

Other issues then emerged in bewildering rapidity: denial of inheritance and land rights, misuse of contraceptives and sex-determination tests (pre-natal female foeticide), the brutality of customs like dowry and sati, forcible prostitution, inadequate divorce and maintenance rights, and child marriages. At the same time the continuing struggle over problems such as housing, access to water and work for the rural poor, developed a specifically feminist orientation while remaining part of the general movement. In urban areas professional women's organizations emerged among journalists, doctors, and so on, which were for the most part but not always concerned with issues of career advancement. Sexism in the print and visual media became issues of debate and mobilization. There has also been an enormous proliferation in various languages of feminist journals, including *Manushi* (English), *Sabla* (Bengali), *Apni Azad Ke Liye* (Hindi), *Samata* (Telugu), *Women's Voice* (Tamil) *Anusaya* (Gujarati), and *Baija* (Marathi). Women's centres offering refuge and support have emerged in cities like Bombay, Pune, Delhi and Kanpur. Cultural forms of mobilization and consciousness-raising such as street theatre groups, songs on tape, posters, exhibitions and jathas (familiarization campaigns) are now part and parcel of feminist activity.

In conclusion, it can be said with confidence that the autonomous women's movement is stronger in India than perhaps anywhere else in the third world. It has a wide geographical range and spans the rural poor and the urban middle class. In Latin America, women are often at the forefront of struggle around general issues. This is true also of India. But the key difference is the existence of a significant and growing movement led by women independent of political parties or other male-dominated structures and focusing on specifically feminist issues. There is also substantial political dispersion in the movement. There are Gandhian/Sarvodaya-influenced groups as well as urban-based socialist feminist groups. To get an idea of the speed with which the women's movement has grown consider the last two all-India conferences. In December 1985 there was a national conference in Bombay of autonomous women's groups committed to women's liberation. There were 350 delegates representing 89 groups throughout the country. These groups ranged in size from a handful to a few thousand. The 1988 conference in Patna, Bihar was attended by some 700 women.

But for all its promise, the autonomous women's movement is not immune to the pressures faced by other specific interest formations. The Indian bourgeois democratic state would not want to confront this women's movement head-on unless absolutely necessary. Such has been its impact that even the CPI and CPM, originally opponents of its autonomy, have allowed the formation of women's caucuses in their mass fronts. But the state and government pursues a calculated strategy of seeking to co-opt such groups with the promise of financial and infrastructural support and through apparent willingness to alter laws in their favour. This is often a double-edged sword. An issue like sexism in the media cannot be tackled by harsher censorship laws which clearly divide feminist responses, for example the Indecent Representation of Women Act. The other problem is that once a law is amended, the struggle which focused on the demand loses its rationale and often peters out, leaving the decisive question of effective implementation by the wayside. Rather than face up to this crucial problem of state power, the dominant tendency within the autonomous women's movement, as indeed among all those groups/movements which go by the name of Non-Government Organizations (or their equivalents), is to ignore it as an unwarranted preoccupation of political traditionalists, Marxist or otherwise.

Regarding the ecology movement, there is some overlap between groups working among tribals and groups concentrating on ecological issues, since betterment of tribal life is intimately connected to preservation of forest cover. Of course, there are many groups addressing themselves to non-tribal environmental issues. Radical groups of hard-core activists concerning themselves with tribal welfare probably number around twenty-five to thirty, which is also the likely number of radical health groups. There is much overlap between ecological, health and popular science groups and between popular science and literary groups. There are close to two hundred literary groups (readers' and writers' groups) operating mainly in the languages of Hindi, Marathi, Bengali, Malayalam and Telugu. Between forty and fifty of these groups have significant popular followings, including the Marathi Granthali in Maharashtra, the Writers' Co-operative in Kerala and a Progressive Writers' Association in the north. Their basic forms of activity are discussion circles and regular publication of books, magazines and pamphlets. Few of them produce regular journals. Invariably, the dominant trend is either liberal or Marxist. Interestingly, these literary movements are relatively strong in parts of the Hindi belt where organized Communism has traditionally been weak. The expansion of these literary groups has been contingent on the spread of literacy since independence. Their audience is mainly among newly educated layers of the 'middle peasantry', Dalits (untouchables), tribals (the effect of the government policy of reservation), urban workers and of course the middle classes.

India's 'combined and uneven development' in the era of late capitalism, with its growing global consciousness of ecological and feminist

issues, has thrown up a variety of problems to which the traditional left
has (with some notable exceptions) responded inadequately. It is hardly
a surprise, therefore, that the regular generational levy of left and far left
recruits has been substantially depleted by this radical exodus into areas
of autonomous activity.

The *economic* reality of India is that people are divided into classes.
The *social* reality of India is that people are divided by caste, sex,
religion, language, region, and so on. The *political* reality is that people
are divided into individual citizens of a bourgeois democratic order who
believe themselves to be self-determining, even though on the economic
and social level they may well recognize and indeed internalize the other,
unequal divisions.

Indian Marxists, however, have too often behaved as if the economic
is the only reality or invariably the most important one. Class has
been allowed to subsume all other divisions. Thus the legitimacy of
autonomous organization by Dalits or women is often denied and the
approach of leftists towards such movements essentially manipulative
and paternalistic, focusing on giving them the 'correct class line' which,
of course, they are best able to provide as a result of their 'superior'
analysis of Indian reality. No wonder participants in such movements
look upon traditional left organizations with suspicion.

To become a part of the tradition of these movements, some of
which have their own long history – for example, the caste struggles in
western India – requires not merely respect for their autonomous forms
of organization but a way of involvement which goes beyond the 'front'
or the 'correct intervention' from outside the tradition itself. One of the
more important historical lessons of the Gandhi-led National Movement
was his ability to incorporate a variety of social movements (particularly
relating to caste and female inequality) into the movement for political
independence. Of course, his thrust was firmly embedded within the
framework of bourgeois principles of equality and legality, but in the
context of Indian social backwardness (the pre-capitalist character of
social and interpersonal relations) this was itself a significant advance.
Interestingly, it has been suggested that the success of the Chinese
Communist Party in rooting itself in the countryside had not a little
to do with its socially emancipatory measures, particularly with respect
to women, even if these were organized and controlled by a male-
dominated party.[18]

In general, the more complex character of state and civil society in a
bourgeois democratic order requires a more sophisticated intervention.
From the beginning of independence the strongly interventionist role
of the state in the economy and in providing a degree of welfare
(institutionalizing a 'social wage' for a section of the population) has

been widely accepted as legitimate. But a sustained programme of left agitation to push the state to socialize health care, for example, on an ever-expanding scale (which would have been a universally popular demand) has been missing. Much the same can be said of the failure to take up consistently issues like continuous expansion of good state-run schools and colleges at all levels, creches, free legal aid, employment schemes, and so on. When such demands have been achieved (such as the Employment Guarantee Scheme) they have become to some extent institutionalized, requiring continuing state support to survive. Withdrawal of this support is then seen as withdrawal of important public rights that have been gained through struggle. Such a perception helps delegitimize, to some degree, the existing state and government.

The same holds true for civil society. In fact, in India, more than in the Western democracies, life for the masses revolves more around culture than politics. Disruptions or agitations at political levels do not automatically filter down to other, more 'lived' levels of civil society, though this is, of course, changing in the wake of mass politicization and the growing reach of the bourgeois democratic state. The left has to think of getting into the pores of Indian society, of setting up a variety of counter-institutions, of *creating* an alternative culture – not just hoping it will spontaneously emerge as a result of the activities of the new social movements.

Much of the work of these new movements has been undertaken or organized by what are called non-government organizations (NGOs), voluntary agencies (VAs) or action groups (AGs). These are a mixed bag ranging from charity groups to development missions (often, in effect, a less bureaucratic and more flexible arm of the state) to militant grassroots organizations to self-conscious non-party political formations with a theorized rejection of traditional forms of left organization and of their supposedly state-centred strategies for social transformation. The CPM, in particular, has reacted with hostility to these NGOs and their dependence on outside, often foreign, funding. But its criticisms have been extreme and often unfair. The most sophisticated defenders of these organizations and their role in civil society are, by contrast, far more balanced in their evaluations.[19]

It is doubtful, however, if they would be prepared to admit that the limitations and weaknesses of the NGO sector as a whole have proved so great that there is little left of its early promise. Criticism of the failed potential of the NGOs is in large measure a criticism also of the new social movements. Today, the overwhelming majority of NGO activists are paid employees rather than genuine volunteers; they have an obvious interest in maintaining the financial lifelines of their organizations.[20] By promoting voluntary service centres in areas such as health, the government is effectively absolving itself of responsibility for socializing health care. What has also become increasingly clear is that these social movements very often have a short life-span, collapsing as a result of loss of cadres or funds or because of various crises affecting individuals, the organizations or their activities.[21] These movements may be against this or that aspect of the system but not necessarily against the system as a whole. Even their gains are not necessarily cumulative nor irreversible.[22]

The best of the voluntary groups and activists involved in the new social movements have proved to be valuable assets and allies in the wider struggle for radical social transformation. But they are not and cannot be a substitute for the proletariat as the strategic locus of this struggle.

One of the main weaknesses of such movements is their tendency to underestimate the power and reach of the Indian state. They maintain illusions about the possibility of achieving social transformation in their field of specific concern without directly confronting this state. This is in keeping with the general tendencies of these movements in Western democracies where they are larger and more developed. But there is less justification for such an approach in India because democracy is weaker and repression stronger and more frequent. This is particularly the case in rural areas where democratic norms are all too often weak or non-existent. In some academic left circles the problem is not so much failure to recognize the capitalist and bourgeois democratic character of Indian society as a tendency to exaggerate the maturity of Indian capitalism and democracy. They have found it possible to combine the latest theoretical concepts from European structuralism and post-structuralism with a Eurocommunist reading of Gramsci to produce their own 'Gramscian' evaluation of the National Movement under Gandhi's Congress. Their sympathy with Gandhi's strategy of 'self-limitation' has led them to propose this as a strategy for the transition to socialism in India today – an India of social movements, hegemonized by a new movement-cum-party (like the pre-1947 Congress) which might emerge as a result of a revamping of today's CPI and CPM (or perhaps even the Congress (I)).

Yet another strand of thinking is represented by Kothari and sympathizers. The principal agency for fundamental social change will be a 'coalition of social movements and mass struggle'.[23] His key statement of faith, shared by many others, is that the 'transformation of the state is to be achieved through the transformation of civil society, not the other way around, in which the state was to be the author of social transformation'.

This caricature of the classical Marxist vision of the relationship between state and civil society really begs all the key questions. Marxism does not claim that the state is the author of all social transformation. But it does claim that without a decisive resolution of the question of state and class power, partial advances in changing civil society cannot even approach the critical point at which their cumulative momentum becomes irreversible. A perspective which fails to grasp this reality reduces the project of socialist transformation to one of gradualist and incremental change in which the state's role as political centralizer for the dominant coalition, linch-pin of the *system* of oppressive structures and wielder of massive violence in the last resort is simply ignored. This refusal to seriously address the question of state power is typical of the radical pluralist vision of how society is to be transformed fundamentally. It can degenerate all too easily into a liberal pluralist accommodation to the reality of state power as it exists, all the more pernicious for not being acknowledged or recognized as such. Kothari argues for making the state minimalist and truly neutral (autonomous of all class interests) so that it can effectively mediate in civil society. This vision floats dangerously close to the 'conservative ideal'. In the quest for a new paradigm of radical politics beyond Marxism, what is ultimately offered is something old and rather stale.

Revolutionary progress will require a structured alliance among all the forces struggling for systemic change. Among the 'specific interest formations' a distinction must, therefore, be made between those which are linked positively to movements of the oppressed and those which are not. Linking the former to each other and to the working-class movement in a collective endeavour for socialist revolution is, of course, of major importance. Indeed, the very process of building the *central* class alliance between the urban and rural proletariat, and unifying a differentiated urban working class itself, requires that the demands raised by the new social movements be taken up by the left as a priority and that links with those movements be set up. A significant minority of the rural proletariat are women. It is the urban and rural poor who suffer most from inadequate health care, housing, education, pollution and environmental degradation. There is no way that revolutionary class unity or alliances can be established without tackling head on the questions of caste and communalism. The cross-class character of these oppressions does not invalidate this perspective even if it makes its attainment more difficult.

The consolidation of a mass vanguard layer requires the linking of all these movements (old and new) without, however, diluting either the content of common struggle through a populist redefinition of the meaning of socialism or promoting illusions that this fundamental breakthrough can be achieved through some gradualist, non-violent path which somehow bypasses the state or peacefully transforms it from within. If these movements on their own cannot establish the necessary links with the working class, the latter also is not, by itself, capable of making such a connection. The bridges have to be provided by those organizations substantially rooted in the working class, partially implanted in these movements and conscious of the need to make the link. The mainstream left, which sees these new movements as rivals, seems less and less capable of doing this. But their failure here is not compensated for by success elsewhere, for example, by a strengthening of the left base within the working class. The reformist retreat of the mainstream left has hampered the workers' ability to fight back – an abandonment all the more serious because the dominant coalition is escalating its assault on the urban and rural proletariat.

Marxist Culture and Discourse[24]

It might be appropriate at this juncture to look at the historical evolution of Marxist culture and its forms of expression. The most striking difference between broadly Marxist and radical cultural production since the mid sixties and the previous three decades is the increasingly autonomous and decentralized character of this production in the later period. Many of the forms – song and dance, theatre and film, publications and discussions – are common to both periods. But in the past, cultural production was more closely connected to the activities and organizational interests of the CPI. To that extent it was more integrated with nationalist and working-class movements. Thus song and dance, skits, and so on, were an integral feature of working-class and Communist demonstrations and morchas, unlike today when autonomous groups render isolated performances.

An outstanding example of early Communist cultural impact at the top was the role of the Indian People's Theatre Association (IPTA), set up in the mid thirties, which engaged the services of outstanding stage and film actors, writers and poets, people like Harindranath Chattopadhyay, Prem Dhawan, Balraj Sahni, K.A. Abbas and Kaifi Azmi. IPTA, largely a CPI front, was without peer the best known and most effective alternative to the big-budget commercial theatre and film world. Today IPTA is a much diminished force mirroring the general dilemma confronting the mainstream Communist parties and their relation to cultural production.[25]

In the last twenty-five years the CPI and CPM have failed to attract creative artists and intellectuals on anywhere near the same scale as earlier. (There are a few among the present crop of CPI and CPM leaders who combine the gifts of organization and mass public appeal, such as

E.M.S. Namboodripad and Jyoti Basu of the CPM; there are none who could be considered theoreticians of any genuine quality or stature.) The growing disillusionment with the Soviet and Chinese post-war experience has obviously been a major reason for the distancing of left intellectuals from close identification with the mainstream Communist parties. In the late sixties and seventies the effusion of street theatre groups (especially in West Bengal) was intimately connected to the revolutionary euphoria generated by Naxalism. This has remained an important form of mass cultural contact. The street theatre movement did not collapse in the wake of the ML decline, but its rate of growth has long since flattened out. Moreover, most of these companies have cast away the moorings that bound them to particular political groups.

Growing ideological uncertainties and cultural fragmentation have gone hand in hand. All this, along with the collapse of an earlier revolutionary optimism, has had an undeniable effect on the content and themes of contemporary radical culture. Before independence and up to the sixties the important, if not always dominant, motifs were: the inequity of British colonialism and its dehumanization of Indians; the centrality of the working class and the dignity of its labour; Marxism as the key to understanding and consciousness; the need for organization and party; the idealization of the party cadre as a self-sacrificing ascetic in Indian conditions of generalized poverty; the glorification of Soviet and then Chinese progress; the certainty of revolution, and clarity regarding its path. This has been replaced by a much broader canvas of concern – the taking up of a whole range of social and ecological preoccupations, tribute to the emergence, for example, of Dalit and women's groups whose own cultural output has had a far-reaching effect. The Stalinist rigidities have been weakened. All this is positive. But in another sense, the focus has become much hazier, less Marxist. A populist rather than class definition of socialism has increasingly become the norm. The focus has shifted from classes to masses, from class struggle to mass struggle, from exploitation to oppression. The impact of the Cultural Revolution on sections of the Indian left reinforced this thematic shift.

Rural India: Class Structure and Conflict

Towards the close of the twentieth century, the peasantry as a social category is proving to be far more stubborn in its efforts to survive than most Marxists at the beginning of this century ever anticipated. Kautsky was among the first Marxists to recognize that the expansion of capitalist relations would affect agriculture very differently from industry and that it need not lead to growing concentration of landholdings. But of all the early left thinkers who turned their attention to the 'peasant question' Chayanov has proved the most enduringly insightful as far as India goes. It is not surprising that Thorner, who foresaw in the fifties and sixties more accurately than most what future course Indian agriculture would take, also played a major role in the revival of Chayanov studies.[26] Traditionally, Marxists saw de-peasantization – class differentiation and polarization – as the inevitable outcome of the expansion of capitalist relations in the countryside. The tempo and forms of such a change might vary from country to country but the end result was not in doubt – rural capitalists on one side and rural proletariat on the other, with a shrinking buffer in between.

Even the most cursory survey of third world agriculture in this century would show that this is far from the norm. In Mexico the relative share of the peasantry in the total population has gone down while its absolute numbers have remained roughly steady. In Brazil the relative share has also fallen but the absolute numbers have risen. Shanin (himself influenced by Chayanov) has argued that capitalist transformation had three distinct inter-related effects: differentiation, pauperization and marginalization.[27] Differentiation was the most important structural consequence of capitalist transformation. Where differentiation at the bottom end of the self-employed peasant householding category was not matched by upward polarization – by an increase in the number of farmers hiring labour – there would be increasing pauperization and migration to the towns. Under certain conditions peasants would neither proletarianize nor become pauperized, but would be progressively marginalized as the weight of peasant agriculture within the national economy decreased steadily over time.

Migration from the countryside to the towns in India has not been remotely of the same proportions as in other third world countries, so pauperization in the sense described by Shanin has been contained. The percentage of people living in the countryside has declined very slowly. While agriculture's share of the total production is bound to decrease there is no sign that the peasant category (self-employed landholder) has diminished significantly relative to other social groups in the countryside. According to the Rudolphs, this group has actually increased its share of the total land operated upon.[28] Clearly, the Indian peasant has not been marginalized. Finally, whether one goes by the dicennial population census (1961, 1971 and 1981), the National Sample Surveys (NSS) or by data from the Rural Labour Enquiries (RLE) it is quite clear that progressive and ever-escalating polarization of social classes has not taken place in India.[29] The completely landless constitute only 13 per cent of all households. A majority of agricultural workers have some barren land, though their principal source of livelihood is waged work. Different methods of tabulation give different estimates for what can loosely be called the poor peasantry.[30] But there is general agreement that together they make up a slim majority; that is to say, at least 40 per cent do not belong to either category and there is little evidence to suggest that this will change.

Why has polarization not taken place and what are the implications of this 'failure' for social conflict and mobilization? Also, how are the 'middle peasants' to be defined and characterized? By a Marxist criterion based on labour hiring and surplus extraction, the 'family farmer' category does not constitute a distinct class. They are self-employed and, as Chayanov has pointed out, do not act according to the operational criteria of the strictly capitalist farm, which takes into consideration wage, interest, rent and profit levels.[31] Family farms will be willing to pay more than capitalist farms for borrowing capital and for rent; they will sell their output for lesser rates and they will work for longer hours. In good years they will get an overall surplus and use it for capital formation and renewal. They may get no net surplus in many years, but they will carry on with great tenacity. Chayanov's analysis provides powerful explanation for why there is neither significant concentration of landholdings or social polarization of a kind that systematically squeezes out the 'middle peasantry'. The sheer size of this intermediate layer in India also means that only a small segment can make the transition to becoming rich farmers.

The family farmer's objective location in the class and social relations of the countryside is contradictory. He does not hire his labour out and hiring in is limited to a certain upper segment, and that too only at peak periods in the production and harvesting cycle. But though he is not, strictly speaking, a capitalist farmer, his objective interests are so closely bound to the basic demands of the rural rich that he is in no way the vacillating figure which the middle peasant is supposed to be. In the absence of polarization and with the steady expansion of capitalist production techniques and market relations of various kinds, it cannot be otherwise. He is as much a prisoner of the capitalist commercialization of Indian agriculture as the rich farmer, and his economic aspirations can only be to join the ranks of those above him. What marks the post-independence from the pre-independence period is the greater economic and social homogenization of roughly the top 40 per cent of the rural population. This economic 'unification' of interests was inevitable once the zamindari system of pre-capitalist exactions was eliminated and agrarian capitalism pushed forward. The social homogenization is the consequence of the spread of relative economic prosperity to the intermediate castes which broadly encompasses the large bulk of the rich farmer class and the family farmer category. The economic bonds are, of course, stronger than the social bonds. It is these developments that have made the new peasant movements such a force to be reckoned with, though there is a tradition of peasant movements led by the rural rich stretching back at least to the beginning of this century.[32]

The central characteristic of the new peasant movement like some of its forerunners is that it locates the principal opponent (this time the Indian state) *outside* the agricultural sector as a whole.[33] Poverty and exploitation are not the consequence of relations internal to the agricultural sector or the countryside but the result of the behaviour of forces outside it. This provides the basic rationale for a multi-class mobilization by the rich peasantry for a programme of demands which will clearly benefit it the most. Except for the northeast and east, the kulak-led movement has had an impact everywhere. To date, the strongest such movements have been regional and in those areas where commercialization of agriculture has been considerable. They have been strongest in western Uttar Pradesh, Haryana, Punjab, Maharashtra, Tamil Nadu and Karnataka. In the eighties farmers' organizations of a similar kind have emerged in Gujarat, Madhya Pradesh and among sugarcane and tobacco growers in Andhra Pradesh.

Though there are demands that unite these regional movements, the prospects for the emergence of a national farmers' movement are still uncertain. The regional movements have different origins, sometimes different general philosophies or 'grand designs' and different perspectives on how to relate to existing political formations. The Shetkari Sanghtana (SS) of Maharashtra led by S. Joshi has a one-point programme giving paramount importance to remunerative prices which it insists will revolutionize the entire rural sector. The Tamil Nadu Vivasayigal Sangam (TNVS) led by N. Naidu has a much more comprehensive set of demands for minimum (but discriminatory) wages for male and female labour and for provision of rural infrastructure and services. The Karnataka Rajya Ryothu Sangha (KRRS), while admitting that low-caste participation at leadership levels is very limited, insists that this is not the case in its ranks. Its constitution specifies that untouchables should have 30 per cent of seats in village councils and it takes Gandhi's programme of class conciliation and social welfare as an ideal. Throughout the seventies and eighties the Bharatiya Kisan Union (BKU) of Punjab fought repeatedly for a variety of demands: the ending of zonal restriction on the movement of foodgrains; lower electricity rates; higher prices for sugarcane and milk; writing off of government levies payable by Punjab farmers for provision of canals, and so on. In every case the government backed down and made concessions. Its programme for the future demands that daughters be denied inheritance rights so that land parcellization may be reduced.[34]

One of the central points of difference within is the question of whether the farmers' movement should link itself to political parties – either those already existing or new ones of its own making. Informally the kulak lobby has been very much involved in the normal practices of electoral politics and power-brokering. But should it openly pursue partisan political alliances? While Charan Singh in Uttar Pradesh was adamant on the need to build and strengthen a farmers' class party, the new leader of the state's farmers, M.S. Tikait, is for the moment determined that farmers' unity and clarity of focus should not be diluted by involvement in partisan manoeuvring. The BKU is independent of the Akali Dal but both have served the interests of the state's Jat farmers well. The TNVS took a conscious decision in 1982 to form its own party, contravening a 1980 collective decision by regional farmers' organizations which had met to consider the prospects for national level co-ordination and the formation of some sort of national organization. The SS, which had for long been just as insistent as Tikait on abjuring contact with political parties, has now adopted a more accommodative stance towards the opposition parties, arguing that in the conflict between ruling and opposition parties the latter are a lesser evil and that temporary political alliances can further the cause of farmers.[35]

The capacity of these movements, hegemonized by the rich peasantry, to incorporate the poorer strata of the countryside should not be underestimated. Viewed from the top, the larger the base that is mobilized the stronger the movement and the stronger its claim to speak for the rural sector as a whole. It is also a powerful diversion of mass sentiment away from the frustrations engendered by the inequities of class and social relations within the countryside. Viewed from the bottom, the success of these movements can well mean some limited but direct improvement in absolute conditions of poverty through trickle-down benefits. After all, even the poor peasant can benefit from cheaper inputs and better social provisions (village schooling, health care, roads, water management and wells, electricity provision, and so on). As net buyers of food the rural poor clearly lose out from higher remunerative prices for foodgrains and their relative position in the rural hierarchy is likely to worsen. But in the absence of alternatives the peasant movements appear better than nothing. Existing relationships of authority and subjectively felt possibilities are in the short run often more important in deciding the orientation and activity of the poor than the fundamental and long-term clashes which correspond to objective class interests.

If the rise of the kulaks and their peasant movements has been widely recognized, a parallel development since independence should also be given careful attention. Class mobilizations and struggles in the countryside which expressly pit the poor against their rural exploiters have also broken out with a frequency and sharpness quite absent during the colonial period.[36] This has been the other side of the coin of growing capitalization and commercialization of Indian agriculture. On the one hand, dependence on wages and cash incomes for assuring survival has increased dramatically; on the other, older sources of security and welfare provision which were connected to the traditional structures of reciprocal obligations between different classes in the village hierarchy have broken down. Where geographical concentration of the rural poor and landless is high then the possibilities for class mobilization are obviously greater. But perhaps the most important factor is the existence (or not) of a political instrument willing and determined to organize on such lines.[37]

The most effective class struggles in the Indian countryside have invariably been linked to the activity of Communist, Socialist or Marxist-inspired groups or parties. The phenomenon of Naxalism in India since the sixties is the most important manifestation of this rising curve of class struggle in the countryside. Agrarian radicalism is not then the sole prerogative of the peasant movements, and the future of rural India is not inevitably 'centrist'.[38] The Naxalite uprising began in 1967. Union home ministry figures from September 1967 till the middle of 1969 showed that incidents of land occupation, land demands by the landless, agitations for increase in wages, and forcible harvesting by sharecroppers showed a sudden and marked increase. Revealingly, most of these struggles were *not* led by Naxalites.[39]

In more general terms, then, what are the key revolutionary alliances in the Indian countryside and what is the strategic war map? The new peasant movements have to be opposed. They are organizations hegemonized by the rich farmers. They consciously pursue class collaborationist strategies which aim to win over or at least neutralize the poor peasantry and rural labourers. In this they enjoy a measure of success which varies from region to region, depending on the relative proportions of the rich farmer/family farmer and the poor peasantry/landless and the extent to which alternative programmes for the poor have been articulated and alternative forms of struggle on a class versus class basis have been organized.[40]

The lines have to be clearly drawn between the rich farmer and aspiring capitalist or family farmer, on the one side, and the rural proletariat and poor peasant on the other. The family farmer category cannot be neutralized and a sizeable segment of it will not be won over prior to the revolutionary overthrow of the bourgeois state. It is part of the 'enemy front'. The basic effort must be directed towards forging an alliance of the rural proletariat and the poor peasant or marginal farmer. Such an alliance has to be centred on a series of economic and non-economic demands and perspectives. Land reform and redistribution of surplus lands expropriated from the rural rich will obviously continue to be a relevant perspective and slogan for mobilization in some areas. But increasingly greater weight has to be given to such issues as higher wages and guaranteed security of rural employment, lower food prices, cooperative forms of land consolidation and cultivation, socialized provision of various productive inputs, social control of water and forest resources with opportunities to the poor to supplement their incomes from collective forms of land upgradation, afforestation and environmental protection. But even this is not sufficiently comprehensive. Perspectives for struggle and mobilization must also include such issues as health care and education, and reduction and elimination of gender and caste inequality. There is a broad overlap between low castes and low classes in the countryside. If revolutionary rural organizations do not raise these issues, some of the peasant movements will, even if they do so in an extremely limited and partial way.

But the family farmer category also imposes two powerful constraints. A rural-centred strategy for revolutionary change or seizure of power at the centre cannot succeed. The sheer size of the 'enemy front' means that though the possibilities for successful class struggle and achievement of partial gains for the rural oppressed are very much there, indeed underestimated, these will vary from area to area and that in many parts the hegemony of the rural kulak will be extremely difficult to dislodge, even when confronted by powerful organizations of the rural poor. It also means that in many cases mass actions will have to be supplemented by armed defence and calculated violence by revolutionary organizations or strongly committed pro-poor groups. The kulaks can fall back on the state's administrative and repressive apparatuses for support, so the question of state power is often posed at a relatively early stage in rural class struggles.

The weight of the urban working class and of urban-based forms of mobilization in any overall revolutionary strategy will almost certainly be decisive, though it will need to be supplemented by powerful upsurges in the countryside. Considerable importance must be attached to the various mechanisms by which urban and rural struggles can be connected and their lessons shared.

Another major caveat is that though the family farmer is part of the 'enemy front' in a pre-revolutionary context, it would be fatal to treat him as such or as no different from the rich farmer in a post-revolutionary context. As a general rule he has no surplus land to be expropriated; he cannot be heavily taxed. He has to be coaxed rather than coerced into more cooperative forms of organizing his agricultural activities. The general perspective for winning him over must be to find ways of increasing the family farm's productivity while simultaneously ensuring a more egalitarian distribution of income among all those who contribute to agricultural production. Rising and better distributed rural incomes will also enhance growth of non-agricultural rural activities and, therefore, of employment absorption in this sector. As farming families grow, outlets are thus provided for those whose employment on the family plot would tend to reduce labour productivity overall.

The Urban Proletariat: A House Divided

In India, as in other industrializing countries of the third world, the urban working class is weakened by the existence of a sizeable unorganized sector: 44 per cent of the industrial workforce is in the small-scale sector; barely 50 per cent of factory workers and only 30 to 35 per cent of the total industrial workforce are unionized. These are disappointing but not perhaps surprising statistics. However, even the organized segment of the workforce is fragmented to a degree not found elsewhere. In 1986, there were 25.04 million people employed in the organized sector – 70.6 per cent or 17.68 million in the public sector (56 per cent in services) and 29.4 per cent or 7.36 million in the private sector, of which 4.44 million were employed in manufacturing. But there are over 38,000 registered unions (1986 figures) and anywhere between a third and half this number of unregistered or 'invisible' unions. At the apex of the union structure, there are some fourteen national federations, most of them formally affiliated to one party or another. In 1947 there was only one, the All India Trade Union Congress (AITUC), dominated by the CPI. The three basic types of unions are firm, craft or category association and a few industry-wide unions, such as textiles. There are federations at the industry, regional and national levels but these are essentially affiliating bodies with no real power to control what happens at the basic unit level. How has such a fractured system emerged?

Historically, unions were set up by outsiders, by socially conscious leaders from the middle class who possessed skills, such as literacy and familiarity with the law, which were lacking within the working-class movement itself. They were usually members of left parties or of the Congress. After independence, as new parties emerged to challenge the Congress and the CPI itself split, new union federations were created.[41]

But though the close connection between party and union explains the origin of these new federations it does not explain how they could all survive and flourish. The same holds true at lower levels. The biggest culprit is the whole legal structure of industrial relations, whose principal pillars are acts passed during the colonial period.[42]

It is not the political character of Indian trade unionism that is the problem but the fact that the system laid down for resolution of trade union issues encourages anything but class struggle methods. It puts a premium on third-party intervention by the state which, time and again, plays a decisive role.[43]

Originally, many trade-union and working-class leaders felt that the working class was so weak in relation to capital that it had to rely on the state to play a major role in enabling labour to achieve some measure of justice. State paternalism has in fact made unions far less sensitive to the need to forge larger structures of unity and class independence. The real beneficiaries of their fragmentation have been the state and the employers. Why then has the labour movement not opposed the present structure of industrial relations more aggressively? It has not done so because it is not united in its hostility.

Those unions affiliated to a party which rules at the centre or in the states or has prospects of ruling can expect to enjoy certain benefits as a result of its privileged links with the party. This does not mean that it necessarily comes off better vis-à-vis capital, since government is firmly committed to raising productivity and preventing industrial stoppages almost as a matter of principle, regardless of the merits of the union case. But unions with links to ruling parties do secure a certain edge over other unions. It is not surprising then that the Indian National Trades Union Congress (INTUC) is firmly opposed to the idea of a secret ballot and that other unions tend to be ambivalent or half-hearted in their support for this method of determining the main bargaining agent. At the other end of the spectrum very small unions can also survive and flourish, engage in negotiation and win occasional battles. The net result is that the present system can benefit certain unions most of the time and other unions some of the time but that the labour movement and the working class as a whole suffers all the time.

There is simply no encouragement to unions and federations, since it is not a matter of their survival, to give primary attention to the organization of their membership and consolidation of their base. It becomes far more important to establish the right political and administrative connections so as to take best advantage of the tutelary relationship with the state. This, incidentally, is why 'outside' leaders remain so important even though the Indian working class is increasingly able to provide its own leadership, to organize industrial action on its own and even to negotiate directly with management. These outsiders are valued precisely because of their capacity to broker, to make use of mechanisms which lie outside the grasp of working-class self-reliance. There is also, clearly, no inducement for unions to democratize their internal functioning and encourage rank-and-file participation. Class strength can only be acquired through the process of class struggle itself. As much is to be learnt from defeats as from victories.

There has to be a major overhaul of the whole system of industrial relations. In particular, a considerable part of the legal paraphernalia which encourages state intervention and paternalism should be dismantled. The initiative here will have to come from the labour movement itself. It will certainly not come from the state or from capital.

The presence of a vast pool of cheap, unorganized labour and a reserve army of unemployed obviously erodes the strength of the organized working class. The majority of industrial disputes are centred on non-economic issues, in particular personnel matters related to questions of employment security (suspensions, fines, dismissals, retrenchments), inter-union rivalries and battles for recognition.[44] This testifies to the problems created by the legal encouragement of fragmentation and by the fear of unemployment in an excess labour economy. Yet another, more recent development is that modern industry is resorting more and more to subcontracting for security, transportation and other service work, to subcontracting production itself to the unorganized small-scale sector, and to investment in the kind of modernization that reduces the permanent workforce. This is true not only in labour-intensive industries like engineering, metal work and textiles, where labour costs are between 25 and 30 per cent of the total bill, but even in capital-intensive processes like chemicals and fertilizers, where labour is around 5 per cent of the total costs and where subcontracting of storage and packaging is increasingly common.

The implications are clear. If the organized working class in even the most modern sectors of industry is to retain its strength it will have to shift its focus from economic to employment related issues, from fighting for compensation for workers' efforts to fighting for control over their efforts in the workplace and indeed to the larger question of how the organized working class, in its own interest, is to help the unorganized working class become unionized, stronger and more secure. In general, especially after the demoralization caused by the defeat of the 1974 railway strike, the trade-union leaderships have preferred to concentrate on organizing the more skilled and better-off sections of the workforce and to compete with each other for shifting loyalties within the existing organized sector. In India, there is an absolute and relative growth of the industrial workforce as a whole and no decline in the rate of growth of white-collar jobs. There has been a remarkable growth of white-collar unionism in the last fifty years. Professions like doctors, researchers, junior scientists, engineers and airline pilots are organized to a greater degree than in many Western countries. Organization itself in these professions is easier and demands are more readily achieved. But the overall result of inter-union raiding and poaching even in a growing workforce is an involution of trade-union activities which does nothing to strengthen the organized working class as a whole.[45]

Within the organized sector there is a further division between public and private sector. The working class in the former is much more strategically located in the economy as a whole and has, on the whole, better and more secure terms of employment. Though over two-thirds of the organized workforce is employed in the public sector, it accounts for only 10 per cent of all industrial disputes. In the early post-independence phase when Congress socialism was the operative ideology, the government, in keeping with its paternalism, cast itself in the role of a model employer and an exemplar for the private sector.[46] Over the years, the private sector not only did not bother to emulate the model employer but the government itself began to re-evaluate its own role, especially after the mid seventies.

India's huge size means that Indian trade unionism is also geographically dispersed. The main centres of working-class organization are Bombay, Madras, Bangalore and Calcutta. The industrial areas in Haryana on the outskirts of Delhi, Kanpur and the rapidly developing industrial belt in Gujarat (Ahmedabad and Baroda) are other centres of importance. The government is also keen on developing backward regions which, in effect, means development of backward districts within the advanced states, thus reinforcing rather than reducing the unevenness of development between the different states. One consequence will be a more socially heterogeneous working-class movement. Bombay's industrial scene is dominated by private-sector (including multi-national) concerns. It is where the working-class movement is most militant, where industrial relations are most unstable, where collective bargaining is strongest. Though party-linked unions are important, the most powerful figures are independents like Datta Samant and R.J. Mehta. The Shiv Sena flourished for a while after the defeat of the textile strike but its growth has flattened out. The 'red' unions, the CITU and AITUC, particularly the latter, have long lost their dominance. Only the Bharatiya Mazdoor Sangh (BMS) has had continued, if modest growth. In Madras, the working class is the most subdued. There is extreme fragmentation; there are no Colossus-like figures as in the Bombay trade union scene; and the unions often suffer severe internal factionalism because of the sharp political rivalry between the two main regional parties, the All-India Dravida Munnetra Kazhagam (AIDMK) and DMK. Madras has not expanded significantly as an industrial centre since the late sixties and this too has put a damper on the possibilities of aggressive working-class activity. According to Ramaswamy, 'Assertive management, unfriendly government, unfavourable economic circumstances and ineffective trade unionism constitute the environment in which Madras workers find themselves.'[47]

Bangalore has perhaps the most stable industrial relations environment. Public-sector industry and unions dominate the scene. There is less fragmentation than elsewhere partly because the state government has avoided the temptation of undue interference and the party in power has generally avoided aggressive protection of its own union wing. The Bangalore unions have a younger, better educated workforce with more democratic internal practices, less reliance on outsiders and fewer shifts of loyalty among the membership. Bangalore is the youngest and fastest growing of the four main industrial metropolises. Calcutta, by contrast, is the oldest and most rapidly declining. Despite the CPM's success in putting a leash on the unions, the party has not been able to attract sufficient private investment to halt its decline. Industrial stoppages have not decreased, nor the flight of capital. CPM control over the workforce has only allowed capital to go on the offensive and to carry out more easily the rationalization it needs. The ratio of strikes to lockouts is more unfavourable in Calcutta than in any of the other three cities.

What on balance then has the Indian urban proletariat accomplished in its decades of confrontation with Indian capital, private and public? Despite the structural dice being loaded against it, Indian labour is in ferment. It has not been tamed; industrial relations overall are neither stable nor peaceful. Since the law has helped to fragment labour, the working class has responded, especially in Bombay, with increasing defiance of and disdain for the law and for the conservative union bureaucracy. This grassroots discontent has been expressed in the willingness of the rank and file to shift its loyalties in search of leaders and unions more willing to fight. The most powerful expression of this militancy was the historic textile struggle when close to 225,000 workers, braving the most remarkable odds, went on strike for well over a year. No fewer than 58.42 million man-days were lost in that strike alone, which must be something of a record. Behind the 'Samant phenomenon' was something far more important. There emerged a new generation of aggressive city born or bred workers, a youthful and militant vanguard which had come to the conclusion that the old trade unionism had to be replaced by much sharper forms of direct confrontation between labour and capital and, if need be, against the state. The textile strike was defeated but the belief that the old forms of unionism and struggle must go remains. The textile strike also set new standards in spontaneous class solidarity and support. This was so despite the fact that other union federations and parties put their narrow interests and fears about Samant first and therefore did not give the kind of support that could have made all the difference. The Samant leadership for its part was also unable to develop a proper strategy for the struggle beyond relying on spontaneous militancy and organization at the base and making sure that its own supremacy at the top remained unchanged. Samant was unwilling to work seriously or consistently for a wider class unity, preferring as he had always done, to go it alone.[48]

Not surprisingly, given the history of steady conservative accommodation by the 'red' unions, their militancy has expressed itself in an anti-ideological orientation which puts a premium on the fulfilment of immediate demands. What kind of unionism will emerge is still an open question. American-style business unionism has some attractions. But the foremost exponents of this approach, like R.J. Mehta, are far from able to maintain a steady loyalty among the rank and file. Distrust of employers runs too deep. Trade-offs with management are unstable as employers, backed by the state, seek to press their workforce to the wall in a variety of ways.

In the aftermath of the defeat of the 1982 textile strike, the Bombay working class as a whole has had to retreat. Prior to the textile strike, at any given point of time, around 25,000 workers would be on strike. By early 1986 the figure had fallen by more than half. But there is considerable unevenness. The strength of the public-sector unions has remained relatively unimpaired. In fact, over the last two decades there has been an uninterrupted trend of more frequent regional and national strikes by government employees. The sixties, seventies and eighties have all witnessed new forms of struggle – from one-day bandhs (stoppage of transport and commercial activities in a city, state, and even nationally) called by opposition parties and union leaders, to gheraos, to direct forms of physical retaliation against management (which has done more than its share in bringing tactics of physical terrorism into industrial disputes).

There have been four landmark strikes in the post-independence history of the Indian working class. In July 1960 a strike was organized jointly by central government employees, the All India Railwaymen's Federation, the Post and Telegraph Union and the All India Defence Employees Federation on a six-point charter of demands.[49] It was the first truly massive show of working-class unity and defiance and it provoked the government to mobilize the Police Home Guard and the Territorial Army. Over 20,000 people were arrested. The strike was called off without success after six days but it did make the centre cautious about over-antagonizing government employees. The Essential Services Maintenance Act was promulgated to illegalize the strike and it is now a vital part of the government's legal arsenal, its provisions having been strengthened since then.[50]

The single most important working-class struggle in the last half-century was undoubtedly the 1974 all-India railway strike. It was a blow directed at the heart of the economy and therefore elicited the most ruthless repression from the state, which sent in the army to crush the strikers and to run the railways. The 1981 77-day strike by 125,000 workers in Bangalore is to date the most powerful struggle ever waged in public-sector industry, while the 1982 Bombay textile strike was the most important struggle ever in the private sector. But even here it was not the resistance of mill-owners but government intransigence that led to defeat. The government was determined to crush the militancy represented by the 'Samant phenomenon'. Any compromise would have had a nationwide impact on the working-class movement which would have been incalculably dangerous for the state and for capital. In this assessment the government was undoubtedly correct.

The most important lesson of all these struggles is a simple one. Despite the state's partially justified image as a better employer than the private sector, once the state is committed to ensuring that a struggle fails, then unless the stakes are raised dramatically and masses of workers mobilized accordingly, the centre will not settle for less than the total defeat of the workers. It nails the lie that a state paternalist pattern of industrial relations can help the working-class movement to advance qualitatively and confirms the role of the state as the most far-sighted defender of the interests of capital, public and private. Indian corporatism is an unbalanced arrangement where the power of the state is far in excess of either private capital or labour.

Since the early seventies, the state has come to see itself as even less of a mediator between capital and labour than in the past. That is to say, where the state was always pro-capital in matters of wages and productivity it partially compensated labour in the area of employment. The labour department and the courts, using their powers of arbitration and adjudication, generally made it difficult for employers to undermine job security. However, the ideological emphasis on rationalization which has taken command since the early eighties means that even this state-endorsed trade-off between capital and labour is being systematically eroded. This erosion will not be confined to the private sector but will also become a much stronger possibility in the public sector as pressures grow for greater efficiency through reduction of 'overmanning'.

The Indian urban working-class movement has as its immediate priority, then, the question of enhancing its own class unity and independence. In the process it will need to make overtures to the rural proletariat and the poor. Given the fragmentation of parties and unions representing the urban proletariat the responsibility for trying to forge such unity and independence weighs disproportionately on the left, which must resist the temptation to prioritize its sectarian interests. If initiatives are not forthcoming from the mainstream left they will have to come from others on the left. One ray of hope is that the working class as a whole has, time and again, shown its interest in such unity and despite all obstacles has, in an uneven, lumbering way, spontaneously moved in that direction.

On what kind of agenda can such an effort be based? Joint action at various levels, involving different unions, local, regional and national federations would automatically throw up co-ordinating committees around single-issue campaigns. There is therefore a vital need to agitate around a series of issues including: (1) elimination of various repressive laws curbing or preventing workers' democratic rights, such as the National Security Act, Essential Services Maintenance Act, and so on; (2) dismantling of the legal set-up which blocks development of a collective bargaining system, that is, pressing for secret ballot, one recognized union, legalization and normalization of strike activity; (3) raising of the social wage for workers in both the private and public sectors through external provision of pensions, housing and health care (there is no reason why such provision should not be extended beyond the urban working class to the rural poor and why the former cannot put itself at the forefront for such demands); (4) provision of proper labour representation on committees responsible for fixing the consumer price index; (5) promotion of the formation of permanent or semi-permanent fronts or co-ordinating bodies of trade unions at various territorial levels as well as demand for a confederation to bring together the various national federations; (6) introduction of employment guarantee schemes in both town and country; (7) establishment of a needs-based national minimum wage and a monitoring body with real powers to penalize institutional defaulters; (8) the demand for equal pay for equal work for male and female workers.

On issues such as sexism, caste and communalism, even the environment, very much more can be done than at present on the propaganda and campaign level by left-controlled unions. Opportunities for such activity exist. The left's failure or refusal to seize them will be all the more serious because the objective weight of the working class is growing *pari passu* with the consolidation of the capitalist mode of production. The unfavourable balance of forces between capital and labour is subject to periodic alteration.

To recapitulate: the sectionalism created by India's enormous social heterogeneity – the sexual, caste, religious, regional, skill and education based divisions of the working class – is reinforced by the fragmentation of trade union organizations and the existence of a 'labour excess' economy. But this weakness is partially mitigated by the importance of state capitalism and, therefore, the relative size of public-sector unionism. It would be incorrect to conclude that working-class consciousness is and must remain entirely fragmented and sectional. The bias of the state against the working class is growing; the struggles of the proletariat against the consequences of this will arise in both the public and private sector. In the public sector, there is a noticeably stronger tendency towards nation-wide mobilizations. Even in the private sector, there will be periodic outbreaks of solidarity-type action.

The broader the scale of strikes (whether in the public or private sector) and the more prolonged they are, the greater their potential to transform consciousness from a fragmented to a more class-based character. In fact, in centres like Bombay the drift of the working class towards a more corporate consciousness is not expressed by its demands as such, but through the forms of struggle adopted when major strikes or a strike wave take place. During the heroic textile strike, territorial support committees were thrown up with great effect. In the most important strike in Bombay's private sector – since the 1988–89 struggle by over 3,000 employees of the soap/detergent multi-national, Hindustan Lever – this organizational form was again adopted as the strategic mainstay. Such corporate forms of organization have in fact lagged behind the average rise in corporate class consciousness in the country's premier industrial metropolis.

In 'normal' times consciousness and organization tend to be sectional but in 'abnormal' times the possibilities of wider forms of organization emerge. If institutionalized, these would increase the frequency of class outbursts of anger and deepen the intensity of their impact on the consciousness of the participants. These would be qualitative advances in the efforts to overcome the fragmentation of Indian unionism. One of the biggest problems facing the working-class movement, especially in the abnormal periods, is the decisive role of the state in defeating struggles. This does politicize the working class. So, for example, after the defeat of the textile strike, Dr Datta Samant's Kamgar Agadi (Workers' Front) emerged as an electoral force and won the main working-class constituency in Bombay during the 1984 general elections, when the Rajiv wave swept everything else before it in Maharashtra. However, this experience can lead to an anti-government rather than anti-state consciousness unless other factors are pushing towards a further evolution.

In particular, since the political crisis of bourgeois leadership is endemic, there are possibilities that dramatic industrial upsurges might coincide with an acute conjunctural political crisis, which would make it that much more difficult for the state to cope. The Indian working class, despite the trade-union structure, is not doomed to sectionalism with all its negative attributes. In normal times it can fight it in various ways, basing itself on the kind of demands outlined earlier. In abnormal times there are very real possibilities for vanguard layers to develop a radical or near-revolutionary consciousness. The constitution of such a vanguard is a vital necessity and is closely connected to the construction of revolutionary formations implanted in the organized working-class movement, in the new social movements and in the rural oppressed, and seeking to make practical and programmatic links among them.

It would be possible to pose much more sharply the crucial questions of class and state power within the framework of broad mobilizations of the working class and other oppressed layers if there was a more coherent and organized vanguard able to take bold political initiatives with a clear overall sense of direction.

India's Permanent Revolution: A Troubling Problematic

In what way, if at all, can Trotsky's thesis of 'permanent revolution' (PR) be said to apply to India? The two most sophisticated attempts at vindicating its contemporary validity are by Michel Lowy and Ernest Mandel, theorists and militants of the Fourth International.[51] Both are insistent that the PR thesis holds for all third world countries as long as there is not a genuine and *complete* solution of the three principal tasks of the bourgeois democratic revolution – the agrarian question, national liberation and unity and the establishment of a bourgeois democratic state and political system.[52]

Has the Indian bourgeoisie solved all three tasks? To begin with, it is as well to remember that Trotsky's own occasional comments about colonial India and its future prospects were among the weakest of his writings on the colonial world. Trotsky excluded the possibility of a British Labour government granting independence to India; he also believed that independence when it was attained would be 'semi-fictitious' and that the internal class contradictions would be so great that there was no chance of a bourgeois democratic system of political rule surviving in the country.[53] Since then, it has been accepted by all supporters of the PR thesis that India has 'resolved' two of the key tasks. Only the agrarian question and its resolution remains in dispute. But what is the agrarian question? And what exactly is meant by the *complete* solution of bourgeois democratic tasks? The difference between a limited solution or the beginnings of a solution and a full solution is sufficiently unclear as to allow for a variety of interpretations and the application of different criteria.[54]

Lowy makes explicit reference to this as a grey area of intellectual judgement and is therefore more cautious and qualified than Mandel in drawing up an historical balance sheet on the validity of the PR thesis. Lowy is at pains to emphasize that 'Trotsky never saw industrialization *per se* as a revolutionary-democratic task'. So unlike Mandel he does not explicitly make the *degree* of industrialization or modernization a decisive criterion for judging the theory of PR, though he does concur with and quote Mandel when suggesting that higher levels of industrialization in the backward countries will invariably be accompanied by higher levels of dependence on imperialism. But can a country with a significant population undergo a complete industrialization and modernization in this manner? While the successes of the city-states of Taiwan, Singapore and Hong Kong can legitimately be ruled out of the reckoning because of their small scale, is it not possible for South Korea to go this route? And what would that imply for the theory of PR? Mandel denies the possibility of South Korea ever achieving such full industrialization by virtue of its very dependence, though some of his formulations on the limitations facing 'backward' capitalist countries are clearly incorrect.[55] Lowy, by his silence on the issue of degree of industrialization, can perhaps argue that as long as it is *dependent* industrialization it does not invalidate the PR thesis.

At bottom, these nuances reflect the unresolved issue of the meaning of the agrarian question. At two points, Lowy seeks to clarify Trotsky's views.

> *The agrarian democratic revolution*: The bold and definitive abolition of all residues of slavery, feudalism and 'Asiatic Despotism', the liquidation of all pre-capitalist forms of exploitation (corvée, forced labour, etc.); and the expropriation of the great landowners and the distribution of the land to the peasantry.[56]

Resolving the agrarian question then would seem to involve two key dimensions – the effective elimination of pre-capitalist relations in agriculture and the establishment of a certain kind of capitalist agriculture without great landowners or high concentrations of landhold-ings and where the bulk of the peasantry have land. Obviously, where rural polarization with a growing proportion of rural proletarians exists, then (according to this definition) even if capitalist relations have become predominant in agriculture there is still no resolution of the agrarian question. Lowy's exposition has the merit of providing a clear basis on which to judge whether there has been a resolution of the agrarian question in independent India. He correctly points out that India's land reforms were slower, more piecemeal and nowhere near as radical as those of Mexico or Algeria, let alone Bolivia. The Indian attempt he therefore judges to have failed. He substantiates his conclusion by a series of observations about the nature of Indian agricultural performance and of the social relations in its countryside, *each and every one of which is wrong*! His main sources for studying the Indian situation were leftists of Maoist persuasion who were strongly inclined to the now discredited view that rural relations were predominantly feudal or semi-feudal, that there was an alliance between the Indian bourgeoisie and such feudal or semi-feudal elements which prevented the necessary social and economic restructuring of the Indian countryside, and that throughout the post-war period Indian autonomy was being progressively weakened. On the basis of faulty or inadequate and therefore misleading data he predicted growing foodgrain deficits, low productivity levels, inadequate food production, growing concentration of landholdings and growing rural polarization, and postulated a grossly exaggerated figure for the total proportion of rural landless.[57] He was further mistaken in underestimating the autonomy of Indian capital and in predicting that Indian industry would grow increasingly dependent on multi-nationals. India would appear to have 'resolved' the agrarian question – if all that is required is to rebut Lowy's brief.

There is another point. When discussing the more backward of the advanced capitalist countries, such as Ireland, Spain and Portugal, Lowy is prepared to accept the impermanence of bourgeois transformations but insists that these countries have been taken out of the ambit of the PR thesis. In the 'relatively backward countries of Europe, bourgeois solutions seem, at least for the moment, to have successfully prevailed'.[58] About Ireland Lowy says: it was able to 'establish "small capitalist agriculture" and preserved bourgeois democracy without interruption for more than a half century'. One could be forgiven for taking this as an apt description of Indian development since independence.

Mandel's approach is different. The failure to resolve the agrarian question will ultimately confirm or reflect itself in the failure of the backward or peripheral country, even if semi-industrialized, to *completely* industrialize (in the manner of the advanced capitalist countries). As long as the conclusion holds, the premise (and therefore the PR thesis) seems to be proven. But the crucial mediations are not clearly spelt out: what are the radical changes in the agrarian structure that would constitute a 'proper resolution' and why are they not possible? The principal criterion for judging failure is the absence of a large and integrated domestic market for industrialization, a market encompassing the overwhelming bulk of the population. This comes suspiciously close to a tautology: there is no complete industrialization because there is no comprehensive domestic market for it and therefore no complete industrialization. The main question, of course, is *why* such a market cannot be constructed and a convincing answer to this has to incorporate both general obstacles and specific ones peculiar to each country. Mandel's most central statement as to why a radical agrarian revolution (so basic to the development of a growing domestic market) is not possible has to do with imperialist domination of the world market. This analysis operates at a level of generality which scarcely makes it useful for the Indian case. Thus, Mandel insists that objective limits to *cumulative* industrialization are imposed by the inability of native capital in the peripheral countries to compete with imperialism. But what if, as in the Indian case, the state decides that the only way to industrialize is by *not* competing with imperialist capital and by not letting it intervene domestically to any significant degree? Partial or 'semi-industrialization' of India is not the result of imperialism *allowing* India to industrialize (because of its own requirements to export producer goods, which is the thrust of Mandel's arguments); rather, imperialism could not have prevented such industrialization by a determined Indian state and bourgeoisie if it had wanted to!

Mandel underestimates the autonomy of Indian capital and its domestic market as well as its potential for growth. The 20 per cent of the population that forms this market constitutes, in absolute terms, a large number, and there is great potential for expanding this market in the countryside through enrichment of the wealthy farmers and their family farmer allies. It is true that a majority, indeed an overwhelming majority, are unable to enjoy the benefits of industrialization or, as Mandel would put it, are unable to become progressively integrated into the internal market and thereby sharply and swiftly raise their living standards. But this would seem to be more a function of domestic factors than of imperialist domination of the world market. It is hardly the case that Indian poverty is 'overdetermined' by what happens on the world market.[59]

China, by breaking away from capitalism, has presumably removed the fundamental impediments to resolving its agrarian question. But can it fully industrialize? Is the measure of this process of cumulative industrialization progressive urbanization and proletarianization? If so, it is obvious that such a scenario, if it materializes in China, will only do so well into the twenty-first century. Ironically, China's high industrial and economic growth rates since the late seventies have had a great deal to do with the introduction of the 'household responsibility system' in agriculture – hardly the kind of radical agrarian measure that Marxists have had in mind. Earlier measures of collectivization and rural development in China provided a basis superior to India's agrarian policies for the massive reduction of absolute levels of poverty (though not its elimination, even forty years after liberation). But they did not, in themselves or in conjunction with the other aspects of 'planned' economic development, lead to particularly rapid rises in the standard of living.

At the very least, it can be said that more weight should be given to certain *internal* characteristics of continental-size economies like those of India and China and that it is not just a question of whether a country has successfully broken away from capitalist constraints, external and domestic. Such factors would include unfavourable and deteriorating land–man ratios, the issue of population growth from an already exceptionally high demographic baseline, the limits to surplus extraction from agriculture (without brutal repression of the peasantry) and the fact that even the optimum level of such extraction may not be sufficient to promote a level of urbanization/industrialization which would drastically reduce the rural sector of both farm and off-farm activities. That is to say, even high levels of industrial growth are not able to absorb labour at the required rate.[60] Once the Stalinist solution of the peasant question is ruled out then there is a very real problem of the persistence of the peasantry both for capitalist India and post-capitalist China, and perhaps for that interpretation of the PR thesis which sees full and rapid industrialization as the inevitable outcome of a successful revolution in a backward country. Rapid is a relative term but surely no Marxist of the classical era, including Trotsky, would have believed that the peasantry would constitute the large bulk of the population in a post-revolutionary society up to eighty years after its inception! If the perspectives of the PR theory concerning industrialization were perhaps over-optimistic for a country like China, could they also be over-pessimistic for a country like India?

Anderson and others have stressed the time factor: that very prolonged periods are required before a sure judgement of the complete validity of the PR thesis can be made. There is merit in this view of a possible 'long march' for countries like India, South Korea and others (under bourgeois rule) towards a 'complete' or 'satisfactory' solution of its key bourgeois democratic tasks. This long march may even witness regressions such as the more or less prolonged breakdown of bourgeois democracy and the rise of internal movements weakening or threatening national unity. Lowy is prepared to concede that such a long march, though highly improbable, cannot be ruled out a priori; Mandel is more adamant and absolute. 'In other words,' he writes, 'the Russian, Brazilian, Mexican, Argentine, Korean and Chinese bourgeoisie no longer could and no longer can create a new Italy, a new France, a new Germany or a new Japan, not to speak of a new United States.'[61]

This way of posing the issue may preserve the formal claims to truth of the PR thesis but robs it of most of its analytical value. All that is left is an assertion, at the most general level, that no backward country can fully industrialize – and even here history will provide the final verdict. There are enough legitimate doubts about the theory's more sweeping claims to justify agnosticism. But the theory also has a more enduring political strategic value. Indeed, the persistence of the peasantry, even in rapidly developing capitalist countries, reinforces the soundness of the theory's injunctions at the level of *tasks* and *alliances*. The poor peasantry is not about to disappear. It will remain a major ally of the working class; the rural proletariat must be joined to its urban counterpart.

The set of slogans and demands required to inspire revolutionary struggle will have to meet the needs and invoke the claims of those seeking to transform agrarian society. Some will be old (like land expropriation and redistribution); others will be new (like calls for socializing water and forest resources, for ecological protection); while the weight of still others (like proper wage levels and employment security for the rural proletariat) will be much greater than in past programmes for carrying out the agrarian democratic revolution. In that sense, for India, certainly in the foreseeable future, the revolutionary process will remain 'combined' and will not be purely proletarian as in the advanced capitalist countries.

The Stalinized left of the CPI and CPM share with some Naxalite groups the traditional schema of a two-stage revolution. Other Naxalites follow Maoist-inspired formulations of the 'uninterrupted revolution' type which are nevertheless still imprecise and confused. In the face of this, the strategic guidelines of the theory of permanent revolution for India need to be strongly and repeatedly affirmed. The last word in this respect can safely be left to Mandel: 'What is important is to see the revolutionary process not as a series of time intervals during which one or another variety of demand is more or less prominent but to see it as a continuous struggle for a mix of slogans and demands in which there is no clear separation between "democratic" and "proletarian" or "socialist".'[62]

Notes

1. C.D. Overstreet and M. Windmiller, *Communism in India*, California University Press, San Francisco 1959.

2. The CPI was officially founded in 1925. In 1926 the CPI had 50 members compared to 30,000 for the CPC and 3,000 in the PKI (Indonesia). During the Comintern third period (1928–34) when the Congress was involved in the mass Civil Disobedience Campaign (1930–34) and the Nehru-led left wing lurched to the left, the CPI allowed Gandhi to reap the benefits uncontested by co-opting the Congress left. The CPI perceived this left as the 'left face of imperialism' just as social democracy was perceived as the 'left face of fascism'. After the Seventh Comintern Congress, the CPI did embark on a very fruitful collaboration with the Congress Socialists. This (1935–47) was when the CPI became a mass party with mass fronts and built an enduring base in the south and east. In 1943 the CPI had 16,000 members of which 26% were workers, 36% peasants (poor and better off), 11% students, 5% women and the rest middle class or intellectuals.

But there was also a rightward shift in its policies at a time when the Congress also shifted to the right. In 1935 Nehru lost the strategic battle to Gandhi by accepting the Government of India Act providing for partial self-government under the aegis of the colonial state. It marked the Congress left's acceptance of the constitutional road to independence through a formal transfer of power. In 1942 the CPI committed its biggest mistake by opposing the Quit India Movement because of Soviet exhortation to subordinate all struggles to the defence of the 'fatherland' and support for the anti-fascist 'democratic alliance' of Allied Powers. Since the colonial state legalized the CPI while repressing the Congress, the former could grow to 60,000 by 1947 but at a huge political price. In Ceylon, by contrast, the Trotskyists who led the anti-colonial struggle emerged as the dominant force in the Ceylon working class after independence and with considerable overall prestige and appeal.

The late formation of the CPI also meant it was Stalinized from the beginning. It did not experience even the limited backwash of the Stalin–Trotsky conflict that took place in the Chinese and Vietnamese Communist parties. A viable Trotskyist current in the CPI would have helped to counter the CPI's pendular political shifts of the thirties and forties. These shifts, reinforced by India's social and geographical heterogeneity, promoted factionalism from the beginning.

3. The objective weaknesses of the Indian working class assured bourgeois hegemony of the National Movement. But every national liberation struggle has an elemental thrust or permanent dynamic towards social liberation. It is this potential that was squandered by CPI policies.

4. See D.N. Dhanagare, *Peasant Movements in India, 1920–1950*, OUP, Oxford 1983, and J. Pouchepadass, 'Peasant Classes in Twentieth Century Agrarian Movements in India' in E.J. Hobsbawm and others (eds), *Peasants in History*, OUP, Oxford 1980. Both Dhanagare and Pouchepadass believe that the CPI Telengana base was class collaborationist, spanning rich peasant to rural poor with the former playing a hegemonic role. This broad front was held together, says Dhanagare, by a three-fold programme of demands for: (i) wage increases and an end to compulsory labour services to big landlords; (ii) opposition to large-scale evictions and a call for a moratorium on all debts; (iii) a dual policy on compulsory levy/procurement of grains, i.e. deploring landlord evasion but encouraging witholding of such levies by rich and middle peasants who supported the Communists.

Pouchepadass and H. Alavi, 'Peasants and Revolution' in K. Gough and H.P. Sharma (eds), *Imperialism and Revolution in South Asia*, Monthly Review Press, New York 1973, agree that when this class collaborationist front broke down and class polarization took place with the poorest strata ranged directly against the rich peasantry, the Communists were unable to unitedly orient towards this development. Differences over strategic line concerning the Congress, internal party disunity, the break-up of the multi-class front and guerrilla focoism proved disastrous in the face of the Indian army's single-minded determination to wipe them out when it intervened in 1948, ostensibly against the Nizam and his paramilitary forces, the razakars. In August 1949 around 25,000 Communists and activists/sympathizers were arrested.

5. Soviet 'experts' on South Asia have now quietly consigned this concept to permanent oblivion but without the slightest self-criticism for the damage it has done in the past.

6. T.J. Nossiter, *Communism in Kerala*, OUP, Oxford 1977. This is a well known reference work.

7. For a representative sample of studies on Naxalism, see S. Banerjee, *The Simmering Revolution: The Naxalite Uprising*, Zed Press, London 1984, M. Ram, *Maoism in India*, Vikas, New Delhi 1971, S. Ghosh, *The Naxalite Movement: A Maoist Experiment*, K.L. Mukhopadhyay, Calcutta 1974, B.D. Gupta, *The Naxalite Movement*, Allied Publications, Bombay 1974, J. Sohail, *The Naxalite Movement in India*, Associated Publishing House, New Delhi 1979. See also R. Ray, *The Naxalites' and Their Ideology*, OUP, Oxford 1988 for a psychological investigation of the Naxalites' 'existential ideology' of near nihilism.

8. Only some 200 of India's 56,000 villages came under the grip of Naxalism. See B.D. Gupta, *The Naxalite Movement*.

9. A.S. Abraham, 'Resurgence of Naxalism', *Times of India*, 12 October 1987.

10. A. Bose, 'Naxalites: A Change of Focus', *Indian Express*, 12 June 1988. Tribals apparently see Naxalites as 'protectors against acquisitive local landed gentry, forest contractors and mindless development programmes'.

11. S. Banerjee, *The Simmering Revolution*, p. 92.

12. In terms of membership the CPI is bigger. In 1986 the CPI had 478,905 down from its peak in 1978 of 546,732 (*India Today*, 30 November 1988, p. 57). In 1985 the CPM's total membership was close to 370,000 with the West Bengal unit having around 137,000 and Kerala with around 122,000, making up together about 70 per cent of the total. Most new recruits are Bengalis and CPM members in the Hindi belt are less than 30,000. Total membership of its mass fronts – CITU, youth, women's, cultural wings – is 1.4 million plus.

13. West Bengal used to account for the single biggest segment of total man-days lost in the country due to strikes. Surely but systematically, the CPM has put curbs on the CITU so that from 1980 lock-outs account for the overwhelming proportion of man-days lost compared to strikes. See Table 1, p. 278 in E.A. Ramaswamy, *Worker Consciousness and Trade Union Response*, OUP, Oxford 1988. The Congress-led INTUC has been able to bounce back into trade-union contention by appearing more radical than the CITU!

14. S. Harrison, *The Dangerous Decades*, OUP, Oxford 1960.

15. In terms of verified membership the INTUC, BMS and Hind Mazdoor Sabha (HMS) are all bigger than the verified membership of the AITUC and CITU. As of 31 December 1980, INTUC had 2,236,128 members, BMS 1,211,345, HMS 735,027, AITUC 344,746 and CITU 331,037. This is somewhat misleading in that verification through a check-off system of membership rolls does not give an accurate picture of actual union loyalties and has been criticized on this count by the left unions whose own estimates for true membership have not been accepted by the centre's labour department. The CITU is particularly influential in Calcutta and Bangalore though not in Bombay and Madras. The AITUC also enjoys considerable strength in key public-sector unions (banks). Both 'red' union federations have a weight and influence in the overall trade union movement which is not captured by the statistics available.

16. A. Jaffry, M. Rangarajan, B. Ekbal, K.P. Kannan, 'Towards a People's Science Movement', *Economic and Political Weekly (EPW)*, 13 March 1983, pp. 372–6.

17. For a compendium survey, see N. Desai (ed.), *A Decade of Women's Movement in India*, Himalaya Pub. House, Bombay 1988.

18. William Hinton, *Fanshen*, Pelican Harmondsworth 1966, and J. Belden *China Shakes The World*, Pelican, Harmondsworth 1973.

19. See H. Sethi, 'Groups in a New Politics of Transformation' in *EPW*, 18 February 1984 and his 'The Immoral "Other"' in *EPW*, 23 February 1985. Also R. Kothari's, 'Masses, Classes and the State' in *EPW*, 1 February 1986 and 'NGOs, the State and World Capitalism' in *EPW*, 13 December 1986. Kothari has been the foremost proponent of the 'new politics' but between these two articles separated by less than a year there would appear to have set in a substantial pessimism about the overall potential of such NGOs. This is no doubt due to the very conscious and largely successful efforts of the government informally and formally to co-opt these

organizations by a bill which will set up national and state councils to regulate NGO affairs. Kothari admits that the foreign institutions of world capitalism do use with some success such NGOs to promote their interests in the third world countryside. To quote Kothari, 'They need to further clarify their goals, discard the now discredited NGO image, resume the original conception of genuine voluntarism' (p. 2182).

Historically, the roots of much of this voluntary sector can be traced back to post-independence Gandhian and Sarvodaya self-help schemes. The NGOs complementary and substitutionist role for the state's development activities has been clearly recognized by the government which has devoted a separate chapter to the voluntary sector in the Seventh Plan Document.

20. According to A.N. Das, 'Politics Without People', *Times of India* 12 January 1988. Foreign inflow to NGOs monitored under the Foreign Contributions Regulation Act is around Rs 500 crores. This does not include domestic private and public support.

21. H. Sethi, 'Groups in a New Politics of Transformation', has done a useful job of detailing some of the main virtues, weaknesses and problems of the NGOs. In these 'specific interest formations' only a minority current is avowedly sympathetic to Marxian socialism. This current has often to restrain itself from forcing the pace or otherwise trying to link up with the working-class movement for fear of weakening the unity of the movement or group to which it belongs.

22. See A.G. Frank and M. Fuentes, 'Nine Theses on Social Movements' in *EPW*, 29 August 1987.

23. R. Kothari, 'Masses, Classes and the State', p. 216.

24. The key compilations (up to the mid sixties) are to be found in S. Pradhan (ed.), *Marxist Cultural Movement in India: Chronicles and Documents*, Vols I, II and III. Published by S. Pradhan, Calcutta 1979 to 1985.

The cultural movement was one of the key mechanisms linking urban middle-class intellectuals and students to the urban and rural poor. Talking of the failure of the Communist party to sustain its cultural activity during the fifties when it went into decline and lost its all-India character, Pradhan says that the 'Metropolitan artist was attracted to the movement not only because he was inspired – genuinely no doubt but transiently in some cases – by anti-fascist and pro-socialist ideals, but also because he found in his close participation in popular causes, a means of enriching his art; in some cases this was an aesthetic equivalent of slumming, or a mere rummaging for newer techniques, in order to attract larger audiences, but there was a deepening of realism in the work of a few. But genuine politicization, a necessary pre-condition of the continuity of a movement of this kind was never systematically attempted and seldom achieved' (Vol. III, p.VI).

25. The IPTA did suffer even early on from a certain metropolitan bias. See ibid., Introduction to Vol.III.

26. See his 'Chayanov's Concept of the Peasant Economy', in the posthumous revival of A.V. Chayanov's writings, *The Theory of the Peasant Economy,* OUP, Oxford 1987.

27. T. Shanin, 'Defining Peasants' in J.P. Mencher (ed.), *Social Anthropology of Peasantry,* Somaiya Publications, Bombay 1983 pp. 60–87.

28. L.I. and S.H. Rudolph, *In Pursuit of Lakshmi,* Orient Longman, Bombay 1988 Table 40 p. 336.

29. According to census data, agricultural proletarian households rose from 16% in 1961 to 26% in 1971 to 25% in 1981 (all figures approx.). Because of a slight change in definition, the percentage of rural proletarians in 1961 may well have been underestimated so the growth between then and 1971 may not have been as great as the figures suggest. Similarly, NSS data give figures of 19–20% for 1961, 22% for 1971 and 25% for 1981 (see L.I. and S.H. Rudolph, *In Pursuit of Lakshmi* pp. 339–40). The RLE figure for 1977–78 is closer to 30% (see G. Omvedt, 'The New Peasant Movement in India', in *Bulletin for Concerned Asian Scholars,* April-June, 1985). But again, RLE figures from the mid fifties onwards do not support a hypothesis of dramatic or progressive proletarianization.

30. See Table 3 and L.I. and S.H. Rudolph, *In Pursuit of Lakshmi,* Table 40, p. 336. In Bardhan's Table the agricultural proletariat and poor peasant would comprise around 60% of the rural population, allowing for some shading off of the top layer of the small

landholder into the family farmer category. By the Rudolphs' estimate, the collective figure, again allowing for some shading off, would be closer to 55%.

Though Bardhan and the Rudolphs differ in their estimates of the size of the 'family farmers' (or 'bullock capitalists' as the latter prefer to call them) and, therefore, also on the size of the rich farmer class, they concur that it constitutes a sizeable chunk of the rural population which (including household members and dependants) runs into tens of millions.

31. See A.V. Chayanov, *The Theory of the Peasant Economy*. His key concept for the family farmer whom, he argues, is interested in maximizing total income rather than profit, is what he calls the consumption needs/labour drudgery ratio. The family farmer household works not only up to the point when marginal productivity of labour reaches zero but beyond. As output increases, the marginal rate of drudgery increases till an equilibrium is reached when the family feels that the unit increase in drudgery would just exceed the unit increase in consumption satisfaction. The labour consumption balance will be affected by demographic differentiation, i.e. family size and the number of working members.

Chayanov disputed the contention of many of his compatriots that a cumulative and unstoppable polarization was taking place in the Russian countryside, arguing that almost 90% of all Russian farmers at the beginning of this century belonged to the peasantry. There is some evidence that Lenin was himself moving away from his conclusions in *The Development of Capitalism in Russia* by recognizing that the 'peasantry' was far more persistent than he had thought (see T. Shanin, 'Defining Peasants').

32. P.K. Bardhan, 'Agrarian Class Formation in India', in P.K. Bardhan and T.N. Srinivasan (eds), *Rural Poverty in South Asia*, OUP, Oxford 1988. I agree with Bardhan that contrary to Wolf (1969) and Alavi (1973) in the Indian peasant movements of this century it was the rich peasantry and not the middle peasants who took the initiative.

33. For a comprehensive survey of the peasant movement as perceived by its defenders, see S. Sahasrabudhey (ed.), *The Peasant Movement Today*, Ashish Publishing House, New Delhi 1986.

34. Ibid.

35. According to P. Seth, 'Socio-Economic Development and Political Process in Rural India: A Perspective', in *Punjab Journal of Politics*, Vol. VIII, No. 1, January–June 1984, in the 1980–85 Lok Sabha, 40% of MPs belonged to farming occupations compared to 22.4% in the 1952–57 parliament.

36. K. Gough, 'Peasant Resistance and Revolt in South India', in *Pacific Affairs*, Vol. XLI, No. 4 (Winter), 1968–69; M. Mies, 'The Shahada Movement', in *Journal of Peasant Studies*, Vol. III, No. 4, July 1976; P. Prasad, 'Agrarian Unrest and Economic Change in Rural Bihar', in *EPW*, 14 June 1975; R. Singh, 'Agrarian Social Structure and Peasant Unrest', in *Sociological Bulletin*, Vol. XXIII, No. 1, March 1974.

37. See K.L. Alexander, *Peasant Organisations in South India*, Indian Social Institute, New Delhi 1981. D.S. Zagoria has argued that successful revolutionary peasant organizations emerge where certain social, political, psychological and technical conditions are satisfied, namely a high concentration of landless labourers, land-poor peasants in a tenancy system, heavy population pressure on land, consciousness of possibilities of change, freedom to organize, leadership and cadre skills. 'Asian Tenancy System and Communist Mobilisation of Peasantry', in J.W. Lewis (ed.), *Peasant Rebellion and Communist Revolution in Asia*, Stanford University Press, 1974. Also his 'The Ecology of Peasant Communism in India', in *American Political Science Review*, Vol. 65, March 1971.

Zagoria is, in fact, too demanding. As the success of the Naxalites in Bihar and elsewhere shows, even in conditions of absence – absence of tenancy system, lack of freedom to organize, a low initial level of class consciousness – it is still possible to generate and sustain powerful class struggles. The decisive factor in these cases has been the subjective one – leftist-inspired cadre training and implantation and their mass organization and mobilization.

38. L.I. and S.H. Rudolph, *In Pursuit of Lakshmi*. The authors do acknowledge the open-endedness of historical prospects and therefore of the possibilities of growing class conflict. But the whole thrust of their work is to deny the significance of class politics and

to point out its diminishing relevance. In fact the rise of kulak power is the rise of a class power. What is at issue is the extent to which class tensions and potential for conflict in the countryside will be contained to the benefit of the dominant classes and their allies.

39. See the government report 'The Classes and Nature of Current Agrarian Tensions', in A.R. Desai (ed.), *Agrarian Struggles in India after Independence*, OUP, Oxford 1986. The report counted 5 such incidents in Assam, 8 in Andhra Pradesh, 9 in Bihar, 7 in Kerala, 7 in Madhya Pradesh, 5 in Maharashtra, 5 in Punjab, 3 in Rajasthan, 3 in Tamil Nadu, 5 in Uttar Pradesh, one each in Manipur, Gujarat and Tripura. Some of these were spontaneous, others organized by the CPM, CPI and SSP (Samyukta Socialist Party) as well as by Naxalites.

40. G. Omvedt, in her 'The New Peasant Movement in India', has sought to make a case from the left as to why these 'peasant movements' should be supported: 'The fact is that the primary effect of the green revolution (and of all associated capitalist development in agriculture) has been the changing relationship of the peasantry to the state and to capital, whereas the changes in internal, intra-village relations have been a secondary effect' (p. 16). Leaving aside her quite arbitrary designation of what is primary and what is secondary, it cannot be argued in Marxist terms that the state *exploits* the family farmer, even indirectly, e.g. through taxation, the principal form of such collective and indirect exploitation. The state has consistently promoted the interests of the rich farmer/family farmer but is unable to give it all or as much as it wants. The family farmer, in particular, is not assured of regularly rising surpluses.

The theoretical rationale for Omvedt's new and more sympathetic evaluation of the 'peasant movements' has, not surprisingly, led her to implicity reject the 'labour theory of value' for a more Weberian concept of 'exploitation'. Politically, the strategic reorientation to class collaborationist alliances in the countryside and fronts could be said to be in keeping with the more diffused notions of revolutionary change and the more negative reflections on the importance and necessity of class struggle (and 'vanguard' political formations) made popular by the rise of the new social movements.

41. The Congress trade union INTUC split off in 1947 from the Communist dominated AITUC. The next year Congress Socialists walked out of AITUC to form the Hind Mazdoor Panchayat (HMP) which joined with the Royist IFL to form the HMS. At its inaugural session, West Bengal Marxists not in the CPI split off to form the United Trades Union Congress (UTUC) which became the trade-union wing of the Revolutionary Socialist Party. In 1955 the Jan Sangh formed its federation, the BMS. The UTUC and AITUC then suffered further splits related to scissions within the parent political organization. The CITU was set up by the CPM in 1970. In 1965, the HMP broke off from the HMS when the Socialists suffered a split. See E.A. Ramaswamy and Uma Ramaswamy, *Industry and Labour*, OUP, Oxford 1981, pp. 92–3.

42. The 1926 Trade Union Act governs registration procedures. The 1947 Industrial Disputes Act allows government to intercede in any dispute either at the request of one or both parties to the dispute or of its own volition.

43. Three issues are crucial – establishing a single bargaining agent, an accepted and fair method of recognition of this agent, i.e. the majority union, and accepting that strike action is a legitimate and necessary mechanism for the resolution of problems. In 1950, the then labour minister, V.V. Giri, later to become president, put forward a bill which addressed these issues directly by endorsing recognition through secret ballot, removing the right of just any and every union to negotiate and widening the scope for legal strike action. The conditions that exist today make legal strikes almost impossible and put a premium on procedures of state arbitration and compulsory adjudication by industrial tribunals and courts. The Congress withdrew the bill for fear of undermining the INTUC and Giri resigned in protest.

44. See Table 5 and 6, E.A. Ramaswamy, *Industry and Labour* pp. 219–22. Up to 1975, wage and bonus disputes account for a little over 40% of all disputes. By 1986 this had fallen to around a third. See *Pocket Book of Labour Statistics*, Labour Bureau, Government of India, Simla 1987, p. 159.

45. There is some evidence of a decline in the average size of unions even as their number and those of the total membership increases. See Table 29, p. 281 in L.I. and

S.H. Rudolph, *In Pursuit of Lakshmi*. However, most of this decline in average size (after independence) took place between the fifties and sixties. From the mid sixties to the early eighties there does not appear to have been a statistically significant trend of decline. See G. Ramanujam, *Indian Labour Movement*, Sterling Publications, New Delhi 1986, Appendix V. This suggests that the degree of involution may be somewhat exaggerated and that union proliferation is greater among registered unions not sending in returns and among unregistered unions.

46. One major manifestation of the government's self-appointed role was the setting up of wage boards for wage determination. By the mid seventies over twenty such wage boards were set up covering almost all the plantation sector, 80% of the mining sector, 40% of manufacturing and journalists.

47. E.A. Ramaswamy, *Worker Consciousness and Trade Union Response*, OUP, Oxford 1988, p. 95. Almost all work on the Indian urban proletariat has fallen into one of two patterns. These are either straightforward historical narrations on the evolution of the trade union movement, or sociological-legal studies of the structure of industrial relations, their mechanisms of dispute resolution and the main problems preventing 'stability' in industrial relations. Ramaswamy's writings have generally been among the most sophisticated studies of the Indian labour scene and indispensable for researchers.

But there is a complete dearth of the kind of studies which can provide an assessment of the revolutionary potential of the urban working class, of how its 'average' consciousness has evolved, of the psychological residues of various victories and defeats, of the lessons learnt and expressed in later rounds of struggle, of the creativity of the working class in action as expressed in original forms of organization and mobilization. This is no doubt due to the simple fact that the working class has not really been perceived as a revolutionary agent. The Naxalites have their eyes fixed on the countryside and most trade union leaders/organizers, including those of the mainstream left, are committed to bourgeois reformism.

48. S. Pendse, 'Labour: The Datta Samant Phenomenon', in *EPW*, 18 and 25 April 1981, and R. Bakshi, *The Long Haul*, Build Publications, Bombay 1986. One of the most important aspects of the textile strike was that for the first time, a unity in action was forged between the poor peasantry and landless of the rural hinterland and the urban textile workers. See R. Bakshi, *The Long Haul* for more details. Furthermore, the strike was waged not primarily for a wage increase but against state legislation which made it virtually impossible for the textile workers to overthrow the hated but 'recognized' Congress and employer's union, the Rashtriya Mill Mazdoor Sangh (RMMS), for a union of their choice, in this case the Maharashtra Girni Kamgar Union (MGKU) led by Samant. In this sense it was as much a direct challenge to state authority as to the textile mill owners.

49. S. Sen, *Working Class of India: History of Emergence and Movement, 1830–1970*, Bagchi and Co., Calcutta 1977, pp. 445–6.

50. In 1968 a one-day strike by 2.5 million central government employees was again met by direct repression, with over 10,000 arrests, 15 deaths from police firing and 48,000 termination notices handed out.

51. Michel Lowy, *The Politics of Uneven and Combined Development*, Verso, London 1981, and E. Mandel, *Revolutionary Marxism Today*, Verso, London 1979.

52. P. Anderson, *Considerations on Western Marxism*, Verso, London 1979, pp. 118–19. For Anderson, the criteria are so extensive as to be possibly too demanding and unfair since judgements about the 'success' or character of bourgeois democratic revolution in countries like Japan and Germany were not based on similarly strict standards. Furthermore, the fulfilment of all three tasks in the advanced countries was extremely protracted.

53. See 'India Faced with Imperialist War', written on 25 July 1939, and the 'Manifesto of the Fourth International', in *Writings of Leon Trotsky, 1939–40*, Pathfinder, London 1969, pp. 29 and 39.

54. Lowy, *The Politics of Uneven and Combined Development*, p. 162.

55. Mandel, *Revolutionary Marxism Today*, p. 79: 'Only in the case of relatively marginal products will they be able to challenge imperialist domination of the market.' South Korean prowess and international competitiveness in the areas of steel production,

shipbuilding and automobiles can by no stretch of the imagination be considered successes in 'marginal' products.

56. Lowy, *The Politics of Uneven and Combined Development*, p. 89. This definition is reiterated in slightly different words on p. 161.

57. Ibid., pp. 175–7. See particularly, his footnotes 32 to 40.

58. Ibid., p. 165.

59. E. Mandel, 'Semi-Colonial Countries and Semi-Industrial Dependent Countries', in *New International*, fall 1985: 'It is not cumulative precisely because it is dependent i.e. *overdetermined by what happens in the capitalist world market, above all in the imperialist countries which continue to represent the major part of that market*' (his emphasis), p. 168.

While a number of 'semi-industrial' countries have confirmed Mandel's prediction of periodic stagnation if not absolute decline in industrial growth, e.g. Latin America, i.e. there has been *absence of cumulative growth*, this has not been the case of South Korea and India where prolonged cumulative growth has taken place, despite the long downturn of world capitalism since the early seventies.

60. It has been a general conviction of Trotskyists that whatever the deformities of bureaucratically planned economies they were superior to even the strongest capitalist countries in their ability to provide full employment. China is better in this regard than India but it is not a 'labour shortage' economy, like the USSR and has a real and growing unemployment problem which cannot be laid to rest simply or primarily at the door of world capitalism and its pernicious influence on even a post-capitalist economy.

61. E. Mandel, *New International*, p. 159.

62. E. Mandel, *Revolutionary Marxism Today*, p. 91.

6

India in the World

Nonalignment: The Nehru Era

If there is one word that is supposed to represent the unchanging essence of Indian foreign policy, it is 'nonalignment'. Obviously, this conceptual characterization could only endure precisely because its meaning was not fixed. It has been invested with different meanings and cadences in response to changing circumstances. But the equally enduring attraction of the nonalignment label (not only to India) would be incomprehensible if it did not possess some minimal consistency of meaning. That constant quality has been nonalignment's endorsement of the important, if rather mundane, principle of maximum national autonomy in the realm of foreign policy, of the right of governments to have the greatest possible freedom to manoeuvre as they see fit rather than subordinating themselves to the imperatives of bloc politics as decided by its most powerful constituents.[1]

'Nonalignment' has generally been used in two distinct though related senses. In its first sense it is a world view or ideology concerning how the global state system should function. It purports to describe a broad movement, the third world Non-Aligned Movement (NAM), which initially sought to play the role of an international buffer between the two cold war blocs. Nonalignment as a normative principle undoubtedly had a certain moral cast. It was supposed to represent an alternative to 'balance of power' and 'alliance' politics.[2] In its second and more important sense, it is a description of the specific foreign policy orientation of a particular nonaligned country. As such, it becomes a loose synonym for the traditional policy of effective pursuit of national interest through the expansion of national power. That there is an irreconcilable tension between these two uses of nonalignment became evident to the Indian state elite as the Nehru era drew to a close, particularly after the debacle of the Sino–Indian war of 1962.

Two of the most striking aspects of the Nehru era were the high visibility of India in UN efforts to intervene in international disputes (Korea, Suez, Congo, and so on) and the complete dominance of Nehru himself in the formulation of foreign policy, at least up to 1962. For fully seventeen years, Nehru combined the positions of prime minister and foreign minister.[3] His personality and predilections had a major impact on the foreign policy behaviour of the country. Newly independent countries, he believed, could individually and collectively play a global role out of all proportion to their actual power. But beyond this, capitalist India's more narrowly conceived national interests were also seen to be best served by nonalignment. This was undoubtedly correct. Nonetheless, the intellectual bedrock for this orientation was a confused mishmash of traditional realpolitik and grandiose assumptions about the cultural, political and moral contributions of India's 'freedom struggle' to the world. The moral and political lessons Nehru drew from the National Movement's success in displacing colonial rule were extended to the international arena. Nehru himself was all too often prone to describing nonalignment as a *philosophy* of foreign policy behaviour, and one which was supposed to be uniquely suited to India's cultural (Hindu tolerance, indeed promotion of variety and coexistence) and political (non-violence as a credo) heritage.

There were numerous and powerful elements of self-deception in this Indian self-image. Post-independence foreign policy was indeed connected to the character of the National Movement's leadership and forms of struggle but not in the way Nehru assumed. Neither the movement nor its leadership was *revolutionary* in character. This had an important impact on its foreign policy which has been passed over in silence by bourgeois and even some left historians.[4] Independence was achieved through a *transfer* of power, not a radical wresting of authority invoking deep anti-autocratic or socially liberating impulses on a mass scale. This had a number of consequences, most notably with respect to Kashmir, the Himalayan states (Nepal, Bhutan and Sikkim) and the Sino–Indian border question. Certain princely states had to be incorporated peacefully into the Indian Union, with due respect accorded to the right of the ruler to decide his allegiance to Pakistan or India in the partitioned subcontinent. Hyderabad, Junagadh and Kashmir created immediate problems because the sentiments of the public and the ruler were at variance. While the first two problems were 'resolved' by fiat, Kashmir was not and became an enduring preoccupation dogging India's and Pakistan's future foreign policy behaviour.[5]

The other aspect of this non-revolutionary transference of authority was Indian willingness to inherit 'colonial rights' and so-called obligations with respect to the Himalayan states, and its essentially legalistic attitude to the British demarcation of the Sino–Indian territorial boundary. The contrast with the post-revolutionary regimes of Russia and China is sharp. Leninist Russia and (to a lesser extent) Maoist China made renunciations of the foreign claims of territory and loyalty of past imperial regimes. Imperial China had exercised vassalage and semi-vassalage over Tibet and the Himalayan states until stripped of this power by the British. Post-liberation China, like post-independence India, denied the full right to self-determination to Tibet and Nagaland respectively. But Chinese attitudes towards the Himalayan states and to border demarcation with Nepal as well as India were largely bereft of imperial hangovers.

India took over from colonial Britain its 'forward defence thesis', which envisaged India's natural defence sphere as extending to the southern watershed of the Himalayas incorporating most of Nepal, Bhutan and Sikkim.[6] Even under Nehru, India sought to discourage Nepali and Bhutanese attempts to legitimize their international status by seeking widespread diplomatic recognition, admittance to the UN and so on.[7] On the Sino–Indian border question, India insisted on the inviolability of colonially demarcated boundaries – a posture that could only be offensive to Chinese sensibilities regarding past impositions by foreign powers. The Chinese favoured a political, rather than technical–legal, approach based on reasonable give-and-take and respect for key geographical features along the border in question. This was a legitimate and reasonable approach and should have been reciprocated by New Delhi. Though periodic tensions between India and China were probably unavoidable given their common interests in consolidating their power in the Himalayan crest, the Sino–Indian war was avoidable.[8] The pertinent argument is not that a non-revolutionary government in India could never have pursued other policies (especially with regard to the boundary dispute with China), but that such a government could have much less readily assumed the mantle of colonial Britain's subcontinental pretensions. It convinced itself that there was no contradiction between disrespecting or discouraging the right of the Himalayan states to maximum national autonomy in foreign affairs and insisting that this was a basic principle of nonalignment. The forcible liberation of Goa in 1961 was perfectly justified as the final step in eliminating colonial rule in India, but it further eroded the moral credibility of India and Nehru as apostles of non-violence.

The relative obscurity (and inconsequentiality) of the Himalayan states in the larger global order and Pakistan's resort to force in 1948 in order to wrest control of Kashmir provided a cover for the more 'imperial' aspects of Indian foreign policy behaviour. But what gave Indian nonalignment even greater credibility was the American post-war decision to situate South Asia within its global strategy of anti-Soviet and anti-Communist containment. The USA sought to include a number of Middle Eastern and Asian countries in various military alliances like the Baghdad Pact, SEATO and CENTO. This went directly against Indian efforts to insulate South Asia from the superpowers as part of its regional strategy and as a general principle of promoting disengagement from bloc politics everywhere.

In the early years of independence, though the Indian state was undoubtedly determined to maintain maximum autonomy, it was by no means as critical of the USA as it was later to become. Apart from cultural and political ties with the West, symbolized by Indian endorsement of the Commonwealth, the USA was widely perceived as a supporter of decolonization. Moreover, Stalin's Russia was still hostile to the 'bourgeois' government of India. Only in the early fifties, when nonalignment and Indian stances on such issues as Korea, Vietnam and Chinese exclusion from the UN, were seen to weaken imperialist efforts to isolate the USSR, did the Kremlin begin to make a dramatic re-evaluation of the character of the Indian state, of the Congress and of its path of economic development.[9]

In pursuit of its global strategy the USA supported Pakistan and its claims to Kashmir while seeking to impose political and economic pressures on India. National and regional self-interest and global hopes for the nonaligned bloc combined comfortably to give Indian foreign policy an overall coherence and legitimacy. It opposed regional military alliances with noticeably greater fervour than it opposed NATO, ANZUS or the Warsaw Pact. It sought to befriend China and the USSR while maintaining good relations with the West. It sought to maximize economic support from all quarters. It was an active champion of de-colonization, disarmament and development in global forums. Even Indian embarrassment at offering only mild criticism of the Soviet invasion of Hungary in 1956 (necessitated by the Soviet Security Council veto on Kashmir in favour of India) was brief and did no lasting damage to India's image or self-perception. What had not been perceived was that Indian nonalignment was not just an 'active' policy particularly suited to a country pursuing economic self-reliance and to its ambitions as an emerging power; it was also a 'reactive' posture whose efficacy was partly dependent on the degree of pressure imposed on it by one or more of the bigger powers. It was Chinese pressure, namely the Sino–Indian war, that led to the first decisive re-evaluation of and readjustment in Indian nonalignment.

The Uncertain Years

China's humiliation of the Indian armed forces in the 1962 border war did not cause India to abandon nonalignment, though it forced it to seek active support from the West (particularly the USA), to give up the wider global pretensions of the Nehru era and to pay much more attention to developing its own military prowess. Henceforth, strengthening Indian nonalignment would mean strengthening the Indian capacity to pursue its national interest. This shift away from international preoccupations also meant a sharper definition of Indian 'interests', which were now seen to be essentially, indeed almost entirely, regional in character. At the same time, ironically, this geographic involution began to release India from its hitherto strongly Pakistan-obsessed foreign policy. It had a new 'enemy' and new alliances to consider. Effective countering of even the Pakistan threat required a broadening of strategic vision and political and military preparations.

Pakistan and China constituted the direct challenges to Indian authority on the South Asian landmass; the USSR and the USA would undoubtedly seek for their own reasons to project their power into this region and into the Indian Ocean. Nonalignment was still a valid framework for policy-making because it was still the only approach compatible with the effort to make India an independent and respected power in the region. After the initial temptation to seek a closer alliance with the USA was resisted, India was in a position to benefit from both the US policy of seeking to contain China and from the deepening Sino–Soviet rift. The American view that capitalist and democratic India was the most important political and economic counterweight to Communist China had an established pedigree. As nonalignment became internationally respectable in the sixties, and with signs of a thaw in US–Soviet relations, the old American policy of forging military alliances to contain the USSR lost a large part of its appeal in regions like South Asia. It was only after the rise of an independent and armed Palestinian resistance in the late sixties and then the Yom Kippur War and oil crisis of 1973 and 1974 that the strategic importance of the Middle East (and in consequence the geo-strategic significance of South Asia and the Indian Ocean) was highlighted.

From the Soviet point of view, the importance of an Indian counterweight to China was reinforced by its own rapidly deteriorating relationship with the latter. To keep India on course and immune to Western blandishments, the USSR had to step up its own commitment to the country. At the same time, seeking improved relations with Pakistan would give it a greater flexibility vis-à-vis China for there was as yet no convincing reason why it should put all its South Asian strategic eggs into the Indian basket. Pakistan and China had obvious reasons for exploring the possibility of improving ties. To compensate for the Sino–Indian imbalance, India sought support from USA, USSR and Western Europe. Its great success story was its developing link with the USSR. To compensate for the Indo–Pakistan imbalance, Pakistan sought support from the USA, Western Europe, the USSR and China. Its great success story was its developing link with China.

The 1965 Indo–Pakistan war (initiated by the latter's 'subversive' manoeuvres in Kashmir) was a small turning point. Militarily, the outcome was a stalemate. But politically it represented a victory of sorts for India. The Pakistani assumption that the war would spark off a rebellion in Indian-occupied Kashmir was belied. Indian nonalignment had resulted in the USSR providing aid to India and the USA remaining neutral. Pakistan's membership of SEATO (it withdrew after the 1965 war) got it nothing. The shift to China became more marked in the wake of this Western 'betrayal'. With the USA increasingly bogged down in Vietnam, it was the USSR that emerged as a truce-maker, getting India and Pakistan to sign an accord at Tashkent. One lesson that was not lost on Washington or Moscow was that the Indian military performance (in contrast to 1962) suggested that the country would soon emerge as the dominant power in South Asia. In the last years of the Johnson administration such a realization was beginning to dawn and was expressed in policy re-examination in the State Department. The 'no arms' policy to both India and Pakistan embodied the new perception. It was given up by the Nixon administration in favour of a tilt to Pakistan because of US overtures to China through Pakistan. Nixon also needed to convince China of his bona fides as a reliable friend in the slowly emerging, anti-Soviet US–China axis. This required a display of loyalty to such a longstanding American ally as Pakistan.

1971 and After: India's Search for Power

In July 1971, Kissinger stunned the world by announcing that the USA and China had been engaged in secret negotiations. A short month and a half later Mrs Gandhi announced the signing of an Indo–Soviet Friendship Treaty. It was her attempt to counter-balance the new US–China–Pakistan line-up. That the Indo–Soviet Treaty violated the spirit if not the letter of the NAM charter was beside the point.[10] While the Soviets have felt that the treaty could even play a role in staving off seemingly imminent war, this was not their main motivation. They undoubtedly saw the treaty as a major component in a long-term effort to establish an Asian Collective Security System – a thinly disguised Soviet policy aimed at isolating China. From Mrs Gandhi's point of view, the treaty was a measured and defensive response to a crisis-ridden conjuncture, a guard against a possible USA-supported Chinese attack on India should war break out with Pakistan in what was later to become Bangladesh. If anything, the treaty hastened Indian armed intervention, which had as its principal purposes the dismemberment of Pakistan, the pre-empting of the liberation struggle in Bangladesh (which was beginning to take on an independent dynamic), and the installation there of a pro-Indian Mujibur Rahman government.[11]

The contrasting perspectives with which the treaty was looked upon only became clear with time. The Soviets have often sought to play it up and to encourage hopes of its renewal when it runs out in the nineties. The Indian government, after its victory in 1971, has consistently sought to play it down. For India the treaty remains the first and only one of its kind. It was clearly necessitated by the politics of its time and it possesses relevance only as long as the pressure of a USA–China–Pakistan axis against India in South Asia exists. But it also represents a limitation on India's longer-term project of securing the removal or at least minimization of superpower presence in the region.

In 1971 Pakistan found support from China and the USA to be more verbal than material. It was unable to prevent Pakistan's defeat by India on the battlefield. The American administration was divided between the Nixon–Kissinger executive and the State Department with respect to its appreciation of the situation and of Indian aims.[12] The Pakistani repression of Bangladesh, after all, received international opprobrium. Furthermore, the USA had no real strategic interest in maintaining the status quo in East Pakistan, a fact which was not lost on Beijing and which must have influenced China's decision at the time not to match its anti-Indian belligerence in words with action on the ground.

Yet realpolitik after 1971 also determined that Pakistan had no choice but to turn to the USA and China again. The major new policy orientation of Bhutto, which was followed and developed by the Zia military regime (which overthrew Bhutto in 1977), was cultivation of closer ties with the Islamic Middle East as a way of widening foreign policy options and restoring prestige. In a sense, General Zia at the time of his death in autumn 1988 had achieved remarkable successes. The loss of East Pakistan was, on balance, a strategic and economic gain, since in the long run even a formally united Pakistan could not have challenged India's regional primacy and would always have been militarily vulnerable. Pakistan had restored its status as a major strategic ally of the USA. It had close relations with China and an excellent standing with the 'moderate' Arab regimes of the Middle East. It was an important factor in the internal politics of Afghanistan, where the Russians had clearly suffered a grievous defeat – symbolized by their belated decision to withdraw from a country in which they should never have intervened in the first place.

But this 'success' is also deceptive. Pakistan's international prestige far outpaces its actual strength. Its diplomatic skill in repeatedly out-manoeuvring India through the technique of offering reciprocal obligations is no substitute and little compensation for the fundamental asymmetry in the distribution of power between the two countries. Moreover, the unresolved 'national question' in Pakistan remains a time-bomb which even the quasi-democratic regime of Benazir Bhutto will have immense difficulty in disarming, if indeed it is capable at all of doing so, which is doubtful.

India's trajectory since 1971 has not been without its ups and downs but the trend has been firm. Following its 1971 victory it was able in 1973 to restore good relations with the Shah of Iran with economic benefit to both.[13] More important, there was the beginning of a common exploration of the role a joint Iran–India axis could play in enhancing the prestige and authority of both in their respective regions. Iran under the Shah was keen to distinguish itself from its Arab neighbours and its close relations with the USA did not prevent it from entertaining ambitions of its own. From New Delhi's angle, a closer relationship with Teheran would be an additional and important counter to the relationship Pakistan was forging with the Arab states of West Asia. The Islamic revolutionary upsurge that began in 1978, culminating in the overthrow of the Shah, abruptly terminated what had earlier seemed a promising development in India's new drive for regional eminence.

The Indian state's growing self-confidence was reflected in other ways. In the late sixties fear of possible Chinese nuclear blackmail had led the Shastri and Mrs Gandhi governments to at least consider the idea of seeking shelter under an American nuclear umbrella. After 1971 such a perspective was abandoned for good. The 1974 Pokharan nuclear explosion was a declaration to the world of Indian capabilities and a warning that India now had the option to join the select nuclear club when and if it felt it was in its interest to do so. Sikkimese aspirations towards greater autonomy were summarily dealt with in 1975 through a constitutional merger which effectively ended its earlier protectorate status. In 1975 a bewildering series of coups took place in Bangladesh in which both the hand of the CIA and of New Delhi could be discerned.[14] By the beginning of the eighties, the Nagaland struggle for independence had been effectively tamed by a combination of sustained repression and economic and political handouts to a carefully nurtured Naga elite. The jungle resistance might continue but an increasingly war-wearied Naga population was slowly coming to terms with the reality of a seemingly unshakeable Indian overlordship.

The shift from Mrs Gandhi's government to the Janata regime and back affected only the nuances of Indian foreign policy.[15] Throughout the eighties the process of regional consolidation continued, with much of the focus on the Pakistan irritant. Despite the outcome of the 1971 war and Pakistan's repeated protestations that it could not hope to match its Indian opponent, its general orientation and behaviour marked it out in Indian eyes as a continuing obstacle to Indian ascendancy. In particular, its alliances with the USA and China constituted a threat to India which the latter felt could not be allowed to pass unchallenged. Without ever breaking into an armed confrontation, Indo–Pakistan relations have been marked by an enduring suspicion and diplomatic efforts at one-upmanship.

As repression of the Tamils in Sri Lanka grew and ethnic strife escalated, India had little hesitation in embroiling itself ever more deeply in the country's affairs. It offered sanctuary and support to Tamil insurgents as well as its services as mediator in forging a settlement between the moderate Tamil United Liberation Front (TULF) and the United National Party (UNP) regime in Colombo. The Indian aim was to use a controlled Tamil resistance as a lever to promote a settlement providing a reasonable degree of Tamil autonomy. This strategy was soon to unravel. After early 1986 the UNP actively embraced a brutal military solution to the Tamil problem, by crushing resistance in the north and northeast of the country. This policy only succeeded in displacing the TULF by the Liberation Tigers (LTTE) as the dominant force among Tamils. The LTTE was more committed to the idea of Tamil Eelam or 'independent homeland' than the TULF and it was less controlled or controllable by New Delhi. The military escalation on both sides forced the Rajiv government to re-evaluate its own perspectives as a desperate Sri Lankan government strove for more active help from outside powers like Israel, Pakistan, Britain and the USA.

India's attitudes were dictated by its own perception of national interest. This did not admit of an independent Eelam and a truncated Sri Lanka left with no option but to fall into the arms of the West. In June 1987, when Colombo escalated its ground and air war against the LTTE, India deliberately and publicly violated the country's air and sea space by air-dropping civilian supplies to the besieged population and insurgents of Jaffna. The point had been forcefully made – there could be no solution of the crisis which was unacceptable to India. When President Jayewardene of the ruling UNP found that the USA was prepared in this case to cede regional authority to India, he carried out a dramatic volte face matched only by the parallel drama of an Indian volte face. On 29 July 1987, the two countries signed an Indo–Sri Lanka Accord wherein the Indian army was for the first time made (in effect) the guarantor of civic peace in a neighbouring and fully sovereign country with which it was not at war. As Premadasa (soon to be the next Sri Lankan president) accurately put it, the protector [of the LTTE] had become the hunter. India gained in a number of ways. Its right to intervene outside its borders in defence of its 'national interests' was emphatically legitimized. In a letter appended to and subsequently incorporated into the Accord, Sri Lanka in effect accepted a partial Monroe Doctrine for India, by renouncing its right to have any alliance with a third party or otherwise engage in activities considered by India to be inimical to its interests.[16] India as a regional power had come of age.

The universally favourable reception to the Accord was particularly pleasing, signalling as it did recognition by East and West of India's sphere of influence.[17] The contrast with the Janatha Vimukti Peramuna (JVP) uprising of 1971, when India was only one among a number of countries, East and West, which rushed to the support of the Bandaranaike Sri Lanka Freedom Party (SLFP) regime, could not have been sharper. To be sure, this time a segment of the population of ethnic Indian origin was involved. But this cannot disguise the fact that the decisive factor behind India's *exclusive* intervention was its growing regional authority. In the same year, in May, a coup in the Fijis led to repression of Fijians of Indian ethnicity. As this was far away from the Indian sphere of influence, New Delhi had little choice but to call on Britain, Australia and New Zealand to exercise sanctions of some sort. When, in November 1988, India airlifted commandos to put down a coup attempt in the Maldives, it was seen as almost a matter of routine.

The fact that, like the original Monroe Doctrine, the Indian version has also run into trouble is a separate matter. This trouble is proof that in the twentieth century, in which mass politicization and mass activity have reached levels undreamt of in past centuries, the authority of major powers is often weaker and more illusory than they imagine.[18] The trade-off involved in the Accord was, after all, contingent on the Indian army doing its job properly, that is, 'taming' the resistance. Having failed so far to achieve this, the UNP itself has come to question the terms of the Accord as involving too many concessions on Colombo's part. The Indian peace-keeping force has been asked to withdraw as internal pressure from the JVP and LTTE has grown. The UNP government has had to explore more seriously the prospects for a direct political settlement between the government and the Tamil resistance groups, including the LTTE. But even this carries the risk of alienating the JVP. An increasingly desperate Premadasa administration has seen no option but to push for Indian peace-keeping force withdrawal – the one policy which meets with the approval of both the JVP and LTTE. India has little choice but to withdraw, though it will try to do this in a manner which best saves its face. The Accord has collapsed.

Finally, what of the complex quadrangular relationships between the USSR, USA, China and India during the seventies and eighties? After the emergence of Bangladesh, American policy towards India, especially in the first years of the Carter administration, showed signs of becoming more balanced. This drift was ended by the fall of the Shah in February 1979 and the Russian invasion of Afghanistan in December that year. Overnight Pakistan became a lynch-pin in a new American strategic perspective as a counter to Soviet expansionism and as a military and political launching pad for the USA's Rapid Deployment Forces into the Middle East.[19] Pakistan's ties with 'moderate' Arab regimes (Pakistani troops have been seconded to some of these regimes) were seen as a valuable counterweight to the pressures for radicalization exerted in different ways by the secular Palestinian struggle and the Shiite Islamic forces of Iran and Lebanon.

This sudden elevation of Pakistan into an immensely important strategic ally of the USA was also accompanied by the continuing entente between the USA and China. The threat of a USA–China–Pakistan axis loomed larger then than at any time in the past. Only with the end of the Brezhnev era and the new improvement in Sino–Soviet relations initiated by Gorbachev and Deng has this threat receded. In such a context, the Indian response to the Russian invasion of Afghanistan was, not surprisingly, rather muted. India could not approve of a Soviet military expansion that brought it to the Durand Line and that much closer to South Asia. But insofar as this exerted pressure on Pakistan's other flank it was not without its benefits. Escalated American military aid to Pakistan, ostensibly for the Afghanistan rebels, could not but be viewed as an unfriendly act in New Delhi, necessitating compensatory military purchases and preparations. India's dismay about the extension of Soviet might in Afghanistan was firmly subordinated to the need to preserve its close relations with the USSR. In the wake of the Soviet withdrawal from Kabul, the Indian government is more than mildly concerned about the prevailing uncertainty.[20]

The most significant development, perhaps, in the quadrangular power game over the last two decades has been the Chinese realization that Indian autonomy and power were real and growing, that India was not a puppet of Soviet 'Social Imperialism' and that its regional hegemony could be contested but not displaced by Pakistan. As early as 1979, Beijing indicated to the Janata regime that Chinese support to the insurgents of northeast India was a 'thing of the past'.[21] In their own search for greater flexibility, both the USSR and China have sought to thaw their mutual relations. China has also been keen on improving Sino–Indian relations while maintaining its political tilt towards the USA and Pakistan. The Sino–Indian border dispute is by no means insoluble. The actual line of control is likely to be the basis for a more permanent treaty solution. This will take some time but there is meanwhile no real barrier to the pursuit of a steady if low-key improvement in Sino–Indian ties. These are likely to be further facilitated by the Chinese recognition that, in the long run, it has to award to Tibet a much more substantial measure of autonomy than it currently enjoys. The return of the Dalai Lama from Indian exile is likely to be crucial. A partial restoration of Tibet's role as an autonomous buffer state between China and India will assuage Indian doubts, especially if it involves the dismantling of a substantial part of China's military apparatus in Tibet.

The Nuclear Dimension

'Nuclear ambiguity' is the best way to characterize the current policies of India and Pakistan. The election of Benazir Bhutto has made no concrete difference in this respect. However, to the extent that establishment of a quasi-democratic civilian regime in place of naked military dictatorship might reduce tensions with India and lessen the probability of an Indo–Pakistan war breaking out, it also tends to somewhat ease the nuclear tension between the two countries. But the tension still exists and will not go away; there is every chance of it periodically rising to more dangerous levels. Both countries have developing programmes for weapons production and deployment. Both resort to public boasting about indigenous technical abilities. Both assert their determination to resist nuclear threats or blackmail. And both countries repeatedly insist that their nuclear programmes are entirely peaceful in character and that they have no ambitions to join the club of nuclear weapons states (NWS).

But there are important differences in the nuclear histories of the two countries. India was the first third world country to embark upon a nuclear energy programme. It is also the only third world country (apart from China) that has officially detonated a nuclear device (in 1974) and thereby publicly demonstrated its nuclear weapons capability. Up to the late fifties India's nuclear programme was entirely civilian, but it soon developed a dual character, though in the Nehru era the official policy regarding nuclear weapons was permanent abstinence. Unlike Pakistan's, the Indian civilian nuclear programme was not essentially a cover for a military programme. But the Indian programme, operating as it has on a broad technological front involving space exploration, development of delivery and command, control and intelligence systems and weapons-grade fuel accumulation, provides the foundation for the exercise of weapons option at progressively higher levels if and when a decision to do so is made.[22]

As far as official policy goes, a break took place after the 1962 Sino–Indian war and the death of Nehru. Officially, policy shifted subtly from permanent abstinence to simple abstinence, subject to review. The Chinese nuclear explosion of 1964 and its development of the hydrogen bomb three years later almost certainly put paid to any real chance of India joining the 1968 Non-Proliferation Treaty (NPT), though it had played a prominent part for many years in its preparation. In retrospect this was a landmark decision. Since then India has consistently refused to forswear the nuclear option. The perceived 'threats' justifying such a stand have varied. Throughout most of the sixties and seventies it was the Chinese threat, potential and actual; since then it has been the Pakistani threat. But over time, self-perceptions have become more important than threat perceptions. Advocates of India going nuclear have increasingly emphasized the importance of nuclear weapons possession as a source of prestige and power in global politics.

The Pakistani route to the nuclear threshold has been more straight-forward and more reactive, that is, to Indian developments. By the mid sixties, India had built a research reactor and a reprocessing plant and the nuclear weapons issue had become a part of the domestic public debate. It is at this relatively late juncture that Pakistan entered the nuclear field. Its preparations had a decidedly military orientation and efforts began in earnest (especially after the 1971 defeat in Bangladesh) to produce indigenously or acquire clandestinely the essential components for such a programme.[23] Early attempts to secure plutonium reprocessing facilities from France fell through because of American objections. But by all accounts, Pakistan in the eighties constructed a uranium enrichment plant (based on stolen designs and illegal imports) which has given it the wherewithal to pile up a small arsenal of bombs.[24]

Islamabad's attitude to nuclear weapons production and deployment is both more consistent and less complex than New Delhi's. It has sought either a military-political parity with both countries having nuclear weapons capability – both reaching the threshold without crossing it – or a non-nuclear parity of mutual renunciation of the nuclear option. Thus Pakistan has over the years repeatedly put forward a variety of proposals for mutual and simultaneous abstinence, ranging from mutual or third-party inspection of each country's nuclear facilities to joint signing of the NPT (this proposal seems to have fallen out of favour with the Benazir Bhutto government) to the establishment of a nuclear weapons free zone (NWFZ) in South Asia.

India's nuclear ambiguity has thus been more ambiguous than Pakistan's. This is a function of the asymmetry in power and potential between the two countries. India has greater difficulty defining its insecurities. To justify keeping the weapons option open, New Delhi has to cite long-term abstract and potential rather than existing dangers, such as the China factor, possible superpower blackmail, the need for leverage to augment global efforts at disarmament, and so on. The one effort to cite an immediate danger, the Pakistan threat, founders on Islamabad's willingness to explore avenues of regional de-nuclearization in contrast to India's unwillingness to entertain any such proposals. Pakistan has greater reason to avoid an open nuclear arms race with its neighbour because the effort to match it in nuclear weapons production and deployment would impose a disproportionately heavier economic, military, social and political burden than on India.

How stable or precarious is the current threshold? In both countries there are factors pushing for and pulling against a crossing of the nuclear Rubicon. In India the most important factor, both accelerating and retarding Indian movement, is China. Any Indian decision to go openly nuclear will result in the inauguration of two nuclear arms races – a primary one vis-à-vis China and a secondary one vis-à-vis Pakistan. China would then clearly perceive India as a nuclear threat to be factored into its strategic nuclear planning. At the same time, if India is to fulfil its apparent destiny as an Asian giant of comparable stature to China, does it not have to make up for lost time by going openly nuclear and at least establish a credible nuclear deterrent against a Chinese threat? As Indian power and ambition grow, pressures for making the second choice are also likely to increase.[25]

For Pakistan, remaining at the threshold is in a sense a 'can't lose' situation. If India agrees to mutual abstinence, non-nuclear parity is automatically established. If both remain at the threshold without crossing it, then despite the asymmetry between the two there is a threshold parity, which has enhanced Pakistan's prestige both in its own eyes and in those of others, for example in the Islamic world. American failure to penalize Pakistan for its flouting of its own laws regarding nuclear proliferation has only increased the incentive for Pakistan not to pull back.[26] In sum, the longer the stand-off, the less stable the situation. Crisis situations between India and Pakistan on even non-nuclear matters – for example, Punjab, Kashmir – can act as dangerous nuclear triggers.[27]

There is a remarkable irony in the fact that the anti-nuclear peace movements are strongest in Europe, where, relatively speaking, the danger of an outbreak of nuclear war is less.[28] There are obvious reasons for this, apart from the fact that the peace movements themselves have lowered the possibilities of such an outbreak. Popular consciousness of the ravages of war is strongest in Europe, the principal site of two world wars. After 1945 it is in Europe that nuclear weapons as instruments of great power politics have been most visible and manifest. But contrary to NATO's claim, it is not nuclear weapons that have prevented a conventional war across the East–West divide but the progressive improbability of such a conventional war, which has rendered the use of nuclear weapons equally improbable.[29] A conventional war in Europe between the USA and USSR has not been a feasible proposition from at least the mid fifties. The initiation of any such conflict would inevitably lead to a war of continental, indeed global dimensions. For a start, the continent of Europe would obviously be embroiled; there would be a rapid 'spillback' into the Middle East and Indian Ocean regions, and the USA's Pacific armoury would be brought into action in keeping with American warfighting perspectives developed since 1945. A major and direct conventional military confrontation between the USA and USSR in Europe could not be limited to that theatre, let alone a small part of it, but would become a global war with multiple goals and dispositions involving many geographical theatres of action. Both superpowers know this: it is this prospect that has deterred. World wars are the result of a complex of factors and require numerous preconditions. Their emergence or avoidance should not be reduced to implausible single-factor explanations like the presence (or absence) of a nuclear deterrent.

In light of the essentially *astrategic* character of nuclear weapons and the growth in popular consciousness that has taken place during the nearly fifty years of the nuclear age, one of the principal lessons that can be drawn is this: it is extremely difficult for nuclear warriors to justify even to their own national public the use of nuclear weapons against non-nuclear adversaries in any circumstances, and against nuclear adversaries in 'cold' situations, outside the context of a 'hot' conventional military conflict. Only in actual wartime conditions can the necessary political, psychological and moral parameters for the actual use of nuclear weapons be constructed. This was the case for Hiroshima and Nagasaki. The reason why the nuclear danger in the subcontinent is greater than elsewhere (if India and Pakistan were to embark on an open nuclear arms race) is because the likelihood of a *conventional* war between the regional rivals erupting at some future point is considerable. After the Middle East (where there is still no nuclear rival to Israel), South Asia boasts the greatest number of wars between the same two combatants (three wars compared to the five Arab–Israel wars). Benazir Bhutto's accession does not remove the basic sources of tension. Apart from the Kashmir question there is the Sikh terrorist and secessionist struggle abetted in some degree by Pakistan. These are the gravest internal challenges that the Indian state has faced since independence. The steady growth of Hindu nationalism is dangerously complemented by the rise of Islamic fundamentalism in Pakistan despite the secular bias of the present civilian regime compared to its military predecessor. There is also the instability of bourgeois political rule in both countries, which makes the temptation to play up an external enemy threat or go in for a unifying and diversionary policy of military brinksmanship an enduring one. It is not necessary to draw from this the conclusion that a war between India and Pakistan is imminent or inevitable, only that it will remain a real and serious possibility.

The search for regional de-nuclearization is therefore an urgent one. Of all the proposals put forward far and away the best is the establishment of a South Asian nuclear weapons free zone (NWFZ).[30] If Pakistan is merely bluffing in repeatedly putting forward this proposal, no Indian government has ever been prepared to call the bluff. Instead it has formulated objections which fall into three broad categories: (a) a NWFZ cannot be fully verified; (b) it renders India defenceless against other NWSs, particularly China; (c) partial de-nuclearization initiatives should not be substituted for global initiatives since this weakens the thrust towards global disarmament.

These are not serious objections and the motivation for putting them forward is clearly to derail serious investigation of the intrinsic merits of the NWFZ proposal. Time and again, resolutions for a South Asian NWFZ have been presented at the UN; time and again only India and occasionally Mauritius, Maldives and Bhutan have voted against it. There is obviously no foolproof guarantee that any treaty will hold or that violation will never take place. Verification procedures work best and will be most trusted when signatories to a NWFZ are most committed to making them work. Verification can provide proof of non-compliance; it can never provide proof of compliance. Verification can never be complete but it can be adequate. This adequacy is more a political matter of trust and a desire to make the arrangement work than a technical matter of equipment and routines. The question then is not how to establish foolproof verification procedures for a South Asian NWFZ (an impossibility) but how to overcome Indian reluctance to commit itself to one. The Indian government has never cited the absence of foolproof verification procedures regarding superpower naval encroachment as a reason why an Indian Ocean 'zone of peace' proposal is not feasible!

With regard to the second objection, the focus is always on China, never on the superpowers, for the simple reason that even if India were to go in for nuclear weapons it could never establish a credible nuclear deterrent against the USA or USSR. Its only effective response to a nuclear threat or attempt at nuclear blackmail from these quarters would have to be non-nuclear, destroying any logic in its arguments for keeping the nuclear option open. As for China, having the option is no answer either; exercising it will only create more problems than it solves, by enhancing not reducing nuclear insecurities.[31]

The third line of argument is the most specious of all and is really nothing more than a token gesture to the ideal of disarmament by those whose primary interests lie rather in the politics of power. Indeed, it is the pursuit of power that is supposed to achieve disarmament – a mind-set entirely typical of nuclear elites everywhere. It represents, ultimately, a refusal to treat nuclear weapons as fundamentally different from conventional ones, as well as a failure or refusal to think through the contradiction between, the transnational effects and astrategic character of nuclear weapons and the 'nationalized' character of their control. The increasing inadequacy of the system of nation-states to resolve the fundamental problems of our age is most starkly highlighted by the nuclear weapons dilemma. Nor is it the first time that larger goals are invoked – such as total nuclear disarmament – with which all can agree, in order to prevent consideration of the process – the necessarily partial acts of renunciation – by which that larger goal is to be reached.

A South Asian NWFZ is clearly necessary and desirable, but is it achievable? How is the Indian government to be brought around? The government is not the bomb lobby. Within the government are those who favour an immediate exercise of the option and others who prefer to leave things as they are in the absence of a demonstrable provocation demanding otherwise. Keeping the option open without exercising it is still the lowest common denominator and, therefore, the beneficiary of governmental inertia in the face of momentous decisions. As long as this position holds there is still space and time for other pressures to develop, namely a movement demanding a NWFZ in South Asia.

The thrust has to come from both internal and external forces. Social democratic parties like the ruling party in Sweden (India and Sweden are both part of the Six Nation Disarmament Initiative) or the Labour Party in Britain (which values its historic ties with the Congress) can embarrass and pressure the Indian government by public support for a NWFZ in the region. They should be pressed to do so by the peace movements of their countries. Within the subcontinent the nuclear weapons question admittedly has little immediate relevance for the vast majority of Indians and Pakistanis – for them the mundane problems of everyday existence have a burning urgency. Nevertheless, the potential urban catchment area for a peace movement is at least several millions of people in both countries. This is a 'public opinion' that the two governments have to take seriously. A history of peace groups and of a peace movement in the subcontinent comprising in the main English-speaking students and middle-class professionals has only just been undertaken. Such a history will obviously be marked by the rise and decline of various small groups of relatively short life-spans. This is a normal part of the history of many movements. The first important step remains to establish the clearest possible agitational focus. This can only be a South Asian NWFZ. Once this focus is secured, the goal of developing a larger and more unified anti-nuclear movement, no matter how seemingly remote, is brought qualitatively closer.

The View from the Left

Both the mainstream left (CPI and CPM) and the Maoists have based their assessment of the Indian state's external behaviour on their ideological dependence on and allegiance to the world view emanating from Moscow or Beijing. The extent to which the post-Mao and Gorbachev changes in these two centres of international communism might shake the Indian left into a new evaluation of India's foreign policy remains to be seen. Silent confusion rather than a dramatic break has been the response so far.

The reigning (and ageing) leaderships of both the CPI and CPM were ideologically formed in the thirties and forties. Stalin's concept of 'socialism in one country' and a two-campist world view of the USSR as the principal bulwark of the socialist world's defiance of American dominated imperialism has remained their basic theoretical and ideological matrix. Soviet-led anti-imperialism is still seen as the dominant axis of struggle in the international arena even as the twentieth century draws to a close. The logic of 'socialism in one country' gradually pushed ruling Communist parties in the third world and the opposition Communist parties of Western Europe to develop perspectives and stances independent of those adopted by the Kremlin or Beijing. This has not happened in India because both the CPI and CPM continue to see the USA as the main destabilizing force in South Asia.

Indian nonalignment in practice, especially after 1971, has involved a pro-Soviet security tilt and a frequent, if often purely formal, opposition to US global behaviour. The CPI and CPM have supported the Indian state's progress towards regional hegemony because they have seen this as the necessary response to American efforts at destabilization – since the USA would obviously aim at setting up client or buffer regimes among the smaller South Asian neighbours. With the significant exception of the CPM's refusal to support the Indian government on the Sino–Indian border question, both parties have endorsed (sometimes with criticism) virtually every major foreign action undertaken by the Indian state – its 1971 intervention in Bangladesh; its absorption of Sikkim; its crushing of Nagaland's nationalist aspirations; the Indo–Sri Lanka Accord; and the prevention of the coup in the Maldives.[32]

This CPI and CPM uniformity cannot be explained simply by the fact that both share a two-stage schema for the internal revolutionary process. The CPI and CPM differ on the class characterization of the Indian social formation and on their characterization of the Congress. The CPM has never considered the Congress to be the 'progressive' representatives of the so-called national bourgeoisie. Yet this has not prevented it from sharing with the CPI a common opinion of the ruling bourgeois party's 'progressive' foreign policy. After the Emergency, the CPI came around to the CPM's view of the Congress as an anti-progressive authoritarian force, but with no effect on its endorsement of the Congress's foreign policy.[33] The changes in Soviet policies after Gorbachev have disturbed both parties more than they care to admit. But it is easier for them to adjust to Soviet foreign policy in the era of Gorbachev than to the anti-Stalinist implications of his internal changes. The basic thread of continuity in Soviet foreign policy from Stalin to Gorbachev – what is good for the Kremlin is good for international socialism – is stronger than in the case of domestic policy, where the ruptures are far sharper. Ideological de-Stalinization has been much slower in external affairs.[34]

While the CPI has been very consistent in its identification with the Kremlin, the CPM arrived at its present alignment with Moscow's world view in the middle and late seventies through a more winding path. In its internal organization the CPM is more Stalinist than the CPI. The left wing within the old undivided CPI reacted more sharply and negatively to Khrushchevite revisionism at the CPSU's Twentieth Party Congress and were sympathetic to the critique of Soviet revisionism that developed during and after the Sino–Soviet split. The CPM, when it emerged in 1964, had to face two competing centres of international Communism with contrasting general orientations. Even though it felt that this rift could only weaken the necessary struggle to maintain a common front of all Communist parties against American-led imperialism, the CPM still had to assess which world view was more accurate, Beijing's or Moscow's. The CPM was not unsympathetic to the Chinese critique of Khrushchevism–Brezhnevism in the sixties. It was the subsequent evolution of Chinese foreign policy, its search for a global entente with American imperialism, rather than Chinese hostility to the Indian government that paved the way for the CPM to move back towards a more uncritical endorsement of Soviet foreign policy. Within the CPM, the pressure exerted by the left wing in support of the Chinese world view disappeared when the Naxalites broke away to form their own distinct movement.

For Naxalites the Chinese critique of Soviet Social Imperialism struck a particularly powerful chord. The USSR had closer relations with its enemy, the Indian state, than with any other country in the third world. The Naxalites, unlike the CPM, were committed to a direct confrontation and overthrow of this state. In fact, the Indo–Soviet connection is the outstanding test case for the general validity of the thesis of Soviet Social Imperialism. Nowhere else have the Soviets invested so much in military and economic support over so long a time. If Soviet Social Imperialism falters as a Marxist characterization of the Indo–Soviet relationship, it can hardly stand on its own anywhere else. According to this view, the USSR is at least as exploitative (usually more so) than imperialism with respect to certain third world countries. It exploits them through economic and military links which create an acute structural dependence on the USSR.

Economic exploitation in the Marxist sense takes place either through unequal exchange, which transfers surplus (value) created in one country to another, or through direct extraction, which is the case when foreign capital owns and controls productive units in another country, by direct investment. Soviet investment in India has been overwhelmingly in the public sector. It never involves equity ownership or control nor direct control over production in industries. The USSR does not directly extract surplus from Indian labour in order to accumulate capital for itself.

What about its trade and aid relationship with India? Early on, India like most developing countries supplied primary products and industrial raw materials. Inasmuch as these reduced Soviet imports of the same from the West it meant a saving in hard currency for the USSR. But the pattern of Indo–Soviet trade has been dynamic. India is increasingly a supplier of semi-processed goods and manufactures. In 1961–62, manufactures were approximately 15 per cent of Indian exports to the USSR. This went up to 35 per cent in 1969–70 and to 48 per cent in 1979–80 and has remained around this level since.[35] With regard to imports from the USSR, the share of manufactures has declined while that of petroleum and petroleum products has gone up, as has that of other primary products.[36] In short, India supplies higher-value manufactures, despite the fact that this trade has facilitated a shift in Soviet domestic production from semi-processed goods to more sophisticated technological products. Indian economic self-reliance has been helped, not weakened, by the Indo–Soviet connection.

Trade benefits are not one-sided. Indian exports to the Soviet Union are not a diversion from, but an addition to exports to hard currency areas. What few studies on this have been carried out show a small diversion in the years 1967–69 but no significant diversion before or since.[37] The rate of growth of exports to convertible currency regions has been higher than the rate of growth of exports to the USSR. For Indo–Soviet trade, this rate of growth during 1969–70 to 1979–80 for exports and imports respectively was 13.7 per cent and 17.0 per cent. For Indian trade with the rest of the world it was 16.7 per cent and 19.4 per cent respectively. Between 1980–81 and 1986–87, the figures for Indo–Soviet trade were 7.3 per cent and 0.9 per cent and for India and the rest of the world it was 11.8 per cent and 8.7 per cent.

With regard to the terms of trade of this bilateral relationship (a crucial element in establishing the degree of unequal exchange), the summary conclusion from a series of comprehensive studies is:

> One of the most important theoretical issues with regard to payments arrangements is that, under it, the terms of trade of the weaker partner deteriorate. Significantly, India's terms of trade with the Soviet Union do not provide any empirical evidence of this. India's trade with the Soviet Union is conducted on the principle of world price. As a result one can expect that the price relationship between India and the Soviet Union will not differ substantially from the price relationships that exist between India and the rest of the world. There have been one or two years when there was a slight departure from the international trend.[38]

Undervaluation of the rupee in the rupee–rouble rate, however, works to the advantage of the USSR. In its essentially barter (rupee) trade with India, the USSR has negative balances. India's idle balances have a lower purchasing power in view of this undervaluation. But the very fact of rupee trade has also meant that India never had to suffer the kind of financial balance of payments problems so characteristic of third world relations with the West.[39] Indian trade with Eastern Europe has long reached a point where both sides see benefit in moving towards hard currency payments. But in the case of Indo–Soviet trade both sides continue to favour the barter system.

Furthermore, there is little doubt that in the decades since independence Soviet purchases have stimulated Indian industry, in areas such as leather, textiles, hosiery and knitwear, and light engineering goods, for example. For engineering products, Indian penetration of Western markets early on was not possible. It was the Indo–Soviet and Indo–Comecon trade that helped Indian entrepreneurs big and small develop brand reliability and skills of all kinds that stood them in good stead when the time came to try to get into the lucrative and beckoning Western market for manufactures.

Adherents of the Soviet Social Imperialist thesis have claimed that the USSR engages in 'switch' trading, that is, purchasing Indian goods and selling them elsewhere for hard currency, thus indirectly depriving India of this currency. Switch trading, however, is done all the time by both sides (for example, India sells Soviet crude oil for hard currency). Even if it is conceded that the USSR does more switch trading, in value and volume terms, than India, this is not a significant aspect of the trade relationship. Such trade has necessarily to be confined almost totally to non-manufacture exchanges, since packaging, advertising, brand names and consumer familiarity become major obstacles to switch trading. Since traditional exports of tea, jute, cashew, and so on, have become relatively less important, switch trading too has been of diminishing importance. Nor is Indian trade with the West free of this phenomenon.

Because of the barter nature of Indo–Soviet trade, Soviet aid and credit has been tied up with it and has been paid back in kind with Indian goods. The economic exchange has been conducted on a state-to-state basis.[40] It has been project-oriented and repayment of principal and interest has been in rupees. Soviet credit is for the purchase of Soviet goods, so there is a tie-up of maintenance imports, but this does not amount to a critical dependence. The state-to-state nature of the Indo–Soviet connection is inevitable given that the USSR has no economic compulsion to export capital. Its aid and credit policies are largely motivated by political and diplomatic considerations. Soviet aid to India is at nominally lower interest rates than most Western aid but this has been offset by other factors so it is unclear what is the effective interest rate. Repayment periods are generally shorter than in the case of loans by the West. But moratoria and adjustments in the schedule of repayments are related to political considerations; the Kremlin can often be more flexible than the West in this respect.[41]

Though Indo–Soviet economic relations will undoubtedly expand, they face certain constraints. With the establishment of the public infrastructure, India's basic import needs from the USSR have declined and its export surpluses have grown. India is turning more and more to the West for imports of the most sophisticated technology. In most years the quantity of Indo–USA trade is greater than that of trade between India and the USSR. Rates of growth of bilateral trade are higher for Indian partners like Japan and West Germany. Nor is the USSR the biggest aid-giver to India, though it remains within the top six. India does have to export to the USSR to meet its debt repayments and to cover defence purchases. No official figures for Soviet defence credit to

India are available but it has been estimated that Indian repayments of military credit average around $300 million a year and will reach around $700 million in the early nineties as a result of military purchases in the eighties.[42]

Both countries are searching for ways to make their two-way trade more meaningful. As long as economic aid and military credit from the USSR remain important, India needs to make the commercial relationship more fruitful by importing more from the USSR; in effect, the latter must be better able to supply the sophisticated technology that India needs. On balance, the Indo–Soviet economic connection will grow because it is to the benefit of both countries.

The military relationship between the USSR and India is of considerable significance. Since the 1962 debacle India's armed forces have relied greatly on the USSR for military hardware. The USSR is India's dominant supplier, but this is not sufficient to fix a permanent political orientation or alignment on the part of India, any more than it was in the case of Sadat's Egypt after the Yom Kippur War. Soviet leasing of a nuclear submarine to India in 1988 (relying on sixties' reactor technology) is the first instance of nuclear military technology being transferred directly to a third world government. India was also the first outside country to be sold MiG-29 fighters, followed by Iraq and Syria.

But the Indian state is now consciously seeking a balanced procurement arrangement, not only because it wants to lessen dependence in this field on the USSR but because the latter is less and less able to provide the state-of-the-art military technology that aspiring powers like India want. The relatively lower cost of arms purchased from the USSR is a factor whose attraction is declining. 'After almost 20 years of buying its most important equipment from the USSR India now turns to the USSR for the bulk of its forces, while it prefers Western suppliers for its most advanced items when possible . . . Now India's best aircraft are generally British and French.'[43]

Unless the USSR is able to develop a wide range of high quality arms it could soon become the 'world's largest marginal supplier'. Since military provision is vital to the Soviet Union's ability to obtain political influence in the third world, this is worrisome to the Kremlin. For the foreseeable future, India will remain the USSR's most important military client. But India's diversification of purchases and indigenization of production will increase. The top military and political elite, which is more pro-Western than pro-Soviet in its cultural and ideological inclinations, can only encourage such a process. But the USSR will remain its single most important military source.

The benefits (to India) of the Indo–Soviet relationship have not then been bought at the expense of damaging political, military or economic payments. The Soviet Social Imperialism thesis as a description of the Indo–Soviet connection is frankly absurd. The rise of the post-Mao, Deng leadership, its repudiation of much of its Maoist heritage and its turn to the market internally have all helped to disorient even those Indian Maoists still sympathetic to Mao. The latter's 'three worlds' theory has come in for some severe criticism. There is a glimmer of awareness that Mao's world view may also have been premised on the subordination of revolutionary developments elsewhere to China's immediate national interests. Indian Maoists have not given up the characterization of the USSR as a state capitalist country practising social imperialism, but it is no longer so loudly proclaimed. There is a new willingness to question older assumptions now that Beijing's appeal as the new and more worthy centre of international Communism has faded. Indian Maoism has become more Indian and less Maoist.

Prospects and Limits

By and large, Indian nonalignment has been a success. While Pakistan has been a strategic adversary, the USA has not. Unlike China, India has never had to face either of the superpowers, let alone both, as strategic opponents. Certainly its relations with the USA have had a fluctuating character alternating between phases of greater or lesser tension, in contrast with its much smoother relationship with the USSR. But this was unavoidable given the USA's perception of Pakistan and its role in US regional and global perspectives. Herein lies the crux of the issue. South Asia in itself is not an area of vital strategic interest or importance to the USA. Only a successful revolutionary upsurge in one of the smaller South Asian countries is likely to alter this perception. Of course, a revolutionary transition in India would have enormous global consequences. But leaving aside such a radical scenario, South Asia's significance for the USA lies more in its location as a staging base or conduit for the exercise of American power elsewhere, for example, in the Middle East. An imperialist naval presence in the Indian Ocean is thus an adequate substitute for an American military presence on the subcontinent itself.

This means that the USA has never had real reason to view bourgeois India as a strategic opponent and some reason to value its potential role as a capitalist rival to Communist China for Asian influence, though now that American fear of Communist monolithism is over, this too is a less significant attraction. The USA can, therefore, accommodate itself to the prospect of growing Indian hegemony in South Asia. At the same time, there persists a basic clash of interests which prevents the possibility of any comfortable accommodation between the two in the next few decades, unless the decline of American imperialism is far more precipitous than can as yet be imagined. The USA cannot act *through* India to secure its interests elsewhere, so it must do so on its own through a continuing presence in the Indian Ocean and through a search for a client regime or ally in or around the region.[44] These American compulsions constitute an obstacle to the Indian state's own aspirations for regional hegemony. Nor does India now need American strategic support to cope with either the Pakistani or Chinese challenge. Only if the latter two are powerfully united would India be tempted to enter a strategic relationship with the USA, if it was available.

What are the basic sources of India's national power? Underpinning Indian nonalignment is clearly substantial economic self-reliance. As the Brazilian example shows, this is not an automatic corollary of having a continental-size economy or population or being gifted with a variety of natural resources. It is also a matter of the specific historical evolution of the indigenous bourgeoisie, of the nature of the leadership of the state elite, and of the policy choices it makes. Besides economic strength and potential, some of the other important components of national power are population size, natural resources, military capacities, the relative strengths of and challenges posed by neighbouring countries, cultural unities even amidst diversity, political stability, diplomatic skills and the accidents of geographical location.

India has been fortunate in being naturally well endowed in many of these respects. These strengths have been reinforced by the state's conscious attempt systematically to enhance its military capacities. In the past decade, India has raised its defence budget by some 250 per cent. It has the world's fourth largest army. It has now overtaken Iraq as the world's largest importer of weapons.[45] But it also has an impressive production base of its own comprising over forty defence plants and thirty-four research and development units. It is able to meet all its own requirements for light and infantry weapons. It can make its own frigates carrying guided missiles. It is producing under German licence patrol submarines and it has made advances in its efforts to produce quality tanks and light combat aircraft. Nor are its successes in rocket and satellite technology to be sneezed at.[46] Progressive indigenization is a conscious policy and is intimately linked to import policy concerning military hardware. India is also likely to enter the export market for small arms in a big way in coming years.[47]

On the cultural and ideological plane, Hindu nationalism, the latest thematic incarnation of Hinduism's promise, lends itself just as easily as earlier Hindu or Buddhist themes did to justifying shifting interpretations of nonalignment. Hinduism, after all, has always expressed a profound ambiguity and flexibility to questions concerning the morality and status of power. Kautilyan realpolitik can be cited as easily as Buddhist or Gandhian *ahimsa* once was. Hindu nationalist sentiments have also been evoked during the last two wars with Pakistan. During and after the 1965 Indo–Pakistan War openly Hindu chauvinist forces like the RSS-Jan Sangh led the campaign for the 'Indianization' of Muslims whose loyalties were presumed to be shaky. After the 1971 war, Mrs Gandhi was widely acclaimed as 'Durga', the Hindu mother goddess of destruction. She and her Congress party did not hesitate to make use of and encourage this Hindu image. After this victory Mrs Gandhi began to make use of Hindu symbols and rituals, to make well-publicized visits to temples, to talk of the 'rights of the majority' and so on. The legitimization of Hindu nationalist sentiment was now being provided by the bourgeois political mainstream, the Congress itself.[48]

The endemic political instability of India's domestic order has had only the faintest of echoes in the realm of external affairs, a situation facilitated by the mainstream left's uncritical endorsement of Indian nonalignment in all its shifting phases. But it is the topographical fortuity of South Asia that provides both assurances and limits to the Indian state's ambitions. South Asia is geographically unique, with the Himalayas as a natural northern cap to the peninsular landmass. This marks out an enclosed space which is the natural sphere of influence of the one continental-size power situated within it. China, by contrast, confronted by Vietnam on one flank, the USSR on the other, and an offshore giant-in-the-making, Japan, has no such comparable natural sphere of influence.

But this very factor of relative isolation not only enhances India's regional potential but also acts as a significant obstacle to its global possibilities. For nations such as the USSR, China, Japan, Germany and France (even Mexico, Brazil and Argentina) the pursuit of regional authority necessarily requires an extension of power and diplomacy to a vastly larger extra-regional, if not global arena. For this very reason, Mexico, Brazil and Argentina find it more difficult than India to become regionally pre-eminent. Where India can safely and piously reject balance-of-power diplomacy in view of its own regional preponderance, such options do not exist for other major nation-state aspirants to regional superiority. For them to achieve accepted regional eminence requires that they be more than just regional powers.

The costs to the USA, USSR or even China of ceding regional (South Asian) dominance to India are thus that much lower, just as the gains to India in terms of global influence are that much less. At the same time, the fact of regional dominance gives it a global status and prestige which is not commensurate with its actual capabilities for intervention on an extra-regional scale. The Indian transition from regional to global power-brokering will be qualitatively harder and more difficult than for some other rising powers, such as Japan, China and West Germany. Indian willingness and ability to attempt such a transition is still a question for the twenty-first century.[49]

The basic challenges to India sustaining subcontinental dominance will arise from within the area rather than from without; but these will not be inconsequential. Indian preponderance is not a synonym for regional stability. The tensions between the smaller nations and India (not to mention those between India and Pakistan) are in many respects sharper than those between India and the superpowers or China. The South Asian mosaic is exceptionally complex, with religious hostilities adjacent to or overlapping with ethnic spillovers, historical patterns of dependence combining with newer forms of economic exploitation, elite nationalism (and therefore anti-Indian resentment) burgeoning in the smaller countries in the wake of partial modernization. Thus Nepal and Bhutan are likely to become more rather than less assertive of their sovereignty. This may involve overtures to China which would disturb India. Indian reactions to any social upheaval of revolutionary dimensions in Nepal need not be spelled out.

In Bangladesh, even under Mujibur Rahman, anti-Indian sentiments had grown. Ziaur Rahman, who came to power in 1975, only tempered his personal hostility to India years later, when he accepted the Janata government's invitation to visit India in 1979. The Bangladesh policy of encouraging Muslim settlement in the Chittagong Hill Tracts has provoked a Chakma tribal backlash and Chakma refugees have sought and obtained shelter in India. New Delhi for its part accuses Dacca of doing little to prevent the Tripura National Volunteers (TNV), rebels fighting to free Tripura from the Indian grip, from taking shelter across the border. Relations between India and Bangladesh are thus destined to have their share of tensions. The same is obviously the case with Sri Lanka.

Defending 'Indian interests' now means that the state must be willing and able to intervene in the internal affairs of neighbouring states if developments there are perceived as representing a serious danger to these interests. Such involvement can take various forms, from supporting one or other political force within the country in question, to blockade (as could be the case for landlocked Nepal), or open military intervention. Any socialist revolutionary perspective must focus on the region as a whole. The Indian state is not only the defender of bourgeois rule in India, it is also the defender of last resort of bourgeois rule in all the neighbouring countries, including Pakistan. If the relationship of forces in India has long been strongly tilted in favour of the bourgeoisie this has not always been so in other countries, where the bourgeoisies are comparatively weaker with respect to their own oppressed classes.

For almost a decade after its birth, Bangladesh represented the weakest link, the site where the frailty of the state and the ruling classes was sufficiently acute as to present, in the short term, the serious possibility of a revolutionary seizure of power by left and progressive forces. The rise of the Jatyo Samajtantrik Dal (JSD) in 1975 in Bangladesh was perhaps the most important expression of this potential, although it was subsequently crushed. Nor can the JVP uprising in Sri Lanka of 1971 be forgotten.[50] Only after this did Sri Lanka establish a significant repressive apparatus of its own. The JVP, which even then showed signs of Sinhala chauvinism, subsequently degenerated into a viciously anti-Tamil sect prone to indiscriminate violence and terrorism in keeping with its eclectic and confused ideological orientation. In Sri Lanka today the challenge posed to India would have been even sharper if the Tamil resistance had given birth to a genuinely Marxist political force and leadership instead of an assortment of radical and not-so-radical nationalist groups or if there was greater clarity on what kind of autonomy had most popular support and needed to be fought for. Should the ethnic Tamils of the north and northeast in their vast majority come to feel that they can have no place within the Sri Lankan Union no matter what the degree of autonomy awarded to them, the Indian state could yet find itself on the wrong side of a national liberation struggle with significant impact on its own body politic.[51]

Ironically, it is Pakistan where the 'national question' could burst out with dramatic force and could turn the country into a powerful revolutionary bridgehead undermining the authority of the Indian state. It has long been assumed, understandably so given the intra-regional rivalry between the two countries, that India only stood to benefit from a further break up of Pakistan. This is no longer necessarily correct. Different times require different responses. An India secure in the knowledge of its overall regional dominance is now more likely to fear the break up of Pakistan if this becomes the prelude to the establishment of a more radical regime in one of the Pakistani 'nations'. The pressures on India to intervene to 'restore stability' would be immense. Clearly, there are promises as well as dangers in such a future scenario for revolutionary movements in the region. If the Indian state can hope to harness 'great Indian' chauvinism to its cause, the revolutionary left can hope to tap the passions of militant nationalism in the classic historical combination of a struggle for both national and social liberation.

One of the great tragedies of the Indian revolutionary left in the last forty years has been its failure to link up with the socialist and Marxist elements within the Naga resistance, which has almost singlehandedly fought the might of the Indian state for nigh on thirty-five years. The programmatic content and political sophistication of such forces, for all their Christian and Maoist inflection, is superior to that of any of the Tamil resistance groups in Sri Lanka. To be sure, the disputed character of Naga nationalism and its small population (less than a million) were obvious barriers to building wider support. But these would not figure if India were to intervene in a country like Nepal or Pakistan which was already recognized as sovereign and independent. In short, the cross-country solidarities among the exploiting, ruling classes of the region must be matched by corresponding cross-country solidarities from below – among the oppressed classes and their representative political formations. These external linkages have to be forged even as the process of national consolidation takes place. The first act in the South Asian revolutionary drama need not take place on Indian soil, but the last most assuredly will.

Notes

1. Even when third world countries actively pursue close alliances with one or the other bloc or are de facto partners, if not puppets, of one or the other superpower, they find it invaluable to endorse this principle of 'nonalignment'. Besides this affirmation of independence, the other main ideological attractions of the label and of membership of the Non-Aligned Movement (NAM) today is that it endorses cultural and racial equality and calls for the kind of reform (however muted) of the world capitalist economy that would, if implemented, give a greater share of the global surpluses to the national bourgeoisies of a number of third world countries. The NAM also provides a diplomatic forum for the exercise of a variety of pressure plays and tactics by individual countries not only vis-à-vis the superpowers and the bloc countries but also in intra-NAM conflicts. These have grown over time and done much to vitiate the effectiveness of the NAM as a whole.

Perhaps the most accurate way of summing up the third world NAM's growing though never complete irrelevancy is to recognize that there is really no third world, no real nonalignment and no movement! In place of the latter there is only rhetoric and resolutions watered down by the need to establish the lowest common denominator. All narrative histories of the NAM thus amount to little more than a statement of its basic principles and a chronological account of its preparatory, ministerial and summit meetings with their accompanying paraphernalia of pious intentions and formal resolutions. Its basic principles – which have been repeatedly violated in spirit if not in letter – are: (1) a country should follow an independent policy of coexistence and nonalignment or should be showing a trend in favour of such a policy; (2) it should consistently have supported movements for national independence; (3) it should not be a member of multilateral military alliances concluded in the context of great power conflicts; (4) if it had conceded military bases these concessions should not have been made in the context of great power conflicts: (5) if it were a member of a bilateral or regional defence arrangement, this should not be in the context of great power conflicts.

These conditions were laid down in the Cairo preparatory meeting (June 1961) for the first summit conference of the nonaligned in Belgrade. An earlier summary of principles was attempted in the famous Panchshila (Five Principles) enunciated by Zhou EnLai at the 1955 Bandung conference. Fred Halliday (in private communication with the author) has made the interesting and persuasive point that the founders of nonalignment, Yugoslavia, Egypt and India, sought to diminish Chinese influence in the third world (each for their own reasons) and in pursuit of this perceived the formal inauguration of the nonaligned bloc (1961) as a way of excluding China and of weakening the Bandung-inaugurated Afro–Asian alliance of which China was a part. Nevertheless, Bandung was a forerunner of nonalignment and India, in particular, had a well articulated foreign policy of nonalignment long before 1961.

In the early phase of the NAM, the internal coherence was greater since there was a common international goal – decolonization (disarmament and development were other themes of secondary importance) – which also lent a certain moral stature and integrity to the movement. The acuteness of cold war politics also enabled certain countries to benefit economically by playing off one bloc against the other. This factor has declined in importance not so much because of the fluctuating character of superpower confrontation (cold wars and detentes) but because of the progressive structural integration of third world countries into the capitalist global order. Beneficiaries of this structural 'lock' like the NICs of East Asia have more to gain from de facto alignment with the West than from equidistance, while losers can less afford to alienate imperialist institutions and governments.

2. For a sound analysis of why the NAM has been progressively enfeebled see A.Z. Rubinstein, 'Does Nonalignment have a future?', in *The Non-Aligned World*, July–September 1984. Rubinstein points to the passing away of charismatic leaders, the preoccupational involution of member countries, intra-NAM discords, and a shift in NAM activities from political brokering to economic lobbying. 'The profusion of high sounding statements of principle and prescription that are the end products of non-aligned conferences signify as Bismarck once observed (in another context) that those professing them have not the slightest intention of carrying them out in practice' (p. 396).

3. Foreign policy is always more autocratically determined than domestic policy. The 'expertise' of individual leaders counts for much more and their popular or mass support for much less. The Indian state represents the interests of the dominant coalition, but it is the state elite that has a monopoly control over issues of foreign policy. Within this state elite, it was the figure of Nehru that towered over others. In most bourgeois democracies there is something that can be called the 'foreign policy establishment'. There is an 'intra-government pluralism' even though it operates within a framework where strict hierarchy and authoritarian commands are accepted as necessary and desirable norms. This pluralism was largely absent in India from 1947 to 1964 and the death of Nehru. The prolonged character of the National Movement enabled the Congress to develop institutions and expertise at various levels to tackle the domestic problems of the post-independence era. The civil service's external affairs wing could see the diplomatic implementation of foreign policies decided elsewhere. But there were no effective policy-making bodies as such. Nehru's dominance in external affairs was an accepted fact in the Congress before 1947 and the pattern was maintained, indeed reinforced by the apparent successes of Indian nonalignment after independence. It is only after the Sino–Indian war and Nehru's death that a degree of institutionalization took place in regard to the making of foreign policy. See K.P. Misra, 'Foreign Policy Planning in India', in K.P. Misra (ed.), *Foreign Policy of India*, Thompson Press, New Delhi 1977 and S. Tharoor, *Reasons of State*, Vikas, New Delhi 1982.

The Indian foreign policy establishment, however, has none of the institutional mediations to big capital that exist, for example, in the USA, where the military-industrial complex exerts constant pressure through various mechanisms and where privately sponsored think tanks and research foundations play a not unimportant role in establishing the menu of foreign policy options and the limits of debate. In India, it is a small and closed affair. The PM's secretariat and inner circle of friends/advisers tend to be far more important than cabinet, parliament, the ministry of external affairs, or the top intelligentsia outside of government.

4. Attempts by certain left historians to ascribe a revolutionary character to the pre-independence Indian bourgeoisie and to the Congress movement-cum-party become particularly threadbare when it comes to analysis of Indian foreign policy. Nonalignment is seen as fundamentally 'progressive' and the logical complement to the bourgeoisie's 'revolutionary' capitalist transformation. See A. Mukherjee and M. Mukherjee,

'Imperialism and Growth of Indian Capitalism in the Twentieth Century', in *Economic and Political Weekly*, 12 March 1988.

5. The moral dimension of foreign policy behaviour in the Nehru era was evident in Nehru's initial promise to the UN that a popular plebiscite would be held in Kashmir once Pakistan withdrew its troops from that part occupied by it during the 1948 war with India. Since that early lapse, Nehru and all his successors have firmly rejected every subsequent attempt by Pakistan to internationalize the Kashmir issue. In the 1972 Simla Agreement with a Pakistan cut down to half its original size, Mrs Gandhi got Z.A. Bhutto to accept the 'bilateral' character of this dispute. This did not, however, prevent successive Pakistani regimes from raising the issue periodically in international fora.

6. China's invasion of Tibet in 1950, which eliminated the Tibetan buffer between China and India, undoubtedly disturbed India and gave greater edge to its efforts favourably to consolidate its relationship with the Himalayan states. The India–Bhutan Treaty was signed in 1949 establishing a relationship 'in perpetuity'. This treaty makes it incumbent on Bhutan to seek India's 'guidance' in external affairs. Ever since, the precise interpretation of what this means has been a bone of contention. The 1950 Treaty with Sikkim reaffirmed its protectorate status until this was ruthlessly and cynically discarded in 1975 by India, which manipulated domestic political divisions in Sikkim to achieve its ends. The Indo–Nepal Treaty of 1950 established the principle of 'mutual defence' for India and Nepal.

7. For a critical and unsentimental account of India's policies with regard to the Himalayan states, see S. Dutt, 'India and the Himalayan States', in *Asian Affairs*, February 1980. See also B. Sen Gupta, *The Fulcrum of Asia* (updated edition, Konark Pub., 1988) and V.J. Belfiglio, 'India's Economic and Political Relations with Bhutan', in *Asian Survey*, August 1972. For more pro-Indian accounts see A. Appadorai and M.S. Rajan, *India's Foreign Policy and Relations*, South Asian Publishers, New Delhi 1985 and R. Gupta, 'Sikkim: The Merger with India', in *Asian Survey*, September 1975. Nehru's most important leadership rival, Sardar Patel (who died in 1950), was in favour of outright annexation of the 'native states'. See S. Dutt, 'India and the Himalayan States'.

8. N. Maxwell's *India's China War*, Penguin, Harmondsworth 1970, puts the blame squarely on India. But even sources more sympathetic to India have accepted that China had a reasonable case and that Indian inflexibility had not a little to do with the final outcome. See B. Sen Gupta, *The Fulcrum of Asia*, pp. 126–31. Sen Gupta calls both India and China 'empire nation states'. While this accurately highlights the realpolitik and more cynical aspects of India and China's policies and behaviour, it doesn't sufficiently respect the differences between a capitalist state, however autonomous, and a post-capitalist state, however bureaucratized, and, therefore, the qualitatively different variables operating on and affecting each regime.

9. Theories of a non-socialist but non-capitalist path of development were developed to justify the USSR's efforts to woo India's bourgeois leaders and government. In time even this theoretical fig-leaf was discarded with no shame whatsoever and with no effect on the USSR's by now well-established policy of supporting capitalist India as its foremost friend in the non-socialist world.

10. 'The word "nonaligned" may be differently interpreted, but basically it was coined and used with the meaning of being nonaligned with the great power blocs of the world. 'Nonaligned' has a negative meaning. But if we give it a positive connotation it means nations which object to lining up for war purposes to military blocs, to military alliances and the like. We keep away from such an approach and we want to throw our weight in favour of peace', *Jawaharlal's Nehru's Speeches*, Vol. 4, Government of India Publications Division New Delhi 1964, p. 361.

Articles VIII to X of the Treaty were the key ones. Collectively they committed each party to avoiding military alliances directed against each other, the use of each other's territories for related purposes and to help each other in the event of an attack on one of them. See A. Kapur, 'Indo-Soviet Treaty and the Emerging Asian Balance', in *Asian Survey*, June 1972 and A. Appadorai and M.S. Rajan, *India's Foreign Policy*. For re-interpretations of nonalignment in the aftermath of the Indo–Soviet Treaty see M.S. Rajan, *India's Foreign Relations During the Nehru Era*, Asia Publishing House, Bombay

1976. For a criticism of such 're-interpretations' stressing their departure from original conceptions see T.A. Keenlyside, 'Prelude to Power', in *Pacific Affairs*, fall 1980.

11. The official reason given for the intervention, namely the 'intolerable' refugee burden, is not convincing. Proportionately speaking, the Afghan refugees have been a much more severe burden on Pakistan doing much more damage to its social fabric. As long as the Soviets were present in Afghanistan there was of course no question of a direct Pakistan intervention in Afghanistan.

Colonel Abu Taher, one of the principal leaders of guerrilla forces fighting for the liberation of Bangladesh, while appreciative of Indian material support was adamant that 'liberation' had to be the work of Bangladeshis themselves and that eventual victory with mass support and resistance was at most a year or two away. See L. Lifschultz, *Bangladesh: The Unfinished Revolution*, Zed Books, London 1979 for an account of this much neglected aspect of struggle for Bangladesh's liberation.

12. C. Van Hollen, 'The Tilt Policy Revisited', in *Asian Survey*, April 1980.

13. V.P. Dutt, *India's Foreign Policy*, Vikas, New Delhi 1984.

14. L. Lifschultz, *Bangladesh*, pp. 47–50, 98–108, 130–49. Also Appendices A, B, C and D.

15. The strategic design – regional dominance – was the same, the operational aspect somewhat different during the Janata's reign. The Janata government was more emphatic on pursuing a 'good neighbour' policy and in pursuing 'genuine nonalignment', i.e. greater even-handedness in its relations with each superpower. This sufficiently disturbed the Russians to send A. Gromyko, the Soviet foreign minister, to New Delhi in April 1977. But Indian reassurances to Gromyko apart, the USA–Pakistan link ensured that the Janata would observe the usual security tilt to the USSR and an economic tilt to the West, though Indo–Soviet trade and technical agreements were also sharply expanded under Janata rule.

16. Two issues particularly perturbed India – the possible setting up of a VOA transmitter and radio-receiver in Jaffna which could be used for military purposes; and the possible leasing out of Trincomalee harbour to the USA which already had a major base in Diego Garcia in the Indian Ocean.

17. The Accord was supported by all major parties in India including the Communist mainstream, which in this case as in others (Nagaland, Sikkim) had no use for Leninist principles of respect for the right to self-determination of oppressed nationalities. The influential media fell over itself in rushing to applaud government behaviour. A few voices raised doubts about the troop commitment involved in the Accord, not because they questioned the morality or political correctness of the action but because of their fears (soon to be realized) that India might be stepping into an Afghanistan-like imbroglio. For virtually the only serious political critique and condemnation (from the left) of the Indian government's action to appear in the English language national media, see my 'For Whose Sake?' in *Illustrated Weekly of India*, 6 December 1987. Demands for a recall of the cynically named Indian Peacekeeping Forces have grown over time as they have got bogged down and have been subsequently voiced by opposition parties. But not one has come out with a principled critique and rejection of the original premises behind India's promotion of the Accord.

18. This is easy enough to understand. The actual power of any particular nation or political unit is not just a function of the power that the wielder can bring to bear on the power 'object', it is also a function of the willingness to comply of the object as subject in its own right.

19. L. Lifschultz, 'From the u-2 to the p-3; The US–Pakistan Relationship' in *New Left Review* 159, September–October 1986.

20. New Delhi would favour the pro-Soviet Najibullah regime over an Islamic fundamentalist regime in Kabul resting on Pakistani or Iranian support, or an unstable coalition of such forces with the Najibullah government. A second-best option would be a stable coalition headed by the former king Zahir Shah sufficiently mindful of Soviet pressure and sufficiently cautious about Pakistan and Iran.

21. W.K. Anderson, 'India in Asia. Walking on a Tightrope', in *Asian Survey*, December 1979, p.1247.

22. L.S. Spector, *The Undeclared Bomb*, Ballinger, Cambridge MA 1988, p. 93, Table 2. For 1992 the low estimate for a stockpile is 60 weapons while the highest estimate is for over 200. The chapters on India and Pakistan provide a comprehensive and balanced summary of their respective nuclear histories. There are a host of studies on India's nuclear policy and development while the single best account of Pakistan's clandestine efforts to secure weapons capability remains S. Weissman and H. Krosny, *The Islamic Bomb*, Vision Books, London 1983. See also the interview given by Pakistan's head of uranium enrichment programme, Dr A.G. Khan to Indian journalist Kuldip Nayar in *The Observer*, London, 1 March 1987.

23. In early 1972, Prime Minister Bhutto had a secret meeting with the country's top scientists at Multan, after which all the stops were pulled out.

24. L.S. Spector, *The Undeclared Bomb*, p. 145, Table 4. For 1992 the low estimate is 5 bombs stockpiled, the high is 24.

25. Even on realpolitik grounds such a decision would be counter-productive. Besides, the heightened levels of nuclear insecurity between India and China and India and Pakistan may well give rise to the following outcomes: (1) Superpower wariness and coolness towards India would grow. (2) Regional neighbours would be alarmed. They are, at least, as likely to seek solace in alliances with outside powers to counter Indian 'hegemony' than to meekly accept it. (3) India may still not succeed in establishing a 'credible nuclear deterrent' against China despite years of effort since China will seek to maintain, if not extend, its quantitative and qualitative 'lead'. (4) The China–Pakistan axis is more likely to be strengthened than weakened by the existence of a nuclearly armed India. (5) Any conventional military dispute between India and Pakistan will carry a new risk of possible escalation into a nuclear war. One can argue that this risk is small but one cannot deny that it is a new and additional risk to the play of possibilities that existed before. To believe that nuclear weapons possession might deter conventional armed clashes between two countries *for ever* is, of course, to swallow the counter-factual myth of deterrence. (6) Finally, once the subcontinent embarks on an arms race, the possibilities of eventual de-nuclearization become more not less remote. The 'leverage' argument is not upheld by historical evidence. It can hardly be seriously contended that the intermediate NWSs have levered the superpowers into acts of partial disarmament.

26. These are the Symington, Solarz and Glenn Amendments, all waived by the US President, the waivers being periodically renewed. The first bars US aid to any non-nuclear weapons state (NNWS) importing uranium enrichment technology. The second bars US aid to any NNWS illegally obtaining nuclear commodities from the USA in nuclear explosives. In October 1984 a Pakistani national in the USA was convicted of attempting to export krytrons (used in nuclear explosive switches). In 1987 a Pakistani-born Canadian national was convicted of exporting beryllium (used in nuclear weapons). The third amendment bars US aid to countries importing plutonium reprocessing technology.

27. For a more comprehensive critical survey of the pitfalls of nuclear ambiguity and of an open nuclear arms race in the subcontinent, see the chapter by P. Bidwai and A. Vanaik in a forthcoming Sipri publication, *Security Without Nuclear Weapons*.

28. In the valuable compendium, *Exterminism and Cold War*, NLB/Verso, London 1982 and in subsequent contributions by E. Mandel and K. Coates in *New Left Review* 141 and 145, this Eurocentric bias among the Western left is very evident. Noam Chomsky is one of the few contributors to refer to the serious possibility of a nuclear exchange in the third world. This is linked by him and some others to the obvious fact of superpower rivalry in the third world. He also mentions in passing the threat posed by the Israeli and South African bombs in their respective regions. But even he manages to completely ignore South Asia. Clearly Indian nonalignment has been something of a mental soporific for Western intellectuals.

29. NATO has sought to erode the practical and theoretical firebreak between conventional and nuclear war. This erosion has taken the form of developing battlefield and tactical nuclear weapons and a theory of graduated nuclear escalation/warfighting/flexible response to correspond to and justify the new array or weaponry. It is the strengthening of the firebreak between peace and conventional war that has more than compensated for

the weakening of the firebreak between conventional and nuclear war. It is not NATO's dangerously irresponsible doctrine of 'first use' (which in theory eliminates the firebreak between conventional and nuclear war) that has kept the peace, but the fact of peace that has kept NATO's doctrine of 'first use' from being put to the test.

30. For a critique of the Non-Proliferation Treaty (NPT), a detailed assessment of a South Asian NWFZ and refutations of objections raised against it, see my articles, 'Why NPT is Unacceptable' and 'The Political Case For a NWFZ in South Asia', in *Economic and Political Weekly* 3 September 1988 and 30 November 1985 respectively. For why a regional test ban is a useful transitional measure see my 'Changing Climate' in *Economic and Political Weekly*, 14 January 1989.

31. See footnote 25.

32. Within the undivided CPI the left wing which eventually broke away to form the CPM in 1964 was opposed to the official stance of support to India during the 1962 war.

33. Before 1978, the CPI had subscribed to the view that the Congress contained a progressive, anti-imperialist wing which was usually dominant within the party, and was identified with Nehru and Mrs Gandhi. This had to be supported at all costs.

34. This is not to say that Moscow's turnaround on Afghanistan or Gorbachev's shift within the framework of 'peaceful coexistence' to a global 'historic compromise' with imperialism has not perturbed the CPI and CPM leadership. The latter seems more comfortable with Brezhnevite perspectives. Since a strong USSR is central to a successful global anti-imperialist struggle, Gorbachev's 'adaptations' can be rationalized as steps undertaken by the Soviet leadership to achieve this end, and surely the CPSU knows better than the CPM its own problems. But insofar as there is no shift in the Soviet view or endorsement of Indian nonalignment and Indian behaviour in South Asia there is no reason for the mainstream left to re-evaluate its traditional postures in this regard.

35. S. Chisti, 'Indo-Soviet Economic Relations', in S. Kumar (ed.), *Yearbook on India's Foreign Policy 1987/88*, Sage Publications, London 1988, Table 2a, p. 156.

36. Ibid., Table 3b, p. 158. Indian imports of metal manufacturers, electrical/non-electrical machinery and transport equipment fell from 50% in 1969–70 to 24% by 1979–80 to 12% by 1984–85.

37. Ibid., p. 145 and Table 1, p. 155.

38. Ibid., p. 145. See also S. Chisti, *India's Trade With Eastern Europe*, IIFT, New Delhi 1973; A. Datar, *India's Economic Relations with USSR and Eastern Europe (1953–1969)*, Cambridge University Press, Cambridge 1972; S. Mehrotra, *India's Economic Relations with the USSR*, Ph. D. Thesis, University of Cambridge, 1985 and his 'The Political Economy of Indo-Soviet Relations', in R. Casson (ed.), *Soviet Interest in the Third World*, Sage Publications London 1986; D. Mukherjee, 'Indo–Soviet Economic Ties', in *Problems of Communism*, January–February 1987.

39. Having to pay for oil imports from the USSR in rupees and not in hard currency has been a major advantage for India, explaining why the import share of petroleum/petroleum products from USSR went up from almost nothing in 1974–75 to 13% in 1979–80 to 23% in 1984–85.

40. With the advent of the Gorbachev era, there is a growing likelihood of joint ventures between the Soviet government and Indian private business, with the latter entitled to up to 49% of equity holding. Some 13 major Indian companies have been attracted to such joint venture possibilities and have submitted proposals accordingly. S. Chisti, *India's Trade with Eastern Europe*, p. 152.

41. Total Soviet aid to India till 1977 was Rs 843 crores. Between 1977 and 1986 the USSR authorized aid amounting to Rs 1,982 crores or Rs 2,825 crores in all. In 1986 the USSR committed itself to supplying another Rs 2,883 crores of which Rs 2,346 crores were lent for 17 years at 2.5% interest. Aid till 1985 was to be repaid in rupees with an average interest rate of 2.5% and maturity period between 10 and 13 years. The grant element in such aid was less than that given by multilateral lending agencies and from some Western countries. S. Chisti, *India's Trade with Eastern Europe*, pp. 140–47.

42. Ibid., p. 146. Soviet defence credit does sometimes have a very substantial grant element.

43. *Sipri Yearbook 1988*, Oxford University Press, New York p. 180.

44. For why India should attach growing importance to the Indian Ocean and how it should expand its sea power, see J. Singh, 'Indian Ocean and Indian Security', in S. Kumar (ed.), *Yearbook on India's Foreign Policy 1987/88*, Sage Publications London 1988. Nor does India welcome a growing Soviet naval presence in the area, hence its advocacy of an Indian Ocean Zone of Peace. Nepal's plea that its own territory be declared a 'zone of peace' has been repeatedly rejected by India.

45. *Sipri Yearbook 1988*, pp. 178–80.

46. R. G. Wirsing, 'The Arms Race in South Asia', in *Asian Survey*, March 1985.

47. 'Heading For a Crisis', *India Today*, 28 February 1989.

48. See M. Hasan, 'In Search of Integration and Identity', in *Economic and Political Weekly*, Special No., 1988, pp. 2468–70.

49. Surprisingly this point has not been grasped by all those, Indian and foreign, who have jumped on to the 'Super India' bandwagon. See, the *Time* cover story of 3 April 1989.

50. F. Halliday, 'The Ceylonese Insurrection', in R. Blackburn (ed.), *Explosion in a Subcontinent*, Pelican, Harmondsworth 1975.

51. This possibility is, as things stand, somewhat remote, although not to be completely ruled out.

Conclusion

One of the most powerful emotional sources of socialist commitment in the subcontinent has been the persistence of widespread and horrendous levels of poverty. The poverty line in the affluent West means a reasonable living standard; here it means an absolute minimum. If Indian capitalism progressively reduces this poverty will there be a corresponding erosion in socialist commitment? To argue that socialism means so much more than the eradication of poverty really begs the question. The *visibility* of injustices connected to poverty and other forms of social oppression has always been among the most powerful stimuli to mass cadre commitment. Whether poverty will decline or not in the coming decades is an important question.

A provisional answer to this was given in Chapter 1. It needs to be fleshed out. The higher the average growth rate the more likely it is that the ultimate dribble of benefits to the poorest strata will be greater. If India has had an average of around 5 per cent per annum during the seventh five-year plan (FYP) and if this average can be maintained or even rise to 6 per cent per annum in the eighth FYP (1990–95) then there will be improvements for the lower deciles of the population which cannot simply be dismissed. But barring an Indian 'miracle' (which even the most optimistic are not prepared to predict) there are many reasons for believing that the absolute numbers of the miserably poor – those many millions of families below or near the poverty line – will remain obscenely high in coming decades.

The long-term growth rate in Indian agriculture has risen from a pre-independence 1 per cent per annum to 2.4 per cent per annum. But this has not led to a significant rise in the long-term rate of growth of rural real wages, which has remained roughly stable at 0.5 per cent per annum. Unless the demand for rural labour from on-farm, off-farm and urban-based industry and services rises dramatically, there is little

scope for a significant rise in rural real wages. Poverty and employment
have a close connection and employment generation, as pointed out
earlier, is the Achilles' heel of the Indian pattern of growth. Since
the proportion of self-employed rural poor is at least as great as the
wage-dependent poor even a significant rise in demand for rural labour
(which is nowhere in sight) would not be enough. There also has to be
a rise in the productivity of the asset base of the self-employed poor.
To put it in more traditionally comprehensible terms, there has to be a
substantial redistribution of wealth/assets. This means land reforms and
collectively organized support packages in the countryside and major
wealth redistribution in the towns and cities.

Who are the Indian poor? In class and occupational terms they
are the agricultural proletariat and the marginal farmers (both also
suffer from heavy indebtedness), the unorganized urban workers, the
self-employed hawkers, cobblers, and so on, who also make up a
large part of the migrant workers among the urban poor. Nor should
non-occupational groups such as beggars, most of whom are disease-
stricken or crippled, be forgotten. In social but non-class terms, there
are disproportionately higher levels of poverty among the Scheduled
Castes, the Scheduled Tribes, the lower rungs of the backward caste
spectrum and among Muslims. Also such social groups as the aged,
deserted wives, widows and orphans suffer disproportionately from
poverty. The bias (especially in the countryside) against women in
matters of nourishment has by now become a widely acknowledged
fact.

Clearly, any programme to overcome poverty requires a holistic
perspective addressing itself not just to questions of income and
purchasing power but also to such matters as socio-economic power,
gender discrimination, social helplessness and illiteracy. This is, of
course, the classical perspective of any revolutionary programme and
as such far removed from the one-dimensional strategy of market-
determined trickle-down. Mass poverty, then, will remain a despairing
reality and a key motivator in the search for revolutionary alternatives.

The segmented character of Indian society, however, generates
tremendous pressures for a corresponding segmentation of left thought
and action. This has to be consciously fought against. A sizeable breeding
ground for the creation of a self-consciously socialist and revolutionary
layer – a mass vanguard of cadres and activists – already exists. Its
individual components are to be found in the left parties, both reformist
and revolutionary, in their mass fronts, in the new social movements and
groups, in Dalit, tribal and anti-communal groups, in the movements
struggling for ethnic and cultural equality, and in the organizations
fighting against genuine national oppression. It is to be found in the

trade union vanguard and among militants in the unorganized sector striving to unionize.

India's history of struggles for progressive ends since independence is a rich and varied one. But both Indian autonomy and bourgeois democracy conspire to eliminate the kind of unifying and centralizing focus provided by a 'nationalist' anti-imperialist or anti-dictatorial struggle. Such a struggle is then more easily hegemonized by a single party or front, as in the Philippines, where this role has been assumed by the Philippines Communist Party, or as in El Salvador, where the Farabundo Marti National Liberation Front (FMLN) has been able to take on this historic responsibility.

The questions of national oppression and corresponding movements for national liberation have become important on the periphery of geographical India, in Nagaland, Sri Lanka, Kashmir, Punjab. Their political and social reverberations on the bulk of the Indian and South Asian population have inevitably been limited.

In the face of these difficulties, exacerbated by the social heterogeneity of the Indian and South Asian mosaic, it is not surprising that many tendencies have, in effect, abandoned altogether the search for a unifying programme or perspective and for the organizational mechanisms which could make the struggle for its implementation effective. But such a search has become more, not less, urgent. It need not and most likely will not take the form of a search to construct a single vanguard party of the revolution. But nor can such strategic unification be provided by some loose federation of movements and groups (parties and non-party formations) whose only common reference point is a minimum programme of reform so diluted as to provide no vision transcending the existing structures of bourgeois rule in India.

Any strategy for revolutionary transformation in India must incorporate certain basic tasks. A corporate working-class consciousness would be substantially transcended in the very process of forging unity between the rural and urban components of the Indian proletariat. This is the key task and it is an impeccably *class* aim and responsibility, though the effort to achieve it will require great attention to and mobilization around a whole series of non-economic issues. The *central alliance* is between this working class and the poor peasantry; this proletariat must place itself at the head of a larger bloc of social forces which should include substantial sections of the urban poor and middle classes.

Not only is this Gramscian perspective not opposed to Leninist vanguardism, but the latter in its broad political sense – the consolidation of a mass vanguard layer – is a precondition for the successful conduct of a 'war of position' in civil society. This cannot be posed against a 'war of manoeuvre'. Indeed, not just one war but many wars of manoeuvre

– directly against the various levels of state authority and also in the interstices of civil society, especially in the countryside – will be a part of the very process of carrying out a larger war of position.

The tasks of unifying the proletariat, cementing its alliance with the poor peasantry or hegemonizing a larger social bloc cannot be accomplished without mediation via groups and organizations that are part of the mass vanguard and which are themselves committed by thought and action to fulfilling these tasks of unification, centralization and coordination. It is at a certain stage of maturation of this vanguard that it becomes possible for objectively determined pre-revolutionary crises to become subjectively transformed into a revolutionary crisis of decisive import. It would be a fundamental error to believe that the class character of the Indian state can be altered by its class opponents without politically preparing for an ultimately decisive (and violent) confrontation with it.

It would be an equally grave strategic error to believe that communalism, casteism and sexism can be eradicated this side of such an eventual transformation of the state or to make the kind of social and political alliances with bourgeois forces that such a barren perspective might suggest. This is nothing less than accommodation in the name of socialism. It is not accidental that some theorists of an indigenous version of 'radical pluralism', such as Rajni Kothari, should have decided in the run-up to the 1989 general election to ally themselves with the Janata Dal of V.P. Singh in preference to association with reformist parties like the CPI/CPM, which were once seen as more natural allies of the social movements. This shift towards bourgeois parties and the bourgeois state has been done in the name of a 'new realism' – in much the same way as some on the American left have come to make their peace with the Democratic Party.

The real intellectual and practical challenges for the Indian left lie elsewhere. Can it begin to generate the kind of collective and strategic discussion and analysis that is required? Does it have the creativity and ingenuity to throw up the various linkages which can provide the basis not just for organizing such a collective debate but also for connecting sectoral struggles, building mutual solidarity and coordinating hitherto isolated actions and efforts? It is only from such experiences that answers will emerge – the 'successive approximations' in the dialectic of theory and practice that remains central to the revolutionary project.

Whatever the difficulties and obstacles, there are grounds enough for informed hope and some optimism. History, after all, will be what we make of it.

Postscript

The ninth general elections since independence, held in November 1989, resulted in the formation of a new, minority government by the National Front (NF), comprising the Janata Dal (JD) headed by the new prime minister, V.P. Singh (141 seats), the Telugu Desam, a regional party in Andhra Pradesh (2 seats), the DMK, a regional party in Tamil Nadu (no seats), and the Congress (S) (1 seat). Crucial outside support was provided by the right-wing Bharatiya Janata Party (BJP) (88 seats) and the Left Front (55 seats). The main constituents of the Left Front are the Communist Party of India (Marxist) and the Communist Party of India, which secured 32 and 12 seats respectively.

The central problem of endemic instability, which earlier could at least be hidden behind single party majority rule, has now been laid bare. A 'centrist' National Front (really the JD) reigns in New Delhi but at the mercy of two sharply opposed forces to its left and right. The only possible working arrangement in this situation is that these two forces support the JD/NF from the outside.

The essentially plebiscitary character of Indian politics has also been re-endorsed, but with a new twist. The pattern of significant vote swings, of strong affirmation or rejection of a party or party leader with little or no reference to the overall programme of that party, was once again clearly evident. The Congress (I) plummeted from its peak of 415 seats in the 1984 Lok Sabha elections to its second worst showing (after 1977), securing only 193 seats; enough, however, to make it still the single largest party. But contrasting with its near total disaster in the Hindi heartland, in the east (Orissa, West Bengal) and in the west (Gujarat), the Congress (I) to its own and to everyone else's surprise swept the southern states of Andhra Pradesh, Karnataka, Kerala and Tamil Nadu. In effect this election witnessed two plebiscites. There was a partial precedent for this in

1977 when the Congress (I) retained a significant electoral base in the south.

How is this contrast to be explained? The Congress (I) clearly benefited from being the only national party, which for all its organizational deficiencies has an historically accumulated network of patron–client relations, political connections, local party bigwigs and vote-gathering structures that spans the country. The south, conscious of its status as a 'poorer relation' to the Hindi belt (and to the north generally) has always had a bias towards a national protector of its interests in Lok Sabha elections. This factor complemented the more regional preoccupations and the general disenchantment with the non-performance of the non-Congress state governments in the south. In Kerala, the ruling Left and Democratic Front performed better in government than its predecessor, the Congress (I) dominated coalition, the United Democratic Front, but was still routed.

The Janata Dal, by restricting itself to standing 240 candidates out of a possible 525 and leaving another 75 to its National Front allies in the south, virtually ensured that even in the best of circumstances the NF could not secure an absolute majority on its own. The wholesale public repudiation of its southern allies (the Telegu Desam and the DMK) and of the Janata Party (of Ramakrishna Hegde) in Karnataka tempts one to speculate that the JD, as the only other centrist and potentially national alternative to the Congress (I), would have done better to follow the logic of plebiscitary politics, disregard its allies, and stand candidates of its own in the south. V.P. Singh could not have been unaware of this potential but given the practical difficulties (the JD has still to establish a national network in any way comparable to that of the Congress (I)) he must have decided that he had little option but to avoid antagonizing his regional allies. Building a truly national network would have to follow the JD's rise to power; it is this power which would give it the capacity to dispense patronage on the scale required.

In the north the massive defeat of the Congress (I) was clearly a tribute to the JD's campaign and to its effective focus on the issue of corruption as the principal factor distinguishing it from the Congress (I). It was further helped by the Congress (I)'s ambivalent response to the rising appeal of Hindu chauvinism as embodied in the remarkable success of the BJP. The BJP is the broad political wing of the Hindu chauvinist and semi-fascist cultural organization, the Rashtriya Swayamsevak Sangh (RSS), which also has as an offshoot, the Vishwa Hindu Parishad (VHP). The VHP, which barely existed at the beginning of the decade, has experienced truly amazing growth by presenting itself as the militant defender of Hindu interests and identity. In the months preceding the election, the VHP made enormous political and emotional capital out of the religious tension surrounding the Ram Janamabhoomi–Babri Masjid affair in Uttar Pradesh. The Babri Masjid, a Muslim mosque, is alleged to be standing on a site (Ayodhya) which is purported to be the original birthplace of Rama, a central figure in Hindu mythology, and on which a temple commemorating his birth was supposed to have stood but which was subsequently razed to make way for the mosque.

The VHP spearheaded a nationwide campaign to rebuild the Ram Janamabhoomi on which the BJP rode piggy-back. In a move which for all its superstitious, mystificatory and reactionary character was nonetheless a stroke of symbolic genius, the VHP organized brick consecration rites in tens of thousands of small towns and villages throughout the country. These bricks were to be carried to the site for a foundation laying ceremony on 9 November. The ruling Congress (I) took an ambivalent attitude toward this campaign and ultimately allowed the foundation ceremony to take place at a certain distance (this is disputed) from the mosque. The anticipated communal clash between Muslims and Hindus did not take place, but this attempt to pander to Hindu sentiment in the north did not gain the Congress (I) new Hindu votes, which went to the BJP, and certainly affected its standing among Muslims, a large section of whom shifted to the Janata Dal. The lessons of this fiasco seem to have hit home. In its post-election declarations, the Congress (I) has again begun to aggressively assert its secular and populist character in a bid to regain its image among the core minorities, especially Muslims.

Certainly, the elections have highlighted the growth and power of Hindu nationalism and the pressures this imposes on even the centrist parties. V.P. Singh himself flirted at times with the BJP and his own response to the *shilyanas* (brick consecration) campaign was well short of the standards demanded by principled secularism. But though the BJP has made remarkably impressive gains (it had only two seats in the last parliament) it is widely perceived as something of a pariah. Neither the Congress (I) nor the JD would want to enter an open alliance with the BJP, despite its parliamentary strength, because this would seriously damage their credentials as centrist and secular forces. The BJP is, therefore, unable to translate its parliamentary strength into a commensurate political ability to influence government policies, especially in areas close to its specifically communal concerns, for example, abrogation of Article 370 guaranteeing special autonomy status to Kashmir, banning cow slaughter, or winding up the Minorities Commission. It is one of the paradoxes of the Indian mosaic that even as serious note must be taken of the dangers of growing Hindu nationalism, the limits to and constraints on it should not be ignored.

What then of the immediate future? Is India entering a new era of near-permanent coalition rule? This time around the permanent crisis of bourgeois political leadership has been given the additional dimension of parliamentary instability. There is virtually no chance of the JD/NF lasting out a full term. It would be remarkable if it could survive in its present form for even two years. Far from coalition rule being institutionalized, the logic of the process revealed by this as well as previous Lok Sabha elections is for a movement towards an ultimate recomposition/realignment of the two centrist forces under a single banner, most likely of Congress nomenclature. The process and mediations by which this denouement is achieved cannot be predicted. There are different paths to the same destination.

From one vantage point, all that holds up a coming together of the JD and the Congress (I) is the leadership of Rajiv Gandhi. Not for nothing did V.P. Singh try to win over the Congress (I) MPs and the MLAs (in Uttar Pradesh) when he first broke from the parent Congress (I) organization. When he finally formed the JD he made it clear then and repeatedly afterwards that he and the JD considered the Rajiv Gandhi leadership, not the Congress itself, as the principal opponent. So one possible post-election scenario could be a further discrediting of Rajiv Gandhi (who was re-elected as leader of the Congress (I) in opposition) through pursuit of the Bofors scandal. Or Congress (I) dissidents might be successfully wooed to join the JD. Two factors work against this outcome. The Anti-Defection Law requires a minimum one-third split in any parliamentary party if its MPs are to avoid mandatory re-election in their constituencies. Furthermore, some 100 Congress (I) MPs are from the south and their loyalty, for the time being, is vested in Rajiv Gandhi in preference to any parochial north Indian figure. This is no guarantee of his permanent tenure. Various manoeuvres are possible. Southern leaders can be elevated to top positions in the party hierarchy in return for abandoning the Rajiv leadership as behind-the-scenes power-brokers work out a merger of the 'centrist' forces with or without split-offs on either side.

Another equally plausible scenario would have the JD splitting and linking up with the Congress. This need not be caused by the pressures of the BJP and the Left Front alone. It could also be the result of severe internal tensions. The JD does not have the relative homogeneity of the Congress (I). The north Indian kulak lobbies represented by the two leaders, Ajit Singh and Devi Lal (currently the deputy prime minister), are uneasily incorporated within it. These lobbies have their specific class interests which are sharply delineated from the more loosely packaged inclinations of other leaders and factions within the JD which do not have such a crystallized social base. A repeat of the Charan Singh-inspired break up of the Janata coalition of 1977 can by no means be ruled out. Leadership rivalries both promote and feed on these factional differences.

A third possible scenario is a collapse of the government and a return to the electorate as the JD and Congress (I) search for a renewed single party majority mandate for themselves. So a JD/NF government could consciously pursue some populist-democratic programmes in the hope of building widespread support for such a mid-term poll. (In any case, the new government will provide a measure of autonomy to television and radio.) What is clear is that a stable two-party competitive system is the most *unlikely* of all possible outcomes. The chances of establishing a stable structure of competing centrisms, as distinct from their mutual recomposition and realignment, are negligible. The capacity of a right-wing party like the BJP to become the nucleus of a second political alternative, either through its own steady electoral growth or as the hub of a relatively stable constellation of other parties, must be judged remote. The segmented character and subcontinental size and variety of India are powerful barriers to such a trajectory. The BJP will, in fact, do well if it succeeds in stabilizing its new found electoral strength. After all, it was its seat adjustments with the JD in the north that helped it to cash in on anti-Congress (I) rather than solely pro-BJP sentiment.

As for the parliamentary left, it has done better collectively than at any previous Lok Sabha election. This may be cited as plausible evidence of the left's potential for rapid growth, given the endemic political instability of the system, but enthusiasm should be tempered by more sober reflection. The mainstream left (CPM and CPI) the fulcrum of the Left Front, remains mired in a regional ghetto. Their national performance was overly dependent on the CPM's base in West Bengal, while their performance in the other stronghold, Kerala, was much worse than expected.

A left which can break out of its regional isolation and double its electoral strength would certainly transform the map of electoral politics in India. The basic mould of plebiscitary politics and centrist rule would not be broken but would be substantially modified. After all, in the last four elections, the Congress (I) has been rejected twice and the Janata party failed to survive. There may be no alternative to centrist rule in New Delhi but it only persists on the sufferance of an increasingly wary and cynical electorate. An informal or formal centre-left alliance in power can, therefore, enjoy the widespread and enthusiastic allegiance of a rejuvenated electorate. Indian bourgeois centrism is less hostile to such an alliance than to one with the right, which would do far more damage to its credentials. In Indian conditions, the left would not then be so much the balancing force between two contending supplicants as the unavoidable reference point for a centrist political formation seeking stable parliamentary rule in New Delhi.

It has surely been the unstated aspiration of the CPI and CPM, both of which have long been completely wedded to the politics of electoralism and little else, to reach such a pivotal position. Such an alliance in power would undoubtedly represent a further and qualitative step forward in the capitalist co-optation of the two Communist parties. It would also, however, give a more meaningful social-democratic and populist angle to the rudder of government as it steered through its various policies. Just how great an angle would depend on the actual relationship of forces prevailing between the left and the centre. A more principled and radical mainstream left than the CPI and CPM have shown themselves to be would resist such co-optation in governance, yet allow the weight of its redoubled force to exercise pressure on government policies. A stronger left would also be a major source of defence, outside the electoral arena, in resisting the tide of Hindu nationalism and communalisms.

But even on the most optimistic reading, it is difficult to see how the left could achieve such a qualitative advance given its present policies. Certainly, to prepare itself for the prolonged effort to achieve such a position, the CPI and the CPM would have to merge and use the strength of this organizational and political unity as a launching pad towards higher ambitions. Of such a merger there is no sign. Indeed, there is a sense in which the two parties could be said to be suffering from a disturbing complacency, especially in the case of the CPM. The mainstream left in India has not experienced the fate of its Communist party brethren in the Western democracies, of progressive electoral, political and organizational decline. But in the face of the momentous changes that are shaking the socialist world, it cannot afford to stand still. It too needs to renew itself if it is not one day to find itself living on time borrowed from the past.

Bombay, 6 December 1989

Tables

Table 1 Indicators of Regional Hegemony: Shares of Regional Aggregates by Country (%)

Aggregates	South Asia	Middle East		Latin America			Africa		Southeast Asia		
	India	Iran	Egypt	Brazil	Mexico	Argentina	Nigeria	S.Africa	Indonesia	Philippines	Thailand
GNP[a]	79.4	34.7	7.6	35.7	19.4	12.0	16.4	23.0	30.3	21.0	18.4
Population[a]	75.7	30.0	31.7	33.7	18.6	8.2	17.8	7.0	42.5	13.0	12.9
Armed forces[a]	67.9	22.8	23.7	35.1	7.3	12.3	26.9	5.0	15.6	7.0	13.5
Military expenditure[a]	81.2	40.5	7.0	38.6	17.3	13.5	22.9	32.5	28.4	11.0	10.7
Installed energy[b]	86.7	42.4	27:5	35.0	19.8	16.6	3.4	56.0	10.8	29.7	24.6
World trade (imports & exports)[b]	63.0	28.3	4.8	32.0	13.3	15.0	21.0	19.0	26.1	13.2	12.4

[a]Figures for 1975; [b] Figures for 1976
Source: L.I. and S.H. Rudolph, *In Pursuit of Lakshmi: The Political Economy of the India State*, Orient Longman, Bombay 1988, Table I, p. 5.

Table 2

	Population (millions) Mid-1986	Life expectancy at birth (yrs) 1986	GNP per capita ($) 1986	Average annual rate of inflation (%) 1965–80	1980–86	Total External Debt ($ million) 1986	Total long-term debt services (as a % of GNP) 1970	1986
India	781.4	57	290	7.6	7.8	41,088	1.1	1.6
China	1054.0	69	300	0.0	3.8	22,724	–	0.9
Indonesia	166.4	57	490	34.3	8.9	42,090	1.7	7.3
Nigeria	103.1	51	640	14.4	10.5	21,876	1.0	3.3
Egypt	49.7	61	760	7.5	12.4	28,556	4.8	4.8
Turkey	51.5	65	1110	20.7	37.3	31,808	1.4	6.2
Brazil	138.4	65	1810	31.3	157.1	110,675	0.9	4.1
Mexico	80.2	68	1860	13.1	63.7	101,722	3.7	10.2
Argentina	31.0	70	2350	78.3	326.2	48,908	5.0	6.8
South Korea	41.5	69	2370	18.8	5.4	45,109	3.1	10.8
Algeria	22.4	62	2590	9.9	6.1	17,929	0.9	8.7

Source: World Development Report, 1988.

Table 3 Distribution of Farm Income by Land Size Classes in 1975

(as % of farm households)

Farm household land size classes	Rural Agricultural population	Area operated	Crop output	Net crop and farm income	Livestock income
Landless	12.3	0.0	0.0	6.2	4.6
Sub-marginal (0.01 to 0.50 ha)	18.6	3.0	4.2	11.6	9.8
Marginal (0.51 to 1.00 ha)	15.7	4.0	5.7	11.2	17.4
Small (1.01 to 2.01 ha)	18.5	12.4	14.9	17.7	19.4
Medium (2.02 to 4.04 ha)	16.3	19.8	22.0	19.7	21.4
Large (4.05 to 8.09 ha)	10.7	20.4	20.0	15.4	16.1
Very Large (8.10 ha and above)	7.9	40.0	33.2	18.2	12.1
All	100.0	100.0	100.0	100.0	100.0

Source: P. Bardhan, *The Political Economy of Development in India*, OUP, Oxford 1984, Table 17, p.107

Table 4 Changes in Major Manufacturing Groups as a Percentage of Industrial Production

Industrial Group	1956	1960	1965	1970	1976
Basic goods	22.13	25.11	26.84	32.28	36.14
Capital goods	4.71	11.76	18.67	15.74	16.76
Intermediate goods	24.59	25.88	23.60	20.95	19.27
Consumer goods:	48.37	37.25	30.80	31.03	27.83
of which, durables	n/a	5.68	6.15	2.92	2.78
non-durables	n/a	31.57	24.75	28.11	25.19
General index	100.00	100.00	100.00	100.00	100.00

Source: S. Mundle, 'Growth, Disparity and Capital Reorganization in the Indian Economy', *Economic and Political Weekly*, Annual No. 1981.

283

Table 5 Distribution of Gross Domestic Product

| | GDP ($ millions) | | % of GDP | | | | | | | | | | | | |
| | | | Agriculture | | Industry | | Manufacturing | | Services | | Gross domestic investment | | Gross domestic savings | |
	1965	1986	1965	1986	1965	1986	1965	1986	1965	1986	1965	1986	1965	1986
India	46,260	203,790	47	32	22	29	15	19	31	39	18	23	16	21
China	65,590	271,880	39	31	38	46	30[b]	34[b]	23	23	25	39	25	36
Indonesia	3,830	75,230	56	26	13	32	8	14	31	42	8	26	8	24
Nigeria	4,190	49,110	53	41	19	29	7	8	29	30	19	12	17	10
Egypt	4,550	40,850	29	20	27	29	–	–	45	51	18	19	14	9
Turkey	7,660	52,620	34	18	25	36	16	25	41	46	15	25	13	22
Brazil	19,450	206,750[a]	19	11[a]	33	39[a]	26	28[a]	48	50[a]	20	21	22	24
Mexico	20,160	127,140	14	9	31	39	21	26	54	52	22	21[a]	21	27[a]
Argentina	16,500	69,820	17	13	42	44	33	31	42	44	19	9	22	11
South Korea	3,000	98,150	38	12	25	42	18	30	37	45	15	29	8	35
Algeria	3,170	60,760	15	12	34	44	11	13	51	44	22	32	19	31

[a] Figures for 1985 [b] World Bank Estimates
Source: World Development Report, 1988.

Table 6a Structure of Manufacturing

| | Distribution of Value Added (%) | | | | % of labour force in | | | | | |
| | Machinery & Transport | | Chemicals equipment | | Agri- culture | | Industry | | Services | |
	1970	1985	1970	1985	1965	1980	1965	1980	1965	1980
India	20	26	14	15	73	70	12	13	15	17
China	–	26	–	10	81	74	8	14	11	12
Indonesia	–	10	–	10	71	57	9	13	21	30
Nigeria	–	17	–	9	72	68	10	12	18	20
Egypt	9	13	12	10	55	46	15	20	30	34
Turkey	8	15	7	8	75	58	11	17	14	25
Brazil	22	24	10	9	49	31	20	27	31	42
Mexico	13	14	11	12	50	37	22	29	29	35
Argentina	18	16	9	13	18	13	34	34	48	53
South Korea	11	23	11	9	55	36	15	27	30	37
Algeria	9	11	4	10	57	31	17	27	26	42

Source: *World Development Report, 1988.*

Table 6b Income Distribution

| | Share of household income by percentile group of households (%) | | | | | |
	(Year)	Lowest 20%	Second 20%	Third 20%	Fourth 20%	Highest 20%	Highest 10%
India	(1975–76)	7.0	9.2	13.9	20.5	49.4	33.6
China	(–)	–	–	–	–	–	–
Indonesia	(1976)	6.6	7.8	12.6	23.6	49.4	34.0
Nigeria	(–)	–	–	–	–	–	–
Egypt	(1974)	5.8	10.7	14.7	20.8	48.0	33.2
Turkey	(1973)	3.5	8.0	–	–	56.5	40.7
Brazil	(1972)	2.0	5.0	9.4	17.0	66.6	50.6
Mexico	(1977)	2.9	7.0	12.0	20.4	57.7	40.6
Argentina	(1970)	4.4	9.7	14.1	21.5	50.3	35.2
South Korea	(1976)	5.7	11.2	15.4	22.4	45.3	27.5
Algeria	(–)	–	–	–	–	–	–

Source: *World Development Report, 1988.*

Table 7 Average Annual Growth Rate (%)

	GDP		Agriculture		Industry		Manufacturing		Services	
	1965–80	1980–86	1965–80	1980–86	1965–80	1980–86	1965–80	1980–86	1965–80	1980–86
India	3.7	4.9	2.8	1.9	4.0	7.1	4.3	8.2	4.6	6.0
China	6.4	10.5	3.0	7.9	10.0	12.5	9.5[a]	12.6[a]	7.0	9.4
Indonesia	7.9	3.4	4.3	3.0	11.9	1.8	12.0	7.7	7.3	5.6
Nigeria	8.0	-3.2	1.7	1.4	13.4	-5.1	14.6	1.0	8.8	-4.0
Egypt	6.7	4.7	2.8	1.9	7.0	6.3	–	–	9.5	4.4
Turkey	6.3	4.9	3.2	3.1	7.2	6.4	7.5	8.0	7.6	4.7
Brazil	9.0	2.7	3.8	2.0	9.9	1.6	9.6	1.2	10.0	3.8
Mexico	6.5	0.4	3.2	2.1	7.6	-0.1	7.4	0.0	6.6	0.4
Argentina	3.4	-0.8	1.4	2.3	3.3	-1.7	2.7	-0.4	3.9	-0.8
South Korea	9.5	8.2	3.0	5.6	16.5	10.2	18.7	9.8	9.3	7.2
Algeria	7.5	4.4	5.8	3.2	8.1	5.2	9.5	–	7.1	3.6

[a] World Bank Estimates.
Source: World Development Report, 1988.

Table 8   Purchasing Power Parity of Selected Items
(cost in Rs for each US$ spent)

Gas	9.05
Liquid fuel	9.14
Electricity	5.51
Engines and turbines	10.77
Electrical transmission equipment	10.94
Communications equipment	9.13
Other electrical equipment	10.63
Office machinery	18.97
Service industry machinery	11.22
Construction and mining machinery	15.29
General industrial machinery	8.59
Special industrial machinery	9.63
Metalworking machinery	8.19
Tractors	9.90
Other agricultural machinery	10.81
Passenger vehicles	10.09
Locomotives	10.85
Other railway vehicles	6.07
Trucks and buses	9.15
Private cars	9.57
Other private transport	5.19
Tyres and inner tubes	11.06
Instruments	7.77
Fridges and freezers	14.06
Televisions and audio equipment	10.92
Cooking appliances	4.97
Heating appliances	8.62
Other household appliances	25.19
Household utensils	4.37
Medical supplies	3.92
Drugs and medicinal preparations	2.47
Toilet articles	5.11
Other personal care goods	3.64
Spirits	8.00
Wine and cider	27.71
Beer	10.20
Non-alcoholic beverages	10.88
Cakes and biscuits	6.85
Sugar	4.46
Confectionery	6.94
Pasta	7.65
Canned fish	4.28

Source: N.K. Chandra, 'Modernization for Export-Oriented Growth', *Economic and Political Weekly*, 19 July 1986, Table 3, p. 1265.

Table 9 Life and Death in China

	Overall death rate (per thousand)	Life expectancy (yrs)	Infant mortality rate (per thousand)	
	(a)	(b)	(a)	(c)
1978	7.5	65.1	37.2	40
1979	7.6	65.0	39.4	41
1980	7.7	64.9	41.6	44
1981	7.7	64.8	43.7	53
1982	7.9	64.7	45.9	61
1983	8.0	64.6	48.0	–
1984	8.0	64.6	50.1	–

(a) Banister's adjusted
(b) Banister's estimates
(c) Young and Dowdle indirect estimate
Source: A. Sen, *Economic Times*, 2 January 1989, derived from Banister (1987) and Young and Dowdle (1985).

Table 10 Mortality Gender Differentials in China

	Life expectancy (yrs)			Infant mortality rate (per thousand births)		
	Females	Males	Female advantage	Females	Males	Female advantage
1978	66.0	64.1	1.9	37.7	36.8	−0.9
1979	65.7	64.3	1.4	42.7	36.3	−6.4
1980	65.3	64.4	0.9	47.7	35.8	−11.9
1981	65.0	64.5	0.5	52.6	35.3	−17.3
1982	64.7	64.7	0.0	57.5	34.9	−22.6
1983	64.4	64.8	−0.4	62.4	34.4	−28.0
1984	64.1	64.9	−0.8	67.2	33.9	−33.3

Source: A. Sen, *Economic Times*, 2 January 1989.

Table 11 Gender Differentials in China and India

		China (1985)	India (1981)
Adult literacy rate	Female	56	26
	Male	82	55
Life expectancy	Female	64	52.1
	Male	64.9	52.5
Sex Ratio	(female/male)	0.935	0.934

Source: A. Sen, *Economic Times*, 2 January 1989.

Table 12 Results in Post-independence Lok Sabha Elections

	1952	1957	1962	1967	1971	1977	1980	1984
				Seats Won				
CPI	26	27	29	23	23	7	11	6
CPM	–	–	–	19	25	22	36	22
Total				42	48	29	47	28
				Percentage of Votes				
CPI	3.3	8.9	9.9	5.1	4.7	2.8	2.6	2.7
CPM	–	–	–	4.4	5.1	4.3	6.1	5.8
Total				9.5	9.8	7.1	8.7	8.5

Source: T.J. Nossiter, 'Communism in Rajiv Gandhi's India', in *Third World Quarterly*, October 1985.

Table 13 Seats Won in Lok Sabha Elections

Name of Party	1952	1957	1962	1967	1971	1977	1980	1984	1989
Congress	364	371	361	283	352	152	352	415	193
Janata/Janata Dal	–	–	–	–	–	297	31	10	141
Swatantra	–	–	18	44	8	–	–	–	–
CPI	26	27	29	23	23	7	11	6	12
CPM	–	–	–	19	25	22	36	22	32
Jana Sangh/BJP	3	4	14	35	22	–	–	2	88
PSP	–	19	12	13	2	–	–	–	–
SSP	–	–	–	23	3	–	–	–	–
Janata(S)/DMKP/LD	–	–	–	–	–	–	41	3	–
Other parties & Independents	106	73	60	80	83[a]	61[b]	43[c]	67[d]	59[e]

[a] DMK—23; National Congress (O)—16; other parties – 30; independents – 14

[b] AIDMK—19; Akali Dal – 8; other parties – 17; independents – 17

[c] DMK—16; other parties – 35; independents – 8

[d] Telugu Desam—30; AIDMK – 12; other parties – 20; independents – 5

[e] Left Front Allies—11; Other National Front constituents – 3; AIDMK – 11; Akali Dal (M) – 6; Other Parties – 12; independents – 16;

Table 14   Companies in India (1986–87)

Rank	Name of Company	Total Capital Employed (crores)[a]
1.	Oil & Natural Gas Corp.	11,621.00
2.	Steel Authority of India Ltd.	9,043.67
3.	National Thermal Power Corp. Ltd.	7,271.82
4.	Coal India Ltd.	6,792.72
5.	Food Corp. of India	6,320.52
6.	Indian Oil Corp.	4,108.20
7.	Bharat Heavy Electricals	3,028.78
8.	National Aluminium Co.	2,769.95
9.	Rural Electrification Corp.	2,377.41
10.	*Reliance Industries	2,002.66
11.	Hindustan Aeronautics	1,912.97
12.	Mahanagar Telephone Nigam	1,763.60
13.	Rashtriya Chemicals Fertilizers	1,579.51
14.	Neyvelli Lignite Corp.	1,554.92
15.	Air India	1,546.29
16.	Bharat Coking Coal	1,471.40
17.	*Tata Steel	1,459.62
18.	Shipping Corp. of India	1,391.98
19.	National Textile Corp. (Holding Co.)	1,296.16
20.	Eastern Coalfields	1,277.28
21.	Indian Telephones Industries	1,269.46
22.	South Eastern Coalfields	1,230.26
23.	Hindustan Petroleum	1,197.24
24.	Central Coalfields	1,135.72
25.	National Hydro-electric Power Corp.	1,110.64
26.	Hindustan Fertilizers Corp.	1,088.47
27.	Mazgaon Dock	1,086.46
28.	*Tata Engineering	1,029.70
29.	Indian Petrochemicals Corp.	939.34
30.	Bharat Petroleum Corp.	931.48
31.	Northern Coalfields	904.39
32.	Housing and Urban Development Corp.	880.61
33.	Hindustan Paper Corp.	874.06
34.	National Fertilizers	842.01
35.	Indian Airlines	802.04
36.	State Trading Corp. of India	796.81
37.	*Larsen & Toubro	788.62
38.	Western Coalfields	757.60
39.	*Southern Petrochemicals	728.31
40.	Kudremukh Iron Ore Co.	698.64
41.	Bharat Aluminium Co.	690.27
42.	*J & K Synthetics	677.94
43.	Indian Dairy Corp.	673.17
44.	Maruti Udyog	646.58
45.	Fertilizer Corp. of India	633.12
46.	Engineering Projects (India)	627.48
47.	Bharat Electronics	625.56
48.	Bharat Earth Movers	618.69
49.	Minerals & Metals Trading Corp. of India	566.57
50.	*Associated Cement Companies	563.80

[a]   Total capital employed represents net block, capital expenditure under construction, capital work-in-progress, inventory and all other assets adjusted for accumulated deficit, if any.

*   These are private-sector companies. In 1989 Larsen & Toubro was acquired by Reliance Industries.
Source: Compiled from the Mid-week Reviews of *Economic Times*, 3 March 1988 (Bangalore edition) and 6 April 1989 (Bombay edition).

Table 15 Companies at Work in India

	Govt Companies		Non-Govt Companies		All Companies	
	No. of companies	Paid-up capital (Rs crores)	No. of companies	Paid-up capital (Rs crores)	No. of companies	Paid-up capital (Rs crores)
Public Limited Companies	480 (0.3)	11,156.5 (22.5)	18,711 (10.9)	7,944.0 (16.1)	19,191 (11.2)	19,100.5 (38.6)
Private Limited Companies	642 (0.4)	27,618.5 (55.8)	151,715 (88.4)	2,771.9 (5.6)	152,357 (88.8)	30,390.4 (61.4)
Total	1,122 (0.7)	38,775.0 (78.3)	170,426 (99.3)	10,715.9 (21.7)	171,548 (100.0)	49,490.9 (100.0)

Figures in bracket represent % of total companies and of their totals.
Data on paid-up capital is provisional.
(Figures for companies at work on 31.12.1988)
Source: 1988–89 Report of the Dept of Company Affairs, Ministry of Industry, Govt of India, Table 6.1, p. 33.

Table 16   Foreign Companies At Work in India

As on	Number of Foreign Companies
31 March 1984	326
31 March 1985	324
31 March 1986	335
31 March 1987	371
31 March 1988	401
31 December 1988	414

Source: 1988–89 Report of the Dept of Company Affairs, Ministry of Industry, Govt of India, Table 6.3, p. 35.

Table 17   Branches of Foreign Companies In India:
Distribution by Industrial Activity

S.No.	Industrial Activity	Industrial code	No. of branches as on 31.3.75	No. of branches as on 31.3.87	No. for which balance sheets are available for 1986–87 or for any previous five-year period	Assets of branches shown in previous column (crores)
1.	Agriculture & allied activities	(0)	112	13	13	5.59
2.	Mining & quarrying	(1)	7	1	1	1.11
3.	Processing & Manufacture	(2, 3 & 4)	80	32	21	89.14
4.	Construction & utilities	(5)	30	11	10	5.68
5.	Commerce (trade & finance)	(6)	144	54	40	6148.88
6.	Transport, communication & storage	(7)	39	34	3	2.58
7.	Community & business services	(8)	84	36	24	56.68
8.	Personal & other services	(9)	14	5	4	1.82
9.	Liaison office/ representation		–	83	67	20.42
	Total		510	269	183	6331.95

Table 18   Indian Subsidiaries of Foreign Companies:
Distribution by Industrial Activity

S. No.	Industry	Industrial Code	No. of subsidaries as on	
			31.3.86	31.3.87
1.	Agriculture and allied activities	0	15	14
	(i) Tea	0.30	15	14
2.	Mining and quarrying	1	1	1
3.	Processing & manufacturing	2, 3 & 4	44	40
	(i) Motor vehicles and parts	3.22	1	1
	(ii) Manufacture of electrical machinery	3.39	9	10
	(iii) Manufacture of explosives & fire works	3.63	1	1
	(iv) Manufacture of aluminium ware	3.51	2	2
	(v) Medical & pharmaceuticals	3.80	8	5
	(vi) Cosmetics & toilet preparations	3.81 & 3.82	2	2
4.	Construction	5	1	1
5.	Commerce (trade & finance)	6	11	10
6.	Community & business services	8	4	3
7.	Personal & other services	9	2	2
	Total		78	71

Index